BOOK OF SERENITY

BOOK OF
SERENITY

One Hundred Zen Dialogues

TRANSLATED AND INTRODUCED BY

THOMAS CLEARY

SHAMBHALA
Boston & London
2005

Shambhala Publications, Inc.
Horticultural Hall
300 Massachusetts Avenue
Boston, Massachusetts 02115
www.shambhala.com

Published by arrangement with Lindisfarne Press, PO Box 799,
Great Barrington, MA 01230

9 8 7 6 5 4 3

Printed in the United States of America

♾ This edition is printed on acid-free paper that meets the
American National Standards Institute z39.48 Standard.

♻ Shambhala makes every effort to print on recycled paper.
For more information please visit www.shambhala.com.

Distributed in the United States by Random House, Inc.,
and in Canada by Random House of Canada Ltd

The Library of Congress catalogues the previous edition
of this book as follows:

Hsing-hsiu, 1166-1246.
    [Ts'ung jung lu. English]
      Book of serenity: one hundred Zen dialogues/translated &
      introduced by Thomas Cleary.—1st ed.
      p. cm.
    ISBN 978-1-57062-381-3 (hardcover)
    ISBN 978-1-59030-249-1 (paperback)
    1. Koan—Early works to 1800. 2. Cheng-chueh, 1091–1157.
    I. Cleary, Thomas F., 1949– . II. Title.
    BZ9289.H7513 1998
    294.3'85—DC21   97-42454
                                              CIP

CONTENTS

TRANSLATOR'S INTRODUCTION

THE *Book of Serenity* is a classic text of Chan Zen Buddhism, a vehicle of an ancient knowledge said to go back to time immemorial and to have been originally transmitted from mind to mind. The continuity of Zen transmission was fostered by periodic revisions and renewals in a body of special techniques and the knowledge subtending them. Many of these techniques are encoded in the *Book of Serenity*, and the use of this kind of literature to help elicit certain perceptions is itself one of these techniques.

The branch of ancient tradition that came to be known as Zen is customarily traced back in Chinese history to the late fifth and early sixth centuries C.E., and was approaching the end of its third overt major phase in China when the *Book of Serenity* was compiled.

These three phases consisted of the era of the founders (6–8 cent.), who worked to establish the principle of experiential internatization of knowledge against a background of excessive intellectualism; the era of the creative proliferation of different transmission lines with particular modes of presentation (8–10 cent.); and the era of dramatic development of Zen literature and the refinement of the use of stories as a medium of teaching and practice (10–13 cent.).

The founding of Zen in China is traditionally attributed to Bodhidharma (d. 535), an Indian yogin, but one of the founders of Zen in Japan, Dogen Zenji (13th cent.) equates the Buddhism transmitted by Bodhidharma with that represented by the earlier Sengzhao, who died in the early fifth century. Sengzhao, an assistant of the famous Buddhist translator Kumarajiva and a great author in his own right, is believed to have actually experienced absolute reality beyond intellect, and his superlative writings were highly esteemed and often quoted in classical Zen lore.

Notably, Sengzhao stated that absolute reality is beyond the grasp of concepts, and therefore can only be experienced intuitively or mystically, not by the discursive intellect. In pursuit of this theme, he wrote that the special knowledge called *prajna* (gnosis) in Buddhist terminology could not properly be called knowledge in the ordinary sense because it is objectless, comprehending no specific concrete thing but rather the nonexistence of inherent identity in objects of conventional knowledge.

Furthermore, Sengzhao discoursed on relativity and absoluteness in time, on the incomparable experience of direct perception, and on the ultimate unity of all existence. He always maintained the limitation of words, however, and noted that any attempt to express the ineffable would inevitably be like setting up a target inviting an arrow. His contributions to Chinese Buddhism made him one of the most highly regarded mystics of all time, and someone with whom the later Zen Buddhists felt a special affinity.

The existence of Bodhidharma, the reputed founder of Zen in China, has been questioned by some scholars; other scholars, however, find what appears to be evidence of the existence of at least one Bodhidharma, possibly two or more. Whatever the historical facts of the matter may be, Bodhidharma certainly exists as a symbol of the Zen tradition of the living exemplar, the bearer of the "mind to mind" transmission. His name, which means "the religion of enlightenment," may be taken as representative of the early emphasis of Zen on using Buddhism not as an object of knowledge (intellectualism) but as a means of knowledge (experientialism).

According to Zen tradition, Bodhidharma used only one scripture in his Chinese teaching activity—the *Lankavatara-sutra*, which he judged to be appropriate to the current state of Chinese civilization. This scripture is one of those used by the school of Buddhism known as "yoga practice" (*yogacara*) or "doctrine of consciousness" (*vijnanavada*).

The doctrine of consciousness represents a quite pervasive thread in Buddhism that is not limited to any one school and very often used in Zen teaching. This doctrine presents the view that phenomena as we conceive and cognize them are not objective realities in themselves, but rather mental constructions made of selected data filtered from an inconceivable universe of pure sense.

To clarify this point, the doctrine defines three natures of phenomena: the imagined, or conceptualized, nature; the relative, or dependent, nature; and the perfect nature. It is held that confusion of these three natures, particularly the habit of holding onto the imagined nature of phenomena as their real nature, inhibits the mind from the freedom and higher development of which it is potentially capable, and restricts the range of experience available to the perceiver.

The imagined nature of phenomena is said to be a representation, a description, which is learned and maintained through conditioning. The world as we know it is therefore looked upon in this teaching as a convention, a set of agreements: thus cultural and individual agreements and differences reach down to the levels of cognition and perception, as anthropological and psychological research have reaffirmed in recent times.

According to the doctrine of consciousness, conventional reality, the imagined nature of things, however important and indispensible for everyday life (and hence not to be abolished by yoga), is not itself objective reality and not the limit of the capacity of consciousness. To misunderstand its representational nature and hold to it fixedly as true reality has a stunting effect on mental activity. Familiar examples of this effect might be such conditions as culture shock and associated misunderstandings, or obstacles to learning behaviors (such as foreign languages) outside of pre-established thinking patterns.

Thus while the process of conventional description and organization of experience in terms mutually coherent to members of a community is by no means to be eliminated from the human repertoire of capacities, being necessary for human life, the doctrine of consciousness recommends that it be recognized as mental representation and that the ability to transcend attachment to mental constructions be cultivated. This is said to allow the development not only of extrasensory perceptions, but of expanded and enhanced descriptive abilities to meet the evolutionary needs of society as well.

The practice of yoga now comes in as a means of actually making this detachment from mental construction a practical possibility. In order that this detachment not become nihilistic or otherwise aberrated, and that altered states of consciousness not merely be substituted as objects of fixation, the doctrine here introduces the principles of the relative and real natures of phenomena concealed beneath the conceptualized description.

The relative or dependent nature is the nature of phenomena as products of interactions of conditions. A generalized example of this commonly used for illustration is the interaction of sense faculties, sense consciousnesses, and sense data. This is the raw material of the selection and organizational process of mental construction. Since the faculties, consciousnesses, and data cannot be apprehended in themselves, outside of their mutual interrelationship, there is no way of grasping their objective nature. Their existence as individual elements, therefore, boils down to a description—a relation of mind and mental object. Hence the principle of the real nature of phenomena states that the imagined nature has no objective reality in the relative nature. This is what is sometimes called "emptiness."

A classic simile is that of a red dye painted on a clear crystal, making it look like a ruby. The red dye represents the imagined or conceptualized nature imposed on the relative nature, represented by the crystal. The real nature is the nonexistence of actual "rubyness" in the crystal. Reflections of this doctrine are to be found throughout Zen lore, and one of the major functions of Zen stories is to help to see through and break up mental fixations.

The Lankavatara-sutra likens the perceived world to waves in the ocean of consciousness. To get to know the real nature of things as they are in the state of "suchness" or "thusness," unpredicated reality, it is essential to still these waves of consciousness. The practice of methods of silencing the mind to see reality without the imposition of conditioned representation is well known in Zen Buddhism. This posed a drawback, however, which is also well represented both in Zen literature and in the writings of outside observers. From the external point of view, the drawback was that this exercise of quiescence gave the appearance of quietism, preventing understanding of the true scope of Zen action. Within Zen schools, emphasis on stilling the mind also led some to regard it as a goal, and successful stilling led some to remain fixated on tranquillity, vitiating their capacity for further progress. In both cases the problem was one of confusing the means with the end. This confusion and its consequences are referred to repeatedly in Zen and other Buddhist lore throughout the ages.

Little is known of the early Zen school in China, but in the record of a disciple of Bodhidharma's successor we can observe the emphasis on the *Lankavatara-sutra* and the doctrine of consciousness, as well as hints of future directions in Zen practice:

> The mind-seal of the founding teacher is not a matter of concentration on ascetic practice, which is merely an aid to the path. If you merge with the fundamental mind and make free use of its true light, then ascetic practice is like picking up earth and turning it into gold; but if you only work on ascetic practice and do not clarify the fundamental mind, thus being bound by aversion and attraction, then ascetic practice is like walking on a dangerous path on a dark night. If you want to clarify the fundamental mind, you should examine carefully—in the midst of sense impacts, before you produce thought and reflection, where does the mind go? Is it nonexistent? Is it existent? Not falling into being or nonbeing, or into any fixed location, the mind-pearl shines alone: it always shines on the world, without a particle of obstruction, without an instant of discontinuity. Therefore our founder also handed on the *Lankavatara* scripture, and said to my teacher, 'As I see China, only this scripture can be used to seal the mind. If you practice in accord with it, you will be able to cross over the world.' Also, whenever my teacher finished lecturing he would say, 'This scripture, after four generations, will turn into literalism and formalism. What a pity.'"

For several generations after Bodhidharma, a "Lankavatara School" centered on the teachings of this scripture did indeed continue to be active and was later identified as an offshoot of the original Zen school. While emphasis on the *Lankavatara-sutra* itself was not prominent in the teaching of the Zen school by the time it came to public attention in the seventh century, nevertheless the doctrine of consciousness remained very much in use in Zen, particularly through certain formulations of the

Avatamsaka-sutra, another major scripture often used in Zen teaching.

A younger contemporary of Bodhidharma, the famous "Mahasattva" (great saint) Fu, is another figure of prominence in the traditions of early Zen Buddhism. Some of his sayings remained favorites of later Zen practitioners. One of those unusual people whom Zen tradition refers to as "responsive manifestations," who are not known to have received teaching from a human mentor but were enlightened through inspirations resulting from their practices, Mahasattva Fu was a philanthropist with a considerable following that included his wife and children as well as other relatives.

A literate farmer, Fu expounded Buddhism to the emperor Wu of the Liang dynasty, and the record of his sayings and deeds is one of the richest sources of teachings surviving from among the early adepts. Perhaps the most famous of his utterances prized in Zen tradition in his verse:

Empty-handed, holding a hoe,
Walking, riding a water buffalo.
Man is crossing a bridge;
The bridge but not the river flows.

The first two lines illustrate the familiar theme in developed Buddhism of being in the world without clinging to things of the world, employing ways and means without becoming possessively attached to them. The second two lines illustrate the contrast between objective and subjective reality: "thusness," naked reality without the screen of mental construction, is in flux (as a river) but does not really change, in that it is always "as is." The mental structures used in crossing over the world, on the other hand, that is, the viewpoints, conceptions, and interpretations are rooted in subjectivity and undergo fluctuation and change, even if they are fixed from their own point of view.

The realistic approach according to this teaching, therefore, would be to recognize the functional value of structures as tools and vehicles, but to also recognize their temporary nature and refrain from attachment to them even while using them. This permits contact with wider reality and freedom to adapt to changing conditions without the impediment of clinging to the familiar or habitual for its own sake. Thus in one single verse Mahasattva Fu summed up a central issue of Buddhism.

Mahasattva Fu is not associated with a particular lineage but is believed to have received the transmission from reality itself through the medium of certain experiences. Bodhidharma, on the other hand, is said to have started the unbroken Zen transmission in China. Among his four enlightened disciples was one Huike, also called Shenguang, who is known as the second patriarch of Zen. Tradition represents one of the main techniques of Zen meditation in the form of a story about Huike's enlightenment: he asked Bodhidharma to pacify his mind, which Bodhidharma agreed to do once Huike brought his mind to him. On introspection, Huike said, "When I look for my mind I cannot find it," to which Bodhidharma replied, "I have pacified your mind for you."

This exercise of "looking for the mind" is an important method common to a number of schools of Buddhism. It appears in various guises and stories designed to foster this special focus of attention. An impossible task per se, it has the function of inducing nonreifying consciousness and is useful in freeing the mind from its clinging habits of thought.

Huike was caught up in the tide of a government persecution of Buddhism and was eventually laicized, never to return to monastic orders. He had ten enlightened disciples, four of them laymen, and after entrusting the teaching to a successor, he is said to have immersed himself in city life, working at various menial jobs as he continued his self-development in secret. One source has it that he went to the city after receiving the Zen transmission from Bodhidharma in order to test his concentration and stability. Like Bodhidharma, Huike's teaching, which was free from academic pedantry, aroused the opposition of established interests in the Buddhist monasteries, and he died through an intrigue.

The one among Huike's disciples who is known as his principal heir and called the third patriarch of Zen is believed to have associated with the teacher during a period of seclusion in the mountains. This man, Sengcan, is reputedly the author of the famous poem *Faith in Mind*, which has been one of the most popular Zen classics throughout its known history.

This poem emphasizes the "middle way" in which there is neither grasping nor rejection, neither inclination nor aversion. In practice this involves neither pursuing mental objects nor remaining fixed on voidness: not trying to stop the mind to gain peace, yet not following perceptions.

Sengcan recommends not fixing the mind on anything but not sinking into oblivion either. If you want to attain the "one vehicle" of enlightenment, he says, do not be averse to sense data—sense data are not bad, he explains, they are the same as true awakening.

The entire poem is in this vein and stresses the ultimate nonduality of the realm of illusion and the realm of enlightenment and the difference lying in the mind itself. The deluded discriminate the two realms conceptually and try to reject one to grasp the other, thus creating their own bonds, while the enlightened have no artifices, so they do not imagine enlightenment apart from direct experience. This teaching tallies with the tenet of the doctrine of consciousness that states that sense experience is itself the matrix of enlightenment, and nonenlightenment is pure fiction whose only binding force is its habitual repetition.

A contemporary of Sengcan was the meditation master and scholar Zhiyi. Although not figuring in the Zen transmission chains emphasized from the ninth and tenth centuries onward, nevertheless he is listed as a Zen master in the model Zen history *Transmission of the Lamp*. One of the most important figures in Chinese Buddhism, this sixth century adept is also known as the founder of the Tiantai school of Buddhism, a comprehensive school of study and practice said to have had an important impact on the development of early Zen.

A number of Zhiyi's schemata are mentioned in the *Transmission of the Lamp*, along with their correlates in Indian tradition . Fundamental to his system was the principle of three levels of truth—conditional, absolute, and mean. The conditional, or artificial, level of truth is also called conventional reality, referring to the everyday world. The truth of it, however, is that all phenomena are conditional, meaning that they have no absolute existence or identity. This insight introduces the level of emptiness called the absolute truth, meaning that conditional phenomena have no independent being.

Thus the meditation proceeds from contemplation of conditionality into contemplation of emptiness, thereby fostering detachment from objects. The next stage is to re-emerge from emptiness into the conditional, whereby temporal knowledge, skillfulness, and compassion are developed.

Finally, by going back and forth between focus on the conditional and focus on its emptiness, the practitioner arrives at the mean, or middle way, realizing that things are neither absolutely existent nor absolutely nonexistent; they can be experienced but not grasped. In the middle way one harmonizes detachment and identification, transcendence and involvement, wisdom and compassion.

This three truth scheme is based on the work of the great Indian Buddhist Nagarjuna (ca. 100 C.E.), who is considered an ancestor of Zen and other schools of Buddhism. It is to be found echoed throughout Zen teaching, though typically not in the form of doctrine but in the form of structural relations within stories and symbols.

Another doctrine of Zhiyi that is brought up in the Zen *Transmission of the Lamp* is that of the so-called "six identities." This refers to six levels of identity of mind and Buddha, illustrating six aspects or stages of enlightenment.

The first level is noumenal identity or identity in principle. This means that all consciousness has inherent within it the very same nature, the nature of enlightenment or buddhahood.

Second is identity in words. This means that insofar as inherent buddha-nature is obscured by distracting conditioned habits, people need to be told about this latent potential in order to start on the path to return to it. This is the level of theoretical teaching and learning.

Third is the level of contemplation practice, where meditation on the three levels of reality is employed to lead to experiential realization.

Fourth is the level of approximation, wherein the senses are purified so as to allow a semblance experience of reality. Since there is still effort involved, it is still not spontaneous mental purity and not considered final realization.

The fifth level of identity is that of partial realization of reality, and the sixth and final level is that of ultimate realization. The final level takes place when the awakened mind is fully uncovered and activated and has become autonomous or free from the influence of artificial conditioning.

While these six levels are not generally named and enumerated in this precise fashion in other Zen lore, they provide a useful scheme for understanding the various standpoints of the transactions of consciousness represented in Zen stories.

One set of meditation exercises formulated by Zhiyi and recommended in Zen commentary on the *Book of Serenity* is what is known as the six subtle methods. A basic form of this practice is indicated in the third story of the *Book of Serenity*, and various modifications of it are found in the exercises of many Zen schools.

The first of the six subtle methods is counting the breath in repeated sets of ten. This is a traditional Buddhist practice specifically prescribed to overcome the tendency toward mind wandering and distraction. This is eventually replaced by following the breath and simply keeping the attention on it continuously without the relatively crude aid of counting. Both of these are widely practiced in modern day Zen.

The third of the six subtle methods is called stopping, or cessation. Here the breath becomes imperceptible and mental activity ceases. This is ordinarily unattainable without careful practice of the first two methods. Cessation, which results in deep tranquillity, is followed up by the fourth method called contemplation, in which the mind is reactivated to visualize the components of the body. This is done so as to internalize the understanding of the organism as a compound that is dependent and subject to disintegration. One purpose of this is to counteract intoxication by the calmness of cessation with the realization that it depends on the body-mind and is thus by nature impermanent and not ultimately reliable.

The fifth subtle method, called returning, similarly cuts through fixation to the standpoint of the preceding stage of contemplation. It accomplishes this by turning the attention away from the object of contemplation to the mind itself that contemplates. This is the aforementioned exercise of looking for the mind, which is one of the main Zen meditation practices. Withdrawal of the mind from objects and focusing it on the ungraspable essence of its own consciousness is intended to free the mind from clinging and return it to its original purity. In the sixth subtle method that follows on this, called purity, the practitioner experiences essential purity and finally attains spontaneity.

A number of meditation methods described by Zhiyi in his works also appear in directions for meditation attributed to the fourth patriarch of Zen, Daoxin (580–651). Daoxin was the first Zen master to establish a settled community of students, and he is said to have compiled manuals of discipline and meditation for his disciples. These methods include incantation, visualization, examination of mental functions, and contemplation of the essence of mind; all of them have precedents in the Tiantai school of Zhiyi. The career of Daoxin is believed to mark the beginning of public recognition of the Zen school.

The fifth patriarch of Zen, Hongren (602–675), was the only one of Daoxin's five hundred disciples given permission to teach. He is said to have used the *Vajracchedika-sutra*, or Diamond Cutter Scripture, in his teaching, and is also the reputed author of a *Treatise on the Supreme Vehicle*, emphasizing discovery and preservation of the fundamental mind without fragmentation of consciousness.

The Diamond Cutter Scripture stresses nonattachment to forms, elimination of religious self-consciousness, relinquishment of means when the end is attained, the distinction between concept and reality, and the ungraspability of mind. All of these themes are prominent in classical Zen teaching and represented symbolically in many Zen stories. This scripture is one of the most popular of all Buddhist texts in East Asia, and innumerable commentaries have been written on it. Hongren's great successor Huineng is said to have been enlightened on hearing a single line from it.

The *Treatise on the Supreme Vehicle*, attributed to Hongren, is a short work whose main point is the original purity of mind. It distinguishes the real mind from conditioned states of mind and says that the essential practice is to maintain this original real mind and keep it unified, not letting it scatter. To find the real mind, the treatise recommends the practice of observing the flow of consciousness, noting its volatility and ungraspability; as a result of persistence in this attentive observation, it states, the flowing stream of consciousness will naturally evaporate and the mind will become clear and stable, so that one can become able to live without being mentally dominated by conditions.

Hongren is said to have had seven hundred disciples, among whom eleven became sufficiently enlightened to become teachers on their own.

Among these were the first Zen masters to go to the capital city and promote the study and practice of Zen in China's imperial precincts. Relatively few remnants of the teachings of these schools survive. In any event, they were eventually superceded by the schools of the so-called southern family of Zen descended from the illustrious Huineng (638-713), one of the most outstanding Zen masters of all time, and recognized in southern tradition as the sixth patriarch of Zen.

Portrayed as an illiterate woodcutter from the underdeveloped south of China, the drama of Huineng's appearance in Hongren's community, his brief apprenticeship, and midnight disappearance is used in Zen lore as a counterpoint to the arrogant self-satisfaction of the learned and the pious, and also as an illustration of the contention that enlightenment, and the aspect of the human being in which the potential of enlightenment resides, transcend conditioned differences such as those produced by cultural and social background.

A collection of sayings attributed to the sixth patriarch Huineng, entitled the *Altar Scripture*, is the only Buddhist text of acknowledged Chinese authorship to be given the title of scripture, usually reserved for works attributed to Buddha. This text presents Zen in simple terms such as outwardly discerning everything while inwardly being unmoved by anything. It has been rendered into English a number of times. A direct successor of Huineng is on record as stating, however, that the *Altar Scripture* contains spurious material wrongly attributed to the patriarch; in any case, its place in the history of Zen study is somewhat problematic, as it does not appear to have been used much in working Zen schools. A commentary on the aforementioned *Diamond Cutter Scripture* is also attributed to Huineng through oral transmission, and this too presents the teaching in a clear and simple manner, without scholastic complications.

Huineng was widely recognized as the master of the age, and it is said that countless people benefited from attending his lectures. He is believed to have taught thirty-three known enlightened disciples who were overt representatives of his school and taught in various places as his successors. It is also recorded that there were a large number of people who attained enlightenment under his guidance but subsequently concealed their identity and remained unknown as heirs of the patriarch. This latter note in the histories points up the fact, commonly encountered in Zen lore but later obscured by institutionalization, that Zen adepts did not all "appear in the world" as teachers, many choosing anonymity, perhaps teaching indirectly, perhaps associating only with the few who recognized their attainment apart from external appearances and reputation. This aspect of the Zen movement is at times only hinted at in the records, at times made explicit. In the case of Huineng's successors, certain ones seem to have had the task of contacting scattered remnants of the school of the fifth patriarch who had become obsessed with trance exercises and thus cut themselves off from the fuller expression of the teaching.

Very little is known of the schools of the heirs of the sixth patriarch, but in the second generation the two great teachers Shitou (700-790) and Mazu (709-788) appeared, who together produced over one hundred and fifty enlightened successors and effected a dramatic expansion in Zen activity. Shitou is the author of *Union of Difference and Sameness*, one of the earliest Zen classics, a short work in verse emphasizing what in modern psychological terms would be referred to in terms of the harmonious operation of the left and right brain in a highly integrated working of the mind.

Mazu did not write anything but was a person of such towering spiritual force that he was able to help over one hundred and thirty people become enlightened. Of these, eighty or so became teachers. Mazu's general teachings present a picture of great simplicity, but most of the information about him is in stories of his encounters with students, showing the way out of particular standpoints. Many of the Zen adepts of that time studied with both Shitou and Mazu; among these was the great layman Pang Yun, one of the more extraordinary lay masters, of whose sayings and compositions a considerable record remains.

Among Mazu's many successors, two that stand out for particular attention are Baizhang Huaihai (d. 814), also known by his honorific title Dazhi, and Nanquan Puyuan (d. 834). Baizhang is nominally the founder of the Chan (Zen) commune system, and the author of the famous saying "a day without work is a day without food." The record of Baizhang's sayings is one of the most extensive of all the classical masters and provides an unusually explicit theoretical basis for understanding Chan teaching and practice, linking Chan with the ancestral tradition of scriptures and ancient adepts.

Baizhang emphasizes the necessity to perceive both absolute and conventional levels of truth and organizes the course of Buddhism into three phases: detachment, not dwelling in detachment, and not making an understanding of not dwelling. He stresses, moreover, that all formulations, of practice and realization for example, are expedients and are by nature incomplete. Baizhang states that a Buddha is a person who has succeeded in getting out of bondage to feelings, thoughts, and other media of conditioning, yet then comes back into the realm of bondage to help others out. He asserts that Buddhas suffer as other beings do, but they are different in that they are "free to come or go." Baizhang speaks of buddhahood largely in human terms but days that the full scope of reality is not available to human beings. It is this realization that highlights the true nature of descriptions and devices reflecting human concerns and does not allow a real Chan practitioner to close his or her mind around any particular formulations. Baizhang points out that authoritarianism is a degeneration of the teaching function. He is one of the most outspoken opponents of proprietary interest in the externals of a school.

The place of Nanquan in Chan tradition is a special one, emphasizing a certain aspect of the teaching. This is pointed out in the *Book of Serenity*, and it should be borne in mind that the representational place of certain teachers in tradition does not necessarily indicate the full scope of their teaching. Indeed, the essential nature of Chan "history" is representational and instructive; the "facts" represented need not be facts in the conventionally understood terrestrial sense, but are rather in the domain of illustration of certain processes and relations.

In the case of Nanquan, he is often cited to fulfill the function of what is called in Chan "upholding the true imperative," which means to remind the student that no formulation is final, that there is no place in absolute reality to set the mind. As the saying goes, insects may land anywhere else, but they cannot land in a raging fire; the mind may fix on concepts, but not on ultimate truth. This kind of teaching is posed as a counterbalance to the ordinary human tendency to seek regularity and familiarity. There are many indications in Chan lore of teachers' attempts to break through these tendencies that lead to and are expressed by mechanical repetition in the form of sloganization, ceremonialism, and general sanctification of means as ends in themselves. There are a number of favorite sayings and stories of Nanquan commonly used in this connection, one of which is the famous tale of "killing the cat." Chan commentary indicates that the meaning is found by perceiving the structure of the stories and perceiving the function through the structure. The surface content is just a vehicle.

Among Nanquan's successors was the very famous Zhaozhou (778–897), one of the favorite figures of Chan lore. Like Layman Pang, Zhaozhou is noted for his extensive travels after enlightenment that helped to consolidate the fabric of the overall Chan activity. Zhaozhou figures in numerous stories of the most esteemed collection of meditation tales, and there is a rather extensive collection of his sayings in the classic *Records of Sayings of Ancient Adepts*. The presence of Nanquan and Zhaozhou permeates Chan lore, and they are universally considered giants in the tradition.

The so-called golden age of Chan was largely dominated by the emergence, over a span of a century or so, of five powerful lineages known to history as the five houses of Chan, descended from Shitou and Mazu through the teachers Yaoshan, Tianhuang, and Baizhang. Each of these houses is associated with particular manners and expressions of teaching; the formulations and anecdotes of their founders became standard reference points in the teaching materials of later generations.

Among Baizhang's numerous successors, the names of Guishan Lingyou and Huangbo Xiyun stand out in Chan history. Guishan (d. 854) and his eminent disciple Yangshan (d. 890) had large communities of students and many enlightened heirs, and their lineage is referred to as the House of Gui and Yang. Much of the documentation of this house is in the form of dialogue between these two masters, represented as two mirrors without an image interposed, and describing one of the methods of teaching and the reality of mind-to-mind communication that underlies it.

Guishan also wrote a short treatise describing the degeneration of contemporary Chan, brought about by the great influx of students with faulty intentions and insufficient grounding in the classical Buddhist sciences and disciplines. Contrary to popular notions of Chan Buddhists as freethinkers and iconoclasts with no regard for scripture or precept, Guishan lays emphasis on the foundation of conduct and the careful study of the principles of Buddhism. He especially emphasizes scripture study for those who cannot achieve the sudden transcendence of Chan mystic method, which means, in other words, for most people.

Yangshan was an extraordinary Chan master, to whom eleven regional military-civil commanders, among the most powerful and arrogant men in China, are said to have paid homage as disciples. As a young man, he studied with ancient masters and was entrusted with an esoteric teaching system said to have been handed down from the sixth patriarch, parts of which appear in the *Book of Serenity* and other Chan texts, communicating the arcana of Chan lore by means of obscure signs and symbols. Aside from the few signs for which explanations are given, a large number of symbols exist that are no longer understood at all. The most extensive explanations of signs used by Yangshan is preserved in the teachings of one of his disciples, a Korean adept, in *Annals of the Halls of the Ancestors*, a text until recently preserved only in Korean tradition. There are also hints of some occult connection between Yang-shan and adepts somewhere to the west, which may help to explain his use of visual symbols to an extent greater than any other Chan master, so far as is known.

Huangbo (d. 850), another of Baizhang's great successors, is said to have been naturally enlightened, and notices of his speech and behavior reflect the irrepressible independent spirit esteemed in Chan Buddhism. Records of a number of his speeches are preserved in two short texts that present the theoretical and practical aspects of Chan in a very straightforward and simple form. His remarkable disciple Linji Yixuan (d. 867), after whom the Linji House of Chan is named, was a similarly dynamic personality, whose collected sayings became one of the major classics of Zen.

Linji further elaborated certain formulations of his teacher Huangbo and the latter's predecessor Baizhang and also clarified a number of specific strategies of Chan teaching method. Linji emphasized the nature of religious and philosophical formulations in Buddhism as originating in or describing mental states and processes and stressed the importance of actually living through these experiences. He was known also for the use of the shout, which he explained could be used as a shock technique to interrupt a useless stream of consciousness; or as a sounding technique to draw a reaction, on the basis of which further interaction could be made; or as a cornering technique to exert pressure on someone in a quandary; or as an expression of what cannot be conceptualized or articulated. This shout was soon imitated by followers of Linji, to the extent that one of his successors had to speak out against this ignorant mime, and one of the greatest masters of his lineage centuries later actually imposed a fine on students who pretended to express their understanding by shouting.

A number of Linji's formulations also became standard items of Chan lore; teaching schemes known as "the three mysteries and three essentials," "the fourfold host and guest," and "the four views." The three mysteries and three essentials are an abstruse elaboration of the three stages of attainment stated by Baizhang, alluding to subtle gradations in the relation of the practitioner to the stage of practice. The "fourfold host and guest" symbolize overall aspects of realization: the "guest within the guest" refers to the state of people alienated from the true self, merely being occupied in the pursuit of externals; the "host within the guest" refers to the elementary stage of Chan practice in which people sense, or believe, in the latent presence of real consciousness and turn away from externals to look for the innermost mind. The "guest within the host" is the awakened person who then returns to the ordinary world to contact others; the "host within the host" is the inner essence, or personal experience of the enlightened. The "four views" is a set of experiential possibilities exercised to help people proceed from the first stage of guest within guest through the second, which is a transition technique to reach the third and fourth, which are complementary. The four views are the state of effacing the environment but not the person, effacing the person but not the environment, effacing both, and effacing neither. The last stage refers to perfect integration of consciousness and objective reality, made possible by gradual removal of subjective biases through purgative, purifying experiences.

Roughly contemporary with Guishan, Yangshan, Huangbo, and Linji, were the noted adepts Deshan Xuanjian (d. 867), Dongshan

Liangjie (d. 869), and Caoshan Benji (d. 901). The two latter masters were the ancestors of the so-called Cao Dong House, while the former was the ancestor of the Yunmen and Fayan houses of Chan.

Dongshan and Caoshan are famed for the creation or development of a number of teaching formulae, known as the five ranks, the three roads, the three falls, the three leaks, and the four types of different kinds. The five ranks device is particularly well-known and formed the basis for the reorganization of Zen study in the Japanese Rinzai school of the eighteenth century.

The five ranks may be viewed as a progression of stages of development or an analysis of different degrees of integration. In the first, called the relative within the absolute, one practices detachment and interruption of mental habits, thereby gaining a measure of freedom and rest from compulsion and confusion. Detachment alone, however, is called a pit or a cave in Chan lore and shunned as a perilous indulgence without positive usefulness in itself. The second rank, therefore, called the absolute within the relative, is a state of merging with the environment, achieving a kind of unity of subject and object, sometimes likened to being like a mirror. This capacity to become totally absorbed in the present, however, while useful for breaking through the mental scattering caused by excessive attention to past or future, is also eventually shunned, called in Chan technical terminology "falling into the present," because it lacks the faculty of discrimination necessary for the person to be fully effective in the world. Thus the third rank, coming from within the absolute, does not remain in this equanimity, and turns to development of observation and action that leads to the fourth rank, arrival in the relative, and mastery of action in the world. The fifth rank, simultaneous arrival in both relative and absolute, refers to the consummation of harmony and integration of transcendence and being in the world. In the *Book of Serenity* this rank is represented as a mirror spinning, the back dark side of detachment and transcendence seeming to merge with the functioning bright side. This scheme of five ranks has early models in the *Lotus of Truth* (*Saddharma-pundarika*) and *Flower Ornament* (*Avatamsaka*) scriptures, both of which were widely read and highly esteemed in Chan circles.

The three roads scheme also presents major stages of Chan practice and realization in general outline and echoes the previously mentioned three phases defined by Baizhang two generations earlier. The first road, called the path of the bird, is detachment, emptying the mind of preoccupations, and is referred to as "walking in the void." The second road, called the hidden path, goes further yet to the state of nonattachment even to detachment, where there is no longer consciousness of emptiness. The third road, called "extending the hands," refers to returning to the world freely, liberated enough to be in the world without being conditioned by worldly things, and now able to complete the cycle of Buddhist life by reaching out to others to help them toward liberation.

The three falls refer to progression beyond certain critical experiences and stages. The "fall of the ascetic" refers to transcending detachment; this is what is called "being a water buffalo," meaning acting in the world of differences. The "fall of the noble" means going beyond the experience of oneness and nondiscrimination, knowing the essence of the self but not clinging to it. The "fall according to kind" is referred to as not obliterating sense experience, but returning, after initial detachment from the senses, to live in the realm of sense without being blinded or impeded by their experience.

The three leaks are impurities or defects in the knowledge of the Chan practitioner. The "leak of views" refers to clinging to a fixed position. The "leak of feelings" means retention of bias. The "leak of words" means excessive explanation that conveys a false sense of understanding that obscures the practical process; intellectual understanding, if exaggerated at the expense of actual application, can produce a false sense of having arrived at the end when one is really only on the threshold of beginning.

The scheme of four types of different kinds describes particular fields of experience and action. First, the "different kinds of coming and going" refers to all sense experiences, all verbalization, all mundane and spiritual states; this is in a sense the field of Chan practice. Second, the "bodhisattva assimilating to different kinds" refers to re-entering the world after having understood oneself, coming back to the mundane after having realized nirvana so as to help others. The "bodhisattva" is one dedicated to the ordinary and transcendental welfare of both self and others equally. Third, the "different kinds for ascetics" refers to re-entry into the world after having forgotten completely about everything in past present and future and having become independent. Fourth, the "different kinds within the Chan school," means going beyond absorption in the present moment, transcending all notions, even of "thusness" and acting in the midst of differentiations with no sense of either relative or absolute, being or nonbeing.

While these diagrams may be useful for general understanding of what Chan is about, in the case of this as well as the other houses of Chan, the transmission of teaching did not simply consist of explanation and elaboration of particular teaching frameworks. Nevertheless, in the Cao-Dong House, there was, at least in some cases, formal transmission of its particular teaching devices, *after* the actual mind-to-mind communication of the essence of Chan. The subsequent ceremonialization of formal tradition became a target of severe criticism, both within and without this particular lineage.

Deshan Xuanjian, a stock figure in Chan lore and one of the most important links in the transmission, usually appears in the function of representing the shift from conceptual and inductive knowledge to nondiscursive knowledge in direct experience. As famous for striking as Linji is for shouting, he is usually pictured as attempting to foster an abrupt switch into the vaster realm of direct perception from the confinement of conditioned thought.

Deshan's most famous successors were the extraordinary Yantou (d. 887) and the great teacher Xuefeng (d. 908). Yantou is one of those Chan masters who is already enlightened when he appears on the scene of Chan lore and often plays the role of the idol breaker. In particular, he opposed quietism, apparently a fairly common degeneration of Chan, and stressed the importance of complete mental freedom, fluidity, and resilience. Xuefeng, on the other hand, whose final enlightenment is said to have actually taken place through the impact of Yantou's guidance rather than Deshan's tutelage, represents the diligent, indefatigable seeker who matures slowly and finally becomes a skillful teacher of vast experience and expertise.

Such was Xuefeng's mastery in his later years that he attracted a community of over a thousand students and had over fifty enlightened disciples who were already accomplished teachers in his lifetime. Very many stories emanate from the school of Xuefeng, his associates and pupils, and it is from this school that some of the earliest indications of the use of ancient and contemporary anecdotes as a medium of study emerge.

Two of Xuefeng's disciples who stand out for particular attention from the point of view of Chan history are Xuansha (n.d.) and Yunmen (d. 949). Xuansha was the ancestor of the Fayan House of Chan, usually named after his spiritual grandson Fayan Wenyi (d. 958), but referred to in an early history as a revival of the sect of Xuansha. Yunmen is the ancestor of the Yunmen House, which flourished enormously for several generations.

Yunmen was one of the first classical masters to make extensive use of anecdotes and specially constructed questions in his teaching. Although he is said to have forbidden the recording of his words, nevertheless over a thousand examples of his sayings come down to us, including some of the most difficult problems of Chan lore. One of his successors formulated the description of "three phrases" that are said to be inherent in each of Yunmen's statements. This came to be known as "the three phrases of Yunmen" and echoes the three levels of truth according to Tiantai Buddhism. The three phrases are known as "cutting off the streams," referring to interruption of trains of thought and mental habits; "covering heaven and earth," referring to direct holistic awareness; and "going along with the waves," referring to compassion speaking to everyone in accord with their understanding. These may be viewed as three facets of the totality of Chan experience and activity.

Near the end of his life, Xuansha also summed up his teaching in terms of three axioms. The first axiom is that one must personally realize the equality and equanimity of absolute reality, experiencing the absolute outside of all patterns, yet subsequently not clinging even to this experience. This is the sphere of the various devices, verbal and otherwise, used to get people to let go of intellectual and emotional holdings. The second axiom is to return to the realm of causality, to be able to adapt effectively to potentials. Here the adept must see both sides, the equality of absolute reality and the differentiations of relative reality, and be unmoved by either side while being able to penetrate both. The third axiom is perfect integration of wisdom and everyday life, being unattached within while capable of fluid response outside, not being confined to arbitrary patterns, acting freely, guided only by wisdom and compassion working together.

Xuansha's school was revitalized by Fayan Wenyi two generations later, thus becoming known as the Fayan House, the last of the Five Houses. Like Yunmen, Fayan had many enlightened successors including four adepts who rose to the status of "National Teacher" in kingdoms in China and Korea and helped protect Buddhism outwardly in those cultural spheres.

Fayan was the first Chan master to compose a commentary on Shitou's classic *Union of Difference and Sameness* and he also wrote a withering commentary on the decadence of Chan in his time. The former work is lost, but the latter is extant under the title *Ten Guidelines for Chan Schools*. In this forthright treatise, Fayan criticizes degenerate trends such as teaching without enlightenment, sectarianism, teaching without really knowing how to employ the Chan techniques, answering questions without true insight and without regard for the circumstances, failure to integrate detachment and identification, arbitrary use of Chan lore and Buddhist scriptures, imitation, hypocrisy, contentiousness, and carelessness in composition of written materials.

Like the early Gui-Yang House, the Fayan House flourished briefly and then became quiescent, but it left a great legacy in its revival of Buddhist studies, which became an important element in latter-day Chan. It will be remembered that Chan Master Guishan had averred a century before that the lapse of Buddhist studies in Chan circles was one of the causes of decline in Chan. Fayan's great successor Deshao (d. 972), one of the National Teachers, now used his prestige to promote the restoration of Tiantai Buddhism (whose founders are considered Chan adepts) by recovery of lost texts from abroad. Furthermore, Deshao's heir Yanshou (d. 976), also considered a patriarch of Pure Land Buddhism, produced a massive amount of written work, organizing and explaining passages from hundreds of scriptures and treatises in such a way as to harmonize the Tiantai, Huayan, Faxiang, and Chan schools of Buddhism. Yanshou's monumental *Source Mirror Collection*, quoted in the *Book of Serenity*, was printed and placed in monasteries throughout China and was also taken to Korea and Japan where it was instrumental in the development of syncretic studies of Chan and other Buddhist formats.

It is typical of all the houses of Chan that with few exceptions the schools of the heirs of the founders did not have energy on a par with the teachers of the parent houses. Chan tradition shows clear consciousness of this phenomenon, which in effect means that there is a difference between the level of self-understanding and the extra capacity to teach others. This does not necessarily imply a hierarchy, however; Xuansha, for example, advised one of his successful disciples not to try to teach because he was too exceptionally enlightened and his self-expression would be too lofty for people to grasp. Records say that he did not try to set himself up as a teacher, and his influence was recognized by a very few in his lifetime.

Then again, there is another significant factor in the expansion-contraction pattern of Chan transmission waves, and that is what might be called the "immunization" phenomenon that invariably follows a creative outburst of the teaching function, when the external vehicles of the expression of the teaching—such as symbols and terminology—become routinized or dogmatized and lose their original impact. This, of course, is the reason why Chan teaching is periodically renewed in different forms, as is well attested by its history, to offset the formalization/fossilization process that results from the reassertion of the human tendency to seek the reassurance of familiarity, repetition, and stasis. It is also worthy of note that precise awareness of this ossification and the measures taken purposely to offset the sterility it brings are clearly articulated in the works of the great Chan masters. Certain features of authentic Chan commentary, such as overturning previous formulations, switching points of view, alternating support and opposition, and so on, are not reflections of sectarian differences or changes in the course of intellectual history, as some outside observers have imagined, but are reflections of the diagnosis and treatment of sclerotic tendencies in the transmission of Chan lore.

Following the inevitable pattern of this "abode of decay," a classical Buddhist term for this world, the Gui-Yang and Fayan Houses, as well as the powerful Nanquan and Shishuang lines of Chan transmission eventually died out. The Linji, Cao-Dong, and Yunmen lines reached the verge of extinction within a short time, but were revived, incorporating the legacies of the quiescent houses as well as other Buddhist traditions, by the vigorous activity of several adepts who flourished from the tenth to the twelfth centuries. A further strategy developed to counterbalance the involutionary pattern of institutionalized Chan at this time was to inject a living element from the core of Chan into Confucianism and Taoism. This latter operation had considerable success that rebounded to produce a certain invigorating effect on outer Chan as well.

The Linji house of Chan was revived by the school of the great Fenyang (d. 1024), who left a rich teaching heritage including commentaries on the methods and devices of all the five houses as well as other important lineages. Fenyang is believed to have been the first master to compose poetic comments on anecdotes from Chan lore, a practice which subsequently became universal. He also gave many examples of alternative sayings and answers for dialogues of the ancients to illustrate specific dimensions of the perspectives being illustrated. Fenyang designed many special questions and answers pointing up key issues of Buddhist understanding as well, and composed a number of songs discoursing on various aspects of Buddhist life and study. Fenyang's work is a treasure trove of Chan lore, but from his time on it is virtually impossible to understand even the surface content of much Chan writing without thorough familiarity not only with Buddhist philosophy but with the constructs of the various houses and lineages of Chan that preceded it.

Fenyang is also known in Chan lore for having used a very deft and humorous technique for deflecting hypocritical students. He had very few disciples, but most of them became renowned adepts. The resurgence of Linji Chan came with the schools of the successors of his successors, particularly those of Huanglong Huinan and Yangqi Fanghui in the 11th century. The records of these adepts are relatively brief and cryptic, but they had many enlightened successors and their lineages are called the Huanglong and Yangqi branches of the Linji House. The Huanglong branch deteriorated notably, but the Yangqi branch, which also eventually dominated Japanese Zen of this school, subsequently produced such giants as Yuanwu (d. 1135) and Dahui (d. 1163), who contributed greatly not only to the renewal of Chan teaching, but also to the preservation of certain techniques within Neo-Confucianism, which was to dominate the Chinese intellectual world for centuries to come.

The Yunmen line was greatly revived by the distinguished fourth generation master Xuedou Chongxian (d. 1052) and flourished over the succeeding generations, particularly through the school of Xuedou's successor Tianyi Yihuai. It eventually died out when the last surviving master of the line did not find anyone he deemed capable of effectively receiving and transmitting the teaching. This event, which is recorded explicitly in Chan history, reflects the unwillingness of ancient Chan adepts in China to continue schools at the cost of reality, preferring to let a lineage die out rather than perpetuate empty forms. According to Japanese books, this tradition was not upheld so strictly in Japan, where there was far more proprietary interest in schools and sects, and even in China there are suggestions of faulty transmission in later times.

Xuedou was highly acclaimed as a poet, and many examples of his work are preserved in a number of texts. He is probably most famous for his collection of poetic comments on one hundred Chan stories enshrined in the classic *Blue Cliff Record* with prose commentaries by Yuanwu. Less well known in his collection of prose comments on one hundred Chan stories, called the *Cascade Collection*, which was also expanded by Yuanwu's commentaries into the classic *Measuring Tap*. Xuedou's work has maintained a lasting influence through these books, particularly the *Blue Cliff Record*, which was for centuries a sort of standard Zen text in Japan. His *Anthology on Outstanding Adepts* was also lauded as a guide for the world by the founder of the southern branch of the Complete Reality school of Taoism, which had enormous influence in China during the Song, Jin, and Yuan dynasties.

Yuanwu (in this *Book of Serenity* known by another of his honorific titles, Foguo) and his successor Dahui, known as outstanding masters in the Linji line, also both studied Yunmen Chan, and the latter studied Cao-Dong Chan as well. One part of their work reveals an aspect of Chan teaching that is easily glossed over in dogmatic and ritualized approaches: cooperation by opposition. So dramatic was the influence of Yuanwu's *Blue Cliff Record* that it came to be widely recognized as authoritative, with the consequence that it was often memorized and quoted without being studied and employed; therefore Dahui, recognized heir of Yuanwu himself, had the book burned and then explained Chan stories in quite a different manner, in order to break up the current fixation on Yuanwu's formulations. The Chan record of this event and its background notes the time and function of both Yuanwu's teaching and Dahui's supercession, and regards both the composition and destruction of the *Blue Cliff Record* as great contributions to Chan teaching.

There are numerous other examples of this kind of point-counterpoint teaching, both on major and minor scales; it is, in fact, a standard device in Chan commentary method. When viewpoint switching has been taken as representative of differences of opinion or doctrine, the effect of this method has been lost. Literalistic interpretation, coupled with primitive concepts of right/wrong, superior/inferior, win/lose, either/or, which Chan commentary explicitly says cannot be applied to such cases, is often seen in external doctrinal/intellectual history treatments of the materials, as well as in sectarian movements, which may virtually freeze for centuries around some of the formulations of one or two "patriarchs." Hence Chan literature repeatedly emphasizes the need to suspend ordinary emotional and intellectual judgements and particularly to suspend the impulse to grasp and reject, in order to derive the intended benefit from the Chan stories.

A similar device, designed to provoke doubt and shake attachments, appears to be at work in the difference between the teachings of Dahui and Tiantong Hongzhi and certain other masters of that era. Dahui and Tiantong, representatives of the Linji and Cao-Dong lines of Chan respectively, are pictured as presenting quite different forms of Chan practice, the former supposedly upholding so-called *kan-hua* or "story contemplation," the latter supposedly upholding so-called *mo-jiao* or "silent illumination." Story contemplation means use of the Chan story or *gongan* (Japanese *kōan*) in meditation; silent illumination means quiet sitting in pure awareness with no object. Since one was known to tend to intellectualism while the other was known to tend to quietism, neither could be emphasized exclusively; while the emphases of Dahui and Tiantong differed, however, both of these masters did in fact use both of these methods in their teaching. Japanese polemic and Western historians have elevated this to the status of a controversy or even a "schism," but this exaggeration has no basis in the actual Chinese records of the original activity, which show that Dahui and Hongzhi approved and supported each other. A parallel phenomenon appears in an apparent opposition between two other Chan masters of that era, centering around the extremes of so-called *gedeng* or "complication" Chan (corresponding to *kan-hua*) and *pingshi* or "ordinary reality" Chan (corresponding to *mo-jiao*). Again records show that these masters did not question each other's attainment but provided a counterpoint to shake the attachments of students who were merely wedded to a particular form of practice or school.

Duhui is well known for his outspoken criticism of quietism, an endemic disease of Chan and Zen so prevalent that Chan and Zen literature abound with warnings against it. Some observers have even called Zen a religion or cult of tranquillity, despite the fact that all of its great teachers are on record to the contrary. Dahui points out that quiescence is a means not an end, and Tiantong also warns against excess in quiet sitting, criticizing those who cannot integrate with the ordinary world. Dahui also criticized formalization of Chan as a religion and its reliance on ceremonial trappings; and he especially repudiated the current belief that the enlightenment experience (*wu*, Japanese *satori*) is not necessary. He further contributed to the enlivening of Chan tradition by collecting unusual stories and writings that bring out perspectives that tended to become neglected in stereotyped schools.

Tiantong Hongzhi is mentioned specifically in Dahui's writing as the reviver of the declining Cao-Dong school of Chan, and also, notably, as one who really understood what Dahui was about. Hongzhi, or Tiantong, as he is known in this *Book of Serenity*, was the crowning master of the restoration of the Cao-Dong house, which had perished and been resurrected by a Linji master of a couple of generations before. He left a rich teaching, which included a set of one hundred poems on selected Chan stories, after the fashion of the earlier Xuedou. He also produced a collection of prose comments on a hundred stories like Xuedou's *Cascade Collection*. Both of these texts were taken up by the later Cao-Dong master Wansong Xingxiu and expounded in a fashion similar to Yuanwu's treatment of Xuedon's work. The prose collection was expanded into the *Record Of Further Inquiries*, while the verse collection was expanded into the *Book of Serenity*, of which the present volume is a translation.

The original text of the *Book of Serenity* was lost due to disturbed conditions in northern China where Wansong worked—successive invasions and occupations by foreign powers. The text was eventually reconstructed by Wansong himjself at the request of one of his disciples, a statesman named Yelu Chucai. Yelu Chucai was descended from the Khitan people who ruled part of north China under the Liao dynasty, received a Chinese education, and was an officer of the Jin dynasty under the Jurchen people who supplanted the Khitan Liao; eventually he was impressed into the service of Genghis Khan, the Mongol conqueror. He was one of several spiritually trained people from North, East, and Central Asia credited with mitigation of the harshness of Mongol rule over Asia.

A Confucian by early training, Yelu openly recognized the greater scope of Chan Buddhism and became an attentive disciple of Wansong. He had originally been sent to Wansong by another Chan master because of Wansong's erudition in the secular Chinese classics and consequent ability to connect with Yelu's educational background. Yelu urgently requested the reconstruction of the *Book of Serenity* during his extended stay at Genghis' headquarters in Mongolia to help him continue his Chan study while separated from his teacher.

The large number of identifications of classical and literary allusions and expressions to be found in the *Book of Serenity* may be connected with the circumstances of its composition and reconstruction. Wansong himself writes that he did it not only to show he had not invented the interpretations himself but also to reveal the depths of Tiantong Hongzhi's own classical learning. This was not an idle exhibition of literary erudition, but was part of a strategy of the time to outwardly protect Chan from the charge of being a haven for anti-intellectual illiterates and dropouts from the orthodox Confucian establishment and to help make Chan teaching more accessible to the Confucian literati, whose mental development was urgently needed for the welfare of the society as a whole in view of their position in the social structure.

The more fundamental purpose of Wansong's commentaries, naturally, is the elucidation of meanings in the text. While the language may often be derivative, the meaning is not. There is no need, therefore, to be concerned with the authorship or ideological systems of the various texts cited by Wansong. It was common practice for Chan teachers to draw expressions from any available source—Buddhist, Confucian, Taoist scriptures, folklore, popular song, secular poetry—and use them freely in their own way, without any necessary connection with the original context. The context in which the meaning intended in Chan usage is defined is the context of the Chan outlook; this becomes perceptible by observing the structure of the sayings or anecdotes presented.

This is aided by a basic device of Chan commentary method, one used frequently by Wansong in the *Book of Serenity*, that of quotation of sayings or stories that are structurally similar to the main topic under consideration. What is of the essence is not the superficial content but the structure, and this is brought out by presentation of the same deep structures through the medium of diverse surface contents. Chan sayings and stories are used as devices for holding certain patterns in mind; structural analysis of such materials dates back at least a thousand years in Chinese Chan, and Japanese Zen later developed a practice of contemplating several stories with the same deep structure at one and the same time.

In reading Chan literature, therefore, it is essential to cultivate the ability to see through and look beyond the stuff of which symbols are made so as to find the underlying design. Following intellectual and emotional associations based on surface content leads to fragmentation far afield of the intent. A general rule sometimes cited in Zen teaching is that before enlightenment one should look into the intent; after enlightenment, one may then look into the expression as a communicative tool.

One reflection of this technique of using relations among certain elements to convey something deeper that is not necessarily at all apparent in the surface content is manisfested in the *Book of Serenity* in a way that will be apparent to those familiar with Chan history. That is, Wansong has chosen materials that cut across sectarian lines, counteracting the degenerate tendency to sectarianism and exclusivism that is known to have grown up in some Chan circles. This highlights the basic

Buddhist hermeneutical principle, first enunciated by the Buddha, that what is important is what is actually being taught, not who is saying it. For those unconcerned with sects to begin with, of course, the issue does not arise, and the only matter of importance is the message, presented by parallel teaching.

This point also calls for emphasis on another aspect of Chan commentary, the offering of different views and the use of praise and censure. These techniques are in fact directed at the reader and have nothing to do with intellectual history or differences of opinion among the Chan adepts. In the Chan understanding, no expression or view can ever be complete, and Chan literature explicitly warns that dialogue and difference among Chan adepts are not to be understood in terms of either/or, win/lose choices. Similarly, Wansong's own added sayings are not necessarily direct comments on or illustrations of the statements they are added to; sometimes they are designed to shift the reader into a different viewpoint or shed light on the same point from a different angle. Then again, sometimes they are directed at incorrect or partial ways of understanding certain patterns that centuries of experience showed were typical of dualistic and fragmentary mentation. A considerable amount of Chan commentary is devoted to prevention of fixation and stereotyping and should be seen as addressing the perspective of the reader, not presenting the personal opinion of the speaker.

This characteristic of Chan literature, engaging the reader in mental dialogue rather than professing doctrines and dogmas, is what gives it its life. This is what also makes it so challenging; but the challenge is part of the dynamic, as Chan calls for effort on the part of the would-be learner, without which it would be sterile and ineffective. As a matter of practical principle Chan commentary refrains from exhaustive explanation, for this would crowd out the learner and undermine the very effort needed for the mental transformation the literature is designed to help effect. So Chan literature should be approached with at least the understanding that the desire for quick and convenient understanding has long been recognized as a major barrier to real understanding; and part of the design of Chan literature is to enforce the demand for patience, suspension of preconceptions and judgements, and sustained concentration, without which progess cannot be made.

The overall structure of presentation of the *Book of Serenity* in this translation is as follows:

Introduction by Wansong, generally alluding to particular perspectives, frames of mind, patterns of thought and action.

Case from Chan lore or Buddhist scripture, a saying or anecdote illustrating some aspect or aspects of Chan awareness and praxis.

Commentary by Wansong, expounding upon the case.

Verse by Tiantong reflecting the pattern of the case in poetic form.

Commentary by Wansong on Tiantong's verse.

Added Sayings on the case and verse by Wansong: line by line remarks reflecting or complementing the line or adjusting the understanding of the reader for increased access to potential meaning and function.

A NOTE ON THE TRANSLATION

Each chapter of the *Book of Serenity* consists of several parts: first, an introduction by Wansong; next, the main case, drawn from Chan lore or Buddhist scripture; next, Wansong's prose commentary on the main case; next, Tiantong's verse on the main case; next, Wansong's commentary on Tiantong's verse; finally, Wansong's added remarks on each line of the main case and of Tiantong's poem on each case.

This text has been translated so as to eliminate unnecessary crypticism as much as possible while retaining the meaning and expression also as much as possible. In order to provide for a free flow in reading, no footnotes have been set in the text; suggestive renderings of technical terms and allusions in the context of a total impression built up throughout the text are intended to allow the reader access to the inner design of Chan Buddhist language and lore after reading through the text as a whole to become familiar with its mode of expression. Nevertheless, the great differences of Chinese and English languages and histories makes a certain discrepancy inevitable in pure translation. This has been dealt with in this case in two ways. The notes contain specific terms and allusions in given cases and a glossary of technical terms and metaphors of the classical Chan language has also been added. The latter glossary does not necessarily indicate in which cases which senses of the multi-level terms apply, for this is to be seen by the reader in accordance with the relations of the terms and their application to situations.

BOOK OF
SERENITY

1 THE WORLD HONORED ONE ASCENDS THE SEAT

Introduction Closing the door and sleeping is the way to receive those of highest potential; looking, reflecting, and stretching is a roundabout way for the middling and lesser. How can it bear sitting on the carved wood seat sporting devil eyes? If there is any bystander who doesn't agree, come forward. You can't blame him either.

Case One day the World Honored One ascended the seat. Manjusri struck the gavel and said, "Clearly observe the Dharma of the King of Dharma; the Dharma of the King of Dharma is thus."
The World Honored One then got down from the seat.

Commentary Completely embodying the ten epithets (of Buddhas), appearing in the world as the sole honored one, raising the eyebrows, becoming animated—in the teaching shops this is called 'ascending the seat' and in the meditation forests they call this 'going up in the hall.' Before you people come to this teaching hall and before I leave my room, when will you attain realization?
This is already falling into three and four. Haven't you read Xuedou's saying, "If there had been someone there who could understand the multiplicity of meanings according to situations, as in the Sanskrit word *saindhava,* what would have been the need for Manjusri to strike a beat?" When you bring it up to careful examination, Xuedou shouldn't ask for salt *(saindhava)*—how could I present a horse *(saindhava)*?
Even Manjusri, the ancestral teacher of seven Buddhas of antiquity, saying, "Clearly observe the Dharma of the King of Dharma; the Dharma

3

of the King of Dharma is thus," still needs to pull the nails out of his eyes and wrench the wedges out of the back of his brain before he will realize it.

Even up till now at the conclusion of the opening of the teaching hall we strike the gavel on the sounding board and say, "Clearly observe the Dharma of the Dharma King; the Dharma of the King of Dharma is thus," bringing up this precedent. The World Honored One immediately got down from the seat at that; he saved a half, and imparted a half to Tiantong, whose verse says,

Verse   *The unique breeze of reality—do you see?*
Continuously creation runs her loom and shuttle,
Weaving the ancient brocade, incorporating the forms of spring,
But nothing can be done about Manjusri's leaking.

Commentary   Tiantong says, "The unique breeze of reality—do you see?" Is it the World Honored One's ascending the seat that is the unique breeze of reality? Is Tiantong's reciting his verse the unique breeze of reality? Is my further inquiry the unique breeze of reality? This way it's become three levels—what is the unique breeze of reality? Indeed, you people each have a share, but you should investigate it thoroughly.

He also says, "Continuously creation runs her loom and shuttle." 'Mother of evolution' and 'Creator' are different names for the creation of beings. Confucianism and Taoism are based on one energy; the Buddhist tradition is based on one mind. Guifeng said that the original energy still is created by mind and is all contained in the imagery field of the repository consciousness. I, Wansong, say this is the very source of the Cao-Dong school, the lifeline of the Buddhas and Patriarchs. As the woof goes through the warp, the weave is dense and fine; a continuous thread comes from the shuttle, making every detail—how could this be even spoken of on the same day as false cause or no cause?

After this the verse eulogizes the World Honored One's easygoing abundance, saying "Weaving the ancient brocade, incorporating the forms of spring." Although this is like insects living on wood happening to make

4

patterns, nevertheless though he makes his cart behind closed doors, when he brings it out it fits in the grooves.

Finally, to Manjusri, he gives a cutting putdown, retorting, "Nothing can be done about Manjusri's leaking." Manjusri struck the gavel and the World Honored One thereupon got down from the platform; when Kasyapa struck a gavel, a billion Manjusris appeared—all are this same kind of situation; why are gathering in and letting go not the same? You tell me, where is it that Manjusri has leaked?

> Carefully to open the spice tree buds,
> He lets out the free spring on the branches.

<table>
<tr><td>Added
Sayings
/Case</td><td>

The World Honored One ascended the seat—Today he's not at rest. **Manjusri struck the gavel and said ". . . . the Dharma of the Dharma King is thus"**—I don't know what's going on in his mind. **The World Honored One got down from the seat**—Deal again another day.
</td></tr>
</table>

Added Sayings /Verse

The unique breeze of reality—Don't let it blow in your eyes; it's especially hard to get out.

Continuously creation runs her loom and shuttle—Various differences mix in the woof.

Weaving the ancient brocade . . .—A great adept is as though inept.

Nothing can be done about Manjusri's leaking—Yin and Yang have no irregular succession; seasons do not overlap.

2 BODHIDHARMA'S "EMPTINESS"

Introduction   A man presented a jewel three times but didn't escape punishment. When a luminous jewel is thrown to anyone, few do not draw their sword. For an impromptu guest there is no impromptu host; what's appropriate provisionally is not appropriate for the real. If unusual treasures and rare jewels cannot be put to use, I'll bring out the head of a dead cat—look!

Case   **Emperor Wu of Liang asked Great Teacher Bodhidharma,**
"What is the highest meaning of the holy truths?"
Bodhidharma said, "Empty—there's no holy."
The emperor said, "Who are you facing me?"
Bodhidharma said, "Don't know."
The emperor didn't understand. Bodhidharma subsequently crossed the Yangtse River, came to Shaolin, and faced a wall for nine years.

Commentary   Prajnatara once instructed Bodhidharma, our great teacher, "Sixty-seven years after my death you will go to China to present the medicine of the great teaching, showing it directly to those of excellent faculties; be careful not to go too fast and wither under the sun. And when you get there, don't stay in the South—there they only like fabricated merit and don't see the inner reality of buddhahood, so even if you go there, you shouldn't stay too long." And after all it turned out that he did travel to Liang (in the South), cross over into Wei (in the North), and remained unmoving for nine years.

In recent times, when Cizhou's robe and teaching were bequested to Renshan, Renshan said, "I am not such a man." Cizhou said, "Not being

6

such a man, you do not afflict 'him'." Because of his deep sense of gratitude for the milk of the true teaching, Renshan raised his downcast eyes and accepted. Cizhou went on to say, "Now you are thus; most important, don't appear in the world too readily—if you rush ahead and burst out flippantly, you'll surely get stuck en route."

This, Prajnatara's three instructions, and Bodhidharma's nine years of sitting, are all the same situation. Zhaxi's verse says,

> *Willing to endure the autumn frost*
> *So the deep savor of the teaching will last,*
> *Even though caught alive,*
> *After all he is not lavishly praised.*

This is suitable as an admonition for those in the future. A genuine way-farer knows for himself the time and season when he appears.

Even though Emperor Wu did not comprehend, still he made a point with his question that can be dug into. Even now everywhere when they open the hall and strike the gavel they still say, "Assembly of dragons and elephants at the seat of the Dharma, behold the highest truth." But if it is the ultimate truth, can it after all be seen? Does it admit Emperor Wu's questions or Bodhidharma's answers?

I say, leaving aside the highest meaning for the moment, what do you want with the holy truths? Tianhuang said, "Just end profane feelings—there is no special holy understanding." The *Heroic March Scripture* says, "If you create an understanding of holiness, you will succumb to all errors." Just this Bodhidharma, saying "Empty—there's no holy," undeniably has expert skill and a discerning eye in the light of a spark or flash of lightning.

Emperor Wu stayed there dribbling like a fool, not backing off; he went on to ask, "Who are you who reply to me?" For Emperor Wu's part, this was still a good intention, but he hardly realized that for Bodhidharma it was like being spit in the face. Bodhidharma couldn't help but again offer an "I don't know." Already this is a case of 'the beauty of the flowers easily fades away; how could you add frost to snow?' Bodhidharma saw his eyes moving and immediately shifted his body and traveled another road. The ancients sometimes came forth, sometimes stayed put, sometimes were silent, sometimes spoke; all were doing buddha-work.

Later Emperor Wu after all 'thought about a superior man after he had gone' and personally wrote an epitaph for him, which said,

I saw him without seeing,
Met him without meeting him—
Now as of old
I regret and lament this.

Even though His Majesty was just an ordinary man, he presumed to consider Bodhidharma his teacher in retrospect. After Emperor Wu was covered with dust and Bodhidharma had returned to the West, since then no one has brought up the highest meaning of the truth; fortunately there is Tiantong, who brings it out for the people. His verse says,

Verse *Empty—nothing holy:*
The approach is far off.
Succeeding, he swings the axe without injuring the nose;
Failing, he drops the pitcher without looking back.
Still and silent, coolly he sat at Shaolin:
In silence he completely brought up the true imperative.
The clear moon of autumn turns its frosty disc;
The Milky Way thin, the Dipper hangs down its handle in the night.
In succession the robe and bowl have been imparted to descendants;
From this humans and divinities have made medicine and disease.

Commentary "Emptiness, nothing holy—the approach is far off." The latter expression comes from Zhuangzi—"Very far off, not near to human sense." At that time the patriarch Bodhidharma may have been a bit lacking in expedient technique, but it is hardly realized that unless the medicine stuns you it won't cure the disease. At first he immediately brought down a thunderous hand, but now he has already gone this way to take a rest; therefore 'succeeding, he swings the axe without harming the nose.' As Zhuangzi was attending a funeral procession, as they passed the grave of Huisi he turned and said to his followers, "As Ying Ren was plastering a wall he splashed a bit on his nose, a spot as big as a fly wing; he had Jiang Shi cut it off. Jiang Shi swung his axe, creating a breeze, and cut it off with a whoosh—closing his eyes, letting his hand swing freely, he cut away the whole spot without injuring Ying Ren's nose. Ying Ren stood there without flinching. Since the death of these people, I have no one capable of being my disciples."

"Failing, he drops the pitcher without looking back." Meng Min of the latter Han dynasty stayed in Taiyuan during his travels; once as he was carrying a pitcher, it fell to the ground, but he went on without looking back. Guo Linzong saw this and asked him the meaning. Meng Min replied, "The pitcher is already broken; what's the use of looking back?" Linzong considered him unusual because of this, and urged him to travel for study. The meaning is that if Emperor Wu had spontaneously acquiesced, Bodhidharma would never have cramped himself to go along with another; if Emperor Wu was baffled, Bodhidharma could brush out his sleeves and immediately leave without regret.

In the golden palace he showed his facelessness, managing to say a half; hanging his mouth up on the wall at Shaolin was only eighty percent. This is like "The clear moon of autumn turns its frosty disc." This indirectly makes use of Fayan's poem, "Everywhere I go, the frosty night's moon falls as it may into the valleys ahead," bringing to light the incomparable Way of ultimate truth.

"The Milky Way thin, the Dipper hangs down its handle in the night." In a talk in the teaching hall, Tiantong has said, "In the spherical dot shines the uttermost subtlety; where wisdom is effortless, knowledge remains. When clinging thought is cleared away nothing else is left; in the middle of the night the Dipper handle hangs down in the Milky Way." These two verses are like a mute serving as a messenger—he points it out to people, but can't express it. How could there be master to disciple transmission, mutual quelling of medicine and disease? This misses the point all the more. How is it possible to bring up the true imperative in its entirety?

How much tortoise hair thread is used for the flowers in the sky?
A stone woman uselessly raises the poison needle.

Tsk!

Added   **Emperor Wu asked Bodhidharma**—Even getting up at the crack of
Sayings   dawn, he never made a profit at the market.
/Case   **"What is the highest meaning of the holy truths?"**—For the time being
turn to the secondary to ask.
"Empty, no holy."—Splits his guts and gouges out his heart.
"Who are you facing me?"—He finds tusks in his nostrils.
"Don't know."—'If you see jowls from behind his head . . .'
The Emperor didn't understand—A square peg doesn't fit in a round
hole.
**Bodhidharma crossed the river, came to Shaolin, and faced the wall
for nine years**—A house with no surplus goods doesn't prosper.

Added   *Empty, nothing holy*—Each time you drink water it hits your throat.
Sayings   *The approach is far off*—Honest words are better than a red face.
/Verse   *Succeeding, he swings the axe without injuring the nose*—In an expert's
hands expertise is flaunted.
Failing, he drops the pitcher without looking back—What's already gone
isn't blamed.
Still and silent, coolly he sat at Shaolin—Old, he doesn't rest his mind.
In silence he completely brought up the true imperative—Still he speaks
himself of military devices.
The clear moon of autumn turns its frosty disc—set your eyes on high and
look.
The Milky Way thin, the Dipper hangs down its handle in the night—Who
dares to take hold of it?
In succession the robe and bowl have been imparted to descendants—Don't
think falsely.
From this humans and divinities have made medicine and disease—When an
act of heaven has already passed, the emissary should know.

3 THE INVITATION OF THE PATRIARCH TO EASTERN INDIA

Introduction The state before the beginning of time—a turtle heads for the fire. The one phrase specially transmitted outside of doctrine—the lip of a mortar bears flowers. Now tell me, is there any 'accepting and upholding, reading and reciting' in this?

Case **A rajah of an east Indian country invited the twenty-seventh Buddhist patriarch Prajnatara to a feast. The rajah asked him, "Why don't you read scriptures?" The patriarch said, "This poor wayfarer doesn't dwell in the realms of the body or mind when breathing in, doesn't get involved in myriad circumstances when breathing out—I always reiterate such a scripture, hundreds, thousands, millions of scrolls."**

Commentary The Twenty-Seventh Patriarch was first called Keyura as a boy. As it came to pass that the twenty-sixth patriarch Punyamitra was riding by in a chariot together with a king of eastern India, who was known as 'The Resolute,' the patriarch asked the boy, "Can you remember things of the past?" The boy Keyura replied, "I remember that aeons ago I lived in the same place as you, Master; you were expounding *mahaprajna,* great wisdom, and I was upholding the most profound scripture; I have been awaiting you here to assist you in the true teaching." The patriarch said to the rajah, "This is not one of the lesser holy ones—this is a bodily reflection of Mahasthamaprapta, 'The One Who Has Arrived at Great Power.'"

The rajah had the boy get into the chariot, took him to the palace and made offerings to him. When the boy put on monastic robes and had his head shaved, the patriarch drew on the connection with the *prajna* or *Wisdom Scripture* to have him named Prajnatara, 'Jewel of Wisdom.'

The Liang Court took Bodhidharma to be Avalokitesvara, in India they considered his teacher Prajnatara to be Mahasthamaprapta—only Amitabha Buddha hasn't come down here to earth so far. (a long pause) 'Fenggan talks too much.'

Later, as it happened that the royal family provided for an assembly, the Honorable Prajnatara presided; this old fellow displayed wonders and fooled the crowd—at that time he should have been knocked over, to cut off the complications; if we wait for the question why the Honored One doesn't read scriptures, after all it can't be let go.

And this old fellow Prajnatara had no signs of greatness, either; he took a gourd horse dipper and flipped it over once. The rajah bowed in respect at that—what does he know? I say, the king of a nation coveted one grain of another's rice, the reverend lost ten thousand years' provisions. He only knew his iron spine held up the sky—he didn't realize his brain had fallen to the ground. If you want to help him up, only Tiantong can do it. His verse says,

Verse
A cloud rhino gazes at the moon, its light engulfing radiance;
A wood horse romps in spring, swift and unbridled.
Under the eyebrows, a pair of cold blue eyes;
How can reading scriptures reach the piercing of oxhide?
The clear mind produces vast aeons,
Heroic power smashes the double enclosure.
In the subtle round mouth of the pivot turns the spiritual works.
Hanshan forgot the road by which he came—
Shide led him back by the hand.

Commentary
The opening two lines eulogize 'not dwelling in the realms of body or mind, not involved in myriad circumstances.' According to the analysis of the canonical teachings, five clusters (form, sensation, conception, conditioning, consciousness), twelve sense media (eye, form, ear, sound, nose, smell, tongue, taste, body, feel, mind, phenomena) and eighteen

elements (twelve media plus six associated consciousnesses), are called three groups. The honored one Prajnatara just brought up the head and tail, implicitly including what's in between.

The Sanskrit word *anapana* is translated as breathing out and breathing in. There are six methods involved with this; counting, following, stopping, contemplating, returning, purification. The details are as in the great treatise on cessation and contemplation by the master of Tiantai. Those whose preparation is not sufficient should not fail to be acquainted with this. Guishan's *Admonitions* says, "If you have not yet embraced the principles of the teachings, you have no basis to attain understanding of the mystic path." The *Jewel Mine Treatise* of Sengzhao is beautiful—"A priceless jewel is hidden within the pit of the clusters of being"—when will you find 'the spiritual light shining alone, far transcending the senses'?

Tiantong says, "A cloud rhino gazes at the moon, its light engulfing radiance." In an ancient song it says that the rhino grew his horn while gazing at the pattern on the moon. Good words are to be treasured, but in the final analysis they tend towards feelings and thoughts based on literary content.

"A wood horse romps in spring, swift and unbridled." This eulogizes "breathing out, not involved in myriad circumstances." One might say that skillful action has no tracks.

"Under the eyebrows, a pair of cold blue eyes." Luopu said, "One who has only understood himself and has not yet clarified the eye of objective reality is someone who has only one eye." If you want both eyes to be perfectly clear, you must not dwell in the realms of the body or mind and not get involved in myriad circumstances. And to realize this you must 'hang sun and moon high in the shadowless forest, implicitly discern the spring and autumn on the budless branches.'

"How can reading scripture reach the piercing of oxhide?" Changqing said, "What fault is there in the eye?" In the *Heroic March Scripture* it says, "Now as you look over this assembly of sages, using the eyes to look around, those eyes see everywhere just like a mirror, in which there is no special discrimination." If you miss it here, as Yaoshan said, "You must even pierce through oxhide." I say, after all he had the adamantine eye.

"The clear mind produces vast aeons." The Third Patriarch said, "Just do not hate or love, and all will be clear." Even if one moment of thought is ten thousand years, this cannot be fully upheld. Lumen said, "The whole earth is a student's volume of scripture, the whole world is a student's eye; with this eye, read this scripture, for countless aeons without interruption." I say, it is not easy to read.

"Heroic power smashes the double enclosure." During the latter Han dynasty Wang Mang sent his brothers Wang Xun and Wang Yi to Kunyang, where they surrounded Guang Wu with dozens of rows of soldiers. Guang Wu's army was weak and he wanted to surrender to Xun and Yi, but Yi refused; thereupon Guang Wu made his generals more determined—they marshalled their troops out to fight back and routed Xun and Yi. The honorable Prajnatara was complete in both respects, cultural and military—out, he is a general; in, he is a minister. The elements of being, of body and mind, and the myriad circumstances, are more than a double enclosure.

"In the subtle round mouth of the pivot turns the spiritual works." In the ancient classic *Erya*, the pivot is called the hinge-nest; Guopu's annotation says that it is a doorhinge; flowing water doesn't go stale, a door hinge is not worm-eaten—this means it is active. The Honored One acted before being directed, turned spontaneously without being pushed; whether on *this side* or *that side*, he was beyond right and wrong. Tiantong separates the sand, picks out the gold, distinguishes the marks and divides the ounces—he has judged the fine points.

In the last two lines, he still has extra talent, and says, "When Hanshan forgets the road whence he came, Shide will lead him by the hand to return." This eulogizes the oceanic congregation of the national assembly boring through paper, piercing windows. The Honored One is so kind, he holds forth in brief; "lifting the blind to return the baby sparrow, from the paper full of holes comes a silly fly." His use of Hanshan's poem is like joining complementary tokens. The poem says,

If you want a place to rest your body,
Cold Mountain is good for long preservation.
A subtle breeze blows in the dense pines;
Heard from close by, the sound is even finer,
Underneath the trees is a greying man
Furiously reading Taoist books.

Ten years I couldn't return—
Now I've forgotten the road whence I came.

"After Lu Qiuling came to call, he went back together with Shide; after going out the pine gate, he never returned to the monastery." One book says, "Volubly reading Taoist books." This versifies a child lost, forgetting how to return, and a lost man pointing the way.

Emperor Zhuangzong of the latter Tang dynasty invited Chan Master Xiujing of Huayan temple into the palace for a feast. The great teachers and great worthies there were all reading scriptures; only master Xiujing's group was silent. The emperor asked, "Why don't you read scriptures?" Xiujing said, "When the way is easy, we don't pass along the imperial command; during the halcyon days we stop singing the song of great peace." The emperor said, "For you not to read scriptures may be all right, master, but why don't your followers read them either?" Xiujing said, "In a lion's den there are no other kinds of animals; where the elephant walks there are no fox tracks." The emperor said, "Why do the Great Teachers and Great Worthies all read scriptures?" Xiujing said, "Jellyfish have no eyes—in seeking food they must depend on prawns." The emperor was delighted.

At that, the honored patriarch Prajnatara has been called Mahasthamaprapta for long aeons, and because he recited the profoundest scripture he was named Prajnatara by his teacher, but really had not yet got rid of habit energy and was bested by that Xiujing, who after all has the nose of a patchrobe monk. At this point I unconsciously let out a laugh—what was I laughing at?

Where the statues of Yunju bare their chests,
When the pitchers of Gongxian close their mouths.

Added Sayings /Case **A rajah invited the Twenty-Seventh Patriarch**—Over and over again he'll be paying back the debt of his mouth.

"Why don't you read scriptures?"—Whoever receives a salary without service is uneasy in sleeping and eating.

"I don't dwell in the realms of body or mind when breathing in, don't get involved in myriad circumstances when breating out—I always reiterate this scripture, hundreds, thousands, millions of scrolls"—The preceding lecture and eulogy was an unlimited excellent cause.

15

Added
Sayings
/Verse *A cloud rhino gazes at the moon, its light engulfing radiance*—He subtly puts a line through; the pattern is already evident.

A wood horse romps in spring, swift and unbridled—Going through a cluster of hundreds of flowers, not a petal sticks to his body.

Under the eyebrows, a pair of cold blue eyes—Never chased a bunch of snakes and ants.

How can reading scriptures reach the piercing of oxhide?—Gone through!

The clear mind produces vast aeons—One arrow before the prehistoric buddhas . . .

Heroic power smashes the double enclosure—. . . shoots through the double barrier.

In the subtle round mouth of the pivot turns the spiritual works—When has it ever moved?

Hanshan forgot the road by which he came—Not being present for a while is like being the same as a dead man.

Shide led him back by the hand—This has to be a man of the same locality.

16

4 THE WORLD HONORED ONE POINTS TO THE GROUND

Introduction   As soon as a single mote of dust arises, the whole earth is contained therein; with a single horse and a single lance, the land's extended. Who is this person who can be master in any place and meet the source in everything?

Case   **As the World Honored One was walking with the congregation, he pointed to the ground with his finger and said, "This spot is good to build a sanctuary."**
Indra, Emperor of the gods, took a blade of grass, stuck it in the ground, and said, "The sanctuary is built."
The World Honored One smiled.

Commentary   When the World Honored One spread his hair to cover mud and offered flowers to Dipankara Buddha, 'The Lamp,' that Buddha pointed to where the hair was spread and said, "A sanctuary should be built in this place." At that time an elder known as the foremost of the wise planted a marker in that spot and said, "The building of the sanctuary is finished." The gods scattered flowers and praised him for having wisdom while an ordinary man. The story Tiantong quotes here is much the same. I say, the World Honored One's ancestral work was given over to Dipankara; then there was the elder—getting the beginning, he took in the end.
Now it is given over to Tiantong, who must produce a matching literary talisman.

Verse   *The boundless spring on the hundred plants;*

Picking up what comes to hand, he uses it knowingly.

The sixteen-foot-tall golden body, a collection of virtuous qualities

Casually leads him by the hand into the red dust;

Able to be master in the dusts,

From outside creation, a guest shows up.

Everywhere life is sufficient in its way—

No matter if one is not as clever as others.

Commentary   Tiantong first versifies the case with four lines, then sets up the main beam and expresses the enlightening way.

Zhaozhou picked up a blade of grass and used it as the sixteen-foot body of gold. The World Honored One pointed the way the wind was blowing, Indra brought forth what was at hand.

Tiantong's verse emerges from the merging of subject and object; it is not just the ancient sages, but you too can be host within the dust right now, and also come as a guest from outside creation.

But tell me; in the current trend, Liu Fuma had this temple built to requite a debt of gratitude; is this the same as Indra thrusting the blade of grass in the ground?

(raising the whisk) A community for a day, abiding forever.

Added Sayings /Case   **As the Buddha was walking with the congregation**—Going along following the heels of another.

He pointed to the ground and said, "This spot is good to build a sanctuary."—Shouldn't move earth on the head of the guardian spirit.

Indra stuck a blade of grass in the ground and said, "The sanctuary is built."—Repairs won't be easy.

The Buddha smiled—Reward and punishment are distinctly clear.

Added Sayings /Verse   *The boundless spring on the hundred plants*—Jiashan's still around.

Picking up what comes to hand, he uses it knowingly—Going into a wild field, not choosing.

The sixteen-foot golden body, a collection of virtues—How are you?

18

Casually leads him by the hand into the red dust—He gives a show wherever he may be.

Able to be master in the dusts—One day the authority is in one's own hands.

From outside creation, a guest shows up—Observe when the imperative goes into effect.

Everywhere life is sufficient in its way—It's not gotten from others.

No matter if one is not as clever as others—No color of shame on the face.

5 QINGYUAN AND THE PRICE OF RICE

Introduction Siddhartha cut off his flesh to give to his parents, yet is not listed in the legends of filial children. Devadatta pushed over a mountain to crush the Buddha, but did he fear the sound of sudden thunder? Having passed through the forest of thorns, and cut down the sandalwood tree, just wait till the year ends—as of old, early spring is still cold. Where is the Buddha's body of reality?

Case **A monk asked Qingyuan, "What is the great meaning of Buddhism?" Qingyuan said, "What is the price of rice in Luling?"**

Commentary When Chan Master Xingsi of Qingyuan Mountain in Ji province first called on the Sixth Patriarch, he immediately asked, "What work should be done so as to be able not to fall into steps and stages?" The patriarch said, "What have you done?" Qingyuan said, "I do not even practice the holy truths." The patriarch said, "If even the holy truths are not practiced, what steps or stages are there?" The patriarch considered him to be of profound capacity. Although there were many people in the congregation of the Sixth Patriarch, the master Qingyuan dwelt at their head. It was also like when the Second Patriarch said nothing, whereupon Bodhidharma told him, "You have my marrow."

Judging by this monk's question about the ultimate meaning of the Buddist teaching, he too was a true-blue newcomer to the monastery—he wants to travel around the iron enclosing mountains with Manjusri. Qingyuan was a man who didn't even practice the holy truths—yet he just makes it an ordinary encounter, looking back and asking, "What is the price of rice in Luling?"

Some say, "The price of rice in Luling cannot be assessed." They hardly realize that they have already entered into bushels and pecks and set up shop. Do you want to be able to avoid entering this company? Ask of Tiantong; his verse says,

Verse   *The accomplishing work of great peace has no sign;*
The family way of the peasants is most pristine—
Only concerned with village songs and festival drinking,
How would they know of the virtues of Shun or the benevolence of Yao?

Commentary   In 832, during the reign of Emperor Wenzong of the Tang dynasty, Niu Sengru was prime minister; the emperor said to him, "When will the land be at peace?" Sengru replied, "Peaceful government has no special form. Now the surrounding nations are not invading and the farmers are not deserting; although it is not the ultimate order, still it could be called somewhat healthy. If your majesty seeks a great peace beyond this, it is beyond my ability." He withdrew and repeatedly petitioned the emperor to be allowed to retire. He was sent out as the inspector of Huainan. I say, he was already creating a model, drawing a likeness.

Therefore, in rustic style, beating the earth and singing folksongs, ritual music and literary embellishment turn into oddities.

The price of rice in Luling is extremely profound and mysterious. The virtue of Shun, the benevolence of Yao—their sincerity had natural influence; could festival drinking and village songs be a match for that? The moon is white, the wind is pure—each rests in its own lot. Do you understand? Then return to the hall.

Added Sayings /Case   **A monk asked Qingyuan, "What is the great meaning of Buddhism?"** —A minor official often thinks of the rules.
Qingyuan said, "What is the price of rice in Luling?"—An old general doesn't talk of soldiering.

21

*Added
Sayings
/ Verse*

The accomplishing work of great peace has no sign—Is the star on the banner showing yet?

The family way of the peasants is most pristine—'How does that compare to me here planting the fields and making rice balls to eat?'

Only concerned with village songs and festival drinking—The poor ghost is not really alive.

How would they know of the virtures of Shun or the benevolence of Yao?—Thus they achieve loyalty and filiality.

6 MAZU'S "WHITE AND BLACK"

Introduction   Where you can't open your mouth, a tongueless man can speak; where you lift your feet without rising, a legless man can walk. If you fall within their range and die at the phrase, how can you have any freedom? When the four mountains all oppress you, how can you penetrate to freedom?

Case   A monk asked Great Master Mazu, "Apart from the four propositions and beyond the hundred negations, please directly point out the meaning of living Buddhism."

The Great Master said, "I'm tired out today and can't explain for you. Go ask Zhizang."

The monk asked Zhizang; Zhizang said, "Why don't you ask the teacher?"

The monk said, "The teacher told me to come ask you."

Zhizang said, "I have a headache today and can't explain for you. Ask brother Hai."

The monk asked Hai; Hai said, "When I come this far, after all I don't understand."

The monk related this to the Great Master; Mazu said, "Zang's head is white, Hai's head is black."

Commentary   The Sixth Patriarch said to Master Huairang, "The Twenty-Seventh Patriarch of India foretold that from your disciples will emerge a young horse who will trample everyone in the land to death. The sickness is in your heart; don't speak too quickly."

Later Huairang polished a tile and beat an ox, and the spiritual horse entered the stable; he was called Mazu, Ancestor Ma ('horse'). He had the stride of an ox and the glare of a tiger. He could extend his tongue over his nose. On his soles were circular marks. One hundred and thirty-nine people succeeded to him in the Dharma, and each became a teaching master in one area. Zhizang and brother Hai were Xitang and Baizhang.

When we look at this monk, he too is a student of Buddhism; he uses the four propositions and hundred negations to make sure of the source essence of the special transmission outside the teachings.

The *Mahayanasamgraha* says, "'Existence' is slander by exaggeration, 'nonexistence' is slander by underestimation; 'both existence and nonexistence' is slander by contradiction, and 'neither existence nor nonexistence' is slander by intellectual fabrication." If you abandon these four propositions (of existence, nonexistence, both, or neither), the hundred negations are spontaneously wiped out.

Huangbo said, "If you want to understand directly and immediately, everything is not it." I say, "If you understand clearly and thoroughly, nothing is not it."

Looking at it the other way around, without abandoning the four propositions or the hundred negations, where is the meaning of living Buddhism not clear?

The Great Master Nagarjuna said, "Wisdom is like a mass of fire—it cannot be entered from any side." Yet he also said, "Wisdom is like a clear cool pool, it can be entered from any side."

This monk said, "Apart from the four propositions and beyond the hundred negations, please point out to me directly the meaning of living Buddhism." Everywhere they call this a question in the mouth of a shackle; but Mazu wasn't flustered—he just said, "I'm too tired to tell you today. Go ask Zhizang." He spared his own eyebrows and pierced that monk's nose; that monk did not escape being sent away—he really went and asked. Zhizang too fit in the groove without contrivance—"Why don't you ask the teacher?" The monk didn't open his eyes; he said, "The teacher told me to come ask you." Zhizang said, "I've got a headache today, I can't explain for you. Go ask brother Hai."

The monk asked Hai, who said, "When I come to this, after all I don't understand." 'I thought it was Houbai (the thief), but here is even Houhei (who robbed Houbai by trickery).'

Although the monk didn't have a sanguine nature, still he saw things through from start to finish—he told all this to Mazu, who said, "Zang's head is white, Hai's head is black." This statement kills everyone in the world with doubt.

A verse of Zhaojue of Donglin says,

> The hundred negations and four propositions gone, wordless,
> Black and white distinctly clear, determining absolute and relative.

I say 'four in the morning, three at night'—they are glad or mad without reason.

One night as these three great men were gazing at the moon along with Nanquan, Mazu said, "What should one do at this very moment?" Baizhang said, "Just right to cultivate practice." Xitang said, "Just right to make offerings." Nanquan brushed out his sleeves and left. Mazu said, "The scriptures go into the treasury (zang); meditation goes into the ocean (hai)—only Nanquan alone transcends utterly beyond things." Even here black and white should be clearly distinguished.

I say, 'Zang's head is white, Hai's head is black'—a duck's head is green, a crane's head is red. The ten-shadowed spiritual horse stands south of the ocean, the five-colored auspicious unicorn walks north of the sky. People everywhere, do not depend on a fox spirit—Tiantong has the real story. His verse says,

Verse

> Medicine working as illness—
> It is mirrored in the past sages.
> Illness working as medicine—
> Sure, but who is it?
> White head, black head—capable heirs of the house.
> Statement or no statement—the ability to cut off the flow.
> Clearly sitting cutting off the road of speech,
> Laughable is the old ancient awl at Vaisali.

Commentary   The four propositions as four repudiations are like 'a mass of fire which cannot be entered from any side'—the four propositions as four gates are like 'a pure cool pool which can be entered from any side.'

When I was scribe at Daming in the old days, Master Heng of Tanshi passed through Daming; I knocked on the door in the dark of night, calling his attendant, burned incense and formed a relationship—then Tanshi allowed me to see him. I asked him to tell me more about what is the living word and what is the dead word. He said, "Scribe, if you understand the dead word, it is the living word; if you don't understand the living word, then it is the dead word." At that time I thought to myself that the methods of an old adept would after all be different.

Now looking at this monk's question today, he stayed anchored, demanding to have the living meaning pointed out apart from the four propositions and beyond the hundred negations. The three old fellows' brains resembled one another—if you immediately understand as abandoning the four propositions and transcending the hundred negations, you will be buried in the same pit with this monk.

Later Tiantong eulogized Yangshan's dream about striking the gavel: "Abandon the four propositions, cut off the hundred negations—in sickness Master Ma and his children stopped doctoring." I say, what mental activity is this?

"White head, black head—capable heirs of the house." In the *Book of Changes,* under the diagram 'covering' it says, "Capable heirs of the house are able to uphold the family work."

"Statement or no statement—the ability to cut off the flow." I say, he has only ripples on still water, no waves flooding the heavens.

"Clearly sitting cutting off the road of speech, laughable is the old ancient awl at Vaisali." The Sanskrit name of Vaisali means 'vast adornment' in translation—this is the name of the city where Vimalakirti lived. Manjusri asked Vimalakirti about the real way to nonduality, and Vimalakirti remained silent; when this monk questioned father Mazu and his sons, elaborations covered the earth.

Tell me, what is it that is laughable?

'If you can just avoid the taboo name of the present, you'll surpass the eloquence of a former dynasty, which cut off every tongue.'

<table>
<tr>
<td>Added
Sayings
/Case</td>
<td>

"Apart from the four propositions and hundred negations, what is the meaning of living Buddhism?"—If they knew the point of this monk's question, it would save people untold mental power.

"I'm tired out today and can't explain for you."—There's already the moon in the boat.

Go ask Zhizang"—He adds wind to the sail.

(the monk asked Zhizang)—After all he accepts people's judgements.

"Why don't you ask the teacher?"—Good texts are much the same.

"The teacher told me to ask you."—How very bright and sharp!

"I have a headache today and can't explain for you."—'I shouldn't be unable to be Master Ma's disciple.'

The monk asked Hai—A bitter gourd is bitter to the root.

"When I come this far, after all I don't understand."—A sweet melon is sweet to the stem.

The monk recounted this to the great master—Get some money for shoes!

"Zang's head is white, Hai's head is black."—Investigate for thirty more years.

</td>
</tr>
<tr>
<td>Added
Sayings
/Verse</td>
<td>

Medicine working as illness—A barbarian drinks milk and then is suspicious of a good doctor.

It is mirrored in the past sages—When the teachers are many, the lineage is confused.

Illness working as medicine—Digesting medicine with medicine, eliminating poison by poison.

Sure, but who is it?—Isn't it Tiantong?

White head, black head—capable heirs of the house—Cooked with one steaming.

Statement or no statement—the ability to cut off the flow—He renews Guishan's laughter.

Clearly sitting cutting off the road of speech—Once dead you don't live again.

Laughable is the old ancient awl of Vaisali—He just got one part.

</td>
</tr>
</table>

7 YAOSHAN ASCENDS THE SEAT

Introduction Eyes, ears, nose, tongue—each has one ability. The eyebrows are above. Warriors, farmers, crafters, merchants—each returns to a job. The unskilled one is always at leisure. How does a real Chan master devise techniques?

Case Yaoshan hadn't ascended the seat (to lecture) for a long time. The temple superintendent said to him, "Everybody's been wanting instruction for a long time—please, Master, expound the Teaching for the congregation."
Yaoshan had him ring the bell; when the congregation had gathered, Yaoshan ascended the seat: after a while he got right back down from the seat and returned to his room. The superintendent followed after him and asked, "A while ago you agreed to expound the Teaching for the congregation. Why didn't you utter a single word?"
Yaoshan said, "For scriptures there are teachers of scriptures, for the treatises there are teachers of treatises. How can you question this old monk?"

Commentary The hungry will eat anything, the thirsty will drink anything. Therefore at five requests from three people bodhisattvas enter the teaching hall, showing their whole bodies with half a verse; demigods take the high seat—how could they begrudge the teaching?
Chan Master Huinan of Huanglong said, "Nowadays many people take the Dharma lightly; I would be like a farmer who lets the fields dry from time to time to make them parched and thirsty—after that, when water is poured on, then the crops sprout." When Yaoshan did not take

the high seat for a long time, however, it was not like this. Jiaofan said, "A hut conceals deep within a thunderous tongue; let the myriad forms explain on their own." Yongjia said, "Speaking when silent, silent when speaking; the gate of great generosity opens, with nothing blocking the way."

The administrator missed every point; he said, "The community has been wanting some instruction for a long time—please expound the teaching for them." In the course of humanity and duty, in the capacity of host and guest, this is not out of line—so Yaoshan had him ring the bell. He only saw the thunderous issue of the command; when the congregation gathered, how could they know the stars would blaze with glory? Yaoshan took the high seat, remained silent, then after awhile got down and returned to the abbot's room—this act of supernormal power is not the same as the little ones.

The superintendent monk followed behind and asked, "A while ago you agreed to expound the teaching for the congregation—why didn't you utter a single word?" Cuiyan Zhi said, "When Yaoshan got down from the seat, at first the superintendent wondered why he didn't say a single word—this could be called misleading his three armies." I say, it's just that the general is not valiant.

Yaoshan said, "For scriptures there are teachers of scriptures; for the treatises there are teachers of treatises. How can you doubt this old monk?" Langya Jiao said, "When Yaoshan got down from the seat, doubt was unavoidable; when he was confronted by the superintendent, he lost one eye." I say, how many could recover completely? Yet he doesn't know how to get back two eyes. Xuedou said, "What a pity that old fellow Yaoshan bit the dust on even ground; no one in the world can help him up." I say, you too should lend a hand.

Wuyu's verse said,

> He had already bit the dust before leaving his room;
> Quietly he returns, with no further mistake.
> Teachers of scriptures and treatises still tell each other;
> When one fact is distinctly clear he'll call them himself.

I say, government officials are easily tested, but the public case is not complete. Giving it to Tiantong, how will he judge?

Verse   *A foolish child troubles over 'money' used to stop crying;*
A good steed chases the wind, looking back at the shadow of the whip.
Clouds sweep the eternal sky; nesting in the moon, the crane—
The cold clarity gets into his bones, he can't go to sleep.

Commentary   In the *Great Demise Scripture* it says when a child cries its mother takes yellow leaves and says, 'I'll give you some gold,' whereupon the child stops crying. The first line versifies "We have been wishing for some instruction for a long time; why didn't you utter a single word?"

An outsider asked the Buddha, "I don't ask about the spoken or the unspoken." The World Honored One remained silent; the outsider then bowed and said, "The World Honored One's great compassion has opened the clouds of my illusion and allowed me to gain insight." After the outsider had left, Ananda asked the Buddha, "What truth did he see that he said he had gained insight?" The Buddha said, "Like a good horse, he goes as soon as he sees the shadow of the whip."

Yaoshan and the World Honored One raised the whip alike; the superintendent led the assembly of monks—there is something to praise. Yet he wondered why Yaoshan didn't say anything—we might say that patch-robed monks in China are not as good as outsiders in India. Tiantong's versification in this way and my explanation in this way are all yellow leaves to stop crying. It is just because you are sound asleep and not yet awakened. Those whose sleep is light will wake up as soon as they're called; those deep asleep can only be roused by shaking them. There is yet another kind who, when you grab them and stand them up like dead trees they still talk in their sleep by themselves, staring. Compared to that Yaoshan, a crane nesting in the clear moon, so clear he can't sleep, the difference is as between clouds and mud. But even so, his sleep talk is not little.

Added   Yaoshan hadn't ascended the seat for a long time—Movement isn't as
Sayings   good as stillness.
/Case   The temple superintendent said to him, "Everybody's been wanting instruction for a long time—please expound the teaching for the assembly."—He relies on the heavy, not the light.

Yaoshan had him ring the bell; when the assembly had gathered—
Gathering together acting as ministers, what matter could be troublesome?
Yaoshan ascended the seat; after a while he got right back down and returned to his room—That's something to talk about!
"Why didn't you utter a single word?"—If the ocean were filled, the hundred rivers would have to flow backwards.
"For scriptures there are scripture teachers, for treatises there are treatise teachers—how can you wonder about this old monk?"—Too bad—a dragon's head but a snake's tail.

Added *A foolish child troubles over 'money' used to stop crying*—What's the use?
Sayings What can he possibly do?
/Verse *A good steed chases the wind, looking back at the shadow of the whip*—He
gets right up and goes.
Clouds sweep the eternal sky; nesting in the moon, the crane—An embarrassment for the one under the tree.
The cold clarity gets into its bones, he can't go to sleep—Dreaming with open eyes.

8 BAIZHANG'S "FOX"

Introduction If you keep so much as the letter *a* in your mind, you'll go to hell like an arrow shot; one drop of wild fox slobber, when swallowed, cannot be spit out for thirty years. It is not that the order is strict in India; it's just that the ignoramus's karma is heavy. Has there ever been anyone who mistakenly transgressed?

Case **When Baizhang lectured in the hall, there was always an old man who listened to the teaching and then dispersed with the crowd. One day he didn't leave; Baizhang then asked him, "Who is it standing there?"**

The old man said, "In antiquity, in the time of the ancient Buddha Kasyapa, I lived on this mountain. A student asked, 'Does a greatly cultivated man still fall into cause and effect or not?' I answered him, 'He does not fall into cause and effect,' and I fell into a wild fox body for five hundred lives. Now I ask the teacher to turn a word in my behalf."

Baizhang said, "He is not blind to cause and effect."

The old man was greatly enlightened at these words.

Commentary On Baizhang Mountain in Hong prefecture, every time Chan Master Dazhi ascended the high seat, there was always an old man listening to his teaching. The old man had dwelt on this mountain in the time of Kasyapa Buddha; because he had answered a student mistakenly, up to the present he had degenerated into a wild fox being. Indeed it was because he himself leaned on a fence and stuck to a wall, sending people off to fall into a pit and plunge into a ditch.

He saw that Dazhi had the skill to pull out nails and draw out pegs, so he forsook himself and followed the other, asking Dazhi to turn a word in his behalf. Dazhi gave a fearless explanation, lightly turning and saying, "He is not blind to cause and effect." The old man was greatly enlightened at these words. He based his logic on actuality; not falling into cause and effect is forced denial, a nihilistic view; not being blind to cause and effect is finding the wondrous along with the flow.

Those who understand the vehicle of the teachings see immediately when this is brought up, but though they shed their hair clothes, they're still wearing scale armor. Have you not heard it told how when Chan Master Yuan was in the assembly of Chan Master Hui he heard two monks bring up this story; one monk said, "Even if he's not blind to cause and effect, he still hasn't shed the wild fox body." The other monk replied, "Just this is not falling into cause and effect—and when has he ever fallen into cause and effect?" The master was startled and considered these words unusual; he hurried to the bamboo cluster hermitage on Mount Huangbo—as he crossed a valley stream he was suddenly enlightened. He saw Master Nan and told what happened; before he finished tears were streaming over his jaws. Master Nan made him sleep soundly on the attendants' bench; but suddenly he got up and wrote a verse:

> *Not falling, not blind;*
> *For monks or layfolk there are no taboos.*
> *The bearing of a freeman is like a king's—*
> *How can he accept the enclosure of a bag or covering by a lid?*
> *One staff can be horizontal or vertical—*
> *The wild fox leaps into the company of the golden lion.*

Master Nan laughed.

Seeing it in this way, when we first see him say, "I now ask you to turn a word for me," hopefully he would have said, "He does not fall into cause and effect," to avoid causing beginners to fall into the pit of understanding.

In the evening Baizhang went into the hall and recounted the preceding events: Huangbo immediately asked, "An ancient answered a turning word mistakenly and fell into a wild fox body for five hundred lives;

what if one is not mistaken, turn after turn?" Baizhang said, "Come here and I'll tell you." Huangbo approached and gave Baizhang a slap; Baizhang clapped his hands laughing and said, "I knew foxes' beards were red—here's another red-bearded fox!"

Yangshan said, "Baizhang attained the great capacity, Huangbo attained the great function." They didn't have the names for no reason; Guishan asked Yangshan, "Huangbo always uses this capacity—did he get it by birth or from another?" Yangshan said, "This is both his receiving a teacher's bequest and also inherent communion with the source." Guishan said, "So it is."

Look at that father Baizhang and son—they roam fearlessly like lion kings—how could they make a living in a wild fox den?

My tail bone is already showing more and more—now I'll let Tiantong loose to ply his claws and fangs. Look—his verse says,

Verse   *A foot of water, a fathom of wave.*
For five hundred lives he couldn't do a thing.
'Not falling,' 'not blind,' they haggle,
As before entering a nest of complications.
Ah, ha! ha!
Understand?
If you are clear and free
There's no objection to my babble.
The spirit songs and shrine dances spontaneously form a harmony—
Clapping in the intervals, singing 'li-la.'

Commentary   Establishing practice and realization, distinguishing cause and effect—a foot of water, a fathom of wave. Falling into the spirit of a wild fox for five hundred lives—even if the two monks at the bamboo cluster hermitage had extraordinary discernment, when we hold them up to examination, they have not avoided plunging into a tangle. In this line of Tiantong's there are two characters which do not rest easy—why doesn't he say, "As before they plunge into a wild fox lair"?

"Ah, ha! ha!" This illustrates Baizhang's enlightenment: Tiantong reveals what's in his own heart, saying, "Understand?" But I ask, does Tiantong understand? "If you are clear and free, there's no objection to my babble." Fortunately he has status—what chore would he not do for others? Babble, "dada wawa," is baby talk—representing that it is not real speech. Also the *Weir of Interpretation of the Lotus of Reality* says, "Dada is a symbol of learning action; wawa is a symbol of learning speech." In the *Great Demise Scripture* there is 'sickness practice' and 'baby practice.' Some books say 'baba wawa.' Chan Master Shandao of Shishi said, "Among the sixteen practices in the *Great Demise*, the baby practice is best." All this is the same meaning as the "spirit songs and shrine dances." But tell me, what is the harmony?

> *Ten thousand pipes you cannot hear if you have mind;*
> *On a solitary cliff without ears then you know the sound.*

Added Sayings / Case

When Baizhang lectured, there was an old man who used to listen and then disperse with the crowd—Finding quiet in the midst of noise.
One day he didn't leave—Been doubting this guy all along.
Baizhang asked him, "Who are you?"—Things can't be mixed up—when a guest comes you should wait on him.
"I lived on this mountain in ancient times."—Originally he is a man of the house.
A student asked, "Does a greatly cultivated man fall into cause and effect?"—Just do good, don't ask about the road ahead.
"He does not fall into cause and effect."—A fitting statement is a stake to tie a donkey to for ten thousand years.
I fell into a wild fox body for five hundred lives—You said one doesn't fall into cause and effect.
Now I ask the teacher to turn a word in my behalf—What reason can you give?
"He isn't blind to cause and effect."—Buried in one pit.
The old man was enlightened at these words—Fox drool is still there.

Added Sayings / Verse

A foot of water, a fathom of wave—Luckily naturally the rivers are clear, the ocean is calm.
For five hundred lives he couldn't do a thing—If he had known what would happen today, he'd regret not being careful to begin with.

'Not falling' 'not blind' they haggle—Stupid slobbering hasn't stopped.

As before entering a nest of complications—wrapping around the waist, entangling the legs.

Ah, ha, ha!—Laughable, pitiable.

Understand?—He holds the cow's head to make it eat grass.

If you are clear and free—Like insects chewing wood . . .

There's no objection to my babble— . . . happening to make a pattern.

Spirit songs and shrine dances spontaneously form a harmony—Each clap is the order.

Clapping in the intervals, singing 'li-la'—Growing finer.

9 NANQUAN KILLS A CAT

Introduction Kick over the ocean and dust flies on the earth; scatter the clouds with shouts, and empty space shatters. Strictly executing the true imperative is still half the issue; as for the complete manifestation of the great function, how do you carry it out?

Case One day at Nanquan's the eastern and western halls were arguing over a cat. When Nanquan saw this, he took and held it up and said, "If you can speak I won't cut it."
The group had no reply; Nanquan then cut the cat in two.
Nanquan also brought up the foregoing incident to Zhaozhou and asked him: Zhaozhou immediately took off his sandals, put them on his head, and left. Nanquan said, "If you had been here you could have saved the cat."

Commentary Chan Master Yuantong Xiu of Fayun saw two monks standing together talking; he took his staff, went up to them and hit the ground several times with the staff and said, "A piece of karmic ground." How much the more so in the case of the leaders of the groups in the two halls, who got into an argument over a cat; Nanquan didn't offer them forgiveness or encouragement, nor did he give them admonition and punishment— a genuine man of the Way, he used the fundamental matter to help people; holding up the cat, he said, "If you can say a word I won't cut it." At that moment all sentient and inanimate beings in the whole universe are alike in Nanquan's hands begging for their lives.
At that point, if there had been someone who came forward and either

37

extended open hands or else grabbed him by the chest and held him tight and said, "After all, we sympathize with the Master's spiritual work," even if Nanquan had specially carried out the true imperative, I dare say (that person) would have been able to save the cat. But this den of dead rats had no energy at all; once Nanquan held forth, he wouldn't withdraw, and acted out the order to the full.

Eminent Xin of the Liao dynasty wrote the *Mirror Mind Collection,* in which he criticizes Nanquan's group for killing a living being, committing wrongdoing. Head Monk Wen wrote *Discerning Errors in the 'Inexhaustible Lamp'* in which he helped (Nanquan) out, saying, "An ancient text has it that he just made the gesture of cutting—how could he have simply cut it in two with one stroke, sending fresh blood gushing?" In these two critiques of the ancient, Mr. Wen's fault is the graver, whereas Mr. Xin's fault is the lesser.

As ever, Nanquan was shaking his head and wagging his tail in a herd of water buffalo. Haven't you read how as Chan Master Fori was having tea with his group he saw a cat coming and tossed a dove from his sleeve, giving it to the cat, which took it and went away. Fori said, "Excellent!" This too cannot be false contrivance of empty action.

Nanquan thought to himself that 'where the tune is lofty, few join in'— reciting the preceding story to Zhaozhou, he questioned him about it, whereupon Zhaozhou took off his sandals, put them on his head, and went out. After all, drumming and singing go together; clapping the interval was accomplished perfectly—Nanquan said, "If you had been here you could have saved the cat." Although this little bit of activity is difficult to understand, yet it is easy to see—just see through it in lifting the spoon and picking up chopsticks, and you will see that the cutting of the cat and the wearing of the sandals on the head are not any different. Otherwise, look again; what tricks has Tiantong specially created?

Verse   *The monks of both halls were all arguing;*
      Old Teacher Nanquan was able to show up true and false.
      Cutting through with a sharp knife, all oblivious of formalities,
      For a thousand ages he makes people admire an adept.
      This path has not perished—

A connoisseur is to be lauded.
In tunneling through mountains to let the sea pass through,
only Great Yu is honored:
In smelting rock and mending the sky, only Guonu is considered best.
Old Zhaozhou had a life:
Wearing sandals on his head, he attains a bit.
Coming in differences, still clearly mirroring;
Only this real gold is not mixed with sand.

Commentary "All the monks of both halls were arguing"—up till now they have never settled their controversy. If not for Tiantong understanding how Nanquan's example evinces the whole from a clue, time and again the mistaken and the correct would not be distinguished. When the false and the true are distinct, how do you judge them? Then you should cut them off with a sharp sword and bury them in one pit. This will not only put an end to a whole lifetime's unfinished business, it will also cause the breeze to be pure throughout the land for a thousand ages.

At Nanquan's the teacher was excellent, the apprentice strong; seeing the group had nothing to say, he recounted it to Zhaozhou, to show that there was a man in the crowd. Zhaozhou took off his sandals, put them on his head and walked out—after all "this path has not perished—a connoisseur is to be lauded." Confucius said, "Heaven is not about to destroy this culture." Observe how the paths of teacher and apprentice merged, singing and clapping following along with each other; nothing can compare.

In the method for making illustrative posthumous names it says that the flowing through of the fountainhead of the spring is called Yu. Also being the beneficiary of abdication and accomplishing good works is called Yu. In the classic geography *The Contributions of King Yu,* it says, "He led the river from Rock Mass Mountain to Dragon Gate Gorge."

According to the book of Huainan, "The army of the Gonggong clan was strong and violent, and they contended with king Yao; when their strength was exhausted they ran up against the Buzhou Mountains and died. Because of this the pillar of heaven broke; the goddess Guonu smelted five-color stones to repair the sky." Liezi says, "When the positive and negative principles lose balance, that is called 'lack'—smelting the essence of the five constants is called repairing."

Master Ben of Yungai brought up the story of Dongshan taking away the fruit tray from the head monk Tai and said, "Though Dongshan has the mallet to shatter the void, still he doesn't have the needle and thread to mend it."

Nanquan is like great Yu, who dug through the montains to let the sea pass through, manifesting extraordinary actions: Zhaozhou is like Guonu smelting stones to repair the sky; he finished the story.

I say, Zhaozhou was able to break up the home and scatter the family eighteen times; I don't know how many lives he had. Wearing sandals on his head amounts to something—tsk! tsk! there's nowhere to go, acting this way.

Baofu Congzhan said, "Even though he's right, it's just worn-out sandals; Nanquan leveled the high and spoke to the low—'If you had been here, you could have saved the cat.'"

Cuiyan Zhi said, "Even the great Zhaozhou could only save himself." He passed up the first move.

Tiantong said, "Coming in differences, still clearly mirroring; only this real gold is not mixed with sand." He only can push the boat along with the stream; he doesn't know how to steer against the wind.

And now this bunch of you are here, and we have no cat; what dog shall we argue over?

(Wansong chased them out with his staff.)

Added Sayings /Case **The eastern and western halls were arguing over a cat**—People on an even level don't speak, water on an even level doesn't flow.

"If you can speak, I won't cut it."—Who dares stand up to his blade?

The group had no reply—Wait till rain douses your head.

Nanquan cut the cat in two—Once drawn, the sword is not sheathed.

Nanquan brought this up to Zhaozhou and asked him—a second try isn't worth half a cent.

Zhaouzhou put his sandals on his head and left—Should cut in two with one sword for him.

"You could have saved the cat."—When the heart is crooked you don't realize the mouth is bent.

Added
Sayings
/ Verse *The monks of both halls were all arguing*—If you have a reason, it's not a matter of shouting.

Nanquan was able to show up true and false—The clear mirror on its stand, when things come they're reflected in it.

Cutting through with a sharp knife, all oblivious of formalities—How much wind of the Dragon King does it take?

For a thousand ages he makes people admire an adept—There is one who doesn't agree.

This path has not perished—What use can the head of a dead cat be put to?

A connoisseur is to be lauded—I don't say there are none, just that they're few.

In tunneling through mountains to let the sea through, only great Yu is honored—The effort is not misspent.

In smelting rock to mend the sky, only Guonu is considered best—It won't do to lack one.

Old Zhaozhou had a life—Picking up whatever comes to hand, there's nothing that's not it.

Wearing sandals on his head, he attains a bit—For the moment I believe a half.

Coming in differences, still clearly mirroring—A wearer of the patch robe is hard to fool.

Only this real gold is not mixed with sand—This is truly impossible to destroy.

10 THE WOMAN OF TAISHAN

Introduction With gathering and with release, the pole is by his side; able to kill, able to give life, the balance is in his hands. Passions, demons, outsiders—all rely on his direction: the earth, mountains, and rivers all become playthings. But tell me, what sphere is this?

Case On the road to Taishan there lived a certain woman. Whenever a monk asked her, "Which way does the road to Taishan go?" the woman would say, "Right straight on." As soon as the monk would go, the woman would say, "A fine priest—he goes that way too."
A monk told Zhaozhou about this; Zhaozhou said, "Wait till I check out that woman for you."
Zhaozhou also asked the woman the same question. The next day he went up in the hall and said, "I have checked out the woman for you."

Commentary The woman on the road to Taishan used to follow Wuzho out and in the temples (on the holy mountain Taishan) and had fully gotten into Manjusri's saying, "Before, three by three; behind, three by three." Whenever she was asked by a monk which way the road to Taishan went, she would point out the 'great road to the capital' right under the sun, saying, "Right straight ahead." This monk did not make an obstacle of doubt and went right off; the woman said, "A fine priest—he goes that way too." This woman too had a hook in her hand—how many intelligent freemen has she ensnared?
Since this monk couldn't cope with her, he related this to Zhaozhou,

42

who said, "Wait till I check her out for you." He slaughters everyone with doubt—the old fellow is aged but doesn't rest his mind; what is he planning?—he wants to determine the eye of the source.

Zhaozhou asked the same question and the woman answered in the same way. Some immediately talk about them as two parts, (saying that) the first time this monk was helping the woman, and that later the woman was helping Zhaozhou. Only Xuanjiao has said, "The preceding monk questioned and was answered in this way and later Zhaozhou also questioned and was answered in this way; but tell me, where was the examination?" I say, 'seen through.'

He also said, "She was not only seen through by Zhaozhou, she was also seen through by this monk." I say, not only has she gotten Xuanjiao involved, but me too.

Langya said, "Even the great Zhaozhou walked into the woman's hands and lost his life. Even so, many misunderstand." I say, don't judge others by yourself.

Muzhe of Daguishan said, "All the monks in the world only know to ask the way from the woman; they don't know the depth of the mud right under their feet. If not for old Zhaozhou, how could the heights of attainment of the sweating horses be revealed?" Even so, we need to borrow Tiantong's eulogy to do it: his verse says,

Verse   *Old in years, attaining the essence, no mistake in transmission—*
The Ancient Buddha Zhaozhou succeeded to Nanquan.
The dead tortoise loses its life due to designs drawn on it;
Even the steeds 'Chariot' and 'Wind-chaser' are encumbered by
halter and bridle.
Having checked out the woman's Chan,
Told to people, it's not worth a cent.

Commentary   Ghosts and spirits attain their essence by weird powers. Spells and drugs form their essence of dependent powers. Divinities and dragons attain their essence by earned powers. Buddhas and Patriarchs attain their essence by the power of the Way. Nanquan and Zhaozhou were people beyond buddhas and patriarchs—how could they grow old? That is why it says, "Old in years, attaining the essence."

The enlightened master Zhaozhou succeeded to Nanquan. Mazu said, "The Scriptures are in Zhizang, meditation rests with Huaihai—only Nanquan is alone transcendent beyond things." Zhaozhou was a companion of Changsha; Nanquan was their teacher. Therefore his discerning examinations are not to be classified or characterized in terms of gain or loss, victory or defeat—everyone calls this the Pass of Zhaozhou; it is unavoidably difficult to get through.

However, Confucius had a saying, "A spirit turtle can manifest a dream in an accomplished sorceress, but can't avoid the entrapment of the rapacious net; its knowledge is capable of seventy-two auguries without making any wrong divinations, yet it cannot escape the calamity of having its guts rent. Being so, that means its knowledge wears out at some point, there is an extent to which its spirit cannot reach."

Zhuangzi said, "The sorceress Song dreamed of a man covered with hair who said, 'I am from the depths of the sovereign road; I was the officer in charge of clearing the rivers for the lord of rivers; a fisherman got me along with his catch.' Later when she awoke she figured it out: it was a spirit turtle—it turned out that a fisherman had actually netted a white turtle, five feet around, along with his catch. The sorceress wanted to revive it; she divined on it and said, 'Killing the turtle augurs good fortune.' So she hollowed out the turtle and drilled auguring holes in it seventy-two times without any mistaken divinations." That's what Confucius was referring to.

Luopu said, "If you want to know the ever-transcending people, they do not stick the words of buddhas or patriarchs on their foreheads—that would be like a turtle bearing a design, by which it brings on itself the sign of losing life, like a phoenix ensnared in a golden net, heading for the sky—how can it hope to get there?"

King Mu of the Zhou dynasty had eight swift steeds, among which were two who mounted the clouds and galloped off, soaring beyond the birds in flight—therefore they were called 'Swift Four Horse Chariot' and 'Wind-chaser.' This part of the verse describes the woman being able to see through the monk and yet not avoiding Zhaozhou's examination. Although Zhaozhou can see through, still he doesn't avoid Langya's check. In intensive meditation this is called the law of gold and manure:

if you don't understand, it's like gold; when you see through it, it's like manure. That is why it says, "Told to people, it's not worth a cent."
You just leave behind emotional calculations of gain and loss, victory and defeat, and you'll naturally always fool the woman and look down on Zhaozhou. But if you come to my door, don't point to yourself while carrying a board.

Added
Sayings
/Case

A woman lived on the road to Taishan—A rabbit on the road between the neighboring city and the farmhouses.
Whenever a monk asked which way the road to Taishan went—Traveling for a whole lifetime, you don't even know where you're going.
The woman would say, "right straight on."—This is not yet quite good-hearted.
As soon as the monk would go—having run into a thief without realizing it.
The woman would say, "A fine priest—he goes that way too."—You're already a swindler.
A monk told Zhaozhou about this—When people are even, they don't talk.
Zhaozhou said, "Wait till I check her out for you."—When water is level it doesn't flow.
Zhaozhou also asked the woman the same question—A trap to fell a tiger.
The next day he said, "I've checked out that woman for you."—I'm an even bigger swindler.

Added
Sayings
/Verse

Old in years, attaining the essence, no mistake in transmission—Just don't bedevil people's sons and daughters.
The Ancient Buddha Zhaozhou succeeded to Nanquan—Zhen province truly produces big turnips.
The dead tortoise loses its life due to designs drawn on it—Subtle ghosts and spirits are after all caught in the net.
Even the steeds 'Chariot' and 'Wind-chaser' are encumbered by halter and bridle—Even 'Running Wind' and 'Galloping Rain' cannot avoid the halter.
Having checked out the woman's Chan—How many men are manly?
Told to people, it's not worth a cent—Obviously the faculties are not those of a sage.

45

11 YUNMEN'S "TWO SICKNESSES"

Introduction A bodyless man suffers illness; a handless man compounds medicine; a mouthless man ingests it; a senseless man is well. But tell me, how do you treat a mortal disease?

Case Great Master Yunmen said, "When the light does not penetrate freely, there are two kinds of sickness.

"One is when all places are not clear and there is something before you.

"Having penetrated the emptiness of all things, subtly it seems like there is something—this too is the light not penetrating freely.

"Also, the Dharma-body has two kinds of sickness: one is when you manage to reach the Dharma-body, but because your clinging to Dharma is not forgotten, your sense of self still remains, and you fall into the realm of the Dharma-body.

"Even if you can pass through, if you let go, that won't do. Examining carefully, (to think) 'What breath is there?'—this too is sickness."

Commentary Master Jianfeng of Yuezhou was a successor of Dongshan Wuben. While he was traveling around, Yunmen saw this teacher, as well as Caoshan and Sushan. This public case came from a preceding one: Jianfeng said to his congregation, "The Dharma-body has three kinds of illness and two kinds of light; you must pass through them all one by one and realize furthermore that there is still an opening going beyond." Yunmen came forward from the assembly and said, "Why does the man inside the hermitage not know what is outside the hermitage?" Jianfeng laughed

46

aloud; Yunmen said, "This is still what the student doubts." Jianfeng said, "What is going on in your mind?" Yunmen said, "I want the teacher to comprehend thoroughly." Jianfeng said, "Only thus can one sit in peace." Yunmen said, "Yes, yes."

Jianfeng said the Dharma-body has three kinds of illness, Yunmen said the Dharma-body has two kinds of illness. When I was traveling, everywhere they were discussing this, saying that the three illnesses are 'going away before arrival,' 'attachment after arrival,' and 'penetrating through having no basis to rely on.' Now the two illnesses spoken of here just omit going away before arrival; the latter two are clearly much the same.

Master Foyan said, "Searching for a donkey while riding on a donkey is one illness; after getting on the donkey, not being willing to get down is also an illness." This just omits the last kind. Teachers give prescriptions in accordance with the disease for a certain time, each employing appropriate techniques. The two kinds of light and the two kinds of illness when the light doesn't penetrate freely are no different.

Now as for 'when everywhere is not illumined and there is something in front of you is one illness,' Dongshan said, "Clearly she sees her face— there is no other reality; but unavoidably she mistakes the reflection for the head." If you have the eye to settle heaven and earth, and are most thoroughgoing, without letting so much as a thread slip out, only then will you attain somewhat.

Also he said, 'penetrating the emptiness of all things, subtly there seems to be something; this too is because the light does not penetrate freely.' As Guishan said, "When there is nothing that can strike the feelings, the view is still in the objective." The *Heroic March Scripture* says, "Even if you extinguish all perception and discernment and keep to inner hidden tranquility, this is still a reflection of discrimination of conceptual objects." Nanyuan Huiyong said, "Before, I was like walking in the light of a lamp." Thus it is said, 'this too is the light not penetrating freely.'

According to the fundamental way of the Dongshan succession, if you're still, you sink into stagnant water, if you move, you are limited to the present. Thus, when going outward, do not react; when going inward, do not dwell in emptiness. Outwardly not pursuing ramifications, inwardly not abiding in trance, naturally you will get beyond the three sicknesses and two lights all at once. After that, putting penetrating or not penetrating to one side, examine carefully: 'what breath is there?'—this too is an illness. How can you rest easy? Ask Tiantong to take your pulse: he says,

Verse   *The dense web of myriad forms is so precipitous;*
Passing through beyond location blocks the eyes.
Sweeping out his garden—who has the strength?
Hidden in a person's heart, it naturally produces feelings.
A boat crosses a rustic ford, wet with autumn's aquamarine,
Sailing into the reed flowers shining on the snow, bright.
With a bolt of silk, an old fisherman takes it to market;
Floating in the wind, a single leaf travels on the waves.

Commentary   The *Statements of Truth Scripture* says, "The myriad forms and multitude of appearances are the impressions of a single truth." The one is many, the many are one; that is this, nothing else. Let them be high and precipitous, an enormous mass; one does not pull weeds in a wild field. The clear ground after all misleads people—even if you can pass through beyond location, this is just what blocks the eye. The *Complete Enlightenment Scripture* says, "Illusory states of mind are not annihilated, either." Dongshan said, "The peasant sadly cuts the spiritual roots of the auspicious grass."

Why sweep the garden and empty all things? When Yunmen said, "When everywhere is not clear and there is something before you, this is one sickness," he was not telling you to get rid of illusory objects, annihilate illusory mind, and seek some other place of transcendence. The Third Patriarch said, "The six senses are not bad—instead they are the same as true enlightenment." Together with the *Complete Enlightenment Scripture's* "Knowing illusion, one is detached; without employing any technique one detaches from illusions, without any process; then one sees doing, stopping, letting be, and extinction," it is like rubbing the back of a clay mannikin with diamond.

Tiantong also said, "Hidden in a person's heart, it naturally produces feelings." This versifies 'subtly it seems like something is there.' This is precisely the subtle four kinds of illness described in the *Complete Enlightenment Scripture:* "Knowing self, aware of self, subtly continuing, like life." That is why Puque said, "the great compassionate World Honored One quickly explained the illnesses of meditation."

"A boat crosses a rustic ford, wet with autumn's aquamarine." This versifies reaching the Dharma-body, mooring the boat on the deep still waters of the clear source: Sushan called the Dharma-body a dead wood post—this is a real donkey-tethering stake.

Even if you get as far as setting the boat in motion, still you can't avoid rowing into the brightness of the white reed flowers reflecting the snow. At this point, "Even though the pure light shines in your eyes, it seems you have missed your home; even turning around in pure clarity, after all you get bogged down in that state." This versifies 'Even if you can penetrate, it won't do to let it go.' Here Yunmen has said it all, Tiantong has versified thoroughly.

Afterwards it is necessary to see Yunmen's essential meaning and Tiantong's eye; here is where the gain or loss is figured. What is Yunmen's essential meaning? Didn't you see how he said, "Examining carefully, 'what breath is there?'—this too is an illness." Yunmen just points out the sickness but doesn't tell how to cure it. What is Tiantong's eye? He tells Yunmen's cure: "With a bolt of silk, an old fisherman takes it to market; floating in the wind, a single leaf travels on the waves." Yunmen's meaning is entering the market place extending his hands, not avoiding the wind and waves: it could be said that with his own sickness cured, he pities others' sickness. This is the heart of Vimalakirti. But do you know? With many sicknesses you learn about medicine, but only if you get results may you dare to pass on the prescription.

When the light does not penetrate freely there are two kinds of sickness—
Do you feel your mouth dry up and your tongue shrivel?
One is when all places are not clear and there is something before you—
Seeing ghosts in broad daylight—isn't it an illusion?
Having penetrated the emptiness of all things, subtly it seems like there is something—It's already gripped your chest—why bother to shut your throat?

Also, the Dharma-body has two kinds of sickness—Disasters don't happen alone.

One is when you manage to reach the Dharma body, but because your clinging to Dharma is not forgotten your sense of self still remains and you fall into the realm of the Dharma body—Not only false idols, even a close relative.

Even if you can pass through, if you let go, that won't do—Nursing sickness, the body dies.

Examining carefully, 'what breath is there?'—this too is sickness—Before the doctor has left the house, convulsions break out.

Added
Sayings
/Verse

The dense web of myriad forms is so precipitous—Let them be—how can they hinder you? If you know them, they're not enemies.

Passing through beyond location blocks the eyes—Adding a flapper to a flail.

Sweeping out his garden—who has the strength?—Sweeping away tracks makes traces—the more you hide, the more it's revealed.

Hidden in a person's heart, it naturally produces feelings—Suspicion in the mind makes ghosts in the dark.

A boat crosses a rustic ford—Submerged in stagnant water.

Sailing into the reed flowers—The stationary bank misleads people.

An old fisherman takes a bolt of silk to market—He puts down his capital, hoping for profit.

Floating in the wind, a leaf travels on the waves—Finding the wonder along with the flow.

12 DIZANG PLANTING THE FIELDS

Introduction   Scholars plow with the pen, orators plow with the tongue. We patch-robed mendicants lazily watch a white ox on open ground, not paying attention to the rootless auspicious grass. How to pass the days?

Case   Dizang asked Xiushan, "Where do you come from?"
Xiushan said, "From the South."
Dizang said, "How is Buddhism in the South these days?"
Xiushan said, "There's extensive discussion."
Dizang said, "How can that compare to me here planting the fields and making rice to eat?"
Xiushan said, "What can you do about the world?"
Dizang said, "What do you call the world?"

Commentary   Chan Master Guichen of Lohan temple in Zhang province was previously asked by the governor of Zhang province to dwell in the Dizang temple, built by the governor in the Rocky Mountains west of Min City. After a year there the Master moved to Lohan. Therefore he is also called Dizang.
The master of Xiushan joined with Fayan, Wudong, and the master of Jinshan, to travel beyond the lake region (of east central China). Coming to Zhang province, they were blocked by rain, snow, and swollen valley streams. They put up at Dizang temple west of the city. There they encircled the brazier and ignored master Dizang.
Dizang wanted to test them, so he also drew near the fire and said, "There's something I would ask about; may I?" Xiushan said, "If there's

51

some matter, please ask." Dizang said, "Are the mountains, rivers, and earth identical or separate from you elders?" Xiushan said, "Separate." Dizang held up two fingers; Xiushan hurriedly said, "Identical! Identical!" Dizang again held up two fingers, and then left. Fayan said, "What was the meaning of the abbot holding up two fingers?" Xiushan said, "He did that arbitrarily." Fayan said, "Don't crudely insult him." Xiushan said, "Are there any elephant tusks in a rat's mouth?"

The next day they took leave and departed; first they went to the house. Fayan said, "You brothers go ahead; I'll stay with Dizang—he may have some strong point. If not, I'll come find you." After Fayan had studied there for a long time, the other three, including Xiushan, also came back to Dizang.

Subsequently Dizang asked, "How's the Buddhism in the South these days?" At that point they just should have said, "Always the same as here," but instead (Xiushan) said, "There's a lot of discussion going on." He doesn't even know how to come forth on his own. Dizang said, "How can that compare to me here planting the fields and eating rice?" At that moment Xiushan should have said, "If so, then it is not just the South," but instead he said, "How about the world?" Dragging in the meditating travelers of the South, his mundane air was not yet gone. Out of compassion Dizang had a discussion in the weeds, saying, "What do you call the world?" It would have been better just to say, "I'm busy planting the fields," so to avoid Tiantong listing his crime on the same indictment.

Verse   *Source and explanation variously are all made up;*
Passing to ear from mouth, it comes apart.
Planting fields, making rice—ordinary household matters;
Only those who have investigated to the full would know—
Having investigated to the full, you clearly know there's nothing to seek:
Zifang after all didn't care to be enfeoffed as a marquis;
Forgetting his state he returned, same as fish and birds,
Washing his feet in the Canglang, the hazy waters of autumn.

Commentary   Qingliang said, "Communion with the source is one's own practice; communion by speech is showing it to those who are not yet enlightened." It originally comes from the *Scripture on the Descent of the Great Vehicle into Lanka;* the Buddha said to Mahamati, "There are two kinds of communion; communion with the source means by way of the character of transcending progress one attains to utterly detach from false conceptions from speech and symbols, and go to the realm of nonindulgence; by the process of self-awakening, light shines forth—this is called the character of communion with the source. What is the character of communion by speech? It means teaching the various inductive doctrines of the nine branches, avoiding signs of difference or nondifference, existence or nonexistence, and the like, using skillful techniques to explain the truth as it is needed. This is the character of communion by speech."

Students of lectures say, "Communion by speech without communion with the source is like the sun being hidden by clouds. Communion with the source without communion by speech is like a snake gone into a bamboo tube. Communion with the source and communion by speech together is like the sun in the open sky. Communion neither with the source nor by speech is like a dog howling in a thicket of reeds."

If we distinguish the source and speech, these already are two pathways; how can Chan be divided into five branches and the teachings arranged in three vehicles? Herein not even one can stand up—all are artificial.

How much the more so is going out the mouth into the ear, asking for instruction, reciting and eulogizing—the vines of entanglements and complications have extended into the next country already. The teapots of Gongxian are not without hot water. It is not just in the South that there is a lot of debate going on—if you are someone who can speak of fire without burning your mouth, your eloquence is like a torrent, but basically there's not so much as a letter. Even though planting the fields and making rice is ordinary, unless you investigate to the full you don't know their import. The ancients would reap and boil chestnuts and rice at the edge of a hoe, in a broken-legged pot, deep in the mountains—their fortune was no more than contentment; all their lives they never sought from anyone. Their nobility was no more than purity and serenity—what need for bushels of emblems? Thus, "Having investigated to the full, you clearly know there's nothing to seek: Zifang after all didn't care to be enfeoffed as a marquis."

According to the *Historical Records,* in the sixth year of the Han dynasty they enfeoffed meritorious ministers; some said Zhang Liang had never achieved anything in war. The emperor said, "Setting forth plans in the tent to decide victory beyond a thousand miles is Zifang's (Zhang Liang's) achievement." Then the emperor had him choose thirty thousand households in Qi for himself. Liang said, "I first served in Lower Pei, where I met a deity in Liu City—this was given to your majesty by heaven through me; using my plans, fortunately the time was right. I wish to be enfeoffed with Liu City, that's enough—I cannot presume to take over thirty thousand households." This verse means it's not necessary to open a hall and expound the teaching as in the South. Leaving the clamor, going by way of a fisherman's song,

> When the waters of Canglang are clear,
> I can wash my tassels.
> When the waters of Canglang are muddy,
> I can wash my feet.

This is the common ground of monkeys and cranes, where birds and fish both roam. But tell me, who is this person? A true boardbearer.

*Added
Sayings
/Case* **Dizang asked Xiushan, "Where do you come from?"**—Can you say he doesn't know where he's come from?

"From the South."—Should unload for him.

"How is Buddhism in the South?"—Action and speech worthy of talking about.

"There's extensive discussion."—Lower your voice.

"How can that compare to me planting the fields and making rice balls to eat?"—Don't brag so much.

"What can you do about the world?"—There's still this?

"What do you call the world?"—In the South it's still ok; the North is more critical.

Added
Sayings
/ Verse

Source and explanation variously are all made up—Today there's no expedient.

Passing to ear from mouth, it comes apart—Monks, don't think it strange.

Planting fields, making rice—ordinary household matters—Couldn't be anything else.

Only those who have investigated to the full would know—Why want to know?

Having investigated to the full, you clearly know there's nothing to seek—You should still ask for more instruction from Tiantong once.

Zifang after all didn't care to be enfeoffed—This is still a sacred tortoise dragging its tail.

Forgetting his state he returned, same as fish and birds—Finding the wonder along with the flow.

Washing his feet in the Canglang, the hazy waters of autumn—The use of it is inexhaustible.

13 LINJI'S "BLIND ASS"

Introduction   Devoted entirely to helping others, you don't know there is self; you should exert the law to the fullest, without concern that there be no people. For this it is necessary to have the ruthless ability to snap a wooden pillar in two. When about to go, what then?

Case   When Linji was about to die, he admonished Sansheng, "After I pass on, don't destroy my treasury of the eye of truth."
Sansheng said, "How dare I destroy the teacher's treasury of the eye of truth?"
Linji said, "If someone suddenly questions you about it, how will you reply?"
Sansheng immediately shouted.
Linji said, "Who would have known that my treasury of the eye of truth would perish in this blind ass?"

Commentary   Linji admonished Sansheng, "Don't destroy my treasury of the eye of the very truth." This was the same kind of action as when Xinghua told superintendent Kepin, "Before long you will be a teacher of the Way," and expelled him from the monastery as punishment for making rich soup rice.
In reality this thing does not increase even though a thousand buddhas appear in the world, nor does it decrease when a thousand sages pass away—how could one Sansheng be able to cause it to prosper or die out? The ancient demonstrated this thing, and also showed that there was someone in the congregation. After all Sansheng came out and said, "How dare I destroy the teacher's treasury of the eye of truth?" It was like

one who did not accept another's revilement, immediately offering his own provisions; the treasury of the eye of truth has not become extinct. Then Linji asked, "If someone suddenly questions you about it, what will you reply?" When you don't stop what should be stopped, instead you bring about disorder—Sansheng immediately shouted. In high antiquity and later times, appearing within this gate, since Baizhang was deafened for three days by Mazu's shout, none have compared to this shout of Sansheng. Linji said, "Who would have known that the treasury of the eye of truth would die out in this blind ass!"
In that time the style of the house of Linji naturally had the true imperative—what a pity to let it go. I don't know how Tiantong will finally judge.

Verse   *The robe of faith is imparted at midnight to Huineng,*
Stirring up the seven hundred monks at Huangmei.
The eye of truth of the branch of Linji—
The blind ass, destroying it, gets the hatred of others.
Mind to mind they seal each other;
Patriarch to patriarch they pass on the lamp,
Leveling oceans and mountains,
Magically producing a roc:
Just the name and word is hard to compare—
In sum, the method is knowing how to fly.

Commentary   After the secret transmission on Mount Huangmei, South and North bickered for twenty years; Linji made a clear transmission, but even now some people don't get it. This kind of technique is like a giant fish becoming a roc, mountains and seas being leveled.
Huaixiu of Dagui said, "The ancient waited till death; why did the treasury of the eye of truth after all die out in the blind ass? Linji carried out his plan in a hurry, and Sansheng too was hasty; because of this the sense of father and son was forgotten, eventually causing people of later times to lose hope. If one doesn't find flowing water, one must go to another mountain."

In the original record, Sansheng finally bowed; this was not quite good-hearted. Linji then bequeathed a verse, saying,

> If one asks how it is along the flow without end,
> Real illumination, boundless, bespeaks it to him.
> Apart from names and characterizations, people don't understand;
> Once the sword is used, it should immediately be polished.

When he finished the verse he calmly passed away.

Tiantong brings this case right up to the good part, then stops—Sansheng bowed, Linji spoke a verse—this is a real letting go of an easy dismissal here; is there anyone who can show some spirit for the ancients? Dangerous!

Added
Sayings
/Case

When Linji was about to die he admonished Sansheng—Kindly as he faces death he takes leave thrice.

"After I pass away, don't destroy my treasury of the eye of truth."—What's the mortal hurry?

"How dare I destroy the teacher's treasury of the eye of truth?"—He feigns a small heart but sure has a lot of guts.

"If someone asks you about it, how will you reply?"—He lays his body in the tiger's mouth.

Sansheng shouted—Taking charge of the situation, he doesn't defer to his father.

"Who would have known my treasury of the eye of truth would perish in this blind ass?"—Where there's been a great reward given there must be a brave man.

Added
Sayings
/Verse

The robe of faith is imparted at midnight to Huineng—A thief's son has a thief's knowledge.

Stirring up the seven hundred monks at Huangmei—The leader isn't right.

The eye of truth of the branch of Linji—Half light, half dark, it's all here in today.

The blind ass, destroying it, gets the hatred of others—The heart is sweet, the mouth is bitter.

Mind to mind they seal each other—He sells his own salt at a high price.

Patriarch to patriarch they pass on the lamp—He bores a hole in the wall to steal some light.

Leveling oceans and mountains—He knocks down Yellow Crane Pavilion with his fist, kicks over Parrot Island with his foot.

Magically producing a roc—Turn the hand over and it's clouds, turn it back and it's rain.

The mere name and word is hard to compare—There's still some dislike for paucity.

In sum, the method is knowing how to fly—The treasure of the eye of truth still abides.

14 ATTENDANT HUO PASSES TEA

Introduction   Probing pole in hand, shadowing grass around him, sometimes he wraps a ball of silk in iron, sometimes he wraps a special stone with silk. To determine the soft by means of the hard is of course right; what about the matter of being weak when meeting strength?

Case   Attendant Huo asked Deshan, "Where have all the sages since antiquity gone?"
Deshan said, "What? How's that?"
Huo said, "The order was for a 'flying dragon' horse, but a 'lame tortoise' shows up."
Deshan let it rest.
The next day when Deshan came out of the bath, Huo passed him some tea. Deshan patted Huo on the back. Huo said, "This old fellow has finally gotten a glimpse." Again Deshan let the matter rest.

Commentary   Deshan usually thrashed the wind and beat the rain, hollering at the buddhas and reviling the patriarchs; this monk's errors filled the sky— why did Deshan let him go? What is hardly realized is that he wrestled down oxen without using rope, killed people without using a sword— how many has he ever let go?
Old Huanglong said, "Deshan keeps deaf and plays dumb, but even so, he gets the advantage unseen. Mr. Huo covered his ears to steal the bell—what can be done for the unseemliness of the onlooker?"
I say, is he just stealing the bell? He is like trying to take the jewel from under the jet-black dragon's jaw at the depths of the abyss, getting there

just when the dragon is asleep—if the dragon wakes up, he'll surely be chopped into mincemeat.

Muzhe of Dagui said, "If you don't go up to the Dragon Gate, how can you know the vastness of the blue sea? Even if the waves crash a thousand fathoms, nevertheless a dragon pays no notice."

I say, the fine-scaled piece of armor is not to be wondered at.

Foguo said, "Deshan really had ruthless hands and feet, but he saw that this monk was not a man to accept the hammer, so he stopped right away."

I say, the ancients each had techniques meeting people in accordance with the situation.

Deshan said to Yantou, "You will shit on my head some day." Later Yantou actually said, "Even the great Deshan does not understand the last word." The ancients censured and extolled, letting go and holding back—how could they be involved in gain and loss, victory and defeat? Huanglong and Dagui just brought up the general outline. Look again—Tiantong has produced the profound details in verse:

Verse   *Coming right up face to face, an adept knows;*
Here, sparks and lightning are slow.
The plotter who lost the moment has a deep intent—
To fool the enemy army into not thinking ahead.
Each shot a sure hit,
Who's fooled any more?
When you see jowls from behind his head, the man is hard to run afoul of;
Setting his eyes under his eyebrows, he got the advantage.

Commentary   "Where have all the sages since antiquity gone?" He sure seems to have missed it right in front of him. Deshan said, "What? What?" Deshan hid his body with a reed shade, bringing forth shining eye-mirrors.

In ancient times, as seven wise women were traveling through a forest strewn with corpses, one woman said, "Here are the corpses—where are the people?" Another woman said, "What? What?" The women looked around at each other and all suddenly realized enlightenment and felt the king of gods showering flowers in offering to them.

61

Deshan used this one device, temporarily taking a shortcut—certainly one can't understand it at face value; that is why Tiantong said, "That moment is quicker than flint sparks or a lightning flash." How could Deshan not have known the attendant wouldn't let him go? He sent a go-between looking for a pigeon, put down his capital planning for a profit, but after all he couldn't get out of the other's target range.

If suddenly someone should ask me where the sages have gone, I'd slap him on the jaw and say, "They're here!" Even if Flying Dragon and Lame Tortoise draw in their heads and hoofs, and the attendant and Deshan lose their points and become tongue-tied, do you yet know the old fellow Deshan? As a young man he used to determine the arrays of dragons and snakes; grown senile, now he listens to a child's song.

Added Sayings /Case

Where have all the sages gone?—They're in your nose.

What? How's that?—Swift thunder—you can't cover your ears in time.

Attendant Huo said, "The order was for a flying dragon, but a lame tortoise shows up."—When the house is rich, the children are haughty.

Deshan let it rest—Overindulging people is folly.

The next day when Deshan came out of the bath, Huo passed him some tea; Deshan patted him on the back—He sends him off up a pole.

This old fellow has finally gotten a glimpse—The overturned cart is in the same track.

Deshan again let the matter rest—The tiger's head and the tiger's tail are taken all at once.

Added Sayings /Verse

Coming right up face to face, an adept knows—The ignorant are not aware.

Here, sparks and lightning are slow—Already gone past the next country.

The plotter who lost the moment has a deep intent—Hiding an army, he picks a fight.

To fool the enemy army into not thinking ahead—He goes far into the foreign court.

Each shot a sure hit—He's used to getting the advantage.

Who's fooled any more?—Caught with the loot.

When you see jowls from behind his head, the man is hard to run afoul of—Been bitten by a snake.

Setting his eyes under his eyebrows, he got the advantage—He feigns not knowing.

15 YANGSHAN PLANTS HIS HOE

Introduction   Knowing before speech is called silent discourse; spontaneous revelation without clarification is called hidden activity. Saluting in front of the gate, walking down the hallway—this has a reason. What about dancing in the garden or wagging the head out the back door?

Case   Guishan asked Yangshan, "Where are you coming from?
Yangshan said, "From the fields."
Guishan said, "How many people are there in the fields?"
Yangshan planted his hoe in the ground, clasped his hands and stood there.
Guishan said, "On South Mountain there are a lot of people cutting thatch."
Yangshan took up his hoe and went.

Commentary   Teacher and apprentice join ways, father and son complement each other's actions; the family style of Gui and Yang is a guide for a thousand ages.

Guishan asked Yangshan, "Where are you coming from?" Could Guishan not have known Yangshan had come from the fields? He was just using this question to have a meeting with Yangshan. Yangshan didn't turn away from the question put to him, simply saying this: "From the fields." Now tell me, is there any Buddhist principle here or not? Guishan entered deeply into the tiger's cave, going on to ask, "How many people are there in the fields?" Yangshan planted his hoe in the ground and stood with clasped hands, immediately meeting as a patch-robe monk.

Xuansha said, "If I had seen him then, I would have kicked over the hoe for him." I say, he can't control his zeal.
Chan Master Touzi Yiqing said in verse,

> *Few really understand the point of Guishan's questions;*
> *When Yangshan answered him by planting the hoe,*
> *Buddhas and Patriarchs disappeared.*
> *Xuansha, kicking it over, as a bystander doesn't agree,*
> *To avoid letting the blue yellow green deepen with spring.*

I say, when the grass is withered, the hawk's eye is swift.
The verse of Chan Master Ping of Falun Temple on Nanyue says,

> *Meeting on a narrow road, escape is impossible;*
> *When planting the hoe, standing with folded hands,*
> *Having come across the Bridge, he walks on the shore,*
> *For the first time realizing his whole body is muddy and wet.*

I say, not worth looking around in the light of the moon.
The versification of these two old adepts (Touzi and Ping) only have the thousand-foot cold pine; look again—Tiantong lets out and draws forth a stalagmite. The verse says,

Verse *The old enlightened one's feelings are many; he thinks of his descendants.*
Now he repents of setting up a household.
We must remember the saying about South Mountain—
Engraved on the bones, inscribed on the skin, together requiting the blessing.

Commentary This verse is like the biography of Maoying in the *Book of the Han Dynasty;* 'real and conventional come up together.' When you take a look, Guishan is the old enlightened one; Yangshan and his successors are his descendants. If you go into it, then it's not so.
A monk asked Tiger Cen of Changsha, "Does the original man attain buddhahood?" Cen said, "You tell me—does the emperor of China cut thatch?" Thus we know that cutting thatch is the business of the minister. "But now he repents of setting up a household." A thousand-year shadowless tree, the bottomless shoe of the present; abiding master of the moon over the thousand peaks, robe and bowl, a valley and clouds.

All these are empowered descendants inheriting the family work.

Thus we know that 'lord and minister, father and son,' as a teaching device, was not particularly first established by Dongshan and Caoshan; father and son Gui and Yang had already carried out this order. If not for Guishan thoroughly checking, Yangshan would have just reeked of gruel and rice in the gate of shadows of a light, ahead of an ass but behind a horse, taking this as his ordinary life—that would have been most regrettable. Therefore Tiantong instructs, "We must remember the saying about South Mountain—engraved on the bones, inscribed on the skin, together requiting the blessing."

Fadeng said, "The old peasants return with bundles of firewood, urging their wives to spin through the night. See how busy they are at home; but tell me, by whom are they empowered? When you ask them, they don't know, and suddenly give rise to doubt and confusion. Ah, how many people past or present know the virtue of gratitude?" How is it after they know of it? Cutting off an arm without feeling pain, standing in the snow without getting weary. That is why since I've grown old I have lived here in this Temple of Requiting Blessings.

Added Sayings / Case

Where are you coming from?—It's not that he doesn't know where he's coming from.

From the fields—Why have you fallen in the weeds?

How many people are there in the fields?—Just two, father and son.

Yangshan planted his hoe in the ground and stood there with clasped hands—His letting go is a bit precipitous.

On South Mountain there are a lot of people cutting thatch—He beats the grass to roust the snakes.

Yangshan took up his hoe and went—His gathering back is too fast.

Added Sayings / Verse

The old enlightened one's feelings are many; he thinks of his descendants—Too doting.

Now he repents of setting up a household—For thirty years there's been no lack of salt and vinegar.

We must remember the saying about South Mountain—Noble people forget much.

Engraved on the bones, inscribed on the skin, together requiting blessing—The bitter feeling is not given up.

16 MAGU SHAKES HIS STAFF

Introduction Pointing to a deer, making it out to be a horse, picking up earth and turning it to gold, rousing wind and thunder on the tongue, hiding a bloody sword between the eyebrows, sitting there watching success and failure, standing there examining death and life: tell me, what state is this?

Case Magu, ringed staff in hand, came to Zhangjing; he circled the meditation seat three times, shook his staff once, and stood there at attention.
Zhangjing said, "Right, right."
Magu also went to Nanquan, circled the meditation seat three times, shook his staff, and stood there at attention.
Nanquan said, "Wrong, wrong."
Magu said, "Zhangjing said 'right'—why do you say 'wrong'?"
Nanquan said, "Zhangjing is right—it's you who's wrong. This is something that can be blown by the power of the wind—it inevitably disintegrates."

Commentary In ancient times Yangshan went to Zhongyi to give thanks for ordination. Zhongyi, on his seat, clapped his hands and said, "Aya, aya." Yangshan crossed from west to east, east to west, then stood in the middle; after that he gave thanks for the precepts. Zhongyi said, "Where did you attain this state?" Yangshan said, "I learned it from the seal taken off of Caoqi." Zhongyi said, "Tell me, who does this state receive?" Yangshan said, "It received the Enlightened Overnight Guest." Yangshan then asked Zhongyi, "Where did you attain this state,

Teacher?" Zhongyi said, "I attained this state at Great Master Ma's place."

Chan Master Baoche of Magu in Pu province came up to Zhangjing holding his staff, just like when Yongjia (the 'Enlightened Overnight Guest') first met the Sixth Patriarch (at Caoqi); he circled the meditation seat three times and shook his staff once, then stood there at attention—this was like "learning from the seal taken off of Caoqi." This is called the state which is the king of all states—all states are produced from this.

Zhangjing said, "Right, right." I say, what could be wrong? Master Shengmo Guang said, "'Right' can affirm nothing, 'wrong' contains no real denial. Right and wrong have no master, myriad virtues are ultimately one. The owl and the chickens for no reason naturally separate by day and by night. I have no tongue—I call a tortoise a turtle. If Kasyapa doesn't agree, let him furrow his brow." I say, when you have many troubles you grow old quickly.

Magu wanted to see if others elsewhere were alike; he also once went to National Teacher Huizhong's place, walked around the seat three times, shook his staff and stood there. The National Teacher said, "Since you are capable of such as this, what further need is there to see me?" Magu shook his staff again; the National Teacher said, "You wild fox ghost! Get out." See how that guest and host saw each other; there was illumination, there was action, there was a beginning and there was an end.

Indeed it was because it is hard to forget that which has become familiar and he was used to getting the advantage, that Magu also went to Nanquan and circled the seat, shook his staff and stood there as before. Nanquan, though, said, "Wrong, wrong," just as if he had plotted with Zhangjing. Dagui Zhe said, "Zhangjing said 'right' and fell into Magu's target range; Nanquan, saying 'wrong,' still fell within Magu's target range. I would do otherwise; if someone should suddenly circle my meditation seat three times carrying a staff and stand there at attention, I'd just say, 'You should get thirty blows of the staff before even coming here.'" I say, don't give lip service to social manners—strike!

Magu said, "Zhangjing said 'right'—why do you say 'wrong'?" He couldn't avoid wondering. Nanquin said, "Zhangjing is right—it's you that's wrong." He sees the situation and acts; in the face of danger he puts another forward.

National Teacher Shen of Yuantong said, "Magu is right, Nanquan is not." This saying is just like when Hermit Yong of Deng Peak asked Seng Shenqi, "I haven't seen you for a long time; what have you been doing?" Shenqi said, "Recently I saw Librarian Wei and found peace." Hermit Yong said, "Try to recount it to me." So Shenqi told of his realization; Yong said, "You're right; Wei's not right." Shenqi could not fathom this, and reported it to Wei. Wei laughed and said, "You're wrong—Yong's not wrong." Shenqi went running to ask Chan Master Nan of Jicui, and Nan also laughed. Hermit Yong heard of this and made a verse:

> Light and dark intermingle in the activity of killing and reviving;
> The sphere of a great being, the Universally Good One knows.
> Born of the same lineage, not dying of the same lineage—
> Falling over with laughter, the old awl in the hut.

Jiaofan said, "As I see his words, they seem like the missing rhyme of that play of joy in the Dharma." I say, the elation of Magu, Zhangjing, and Nanquan was also not slight. Hearing 'this is something that can be blown by the power of the wind—it eventually disintegrates,' it would be an even better laugh.

This Nanquan, 'Old Teacher Wang,' not only held sky and earth steady, he also had a road to go out on himself. Master Baoning Yong's verse said,

> The color and form are just like real,
> Displayed before people, even more it shines new.
> When smelted and forged in the fire again,
> Going back after getting there, this is false silver.

When Magu got here, the tiles crumbled, the ice melted. If you want the frozen river to burst into flame and the iron tree to bloom with flowers, we need Tiantong to add another word:

Verse   *Right and wrong—*
Watch out for the trap.
Seeming to put down, seeming to uphold,
It's hard to tell who is the elder brother, who the younger.

Conceding, he adapts to the time;
Denying, what's special to me?
One shake of the metal staff—standing out all alone;
Three times around the seat, a leisurely romp.
The monasteries agitated, 'right' and 'wrong' are born;
It seems like they are seeing ghosts in front of their skulls.

Commentary This public case is entirely in the 'right' and 'wrong.' These days everybody says Magu was being teased by Zhangjing and Nanquan; only Dagui Zhe has said, "Zhangjing saying 'right' fell into Magu's target range; Nanquan saying 'wrong' also fell within Magu's target range." It's like a diamond in the sun—its color is not fixed. Tiantong said, "Watch out for the trap; seeming to put down, seeming to uphold, it's hard to tell who is the elder brother, who the younger." Tiantong is saying that when you take a look they seem to be putting down, seem to be approving; when you examine further, it's hard to consider one elder, hard to consider one younger.

Changwen, son of Chen Yuanfang of the eastern Han dynasty, was Chen Jun; he and Jifang's son Ziaoguang were each discussing their fathers' respective merits. As they argued, they couldn't decide the issue, so they asked Taiqiu. Taiqiu was Chen Shi, father of both Yuanfang and Jifang. Taiqiu said, "It is hard to consider Yuanfang the elder, hard to consider Jifang the younger."

This means that Zhangjing was 'half a pound in the left eye,' Nanquan was 'eight ounces in the right eye.'

"One shake of the metal staff—standing out all alone." Yongjia's *Song of Enlightenment* says, "This is not showing form for useless concern with control; the precious staff of those who arrive at thusness itself leaves its mark." Xuedou said, "The way of the ancient rod is lofty, with twelve gates; in each gate there is a road, empty and desolate." The *Ring Staff Scripture* says, "The twelve rings (on the head of the staff) are used for remembrance of the twelve causes of conditional existence and cultivation of the twelve gates of meditation." The twelve conditions are well known; the twelve gates are the four meditations, four immeasurables, and four formless states. "The way of the ancient rod is lofty, with

69

twelve gates" is the same as "standing out all alone." The Sixth Patriarch also said, "A monk fulfills three thousand standards of conduct and eighty thousand refinements of action; where do you come from, Great Virtuous One, conceiving such self-conceit?" Tiantong means to say that this is neither representing a form nor self-conceit; "Three times around the seat, a leisurely romp."

Zhangjing said right, Nanquan said wrong—being agitated in the monasteries, going off balance inside yes and no, all those without the eye to hold sky and earth steady will see ghosts before their skulls. Haven't you heard how a monk asked Jiufeng, "What is the eye which holds sky and earth steady?" Jiufeng answered, "Sky and earth are within it." The monk said, "Where is the eye of sky and earth?" Jiufeng said, "Just this is the eye of sky and earth." The monk said, "Why did you just say sky and earth are within?" Jiufeng said, "Otherwise you'd see countless ghosts in front of your skull." I say, here there is a teacher of the prohibitions; (shaking his staff once) hurry and give the order according to the rule.

Magu, ring staff in hand, came to Zhangjing, circled the seat thrice, shook the staff once, and stood there at attention—He sure has a lot of Chan.

Zhangjing said, "Right, right."—For the moment I believe in half of it.

Magu also went to Nanquan, circled the seat, shook his staff, and stood there—Tomorrow morning, try to make yet another presentation, to the king of Chu.

Nanquan said, "Wrong, wrong."—I believe half of this for the moment too.

Magu said, "Zhangjing said right—why do you say wrong?"—He's bulging his eyes inside his coffin.

Zhangjing is right—it's you that's wrong—He adds frost to snow.

This is something that can be blown by the power of the wind—it inevitably disintegrates—When you kill someone, you should see blood.

Right and wrong—A narrow drum beaten on both sides.
Watch out for the trap—Thorns are inside.

Seeming to put down, seeming to uphold—One hand holds up, one hand puts down.

It's hard to tell who is elder, who younger—Head high, head low.

Conceding, he adapts to the time—Turning the hand over, it's clouds . . .

Denying, what's special to me?—. . . turning the hand back, it's rain.

One shake of the metal staff—standing out all alone—He sheds the dusts and departs the mundane.

Thrice around the seat, a leisurely romp—He swings his arms as he goes.

The monasteries agitated, 'right' and 'wrong' are born—A midget watches a play.

It seems like they are seeing ghosts in front of their skulls—The house has a sign of good omen—there are surely no such maleficent strangelings.

17 FAYAN'S "HAIRSBREADTH"

Introduction   A pair of solitary wild geese flap on the ground and fly up high; a couple of mandarin ducks stand alone by the bank of the pond. Leaving aside for the moment the meeting of arrow points, what about when a saw cuts a scale beam?

Case   Fayan asked Xiushan, "'A hairsbreadth's difference is as the distance between heaven and earth'—how do you understand?"
Xiushan said, "A hairsbreadth's difference is as the distance between heaven and earth."
Fayan said, "How can you get it that way?"
Xiushan said, "I am just thus—what about you?"
Fayan said, "A hairsbreadth's difference is as the distance between heaven and earth."
Xiushan thereupon bowed.

Commentary   The Master of Xiushan and Fayan both studied with Dizang, deeply benefiting from the power of refinement of 'studying from the side.' This public case is the same as when Fayan broke down Superintendent Ze, who was thereupon enlightened. Superintendent Ze was Chan Master Xuanze of Baoen Monastery in Jinling; Fayan asked him, "Who have you seen?" Xuanze said, "I saw Master Qingfeng." Fayan said, "What did he say?" Xuanze said, "I asked what is the student's self," and Qingfeng said, "The god of fire comes seeking fire." Fayan said, "How do you understand this?" Xuanze said, "The god of fire is in the province of fire; to seek fire by fire is like seeking the self by the self." Fayan said, "Even understanding in this way, how could you get it?" Xuanze said,

"I am just thus; I don't know what your idea is, Master." Fayan said, "You ask me and I'll tell you." Xuanze asked, "What is the student's self?" Fayan said, "The god of fire comes seeking fire." Xuanze was suddenly enlightened at these words. Fayan had chisel and awl in his hands; 'taken away, the seal remains; left there, the seal is ruined'—he broke up Superintendent Ze's barrier of feelings and pulled open Master Xiushan's chains of consciousness.

In the Third Patriarch's *Poem on the Mind of Faith* it says, "The ultimate way is without difficulty; it is only avoiding being choosy—just don't hate or love, be naturally open, clear and pure. If there is even a hairsbreadth of difference, it is as the distance between heaven and earth." Fayan used this to question the Master of Xiushan, making of it a piece of tile to knock on the door. Nowadays if you asked people about it, a thousand out of a thousand would make a logical understanding, or else just stay in the realm of nonstriving.

This one here didn't fall into speculative thought—he just said, "A hairs-breadth's difference is as the distance between heaven and earth." He quite evidently had the relaxation of mastery, but then Fayan after all didn't accept him, but said, "How can you get it that way?" This is why he was the fountainhead of the Fayan stream.

At this point, here I always tell the students to divide their bodies into two and look—when Master Xiushan said this in the first place, why was it not accepted? Then afterwards, why did Fayan turn around and say the same thing? In the meantime, Xiushan said, "I am just thus—how about you?" He was looking for an utterly new sun and moon, to make a separate life. Now Fayan didn't slip a bit—like before he said simply, "A hairsbreadth's difference is as the distance between heaven and earth."

Dongshan Ji said, "The master of Xiushan responded in this way—why didn't Fayan agree? And then when he questioned further a second time, Fayan just said the same thing, whereupon Xiushan got it. Tell me, where is the puzzle? If you can see through, I would say you've got something to go on." I say, how could you get it that way?

This is why it is said, "It is the same way as ever—when you meet someone and talk about it, it becomes confusing." Xiushan thereupon bowed—he understood, all right, but intellectual reasoning is hard to admit; Wuzu Jie 'would have struck Xiushan right across the back in

Fayan's stead'—I say, so it turns out.

Some books have Fayan saying, "The Master of the Mountain has penetrated." I say, neither of these fellows has done with playing with a mud ball. If at that time Fayan had said to me, "How could you get it that way?" I would say to him, "Long have I heard that you have this functional key, Teacher." Or else, I would join hands and go right along, seeing to it that it is settled all at once. When he doesn't believe, let's ask Tiantong—his verse says,

Verse   *When a fly sits on the balance, it tilts;*
The balance scale of myriad ages shows up unevenness.
Pounds, ounces, drams and grains—you see them clearly;
But after all it finally reverts and gives up to my zero point.

Commentary   Tiantong's opening line immediately versifies "a hairsbreadth of difference is as that between heaven and earth." Master Huiyuan of Lushan said, "Ultimately, how can basis and aspect come from the realm of origin and destruction, being and nothingness? A slight involvement with the shifting environment shows a force capable of disintegrating this mountain."

The Third Patriarch said the word 'avoid,' himself already hating and loving from the first—but then he says, 'Just don't hate or love, and be naturally open, clear and pure.' You people, step back and examine yourselves carefully.

The Sanskrit word *samadhi* means equilibrium—not oblivious, not agitated, remaining equanimous. This can be the 'balance scale of myriad ages' that 'shows up unevenness.'

In the pictorial explanations in the *Essentials of Government for Ministry Presidents* it says that weighing has three senses: a level is for conjoining, a balance evens, a scale equalizes.

In the *Heroic March Scripture* it says, "In that self-sustaining stable state of *samadhi*, perception and objects of perception, including all forms conceived of, are like flowers in the sky, fundamentally without any existence. This seeing and its objects are originally the wondrous pure radiant body of enlightenment; how could there be any affirmation or denial there?" At this time you don't need to be choosy—you are aloof of dislike or like; there is not even a hairsbreadth of difference—how could there be separation between clouds and mud?

As for 'pounds, ounces, drams and grains' (units of weight measure, in the Chinese system), eight *shu* equals a *zi*, three *zi* equals a *liang* (ounce), sixteen *liang* equals a *jin* (pound). Now as one with balance in hand, if you bring a pound, I shift a pound to make it even; if you bring two pounds, I too shift to balance. If there be so much as a dram or a grain increase or decrease, it tilts. Everywhere they say, 'Get the meaning on the hook—don't go by the zero point,' but after all there have never been any pounds or ounces on the zero point. It is also like the North Star maintaining its abode in its position. The more or less on the hook are accounted only according to the time.

I say, evenness with mind is not comparable to mindlessness in unevenness. That is why 'Selling people what they want from a markless scale, in both pans profit is made whatever the situation.'

But do you understand Fayan's saying, "The Master of the Mountain has penetrated"? The balance weight has shifted to the very tip, suddenly pushing and overturning pounds and pecks.

Added Sayings / Case	**A hairsbreadth's difference is as the distance between heaven and earth —how do you understand?**—Who dares to budge? **A hairsbreadth's difference is as the distance between heaven and earth**—What's difficult about letting the hundred plants contend? **How can you get it that way?**—An iron mountain lies across the road. **I am just thus—what about you?**—He turns his nose around. **A hairsbreadth's difference is as the distance between heaven and earth**—I had thought there would be something else. **Xiushan thereupon bowed**—He adds error to error.
Added Sayings / Verse	*When a fly sits on the balance, it tilts*—You can't fool it a single point. *The balance of myriad ages shows up unevenness*—When the measure is full the balance arm stops. *Pounds, ounces, drams, grains—you see them clearly*—Don't misapprehend them. *After all it finally reverts and gives up to my zero point*—Get the meaning on the hook.

75

18 ZHAOZHOU'S "DOG"

Introduction   A gourd floating on the water—push it down and it turns: a jewel in the sunlight—it has no definite shape. It cannot be attained by mindlessness, nor known by mindfulness. Immeasurably great people are turned about in the stream of words—is there anyone who can escape?

Case   A monk asked Zhaozhou, "Does a dog have a buddha-nature or not?"
Zhaozhou said, "Yes."
The monk said, "Since it has, why is it then in this skin bag?"
Zhaozhou said, "Because he knows yet deliberately transgresses."
Another monk asked Zhaozhou, "Does a dog have a buddha-nature or not?"
Zhaozhou said, "No."
The monk said, "All sentient beings have buddha-nature—why does a dog have none, then?"
Zhaozhou said, "Because he still has impulsive consciousness."

Commentary   If you say a dog's buddha-nature surely exists, afterwards he said 'no'—if it surely does not exist, still previously he said 'yes'. And if you say that to say 'yes' or 'no' is just a temporary response spoken according to the situation, in each there is some reason. That is why it is said that someone with clear eyes has no nest.
The point of this monk's question was to broaden his perspective and learning; he didn't base it on his own fundamental endowment. Zhaozhou said 'yes', using poison to get rid of poison, using sickness to cure sickness.

This monk also said, "Since it has, why is it then in this skin bag?" He didn't realize he himself had been born in the belly of a dog. Zhaozhou said, "Because he knows, yet deliberately transgresses." One mallet strikes twice; a fleeting opportunity is hard to catch.

This monk might have thought that he was judging the result on the basis of the cause, but if you understand in this way, you cannot even be the slave of a professor.

Later a monk asked this again, whereat Zhaozhou said 'no'. He was one who had attained—whether he said 'yes' or 'no' he had a way out. This monk judged the fundamental way on the basis of words: "All beings have buddha-nature; why doesn't a dog have it?" Thus challenged, I dare say that even the hand that can move the North Star has no way to turn around, but Zhaozhou answered sincerely with this "Because he still has impulsive consciousness." Now you tell me—did this monk have blood under his skin after all? Tiantong cannot avoid putting more *moxa* to burn on the scar on the red flesh:

Verse *A dog's buddha-nature exists, a dog's buddha-nature does not exist;*
A straight hook basically seeks fish who turn away from life.
Chasing the air, pursuing fragrance, cloud and water travelers—
In noisy confusion they make excuses and explanations.
Making an even presentation, he throws the shop wide open;
Don't blame him for not being careful in the beginning—
Pointing out the flaw, he takes away the jewel;
The king of Chin didn't know Lian Xiangru.

Commentary "A dog's buddha-nature exists, a dog's buddha-nature does not exist"— the two parts are not the same; he brings them out together, just like Xuedou's "One has many kinds, two have no duality." Tiantong wants to meet with Zhaozhou, that's why he versifies in this way. Yingtian Zhen said, "A straight harpoon catches ferocious dragons, a curved hook catches clams."

Afterwards, "chasing the air, pursuing fragrance," like hunting dogs they make excuses and explanations in noisy confusion. What juice is there in a dry bone?

Although Zhaozhou threw his shop wide open, basically he just wanted to trade on an equal basis. Tiantong frees Zhaozhou's arm for him; "Don't blame him for not being careful in the beginning."

Guizong asked a scholar, "What classics and histories do you work on?" The scholar said, "I have mastered twenty-four styles of calligraphy." Guizong made a dot in the air and said, "Understand?" The scholar said "No." Guizong said, "And you said you knew twenty-four styles of calligraphy—you don't even recognize the first stroke of the character *always* (used as a model containing all elemental stroke patterns)."

Inspector Li Bo asked, "I don't ask about the twelve-branch teachings of the three vehicles—what's the meaning of Chan?" Guizong raised his fist and said, "Understand?" Li said, "No"; Guizong said, "This great scholar doesn't even recognize a fist?" I say, everybody watch the lion turning.

It is not just saying a dog has buddha-nature or not; especially this "he knows but deliberately transgresses" and "he still has impulsive consciousness" too are extremely careful to look ahead and behind, careful in the beginning, safeguarding the end.

According to the *Historical Records*, King Hui of Zhao got the jewel of the Ho clan of Chin and offered it to King Zhao of Chin in exchange for fifteen cities. Lian Xiangru conveyed the proffered jewel; the king of Chin joyfully showed it in turn to his beauties and attendants—all around him cried, "Long live the king!" Xiangru saw that the king had no intention of ceding his cities, so he came forward and said, "The jewel has a flaw—let me show you." The king handed over the jewel to him. Xiangru took it, got up, and butted his head with it against a pillar and said, "The king of Zhao fasted for five days before he bade me, his minister, to present the jewel and deliver his letter to this court, adorning the majesty of your great nation to practice respect. Now I see your majesty's manners are quite haughty—when you got the jewel you turned it over to show your favorites, as though making sport of me, with no intention of ceding the cities. Therefore I have taken the jewel back—if you try to press me, my head and the jewel will both smash on the pillar!" The king apologized, drew a map and partitioned off the cities; he also fasted for five days. Xiangru had one of his company hide the jewel in his sleeve and head right back to Zhao.

Zhaozhou first gives, then takes away—he had the technique of Xian-gru. Tiantong once wrote another verse on it, saying,

> *Zhaozhou said yes,*
> *Zhaozhou said no;*
> *A dog's buddha-nature—*
> *All over the world, excuses and explanations.*
> *A red face is not as good as honest speech—*
> *When the heart is true the words are surely coarse.*
> *Old Chan uncle of over a hundred years—*
> *Donkey manure is changed for eyes*
> *When he meets with someone.*

Zhaozhou's heart was true and his words honest—this is the 'straight hook basically seeks fish who turn away from life.'

King Wen of Zhou went hunting and saw Qiang Ziya in the valley of the Bowl River, three feet away from the water, fishing with a straight hook. The king thought this strange and said, "How can you catch a fish with a straight hook?" Ziya said, "I only seek fish who turn away from life."

"Donkey manure is exchanged for eyes when he meets someone" is like Lian Xiangru taking the jewel. Fojian raised his rosary, made of stones of the 'sorrowless' fruit, and said, "Do you all see?" After a good while he said, "This is what I got in exchange when I came to the capital; each of you go back to the hall and search." Fojian used 'sorrowless' stones, Zhaozhou used donkey manure; since I have nothing to use, I have never exchanged—if you people can believe completely, as before, your eyes are under your brows.

Added Sayings /Case

A monk asked "Does a dog have buddha-nature?"—He blocks the alley chasing a clod of earth.

Yes—Yet it's never been added.

Since it has, why is it then in this skin bag?—Checking once, he beckons, coming out with what pertains to himself.

Because he knows yet deliberately transgresses—Don't assume he's not talking about you.

Another monk asked, "Does a dog have buddha-nature?"—Born of the same mother.

No—Yet it's never been removed.

All sentient beings have buddha-nature—why has a dog none?— Stupid dog chases a hawk.

Because he still has impulsive consciousness—The foregoing is like before in every way—he settles the case on the basis of the facts.

Added Sayings /Verse

*A dog's buddha-nature exists, a dog's buddha-nature does not exist—*He beats them into one lump, forges them into one mass.

*A straight hook basically seeks fish who turn away from life—*These monks should die today.

*Chasing the air, pursuing fragrance, cloud and water travelers—*He's pierced their noses, unbeknownst to them.

*In noisy confusion they make excuses and explanations—*They fight like dogs over a dry bone, yelping and howling.

*Making an even presentation—*No easy fooling—stop deceiving each other.

*He throws the shop wide open—*When the intelligence is lofty, the words are powerful.

*Don't blame him for not being careful in the beginning—*Once a word comes out of the mouth, the fastest horse cannot overtake it.

*Pointing out the flaw, he takes the jewel away—*A daylight thief steals skillfully.

*The king of Chin didn't know Lian Xiangru—*He misses what's right in front of him.

19 YUNMEN'S "SUMERU"

Introduction I always admire the novel devices of Yunmen; all his life he pulled out nails and wedges for people. Why did he sometimes open the door and set out a bowl of glue, or dig a pitfall in the middle of the road? Try to discern.

Case **A monk asked Yunmen, "When not producing a single thought, is there any fault or not?"**
Yunmen said, "Mount Sumeru."

Commentary National Teacher Yuantong Shan said, "This case is debated everywhere: some say as soon as one questions in this way, already this is raising thought, a fault as big as Mount Sumeru; some say it is like Mount Sumeru, unmoved by the eight winds, remaining steadfast for a thousand ages; some say that because it is difficult for people to pass through, it is like Mount Sumeru. Such assessments have not yet comprehended Yunmen's meaning; only if the bottom of the bucket has fallen out and the red thread is broken off will you realize it is not so at all. Haven't you heard it said that three phrases illumine one phrase, one phrase illumines three phrases; three and one do not intermingle—distinctly clear, the road going beyond."

Foguo said, "Yunmen's answer has provoked conscious feelings in many people." I say, he uses conscious feelings to get rid of conscious feelings—if he did not help people in a great way, he would be unable to assist.

This Mount Sumeru cannot be covered by the sky, earth cannot support it, wind blowing cannot enter, water poured on cannot wet it. Only the diamond eye can see through it at a glance, whereupon one sees seven openings and eight holes, and straightaway finds that it's shattered to smithereens. Then after that it's on the eyebrows and eyelashes, solitary and beyond transcendence, lofty, steep, magnificent.

The Verse of Chan Master Baiyun Duan said,

> *Mount Sumeru—it fills the universe;*
> *Even the Thousand Armed Great Compassionate One cannot*
>   *see through it.*
> *If you know on your own how to ride an ox backward,*
> *You'll never stick to following people all your life.*

I say, looking up, he raises his eyebrows alone; turning his head, he claps his hands.

Master Qishan Zhen's verse on the case said,

> *The unconcerned surrenderer seeks a criminal name;*
> *At the moment of his capture, he loses his whole body.*
> *As for those who rush in pursuit before the true facts*
>   *are called forth,*
> *I don't know how many are standing outside the gate.*

There is only Tiantong who is not within these bounds; his verse says,

Verse *Not producing a single thought—Mount Sumeru;*
Yunmen's gift of teaching is not stingy in intent.
If you come with acceptance, he imparts with both hands;
If you go on doubting, it's so high you can't get a hold.
The blue ocean is wide,
The white clouds are peaceful;
Don't put so much as the tip of a hair in there.
A phony cock crow can hardly fool me—
I still won't agree to let you pass through the gate in the confusion.

Commentary 'You ask me whether there is any fault or not when not raising a single thought—I will bring out a Mount Sumeru, as though right before your eyes'—the benefit of that gift of teaching is certainly not stingy. Yongjia said, "When the gate of generosity opens, nothing can block it." It is not only today.

In Sanskrit, *Sumeru* means Wonderfully High. Being composed of four precious minerals, it is called Wonderful; standing out alone above all peaks, it is called High. Of the mountains of the four quarters, the Sumeru is the supreme.

"If you come with acceptance, he imparts with both hands." An ancient poem says, "Wait till they agree in their hearts—that's when my command carries through." In actuality this thing is always obvious, out in the open, like a black mountain high and steep. Who can cover it? Before it is imparted, do you really have no share? Imparted to you, is it newly gained? Haven't you read Changqing's saying, "The sole body revealed in myriad forms—only if people themselves accept it will it be near." Tiantong's verse at this point has an all-encompassing effect—if you hesitate and don't come forth, a thousand, ten thousand miles—you'll be unable even to see it from afar.

Juyuan said, "This thing is like cliffs crumbling, rocks splitting, standing like a mile-high wall, impossible to get a hold on." In reality, you have never been apart from it. I have never taken it away. This and the above phrase are opposite in illusion and enlightenment; their complementary opposition is distinctly clear.

In the teachings it says that Mount Sumeru goes eighty thousand leagues below the water and eighty thousand leagues above the water—only an ocean could accommodate it. The mountain has never moved for all time, and the clouds appearing and disappearing are always peaceful. Dongshan said, "The green mountain is the father of the white clouds, the white clouds are the children of the green mountain—the white clouds hang around all day, the green mountain doesn't notice at all."

Tiantong has extra ability, and eulogizes Mount Sumeru being vast as the ocean, peaceful as the clouds, going into thorough detail about its marvels. Can a single thought rising and passing away be contained here? That's why he said, "The blue ocean is wide, the white clouds are peaceful—don't put so much as the tip of a hair in there." This contains the same lesson as Xuedou's saying, "Don't put sand in the eye." If you contend that Shaoyang (Yunmen) was not stingy in giving teaching, yet he put even Mount Sumeru in the eye.

83

In this verse on Mount Sumeru, we are faced by every point—the blood line goes through, every beat is the order. It does not arbitrarily produce rationalizations increasing conscious feelings. Really, how can someone who doesn't produce a single thought still ask if there is any fault or not? Even if you always remain in the state of not producing a single thought, when you bring it up to examination, what can it do? That is why it says, "A phony cock crow can hardly fool me—I still won't agree to let you pass through the gate in the confusion."

Meng Changjun went into Chin and became an official. People said to the king, "Meng Changjun is intelligent, but he is of the Ji people; now as a Chin official he will surely put the interest of Ji before that of Chin—Chin is in danger for that." The king imprisoned Changjun and was going to execute him. Changjun sought release through a favored concubine. The lady said, "I want your white fox coat." Now the coat had already been presented to the king; one of Meng's company was able to sneak in and steal it, so that Changjun got out. In the middle of the night they came to a barrier pass in an enclosed valley. The rule of the pass was that travelers were let through the gate at cock crow. Changjun's follower, hoping to fool them, used his skill at imitating a cock crow, and all the chickens began to cry. Changjun escaped trouble in Chin.

(Wansong raised his staff) Today I am in charge of the pass. If there are any students of crowing, come forth. (Also he leaned on his staff and said,) let the first move go.

Added Sayings / Case

A monk asked Yunmen, "When not producing a single thought, is there any fault or not?"—A fellow whose words are pure but whose conduct is impure.

Mount Sumeru—Dangerous!

Added Sayings / Verse

Not producing a single thought—Mount Sumeru—Finished in one line.

Yunmen's gift of teaching is not stingy in intent—Tiantong's is not little either.

If you come with acceptance, he imparts with both hands—I'm only afraid you can't take it on.

If you go on doubting, it's so high you can't get a hold—It's a wasted effort to shade your eyes and gaze at it.

The blue ocean is wide—Flooding the heavens and bathing the sun, it has no shore.

The white clouds are peaceful—Following the wind along with the waves, they are free.

Don't put so much as the tip of a hair in there—Already too much.

A phony cock crow can hardly fool me—The true doesn't cover up the false.

I still won't agree to let you pass through the gate in confusion—The order in India is strict.

20 DIZANG'S "NEARNESS"

Introduction   The profound talk entering into noumenon decides three and weeds out four; the Great Way to the Capital goes seven ways across and eight ways up and down. Suddenly if you can open your mouth and explain fully, take steps and walk, then you can hang your bowl and bag up high and break your staff. But tell me, who is this?

Case   Dizang asked Fayan, "Where are you going?"
Fayan said, "Around on pilgrimage."
Dizang said, "What is the purpose of pilgrimage?"
Fayan said, "I don't know."
Dizang said, "Not knowing is nearest."

Commentary   Yang Wuwei asked Master Furong, "How long has it been since we last met?" Furong said, "Seven years." Mr. Yang said, "Have you been studying the Way? Engrossed in meditation?" Furong said, "I don't play that fife and drum." Mr. Yang said, "Then you wander for nothing over mountains and rivers, incapable of anything." Furong said, "While we haven't been apart for long, you can sure reflect on high." Mr. Yang laughed aloud.

Nanquan said, "The Way is not in knowing or in not knowing. Knowing is false consciousness, not knowing is indifference." Now when people hear it said that not knowing is nearest, and that this is where Fayan was enlightened, they immediately go over to just not knowing, not understanding—"just this is it." They hardly realize that a phrase of the ancients covers everywhere, like the sky, supports everywhere, like the earth. If not knowing is nearest, then what about Heze's saying, "The one word 'knowing' is the gate of myriad wonders." Just affirm totally when affirming, but don't settle down in affirmation; deny totally when denying, but don't settle down in denial. Passing through all the five ranks, absolute and relative, how could you die under a phrase?

But this enlightenment of Fayan's too just spontaneously creates a pattern. Master Dayin of Boshan said, "He is still making a fortune out of a disaster." In Dizang's method of guiding people, the hook is in an unsuspected place—suddenly he gives a yank, and Fayan has a powerful insight; after all it was right to begin with.

Old Master Cizhou said, "In walking, in sitting, just hold to the moment before thought arises, look into it, and you'll see not seeing—and then put it to one side. When you direct your effort like this, rest does not interfere with meditation study, meditation study does not interfere with rest."

Master Touzi Qing said, "Once the golden dragon strays from the water, the giant garuda bird quickly picks it up." Dizang's timing of cause and condictions had not a thread of gap. There is a tongue on Tiantong's brush, to reiterate:

Verse
Now having studied to the full, it's like before—
Having shed entirely the finest thread, he reaches not knowing.
Let it be short, let it be long—stop cutting and patching;
Going along with the high, along with the low, it levels itself.
The abundance or scarcity of the house is used according to the occasion;
Roaming serenely in the land, he goes where his feet take him.
The purpose of ten years' pilgrimage—
Clearly he'd turned his back on one pair of eyebrows.

Commentary
The *Source Mirror* says, "Hitherto deluded about enlightenment, seeming deluded; now awakened from delusion, it's not enlightment. Therefore it is said, 'After complete enlightenment one again is the same as someone who is not yet enlightened.'"

When Dizang asked the question, he wanted to know the reason for setting out. In Fayan's answer he is not modestly deferring, either. Dizang then took advantage of the opportunity and all at once said, "Not knowing is nearest." Fayan was greatly enlightened, that actually this not knowing is the nearest.

Linji asked Luopu, "Where do you come from?" Luopu said, "From Luan city." Linji said, "There is something I would ask about—may I?" Luopu said, "I don't understand." Linji said, "Even searching throughout the whole of China it's hard to find one who doesn't understand." Linji always used the killing sword, and he also had the sword to give life, but was not comparable to Dizang's seeing blood when he killed people, doing his utmost to help people. This 'I don't know, don't understand' is entirely transcendent; you must be utterly free from the minutest obstacles before you will reach the point of not knowing and not understanding.

Once when Guishan had requested everyone to work the fields, there Yangshan asked, "Here is so low, there is so high." Guishan said, "Water can level things. Just level them with water." Yangshan said, "Even water has nothing to depend on—Teacher, the high places are just high level, the low places are low level." Guishan said, "So it is."

In Sengzhao's treatise *Wisdom Has No Knowledge* it says, "The nondifference of all things doesn't mean that you add to a duck's legs and cut a crane's legs, level mountains to fill valleys, thereafter considering them no different." Thus it says, "Let it be long—stop cutting and patching; going along with the high, along with the low, it levels itself."

Zhang Wujin said, "Myriad kinds of preparations are a waste of time. Adapting to everything becomes a fine skill." Thus one speaks freely and acts freely, goes where his legs go; in the spring moon the flowers bloom, in the autumn the leaves fall. If you can understand in this way, what donkey legs would you move? This is why Xuansha did not leave the mountains, Baoshou didn't cross the river—without going outside the gate they knew everything in the world.

Jiaofan's verse said,

> One face, big as a slat;
> Eye, ear, nose, tongue, distinguish territories—
> Inside the skull, no knowledge at all.
> I leave to you the outside—how can you hoke up wonders?

Mouth asked nose, "Eating is up to me, speaking is up to me—what good are you that you are above me?" Nose said, "Among the five mountains, the central one occupies the honored position." Nose then asked eyes, "Why are you above?" Eyes said, "We are like the sun and moon—truly we have the accomplishment of illumination and reflection. We dare ask eyebrows, what virtue do they have to be above us?" Eyebrows said, "We really have no merit; we are ashamed to be in the higher position. If you let us be below, let the eyes look from above— what face-holes are you?" So Baoyue Ming the Chan master said in a lecture, "An ancient said, 'In the eyes it's called seeing, in the ears it's called hearing'—but tell me, in the eyebrows what is it called? (a long silence). In sorrow we grieve together, in happiness we rejoice together. Everybody knows the useful function, but they don't know the useless great function. But tell me, what was the meaning of Venerable Pindola's brushing his eyebrows with both hands?" (Wansong brushed his eyebrows and said 'Cat.')

Added Sayings /Case

Dizang asked "Where are you going?"—Why frame the man?
Fayan said, "Around on pilgrimage."—He goes looking for money to buy sandals.
Dizang said, "What is the purpose of pilgrimage?"—After all he doesn't let him go.
Fayan said, "I don't know."—Why didn't you say so earlier?
Dizang said, "Not knowing is nearest."—He goes right up and bumps him off.

Added Sayings /Verse

Now having studied to the full, it's like before—I'm like the people of yore, not one of the people of yore.
Having shed entirely the finest thread, he reaches not knowing—There is still this?
Let it be short or long, stop cutting and patching—A waste of effort.
Going along with high and low, it levels itself—Don't bother to exert your mind.
The abundance or scarcity of the house is used according to the occasion—Can't lack salt and vinegar.
Roaming serenely in the land, he goes where his feet take him—If you want to go, go.

The purpose of ten years' pilgrimage—Inconceivable.
Clearly he'd turned his back on one pair of eyebrows—As before they're above the eyes.

21 YUNYAN SWEEPS THE GROUND

Introduction Having shed illusion and enlightenment, having cut off holy and ordinary, although there are not so many things, setting up host and guest and distinguishing noble and mean is a special house. It's not that there is no giving jobs on assessment of ability, but how do you understand siblings with the same breath, adjoining branches?

Case As Yunyan was sweeping the ground, Daowu said, "Too busy." Yunyan said, "You should know there's one who isn't busy." Daowu said, "If so, then there's a second moon." Yunyan held up the broom and said, "Which moon is this?"

Commentary Daowu bore down on Yunyan, like Foguo urging on Fojian—as it is said, 'Without upset there is no solution, without struggle there is no expression.' Here as Yunyan was sweeping the ground Daowu casually tested him; Yunyan said, "You should know there is one who isn't busy." Good people, as you eat, boil tea, sew and sweep, you should recognize the one not busy—then you will realize the union of mundane reality and enlightened reality; in the Dongshan progression this is called simultaneous inclusion, naturally not wasting any time.

Daowu immediately saw the open seam and said, "If so, there is a second moon." Xuedou said as an alternative, "Almost might have been let pass." The two old men feared that people would set up a reality-body as apart from the physical body. National Teacher Huizhong said to a Chan traveler from the South, "For us here the buddha nature is completely unborn and undying; your buddha nature in the South there is half born, half dying, half unborn and undying." The traveler said, "How do you

91

distinguish?" The teacher said, "Here we say body and mind are one suchness; there's nothing outside of mind—therefore it's completely unborn and undying. You in the South say body is impermanent while the spiritual nature is permanent; there it's half born, half dying, half unborn and undying." When you get here you must realize there's a time to turn around to the father.

Yunyan then held up the broom and asked, "Which moon is this?" This expression originally comes from the *Heroic March Scripture,* which says, "Like the second moon, who will say it is the moon, who will deny it? For Manjusri only one moon is real—in between there is naturally nothing that is or is not the moon." Daowu immediately stopped. According to one version Daowu brushed out his sleeves and left. I say, completely exposed. But tell me, is it Yunyan exposing Daowu or Daowu exposing Yunyan? Those who have clear eyes try to check it out and see.

Xuansha said, "Indeed this is the second moon." This old fellow has correction fluid in his mouth, a sharp sword on his tongue. Changqing said, "What if he had the broom turned on him and shaken in his face?" Xuansha then stopped. Luoshan said, "Ah, these two old guys don't know good from bad! This fellow Yunyan, bound hand and foot—how long has he been dead?!" I say, I wouldn't say this wouldn't make it in the school of Deshan, but really it still wouldn't yet in the school of Dongshan.

When Xuefeng was traveling, he went to Touzi three times and climbed up to Dongshan nine times. One day as he was cleaning rice, Dongshan asked him "Are you cleaning the grit getting rid of the rice or cleaning the rice getting rid of the grit?" Xuefeng said, "Grit and rice are gone at once." Dongshan said, "What will the community eat?" Xuefeng then turned over the bowl. Dongshan said, "You've got it, all right, but you need to see someone else before you realize it." Xuansha and Changqing succeeded to Xuefeng, Luoshan succeeded to Yantou—all of them came from Deshan's gate; therefore one puts down, one uplifts—their words go against but their meanings accord. Now both streams, Dongshan and Yunmen, are equally active—how could there be superior or inferior?

Yunmen also said, "The butler, seeing the maid, takes care." Baofu said, "Yunyan is a lot like someone pushing a cart through mud, working hard every step of the way." These two old adepts also succeeded to Xuefeng—their speech and character naturally concur. What they mean to say is that Yunyan couldn't use the shaking of the broom to cut off complications; they still don't realize that there are thorns in the soft mud.

As Wansong unfolded this story, before he had finished reciting it, he unconsciously let out a laugh and said, Yunyan and Daowu were illustrating the active conditions of the Dongshan progression. As for that other bunch of old guys, all their mouths consumed the gold, but none cleared the straits for him. Fortunately there is Tiantong, who comes to the rescue, pulling out the sword:

Verse *Borrowing temporarily, Yunyan comprehends the gateway;*
Realizing the function as is appropriate, Daowu then rests.
The snake handler on Elephant-Bone Crag—
The doings of childhood seem shameful when you're old.

Commentary If you discuss this matter, it is like sparks, like lightning. Yunyan lifted it up to show the man, Changqing shakes it right in his face—though their uses are different, they return alike to change and extinction. The Dongshan progression therefore esteems the shift of potential and revolution of state.

On Xuefeng Mountain there is an Elephant Bone Crag. Xuefeng once instructed his congregation, "On South Mountain there is a turtle-nosed snake—you people should watch out for it carefully." Yunmen threw down his staff before him and made a gesture of fright. Is this not "When the butler sees the maid, he takes care"?

Yunyan was sweeping the ground—he raised the broom and said, "Which moon is this?" All have turned into empowered descendants along with the freed singing girl.

Yunmen even up till now is still under the awning—that is why Tiantong won't let him go, saying, "The snake-handler on Elephant Bone Crag— the doings of childhood seem shameful when you're old." Master Shengmo said, "This verse has a way of searching out people's shortcomings and helping their strengths." Here Tiantong and Shengmo condemn

Yunmen, but today I am overturning the decision—don't you see how Tiantong's line about the snake-handling praises Yunmen's great function of his whole potential, not coming down from the clouds? Why is it like this? Putting down and upholding both rest with oneself—who else do killing and reviving depend on?

Added
Sayings
/Verse

As Yunyan was sweeping the ground—Novices and workmen don't have the strength.

Daowu said, "Too busy."—Hiding an army he picks a fight.

Yunyan said, "You should know there's one who isn't busy."—Too bad, the story has become dualistic.

Daowu said, "If so, then there's a second moon."—Only two? There's hundreds, thousands, myriads.

Yunyan held up the broom and said, "Which moon is this?"—He appears from within the crystal palace.

Daowu then stopped—It's all in the unspoken.

Xuansha said, "This is precisely the second moon."—When one person transmits a falsehood, ten thousand people transmit it as truth.

Yunmen said, "When the butler sees the maid, he takes care."—Following the error, he beats the strainer.

Added
Sayings
/Case

Borrowing temporarily, he comprehends the gateway—Giving birth on the spot.

Realizing the function as is appropriate, then he rests—Passing away on the spot.

The snake-handler of Elephant Bone Crag—If you want to speak of others . . .

The doings of childhood seem shameful when you're old—First manage yourself.

22 YANTOU'S "BOW AND SHOUT"

Introduction   People are probed with words, water is probed with a stick. Pulling out the weeds looking for the way is what is ordinarily applied; suppose suddenly there leaps out a burnt-tail tiger—then what?

Case   When Yantou came to Deshan, he straddled the threshold and asked, "Is this ordinary or is it holy?"
Deshan immediately shouted.
Yantou bowed.
Dongshan heard of this and said, "Anyone but Yantou would hardly get it."
Yantou said, "Old Dongshan doesn't know good and bad; at that time I was holding up with one hand and putting down with one hand."

Commentary   Deshan ordinarily beat the wind and hit the rain. One day Yantou spread his sitting mat; Deshan pushed it downstairs with his staff. Yantou went down, gathered up the mat and went off. Next day he went up and stood by Deshan. Deshan said, "Where did you learn this empty-headedness?" Yantou said, "I never fool myself." Deshan said, "Later on you will shit on my head." 'When the father hears his son is strong, he regrets not being killed himself'—'only when one's view surpasses the teacher is one capable of passing on the transmission.'
This question is referred to everywhere as the state of straddling the gate, but he did not necessarily actually straddle the gate to ask at first. In olden times an outsider concealed a live sparrow in his hand and asked the Buddha, "Is the sparrow in my hand alive or dead?" The Buddha strad-

95

dled the gate with his feet and asked, "Tell me—am I about to leave or enter?" The question "Is this ordinary or holy?" truly contains this principle.

In the old days it is said Puhua pointed to the sage monk (Manjusri) statue (in the meditation hall) and asked Linji, "Tell me, is this ordinary or holy?" Linji immediately shouted; Puhua said, "Heyang is a new bride, Muta's is 'old lady' Chan; along with the little pisser of Linji, after all they have one eye." Linji said, "This old thief!" Puhua left the hall saying "Thief! Thief!" Shoushan said, "Of these two thieves there is a real thief; tell me, which is the real thief?" Then in everyone's behalf he said, "Liu Benzi" (who was installed as second successor to the throne of China after Wang Mang, usurper of the Han dynasty claim to rule).

When Yantou asked, "Is this ordinary or holy?" and Deshan immediately shouted, it was just like sizing up and matching Linji; when Yantou bowed, this too was like "the little pisser of Linji after all has one eye."

Xuedou said, "At that point, as soon as he bowed, to have hit him right on the spine would not only have cut off Dongshan, but would have have held old Yantou still." This gets at the same thing as Linji's saying, "This old thief!"

Dongshan heard this recounted and said, "Anyone but Yantou would hardly get it." Foguo added the remark, "The bystander has eyes." He also said, "He only knows the one, not the two." My view is not the same: Foguo says that though the bystander Dongshan has eyes, he only sees that the awl is sharp; I say, though Master Foguo has eyes, he does not see that the chisel is square.

Dongshan purposely took it up and falsely accused Yantou, wanting to show that at that time in the bow there was the provisional and the real. And after all when the fire reached Yantou's head, he hastily beat it out, saying, "Old man Dongshan doesn't know good from bad—at that time I was holding up with one hand and putting down with one hand." Thereat he finally lit the lamp and began to eat dinner. Both houses are distinctly clear.

Haven't you heard the verse of Master Baoning Yong:

> Over the even river runs the rabbit—the blue falcon is released;
> (This versifies the question straddling the gate)
> One push—feeding and eating both eyeballs.

(This versifies Deshan's shout and Yantou's bow.)
A poison hand comes plundering—people buy and leave;
(This versifies Dongshan adding interest to the price.)
What can they do?—Pounds and ounces are not yet distinctly clear.

This is exactly what I'm saying. Do you want pounds and ounces to be distinctly clear? In reality Foguo and I are not contesting who is higher or lower. Look, further, at Tiantong weighing the scale pan:

Verse   *Demolishing the oncomer,*
Holding the handle of authority;
Tasks have a manner in which they must be carried out,
The nation has an inviolable law.
When the guest serves reverently, the host becomes haughty—
When the ruler dislikes admonition, the ministers flatter.
The underlying meaning—Yantou asks Deshan;
One upholding, one putting down—see the action of mind.

Commentary   This eulogizes three people all demolishing the oncomer, each holding the handle of authority. Only Yantou and Deshan had a manner which had to be carried out and an inviolable law. "When the guest serves reverently, the host becomes haughty" refers to Dongshan and Yantou. "When the ruler dislikes admonition, the ministers flatter" refers to Yantou and Deshan. The final two lines refer to Dongshan and Yantou. This style is generally called 'discrimination of the lessons of the ancients'— to pick milk out from water you must be a king goose; then you will see the work of Tiantong's needle and thread.
Yantou knew Deshan had a manner that had to be carried out and an inviolable law, therefore he didn't deny his potential and bowed according to sense. Dongshan knew that Yantou wouldn't be searched, that he wouldn't accept judgement, that as a son inheriting his father's work, he also had a manner that had to be carried out and an inviolable law; so he put bait on the hook by saying, "Anyone but Yantou would hardly get it." Is it not a case of 'served reverently, the host becomes haughty; their admonitions resented, the ministers flatter'?

In the Linji style this is called a long red thread, a green jade pitfall, a device to fell a tiger, a concerted struggle to bury an army. Everywhere they say that Yantou was upholding with one hand and putting down with the other, that Dongshan misconstrued it; they hardly realize that Dongshan's upholding with one hand and putting down with the other is even more distinctly clear. Unless one is an adept who has investigated for a long time, it will certainly be difficult to comprehend the essence of this.

In the present time, all novices who've just shed their civilian clothes see Tiantong's verse saying, "One upholding, one putting down—see the action of mind" and say how strange it is that Chan folk do not consent to explain things through for people—after all, all of it is the action of mind. So they become students clever at deceit. I say, one bit of mental action is a bit of compassion; if you don't encounter something, you don't learn to cope with it. You might say that the fruit comes from within the flower; sweet comes from bitter.

Yantou upheld and put down—Dongshan tries to pass it off for more than it's worth. Dongshan upheld and put down—I explain it through. If someone came forth and bowed, I would let them go—I wouldn't hit them. Why? Because there'd be no blood under their skin.

Added Sayings /Case

Yantou straddled the threshold and asked "is this ordinary or holy?"—This thief!

Deshan shouted—Bursts his brain.

Yantou bowed—This is not yet being good-hearted.

Dongshan heard of this and said, "Anyone but Yantou would hardly get it."—A rich reward, sweet words.

Yantou said, 'Old Dongshan doesn't know good and bad.'—After all he's in a rush again.

At that time I was holding up with one hand and putting down with one hand—Don't I know!

Added Sayings /Verse

Demolishing the oncomer—When the wind blows the grass bends.

Holding the handle of authority—Where the talisman goes, it is put into practice.

Tasks have a manner which must be carried out—Even the Buddha's hand cannot block it.

The nation has an inviolable law—Who dares to confront it head on?

When the guest serves reverently, the host becomes haughty—Those below use manners to stab those above.

When the ruler dislikes admonition, the ministers flatter—Those above use manners to educate those below.

The underlying meaning—*Yantou asks Deshan*—Even though father and son raise an army, . . .

One upholding, one putting down—*see the action of mind*—. . . they don't avoid spear and shield depending on each other.

23 LUZU FACES THE WALL

Introduction Bodhidharma's nine years is called wall-gazing—Shenguang's three bows divulge the natural potential. How can you sweep away the tracks and obliterate the traces?

Case **Whenever Luzu saw a monk coming, he would immediately face the wall. Nanquan, hearing of this, said, "I usually tell them to realize mastery before the empty aeon, to understand before the buddhas appear in the world; still I haven't found one or a half. Luzu that way will go on till the year of the ass."**

Commentary Chan Master Baoyun of Mt. Luzu in Zhi province used to face the wall whenever he saw a monk coming. After Bodhidharma sat for nine years, there was no one to re-enact this law; for the time being they have had everyone ask about buddhas and patriarchs, about transcendence and accommodation—everybody recognizes a little pain and itch.

Nanquan was a peer of Luzu; seeing people's needle and awl not moving, he immediately gives a penetrating comment from the side—"I usually tell them to realize mastery before the empty eon, to understand before buddhas appear in the world; but still I haven't found even one or half a man." His meaning is like letting out a thread; in reality he has transmitted the essence of the teaching in behalf of the other's attendant. He also said, "Luzu that way will go on till the year of the ass." His meaning seems to be blaming Luzu for being too strict, but in reality he's praising his direct imparting right there. Haven't you heard it said that even if you can explain thoroughly, it can't compare with personally arriving once. That is why "On Spiritual Mountain it was like drawing the moon, at

Caoqi it was like pointing at the moon"—how can they compare to Luzu in the crystal palace, in the hall of far-reaching cold, meeting with bared breast?

Baofu saw Nanquan and Luzu's open seam and asked Changqing, "In Luzu's case, where was he being discreet, that he was spoken of by Nanquan in such a way?" I say, why does Baofu say the words 'being discreet'? Unless you know how to discern spring and autumn on the budless branches it is difficult to pose this question. Changqing replied, "Retreating into oneself, conceding to others—not one in a thousand does." I say, the ancient had such clarity of eye!

Xuanjiao said, "Was Nanquan chiming in words of agreement or words of disagreement?" I say, half blocking, half covering—you can't fool him a bit.

Cuiyan Zhi said, "Why go to such trouble?" I say this is already setting up a model, drawing a likeness. He also said, "If a monk comes, what is seen?" I say, you still don't know how few they are. He also said, "One should know the time." I say, if it were Dao Yuanming, he would furrow his eyebrows and go right back. Also he said, "I am not thus—before the womb it's impossible to understand; if you understand, I'll break your waist." I say, Master, who would you have receive the blow of your staff?

Luoshan said, "If old teacher Wang (Nanquan) had seen him then, he'd give him five on the back with his fire tongs, because he knew how to let go but not how to gather in." I say, even getting up early at dawn, already there is someone who's been traveling by night. Xuansha said, "If I had seen him then, I too would have given him five fire tongs." I say, disturbing the spring breeze, never yet ceasing.

Yunju Yang said, "Both Luoshan and Xuansha said this—are they the same, or is there a separate reason?" I say, together it amounts to ten fire tongs. He also said, "If you can pick it out, I'll allow as your Buddhism has some direction." I say he should be given five fire tongs.

People, you look—as Nanquan belittled Luzu in this way, yet Changqing said, "This is retreating into oneself and conceding to others." Luzu held down the barrier crossing, yet Luoshan said, "He knows how to let go, not how to gather in." All this is spreading the net before the fish, drawing the bow after the brigand has gone. Then look at Tiantong—what special approach has he made?

Verse   *In plainness there's flavor*
Subtly transcending thought and expression
Continuously seeming to exist before any sign.
Unbending, like an idiot, his path is lofty:
Jade, when a pattern is carved, loses its purity;
A pearl in an abyss attracts of itself.
A thoroughly clear air burnishes sweltering autumn pure;
A bit of cloud at leisure divides sky and waters afar.

Commentary   In ancient times Xiduan Er the royal courtier was going to take up his post at the capital, when on the way he passed by Daming monastery in Cizhou and went into the hall there; he rejoiced as he saw a monk sitting facing the wall—"Here's a fellow who likes plainness." Great Master Quan said, "There is flavor in plainness. The nature of water is originally plain—when you add tea or honey, bitterness or sweetness are produced therein. Nature is also still and calm—if you make waves with 'delusion and enlightenment,' then 'ordinary and holy' are established therein." Though he says that the plain has flavor, this is flavorless flavor—the flavor is everlasting, subtly transcending thought and expression. Thought and expression come from mind and speech—when you get here, the path of words ends, the trend of mental action dies out. Fayan said, "When reason is finished you forget thoughts and expressions— how can there be any comparison?"

In the classic *Power of the Way,* in the chapter on the undying of the valley spirit, it says, "The gate of the mysterious cow is the root of heaven and earth; continually it seems to exist." Also it says, "I don't know whose child it is—it is before images." For patchrobe monks, to say "continually it seems to exist" means that you shouldn't utterly cut off; "before images" means the time before the empty aeon, before the Buddha has appeared in the world.

"Unbending, like an idiot, his path is lofty" subtly uses Xuedou's "The way is lofty, though seeming foolish." This verse said, "The rain has passed, the clouds are shrinking, dawn has halfway broken through; the multiple peaks are like a drawing of bluegreen rocky crags. Subhuti did not know how to sit on a cliff; he brought on the heavenly flowers and the shaking of the earth." This eulogizes Subhuti sitting peacefully and the emperor of gods showering flowers. Now Luzu, unable to end matters, brought on the examination of this group of old guys, Nanquan and Xuansha. This is indeed a case of "Jade, when a pattern is carved, loses its purity"—it is not as good as "A pearl in an abyss attracting of itself." In the *Book of Jin* there is a poem by Liu Ji which says, "As the stones are full of jade, the mountain shines; as the water contains pearls, the river attracts." In the rock is hidden a jade—it is cut out by Nanquan; in the water is embraced a pearl—it is strained out by Xuansha. Fortunately there is naturally "a thoroughly clear air burnishing sweltering autumn pure," in which just now "a bit of cloud at leisure divides sky and waters afar."

I have never faced the wall; what good measure do you all come here for? (in everyone's behalf) Hear tell Tiantong's eulogy of the ancients.

Added Sayings /Case

Whenever Luzu saw a monk coming he would face the wall—The meeting is done.

Nanquan, hearing of this, said, "I usually tell them to realize mastery before the empty eon."—Without thinking, he calls himself.

"To understand before the buddhas appear in the world."—Does the Master understand?

"Still I haven't found one or a half."—Just because he left a loose thread hanging out.

Luzu that way will go on till the year of the ass—One in a hurry does not understand.

Added Sayings /Verse

In plainness there's flavor—Who told you to add salt and vinegar?

Subtly transcending thought and expression—Deal again another day.

Continuously, seeming to exist, before any sign—Already fallen into the secondary.

Unbending, like an idiot, his path is lofty—No one puts a price on it.

Jade, when a pattern is carved, loses its purity—The master's high-handed.

A pearl in an abyss attracts of itself—Don't brag so much.

A thoroughly clear air burnishes sweltering autumn pure—The body is exposed in the autumn wind.

A bit of cloud at leisure divides sky and waters afar—Around good things there are many devils.

24 XUEFENG'S "LOOK OUT FOR THE SNAKE"

Introduction The whale of the Eastern Sea, the turtle-nosed snake of South Mountain, Puhua's donkey brays, Zihu's dog howls—they don't fall into ordinary ways, and don't travel among different kinds. Tell me, whose way of practice is this?

Case **Xuefeng said to the congregation, "On South Mountain there's a turtle-nosed snake; you people must watch out for it."**
Changqing said, "Today in the hall there are many people losing their bodies and lives."
A monk quoted this to Xuansha; Xuansha said, "Only brother Changqing could say this. However, even though he's right, I do not concur."
The monk said, "What do you mean, Master?"
Xuansha said, "Why use 'South Mountain'?"
Yunmen threw down his staff in front of Xuefeng and made a gesture of fright.

Commentary Although the viper of South Mountain is a dead snake, in front of Elephant Bone Crag if you can handle it, it's alive.
Xuefeng brought it up to show the assembly—basically he wanted to use poison to get rid of poison. Changqing only knew how to push the boat along with the current, saying, "Today in the hall there are many losing their lives." If he had known how to steer the rudder against the wind, Xuefeng would have had to enter the Hall of Extinction.
Xuansha heard this quoted and said, "Only brother Changqing could

say this." Here there is a little difficulty; if you say Xuansha is approving Changqing, why does he then say, "I do not concur"? He not only propels the boat along with the current; he also knows how to steer the rudder against the wind. This monk was heedless of danger and death; he asked Xuansha what he would say. Xuansha just said, "Why use 'South Mountain'? Here we see the hand that manages to bring the snake to life.

Yunmen threw down his staff and made a gesture of fright; he used it most familiarly. In the verse on the story of Yunyan sweeping the ground was cited "the snake-handler on Elephant Bone Crag—the doings of childhood seem shameful when you're old." And for Yunmen he said, "When the butler sees the maid, he takes care," thereupon riding a thief's horse to chase the thief, also ineluctably deadly in his actions.

Today again eulogizing the story of handling the snake, boasting of the hand to capture dragons, see how once the great axe has cut, the hand rubs.

Verse   *Xuansha's great strength*
Changqing's little courage
The turtle-nose on South Mountain, dead, has no use
Wind and clouds meet, horns on the head are born
After all we see Yunmen pitching in to play:
Pitching in to play—
In a flash of lightning, see the change and movement.
With me, it's possible to send away and to summon;
With him, there's capture, there's release.
The underlying matter—to whom is it imparted now?
The cold mouth wounds people, yet they don't feel the pain.

Commentary   Xuansha sent a messenger with a letter to Xuefeng. Xuefeng opened it up and saw three sheets of blank paper. He showed them to that messenger monk and said, "Understand?" The monk said, "No." Xuefeng said, "Haven't you heard it said that nobles are the same all over?" That monk reported this to Xuansha, who said, "The old teacher on the mountain has stumbled past without realizing it." Xuansha succeeded to Xuefeng—he always 'bore witness on his father for stealing a sheep,' and 'in benevolence did not defer.' He said, "Why use 'South Mountain'?" This too is valor without an opponent, great power in the extreme.

Changqing went along with the misdirection and said, "There are many people losing their lives." He did not know how to spring back like a lion; this is truly a case of 'seeing what is proper, not to do it is lack of courage.'

"Wind and clouds meet, horns on the head are born—after all we see Yunmen pitching in to play." This eulogizes Yunmen bringing out a living snake right before your eyes—he wasn't like the other masters, with a bow showing a reflection (looking like a snake) in their cups.

As for "With me, it's possible to send away and to summon," in folklore it says, "Calling snakes is easy, sending away snakes is hard."

"With him, there's capture, there's release" eulogizes Yunmen, who also made a gesture of fright after he had thrown the staff down in front of Xuefeng—once one can capture and release, one surely can send away and summon.

Finally Tiantong says, "The underlying matter—to whom is it imparted now? The cold mouth wounds people, yet they don't feel the pain." Only when one always returns the verse to oneself and brings it out up front, is one an adept.

Xuedou also said, "Now it is hidden here on Ru Peak; those who come, one by one observe expedient methods," and he shouted loudly, "Look right where you are!" I say, Xuedou indulges in looking where he is, not realizing it has pierced his skull. Tiantong rends people with his cold mouth; clear people do not muddle things. If I had been Yunmen at the time, I would thrust the staff at Xuefeng's chest, and if he hesitated without coming forth, I would follow up behind and teach him to accept what he has done himself and personally get bitten. Why so? Now it is the second day of the second month—for the moment we let dragons rear their heads.

Added Sayings /Case   **On South Mountain there's a turtle-nosed snake; you people must watch out for it**—Holding up a sitting mat, I say, 'This isn't borrowed.'

Today in the hall there are many people losing their bodies and lives—Hearing the wind, he raises his voice.

A monk quoted this to Xuansha—Staked up no more than three.

Only brother Changqing could say this—Foxes associate with foxes, dogs with dogs.

Even though he's right, I don't concur—If there's a longer snake than this, bring it out.

What do you mean?—A poison insect on the head makes an itch.

Why use South Mountain—Just this turtle-nose is still beyond the pale.

Yunmen threw down his staff and made a gesture of fright—How can you injure your own life?

Added Sayings /Verse

Xuansha's great strength—In charge of the works, he doesn't defer to his father.

Changqing's little courage—Seeing his duty, he doesn't do it.

The turtle-nose on South Mountain, dead, has no use—He carries a length of broken money-string.

Wind and clouds meet, horns are born on the head—When the time comes, even earthworms become dragons.

After all we see Yunmen pitching in to play—He's too sharp to hold back.

Pitching in to play—If you can't play, stop repeating and repeating.

In a flash of lightning, see the change and movement—In the blink of an eye you've lost your body and life.

With me, it's possible to send away and to summon—Don't brag so much.

With him, there's capture and release—The sceptre's in his hands.

The underlying matter—to whom is it imparted?—To me, old man Wansong.

The cold mouth wounds people, yet they don't feel the pain—Ow! Ow!

25 YANGUAN'S "RHINOCEROS FAN"

Introduction   Oceans of lands without bound are not apart from right here: the events of infinite aeons past are all in the immediate present. Try to make him present it face to face, and he won't be able to bring it out in the wind. But tell me, where is the fault?

Case   One day Yanguan called to his attendant, "Bring me the rhinoceros fan."
The attendant said, "The fan is broken."
Yanguan said, "If the fan is broken, then bring me back the rhinoceros!"
The attendant had no reply.
Zifu drew a circle and wrote the word 'rhino' inside it.

Commentary   (Yanguan was) Chan Master Jian of Zhenguo Haishang Temple in the *Yanguan* (saltworks) district of Hang province.
Originally an offspring of the imperial family of the Tang dynasty, Xuanzong, while in hiding as a monk, was going to call on Master Yanguan. The Master knew about this beforehand, and told the director of duties to tell everyone not to talk at random and to stop any wayward doings. The (future) emperor stayed there a long time, then suddenly left; the Master said to him privately, "The time has come—don't stay curled up in the mud." And he also entrusted to him future responsibility for Buddhism. In the sixth year after the former emperor Wuzong had destroyed the teaching of Buddhism, Xuanzong had restored it—the Master Yanguan had a strong influence in that. The emperor was going

to summon the master to the palace to provide for him, but the master had already long passed on. The emperor lamented and gave him a posthumous title, 'Chan Master Awakened to Emptiness.'

The master one day called to his attendant, "Bring me the rhinoceros fan." The attendant said, "The fan is broken." Still this is talk about ordinary reality between father and son. The master said, "If the fan is broken, then bring me back the rhinoceros." This is going into the weeds with his whole body, in a relationship with an adopted child. The attendant had no reply—after all he had hit upon the true by way of the false; it's just that he himself didn't know he had it. Touzi said on his behalf, "I don't decline to bring it out, but I'm afraid the horn on the head will be lacking." I say, he can repair it. Xuedou brought this up and said, "I want the lacking horn." I say, this is a family heirloom. Shishuang said, "If I give it back to you, master, then I'll have none." I say, he avoids it though face to face. Xuedou said, "The rhino is still there." I say, a clear eye is hard to fool. Baofu said, "The master is old—better ask someone else." I say, much indebtedness leads to deep resentment. Xuedou, bringing this up, said, "What a pity to work so hard without accomplishing anything." I say, a good intention doesn't receive a good reward.

According to this bunch of old guys' empty explanations of the principle, the fan and the rhino ultimately can't be brought out. Only Zifu drew a circle and wrote the character for such a beast; the fan, the rhino, are utterly new, immutable. Xuedou said, "Why didn't you bring it out before?"

Really he says, "The fan is broken"—when has so much as a bit of hair been moved? Before when he didn't bring it out, when had it ever been lacking, either? And now that it's brought out, it's still never increased.

Tiantong praises Zifu for being able to bring it out and use it knowingly, elevating the name and seeking out (one who knows), especially boiling some tea for him.

Verse   *As the fan is broken, he seeks the rhino*
The word in the circle has a reason
Who would have known the thousand-year light of the full moon
Would subtly make a pervasive luminous spot of autumn?

Commentary In various places they say on the fan was drawn a rhinoceros gazing at the moon; some say the fan was made of rhinoceros horn, some say it had a rhinoceros handle. All of these could be called rhinoceros fans. Yanguan at the time opened a shop, and everyone brought out a handle. Only Zifu handled it intimately in a refreshing way—the whole thing is totally distinct.

Master Zifu once said to his congregation, "After returning immediately upon seeing the banner pole at Zifu's monastery from across the river, right where you are you deserve thirty blows of the cane—how much the more so since coming across the river!" At that point a monk started to come forth, but as soon as he did the master said, "Not worth talking with."

In general, the lecturing shops esteem attainment in explanation, the fundamental schools esteem attainment in application. Therefore, 'The word in the circle has a reason.'

Xuansha said to his congregation, "'I have the treasury of the eye of truth; I entrust it to Mahakasyapa' is like drawing the moon; the Sixth Patriarch raising the whisk at Caoqi was like pointing at the moon." In his final discourse before his demise the World Honored One emanated a light as lovely as the moon, and King Ajatashatru's torrid afflictions cleared and cooled. That's why it says, "Who would have known the thousand-year light of the full moon would subtly make a pervasive luminous spot of autumn?" This can be called 'if the great handle is in hand, the pure wind always reaches one.'

The story of the rhinoceros fan has been brought up and eulogized most, but when you get right down to the real point, they haven't ever met with Yanguan. If I were the attendant, when I was told to bring the rhinoceros fan, whatever feathers, reeds, bamboo, silks, or yak hair came to hand, I would bring forth and give him the handle. Why? Because though there may be a thousand varieties of technique, ultimately there are not two kinds of wind.

Added Sayings / Verse **One day Yanguan called his attendant to bring him the rhinoceros fan**—Essentially he can't be missing it.
The attendant said it was broken—But before it was brought up it was whole.

If the fan is broken, then bring me back the rhinoceros—Didn't you hear him say it was broken? Why don't you understand what he says? **The attendant had no reply**—The fan survives. But though it exists, it's as though it didn't.

Zifu drew a circle and wrote the word 'rhino' inside it—Exercising skill, renewing his action, he is capable of making it and knows how to sell it.

Added Sayings / Verse

As the fan is broken, he seeks the rhino—One won't do, two won't stop.
The word in the circle has a reason—It's like he forcibly explains the reason.
Who would have known the thousand-year light of the full moon—Burying the root ten thousand feet, . . .
Would subtly make a pervasive luminous spot of autumn— . . . in the present age it produces sprouts.

26 YANGSHAN POINTS TO SNOW

Introduction Ice and frost are one color; snow and moon merge their light. Freezing the reality-body to death, purifying the fisherman to the extreme. Is there anyone who can appreciate?

Case **Yangshan pointed to a snow lion and said, "Is there any that can go beyond this color?"**
Yunmen said, "At that point I'd have pushed it over for him."
Xuedou said, "He only knows how to push down, he doesn't know how to help up."

Commentary The ancients, in confronting situations, encountering beings, brought to light the one great matter before the empty aeon. The *Lotus Scripture* says, "Pure, uniform unmixed complete plainness is the character of pure conduct." Those who explain it say that white is the basis of all colors, as the one vehicle is the source of all vehicles—yet they don't explain that there is still something beyond white. That is why Yangshan pointed at the snow lion and said, "Is there any that can go beyond this color?" Now white is the basis of all colors, and the color of snow is sheer white—how can there be any going beyond this? I say, since it's called 'color' it must relate with the eye—the color that goes beyond white is only the colorless—it does not relate to the eye. Yunmen therefore said, "At that point I'd have pushed it over for him." If you then grasp the point of ultimate blankness, where there isn't even white, this indeed is falling into the formless realm—that is why Xuedou pointed out a living road besides, having him help up what he pushed down. Foyan said, "If you raise it up here, it will sure make a step by step task." I say, if it were other schools, different streams, I wouldn't say this isn't all right, but you should know in the style of the Dongshan progression there is a time when just when you push down you immediately raise up and just when you raise up you push down—after this, raising up and pushing down are simultaneous, raising up and pushing down are not established—buy some more sandals and travel for thirty years more.

Haven't you seen Fojiao's verse:

> *Uniform, none surpassing, he shows it to people,*
> *Stretching in a world of white silver.*
> *Aloof, they push down and then raise up,*
> *But how can that compare to the freshness of the spring breeze and warm sun?*

I say, 'after the sun comes out, an embarrassing situation.' One kind of student sees Yunmen pushing down and Xuedou helping up, and understands it as exchange of points of action, the great function without convention; seeing that one shouldn't understand uniformity as referring to color or form, they consider it the bloodline of the fundamental essence. Already there is Fojiao as proof; if you don't believe, ask then of Tiantong.

Verse   *One knocks down, one sets up—the lion in the snowy garden.*
Careful about transgression, he embosoms benevolence.
Courageous in action, he sees his duty.
Pure light shining in the eyes is like being lost from home—
Turning around in clear purity is after all to fall into that state.
Patchrobed mendicants ultimately have nothing to rely on:
Dying the same, born the same, which is 'this,' which 'that'?
News of warmth bursts the plum—spring comes to the cold branches.
A freezing gale makes the leaves drop—autumn clarifies the runoff water.

Commentary   Yunmen knocks down, Xuedou sets up; Yangshan points to the lion and wants us to transcend this color—three legs of the pot, it won't do to lack any of them. The three mysteries and three essentials are all herein.

Yangshan feared people would settle in clear blankness—isn't this "careful about transgression, he embosoms virtue"? Pointing it out, he makes people go beyond this color—is this not "courageous in action, he sees his duty"?

Yunmen also feared settling down in uniformity—is this not "careful about transgression, he embosoms virtue"? So he then pushed it down for him—this too is "courageous in action, he sees his duty."

Xudeou feared people would just know how to push down—this is "careful about transgression, he embosoms virtue." Beyond this, he can raise up—this is "courageous in action, he sees his duty."

Haven't you heard how Zhaozhou said, "I do not abide in clarity"—indeed, it's because "pure light shining in the eyes is like being lost from home—turning around in clear purity is after all to fall into that state." If you only know how to push down and don't know how to set up, what are you capable of? A genuine monk is like a pearl rolling in a bowl—although born the same and dying the same, yet they do not dwell in birth and death; although there is no 'this' or 'that,' provisionally we establish 'that' and 'this.'

As for the final two lines, 'sometimes under the gate of the great sun, sometimes before the hall of the bright moon.' In the eternal sky of ten thousand ages, one morning's wind and moon, morning mushrooms and cicadas. Tell me—what time and season is this right now? 'For a time, be like an old tree, like wintry skeletal branches; be about to pursue the spring breezes, about to enter the burned-out fields.'

<table>
<tr><td>Added
Sayings
/Case</td><td>Yangshan pointed to a snow lion and said, "Is there any that can go beyond this color?"—Yangshan unawares has bit the dust on even ground.
Yunmen said, "I'd push it down."—Unable to do anything about the boat, he smashes the bailing bucket.
Xuedou said, "He only knows how to push down, not how to help up."—Seeing iniquity on the road, he draws his sword to help out.</td></tr>
</table>

Added Sayings /Verse

One knocks down, one sets up—the lion in the snowy garden—Just like a living one.

Careful about transgression, he embosoms benevolence—Those who know the law fear it.

114

Courageous in action, he sees his duty—Seeing inequality on the road.
Pure light shining in the eyes is like being lost from home—East and West are not distinguished.
Turning around in clear purity is after all to fall into that state—Climb a story higher.
Patchrobed mendicants ultimately have nothing to rely on—Temporarily passing a lifetime.
Dying the same, born the same, which is this, which that—Neither sword nor axe can cut them apart.
News of warmth bursts the plum—spring comes to the cold branches—Getting revivifying incense.
A freezing gale makes the leaves drop; autumn clarifies the runoff water—He comes and beats the poison drum.

27 FAYAN POINTS TO A BLIND

Introduction   When the teachers are many the line is confused; when laws are issued crime is born. Though curing sickness where there is no sickness may be extreme kindness, how does going by the rule where there is a rule preclude citing a story?

Case   **Fayan pointed to a blind. The two monks went at the same time and rolled up the blind. Fayan said, "One gain, one loss."**

Commentary   Before the noon meal, Fayan went up to a meeting. He pointed to a blind, and two monks both went to roll up the blind. Fayan said, "One gain, one loss."

Dongshan Ji said, "Elders, how do you understand? Some say that because they didn't understand the message they immediately went and rolled up the blind. Also some say that the one he directed understood, but the one who went without being directed lost. Is it possible to understand this way? Since you can't understand this way, I ask you elders, which one's gained, which one's lost? I say, 'washing a clod of earth in mud.'

This is not only Fayan. One day Nanquan said to a monk, "Quite a wind last night." The monk also said, "Quite a wind last night." Nanquan said, "It blew over a pine in front of the gate." The monk also said, "It blew over a pine in front of the gate." Nanquan next said to a monk, "Quite a wind last night." The monk said, "What wind?" Nanquan said, "It blew over a pine in front of the gate." The monk said, "What pine?" Nanquan said, "One gain, one loss."

The story of pointing at the blind absolutely has a strategy for helping people. The two monks rolled up the blind—on the part of the people involved, there are naturally two paths; Fayan first gave a seal that sealed fast and never moved—on the part of Fayan, light and dark intermingle, with killing and enlivening action. The sphere of great being, the universally wise know.

Everywhere they consider detachment from gain and loss and forgetting right and wrong to be superior; Fayan runs into the ocean of right and wrong, the pit of gain and loss, and makes a living there—in sum, someone without gain or loss can determine the gain and loss everywhere in the world.

In my commenting like this too there is gain and loss; in your coming here too there is gain and loss; only those with profound insight into the point of advantage or disadvantage can compare their benefit or loss. As this is called a case of being in the present, there is no need to bother to reexamine it, but because he couldn't flatly settle it, he couldn't avoid bringing on Tiantong's suit: the verse says

Verse   *Pines are straight, brambles are crooked; cranes are tall, ducks are short.*
In the age of the ancient emperors, people forgot about both government and anarchy.
Such peace—a hidden dragon in the abyss;
Such freedom—a soaring bird sheds its tether.
Nothing can be done about the Patriarch's coming from the West—
Within, gain and loss are half and half.
Reeds go along with the wind, turning in the air,
The boat cuts off the flow and reaches the shore.
Spiritually-sharp mendicants here,
Observe Fayan's method.

Commentary   The ancients couldn't help but give the forced name 'the fundamental lot'—"Pines are straight, brambles are crooked," herons are white, ravens are black; this originally comes from the *Heroic March Scripture*—Tiantong changes it to "Cranes are tall, ducks are short." Zhuangzi said,

117

"The long do not have excess, the short are not lacking; therefore, though ducks' legs are short, they'll be miserable if you add to them, and though cranes' legs are long, they'll be unhappy if you cut them off." A proverb says, "If you want to avoid misery, rely on your own lot." Would it be only the people in the age of the ancient emperors who forgot about both government and anarchy? Confucius said, "In the West there is a great sage—he doesn't govern and yet there is no anarchy." "Government and anarchy" refer to "gain and loss." The Third Patriarch said, "Gain and loss, right and wrong—let go of them all at once."

In the *qian* hexagram of the *Book of Changes*, in the first nine it says, "Hidden dragon—don't act." In nine in the fourth place it says, "Sometimes it leaps in the abyss."

In the *Record of the Platform of the Chin Dynasty* it says that Wang Cizhong, while young, changed Cang Jie's ancient symbols into the classical form of writing Chinese characters. The first emperor of Chin called for him, but he didn't come. The emperor, angry, had him imprisoned in a cage on a cart and taken to Chin. On the way, Wang turned into a bird, shed his bonds and flew away. As he reached West Mountain he dropped two quills: in Guiquan district there is a huge mortar stone—that's the place.

This eulogizes the way of high antiquity, its provenance and treasury of deeds, each resting in its own lot. Before the Buddha appeared in the world there were not so many scriptures, treatises, and public cases—when the Patriarch came from the West, then there was gain and loss. Why not comprehend before the pointing to the screen?

"Reeds go along with the wind, turning in the air, the boat cuts off the flow and reaches the shore." These two lines mark out the gain and loss of the two monks. Tiantong here has great effect; it is not easy to say this. If one has not the ability to bring people to life, how could one be able to kill people? For this reason Tiantong also said, "Spiritually-sharp mendicants here, observe Fayan's method." Tell me, based on what law can he say so? Wait till you've been hit, then I'll tell you.

Added Sayings /Case	**Fayan pointed to a blind**—Don't say you don't know, don't say you don't see.

Two monks then both went and rolled up the blind—They walk the same but don't step the same.

Fayan said, "One gain, one loss."—He divides the body under the sword.

Added Sayings /Verse

Pines are straight, brambles are crooked; cranes are tall, ducks are short—Can't move it.

In the age of the ancient emperors, people forgot about both government and anarchy—The gourds, picked up and dug into, are ripe.

Such peace—a hidden dragon in the abyss—Even the Buddha's eye looking cannot see.

Such freedom—a soaring bird sheds its tether—The gaze cannot reach it.

Nothing can be done about the Patriarch's coming from the West—The top beam isn't straight.

Within, gain and loss are half and half—The pillars below are uneven.

Reeds go along with the wind, turning in the air—Active consciousness chaotic, there's no basis to rely on.

The boat cuts off the flow and reaches the shore—Going downstream full sail, it's so fast it's hard to catch.

Spiritually-sharp mendicants here—A drunk railing on the corner—who would take him seriously?

Observe Fayan's method—I too have some here, but it's rare to meet a suitable person.

28 HUGUO'S "THREE EMBARRASSMENTS"

Introduction   One who doesn't wear even an inch of thread is truly a naked heretic; one who doesn't chew even a grain of rice surely returns to the burnt-faced ghost king. Even being born in a holy situation, you still don't escape the dangerous fall of the pole-top. Is there anywhere to hide disgrace?

Case   A monk asked Huguo, "How is it when a crane stands on a withered pine?"
Hugo said, "An embarrassment on the ground below."
The monk asked, "How is it when a drop of water's a drop of ice?"
Huguo said, "An embarrassment after the sun comes out."
The monk asked, "At the time of the purge (of Buddhist establishments) in the 840s, where did the good spirits who guard the Teaching go?"
Huguo said, "An embarrassment for the two of them at the temple gate."

Commentary   Great Master Jingguo of Huguo (monastery) on Suicheng Mountain in Sui province was named Shoucheng; he was together at Baoci in Hunan with the second generation master of Huguo, who was Great Master Yanhua, named Zhiyuan. When Baoci ascended the high seat, Yanhua asked, "What is the buddha-nature of true thusness?" Baoci said, "Who doesn't have it?" After leaving the gathering, the leading monk asked Yanhua, "Do you understand what the teacher said when you questioned him just then?" Yanhua said, "No." The leading monk said, "The teacher was so compassionate—why don't you understand? Who does not have the buddha-nature of true thusness? Even all those born in the four ways in the six dispositions all are fully endowed." Yanhua said, "Thanks for explaining it for me." Jingguo, who was nearby, gnashed his teeth and said, "This old guy not only has no eyes himself, he goes on to blind others." Then he called Yanhua and asked, "What was the leading monk talking about?" Yanhua said, "Before, I didn't understand, and he explained for me," and then he recounted the preceding events. Jingguo said, "Elder, Buddhism is not this principle. If you don't believe me, ask the teacher in the hall." Yanhua went up to the hall and told all about his previous understanding; Baoci also said, "Buddhism is not this principle." Yanhua said, "I just asked the third-seated monk, and he didn't agree either, so he told me to come ask you. I hope you will be so compassionate as to settle this thoroughly for me." Baoci said, "Go ask the monk in the third seat." Yanhua went down and bowed and asked Jingguo, who said, "Just ask." Yanhua then asked, "What is the buddha-nature of true thusness?" Jingguo said, "Who has it?" At these words Yanhua realized enlightenment. He bowed again in gratitude and then said, "Whether you remain one of the crowd or appear in the world as a teacher, I pledge to assist you." Later he actually succeeded Jingguo as abbot of Huguo.

Everywhere they call this story 'Huguo's Three Embarrassments'. It compares with Baofu's 'Four Deceptions'. Those who have not yet passed through the barrier have utmost difficulty catching on.

Haven't you seen how a monk asked Chan Master Yunju Jian, "When dwelling alone on a solitary peak, how is it?" Jian said, "Not lying in a monks' hall big as nine rooms—who told you to stay alone on a solitary peak?" Although this story has no mysterious marvel, it is very enlightening; raising this one corner, the other three corners can be seen.

In Dongshan's *Seal in the Mystery* it says, "The peak stands out unique, but the crane doesn't stay there; the spirit tree is sublime, but the phoenix doesn't alight there." This monk instead asked, "When a crane stands on a dead pine, how is it?" This monk's effort in his ignorant sitting was consummate—he took this little bit of the scenery of the fundamental ground and stuck it on his forehead, showing everyone he met. He hardly realized that 'when the solitary is not established, then is the way lofty.' In the Tiantai teachings this is called the fall at the pinnacle. That is why Huguo said, "An embarrassment on the ground below."

This monk didn't go make a living in solitary destitution; he also presented the drying of ice and aging of snow, again not realizing that when dry and parched yet moisture is born, where cold and clear, yet you need warmth. That is why Huguo said, "An embarrassment after the sun comes out."

The monk came flying up with his spear and armor twice and was beaten down by Huguo both times. Since he was getting nowhere, instead he asked about the rise and decline of the Teaching—challenging with his doubt, he said, "At the time of the purge of the 840s, where did the good spirits who guard the Teaching go?" Emperor Wuzong of the Tang dynasty liked Taoism and purged 260,500 monks and nuns—in the eighth month of the fifth year of the Huishang era (845) he sent down an imperial command that they all be returned to lay life. The emperor drank an alchemist's cinnabar elixir and his temperament became even more excitable, inconstant in joy and anger. By the beginning of the third month of the next year, when hardly half a year had passed, Wuzong died from cinnabar elixir and Xuanzong assumed the throne. The Buddhist temples were restored, three times as many as before.

To discuss it in terms of the way of the spirits, without using Wuzong's little destruction, how could they effect Xuanzong's great revival? The skillful methods of good spirits are certainly not within reach of the ordinary and lesser. Seeing it from the point of view of a patchrobed monk, though, the Teaching basically has no rise and decline—how can the good spirits have any going or coming? That's why Huguo said, "An embarrassment for the two of them at the temple gate."

As I speak in this way, I have wrongly added footnotes for people. Haven't you also read how a monk asked, "When mind and things are both forgotten, what then?" Huguo said, "You don't wash your face." The monk said, "How about when the moonlight falls into the cold pond?" Huguo said, "You don't wash your face." The monk said, "How is it when the light and objects are both forgotten?" Huguo said, "You don't wash your face." One can't always keep adding explanations from the outset. What about when I don't add explanations? There is Tiantong's eulogies of the ancients themselves.

Verse   *The mature man, dignified and imposing, his temples are not yet grey:*
          The youth, if he doesn't bestir himself, won't be enfeoffed.

I think back to the inheritors of a pure family tradition,
And to not watering the ox in the stream where ears were washed.

Commentary   The Third Patriarch said that the body of the great Way is open and has no ease or difficulty—small views and foxy doubts lag the more they hurry. In ancient times two monks were traveling together; the one whose temperament was more hurried was in front, and called back to the one behind, "Time passes quickly—run on up here!" The monk behind said, "The great way is wide and vast—what's the rush?"

I once saw two verses handwritten by National Teacher Yuantong Shan:

> *'Time flies—run on up!'*
> *Stepping on the road,*
> *The rarest flower blossoms.*
> *'The great way is vast—what's the rush?'*
> *Opening up his belly skin,*
> *He engulfs all at once.*

These two verses of National Teacher Shan, like the monk asking in this way and Huguo answering this way, each have one eye.

In Tiantong's verse, the first two lines are like a keen spirit craving glory; the last two are like resigning and retiring.

According to the *History of the Latter Han Dynasty,* Ban Chao's family was poor and he always took employment copying books. Finally he threw down his brush and said, "A man should emulate Zhang Mo and Quan Jiezi, who established their careers in foreign lands, to obtain enfeoffment to a barony ten thousand miles away. How can I work forever between brush and inkstone?" Later he went to the western lands and was enfeoffed as baron of Dingyuan. This symbolizes the monk's three questions, seeking too far.

During the latter Han dynasty (1-2 cent. AD) Yang Zhen was appointed governor of Jing province. He was by nature impartial and pure, and didn't allow private audiences. His descendants ate vegetables and traveled on foot. Therefore an elder wanted them to start productive work, but Zhen would not consent, saying, "To cause later generations to call them descendants of a pure official, and leave them with this, would also be kind, wouldn't it?"

According to the *Historical Records,* Xu You was a recluse on Mount Qi, getting food from the mountain and drinking from the river. Emperor Yao (24-23 cent. BC) wanted to abdicate the throne to him, but when Xu You heard of this, he washed his ears in the river. Chao Fu, watering his ox, asked him, "Usually people wash their faces—you just wash your ears?" Xu You said, "I heard Emperor Yao is asking me to be chief of the nine provinces, so I am washing out 'right' and 'wrong'." Chao Fu said, "The trees of Yuzhang grow in the high mountains—the craftsmen can't get at them. If you want to avoid society, why not hide away deep in the mountains? Now you are wandering in the human world, merely seeking fame and honor. If I go down river to let my ox drink, I fear it may foul the ox's mouth." So he led it upstream to water the ox. Tiantong uses Yang Zhen, Xu You, and Chao Fu to eulogize the three embarrassments. Yet it was said by Tongan, "The defiled are of themselves defiled, the pure of themselves pure—enlightenment and affliction are equally empty and equivalent." This monk and Huguo have been let go. It is no business of yours—each of you, do whatever is appropriate.

Added Sayings /Case

How is it when a crane stands on a withered pine?—Climbing higher with every step is easy.

An embarrassment on the ground below—Letting go every state of mind is hard.

How is it when a drop of water is a drop of ice?—The Reality Body without clothing cannot ward off the cold.

An embarrassment after the sun comes out—When the snow melts it exposes the dead.

At the time of the purge, where did the guardian spirits go?—When you check you don't get there.

An embarrassment for the two of them at the gate—When you get there you don't check.

Added Sayings /Verse

The mature man, dignified, imposing, his temples are not yet grey—He regrets heaven doesn't arrive.

The youth, if he doesn't bestir himself, won't be enfeoffed—He's in too much hurry to be on his way.

I think back to the inheritors of a pure family tradition—Already too many.

And to not watering the ox in the stream where ears were washed—At the very end, too much.

29 FENGXUE'S "IRON OX"

Introduction   Slow play in a game of chess rots the axe handle; while your eyes revolve and your head is lost, the dipper handle is taken away. If, while being in a ghost cave, you can hold a deadly snake still, do you still have the capacity to transform a leopard?

Case   When Fengxue was staying at the government headquarters of Ying province, he said in an address, "The mind seal of the Patriarchs is like the workings of the Iron Ox; when it's removed, the impression remains; when it's left there, the impression is ruined. Just suppose it's neither removed nor left—is sealing right or is not sealing right?"
At that point a certain elder Lu Pi came forth and asked, "I have the working of the Iron Ox; I request the master not to impress the seal."
Fengxue said, "Used to fishing whales, scouring the ocean, instead I regret to find a frog crawling in the mud."
Lu Pi stood there thinking.
Fengxue shouted and said, "Elder, why don't you speak further?"
Lu Pi hesitated.
Fengxue hit him with the whisk and said, "Do you still remember the words? Try to quote them."
As Lu Pi tried to open his mouth, Fengxue hit him again with the whisk.
The governor said, "The Buddhist law and the law of kings are the same."
Fengxue said, "What have you seen?"
The governor said, "When you do not settle what is to be settled, instead you bring about disorder there."
Fengxue then got down from the seat.

125

Commentary Layman Wujin recounted, "When Linji took leave of Guishan, Yangshan was standing by. Guishan said to him, 'How will this man's teaching be in the future?' Yangshan said, 'His teaching will be very effective in Wu-Yue; meeting a wind, it'll stop there.' He also asked, 'Who will succeed to him?' Yangshan said, 'The age is distant and just should not be spoken of yet.' Guishan insisted on asking, saying, 'I still want to know.' Yangshan said, 'Doesn't a scripture say that to serve innumerable lands with this profound heart is called requiting the benevolence of the Buddha?'" The layman said, "By this I know that Fengxue ('Wind Cave') was a later embodiment of Yangshan."

Fengxue first studied from Xuefeng for five years. One day he asked about the story of when the two assembly leaders in Linji's community looked up, saw each other and each shouted; a monk told this to Linji and asked, "Is the eye of host and guest there or not?" Linji said, "Even like this, host and guest are clear." Xuefeng recounted to Fengxue how he and Yantou and Qinshan were on the way to Linji when they heard Linji was already gone and couldn't be met with; then he said, "If you want to understand, ask one of Linji's descendants." Fengxue then told Nanyuan Yong about this—Nanyuan said, "Xuefeng is an old Buddha."

Later the master stayed in the Guanghui Chan monastery on Fengxue Mountain in Ru province. The era of the five dynasties was then torn with strife and the governor of Ying province invited the master to stay for a summer in the government headquarters.

One day the governor asked him to ascend the high seat; Fengxue said to the assembly, "The mind-seal of the patriarchs is like the workings of the Iron Ox." It is not the same as a stone man or wooden horse, mysteriously singing, mysteriously preaching; it is just like the iron ox—no way for you to get near; as soon as you go it hooks you back, as soon as you stay it smashes you to pieces. But if you don't take the seal away and don't leave it there, is it right to seal this or not? You might say there's bait on the hook.

Venerable Lu Pi was also a descendant of the Linji succession—he immediately picked up and turned around the other's words and posed a question that was undeniably special. He said, "I have the working of the Iron Ox; I request the master not to impress the seal." Notwithstanding that, Fengxue acted according to the imperative and said, "Used to fishing whales, scouring the ocean, instead I regret to find a frog crawling in the mud." Whales are huge fish that traverse the oceans; it says in Zhuangzi that Mr. Ren once caught a whale using fifty oxen for bait.

As for 'a frog crawling in the mud,' some say, "In the time of Emperor Wu of the Han dynasty, Bao Lichang saw a flock of wild horses by the Wuai River; among them was an unusual one who came and drank water. So he made a clay man and tied it down on the bank, so it would become familiar; then he replaced it with a real man, who managed to catch that horse. He wanted the horse to be thought supernatural and said that it came out of the river; eventually in legend it came to be considered related to the dragons. Fengxue meant that a horse coming out of clear water turned around and lay down floundering in the mud."

This explanation is roundabout; in Fengxue's Collection of Roars it clearly says 'a frog crawling.' Haven't you seen how Xuedou eulogized the story of the rhinoceros horn fan, then said, "If you want the pure breeze to rise again and the head's horn to regrow, I ask you Chan students to each turn a word. Since the fan is broken, bring me back the rhinoceros." Then a monk came forward and said, "Everyone go to the hall." Xuedou shouted and said, "Casting a hook fishing for whales, I've caught a frog." Comparing these two phrases to Xuefeng's corresponding phrases, the word 'frog' is unquestionable.

Lu Pi was bewildered—he had asked a question, showing his capability, wanting to meet with Xuefeng, but he suddenly got a rap. If you want to specially seek out an enduring surrender, when you display your lance method, you get picked up and dumped over all at once. This is the fault of not knowing how to control the action and carry out the law, guest and host interchanging.

The governor had studied from Xuefeng for a long time—he was not without insight. He said, "The Buddhist law and the law of kings are the same." Fengxue, having wrapped up Annan, now worries about Jibei—immediately he questioned the governor, "What have you seen?" Here's where he should have cleared up Lu Pi's cramp for him, but instead he just said, "If you don't settle what is to be settled, instead you bring about disorder there." Undeniably he spoke to the point. Because he was a lay official, Fengxue swallowed his breath and voice and immediately got down from the seat.

The two venerable adepts, as a dragon and snake, acting hard, acting soft, strummed the reed of the basic style of Linji; added to this is Tiantong's definitive harmony—his verse says,

Verse *The works of the iron ox—*
When the seal remains, the impression's ruined.
Passing through to go beyond the crown of Vairocana,
Coming back to sit on the tongues of manifestation buddhas:
Fengxue is in charge of the scales,
Lu Pi sustained a fall.
On the cane, at the shout—
A lightning flash, a spark.
Evident, distinctly clear, the pearl in the bowl;
But when you raise your eyebrows, you've missed it.

Commentary "The works of the iron ox—when the seal remains, the impression's ruined." When the king of Min sent an emissary bearing a vermilion seal, Baofu went into the hall and said, "Take it away and the impression of the seal remains; leave the seal and the impression is ruined." A monk said, "Not taking away or leaving it, what is the use of the seal?" Baofu hit him. The monk said, "In that case, being inside a ghost cave on a mountain is entirely due to today." Baofu was silent. I say, what a pity—a dragon's head but a snake's tail.

If Fengxue had not transcended to realization of the gate of non-abiding independent great liberation, he could not 'pass through to go beyond the crown of Vairocana.' Emperor Suzong of the Tang dynasty asked National Teacher Zhong, "What is the state of noncontention?" The National Teacher said, "Patron, walk over Vairocana's head." This makes it clear that transcendence of the reality-body is not something in the realm of the 'withered tree.' Fengxue first carried out this order, then came back within the gate of buddha-work to handle immeasurably great authority and settle an unfinished public case, wipe out common-sense assessments of ordinary and holy and cut off the heads of the reward-body and manifestation-body buddhas. In Linji's extensive sayings it says, "This mountain monk's perspective sits on and cuts off the heads of the reward and manifestation buddhas."

With weighing in the balance done in this way, even an adept like Lu Pi too sometimes suffers a fall. In India, when the non-Buddhists stood up for their doctrines, those who were unsuccessful were said to 'suffer a fall.' They would have their heads and arms cut off to pay for not being clever.

This hammer in the cane and shout, the changes of action in lightning flashes and sparks, are all momentary light and scenes—be careful not to use assurance or denial or gain or loss to decide victory and defeat. It's like a pearl rolling in a bowl—blink your eyes and you miss it. (Wansong struck the meditation seat with his whisk and said) 'Done.'

Added Sayings /Case
The mind-seal of the patriarchs is like the workings of the iron ox—Even a needle cannot be inserted.

When it's removed, the impression remains—The nose is pulled around.

When it's left there, the impression is ruined—Cutting off the footsteps.

If it's neither removed nor left, is sealing right or is not sealing right?—Washing a clod of earth in mud.

Lu Pi asked, "I have the working of the iron ox; I request the master not to impress the seal."—Clearly he has waves against the current.

Used to fishing whales, scouring the ocean, instead I regret to find a frog crawling in the mud—A spirit-leading banner, a breath-catching bag.

Lu Pi stood there thinking—He's already past the ghost's door.

Fengxue shouted and said, "Why don't you speak further?"—Already at the edge of the cliff, he gives him one more push.

Lu Pi hesitated—So much time—where's he going and coming?

Fengxue hit him and said, "Do you still remember the words? Please try to quote them."—When you help people, do so thoroughly; when you kill someone, be sure to see blood.

As Lu Pi tried to open his mouth—He still doesn't submit to being burnt and buried.

Fengxue hit him again—He's still short thirty blows of the cane.

The governor said, "The Buddhist law and the law of kings are the same."—If you don't know how to be an official, look at the examples of a neighboring state.

"What have you seen?"—He should give him a whack of the whisk.

The governor said, "When you do not settle what is to be settled, instead you bring about disorder there."—He scolds himself, brings it on himself.

Fengxue then got down from the seat—When you're fully satisfied, that's a good time to stop.

Added Sayings / Verse

The works of the iron ox—The howling still hasn't stopped.

When the seal remains, the impression's ruined—Hook and awl are in one's own hands.

Passing through to go beyond the crown of Vairocana—Trying for what's above, not enough.

Coming back to sit on the tongues of manifestation buddhas—Compared to what's below, too much.

Fengxue is in charge of the scales—Mundane feelings; see cold and warmth.

Lu Pi sustained a fall—People's faces follow high and low.

On the cane, at the shout—How can they be individually explained?

A lightning flash, a spark—They don't await extinction and cessation.

Evident, distinctly clear, the pearl in the bowl—It rolls by itself without being pushed.

But when you raise your eyebrows, you've missed it—I strike while he's still speaking.

30 DASUI'S "AEONIC FIRE"

Introduction   Obliterating all oppositions, cutting off both sides, smashing the mass of doubt—how does that require a single phrase? The Capital is not an inch of a step away—the great mountain only weighs three pounds. But tell me, based on what order can one dare to speak this way?

Case   A monk asked Dasui, "When the fire at the end of an aeon rages through and the whole universe is destroyed, is *this* destroyed or not?"
Dasui said, "Destroyed."
The monk said, "Then it goes along with that?"
Dasui said, "It goes along with that."
A monk asked Longji, "When the fire ending the aeon rages through and the whole universe is destroyed, is *this* destroyed or not?"
Longji said, "Not destroyed."
The monk said, "Why is it not destroyed?"
Longji said, "Because it is the same as the universe."

Commentary   Chan Master Dasui Fazhen of Yi province, also called by the name of Xiyuan of Fu province, and also called Changqing, was a successor of Daan and a spiritual grandson of Baizhang Dazhi (Huaihai). He met more than sixty venerable adepts. While in the community of Guishan he worked as keeper of the fire. Guishan asked him, "You have been here for several years and don't know how to pose a question?" Dasui asked, "What would you have me ask that would be appropriate?" Guishan said, "You don't know how to ask, 'What is Buddha?'" Dasui covered Guishan's mouth with his hand. Guishan said, "Later on you'll have a

131

piece of tile to cover your head; you won't even be able to find anyone to sweep the ground." Later he made tea in a booth by a road and served passersby for three years. He opened the mountain monastery of Dasui and lived there.

A monk asked, "When the fire at the end of an aeon rages through and the whole universe is destroyed, is *this* destroyed or not?" This question originally comes from the *Scripture on the Benevolent King Safeguarding the Nation:* King Kalmashapada, believing in the words of the non-Buddhist Rata, took the heads of a thousand kings to sacrifice them in a graveyard to the god Mahakala, the Great Black One, hoping to prolong the fortune of his nation. King Samantaloka begged a day's reprieve and provided a meal for a hundred (Buddhist) Dharma teachers, in accordance with the teaching of the seven Buddhas. The first Dharma teacher spoke a verse for the king: "In the raging of the aeonic fire the whole universe is destroyed. . . ." The verse is thirty-two lines in all. As King Samantaloka was going to his death, he recited it for the other kings. Kalmashapada, in doubt, asked about it, and he too heard this verse. When he did, his mind opened up to understanding; he gave the kingdom over to his brother, left home and society, and attained forbearance.

According to what it says in the teachings, thousands of thousands of thousands of worlds become and disintegrate as one at the same time. When Emperor Wu of the Han dynasty had Kunming Lake dug, they found ashes; he asked Dongfang Shuo, who said, "Please ask people of the Way from India." During the reign of Emperor Ming of the latter Han dynasty, Kasyapa Matanga and Falan (Buddhist monks from India) arrived; he asked them about the ashes, and they said, "They're ashes of an aeon." Yunan asked professor monks, "When the holocaust happens the world is emptied—where are all those ashes put?" Few had any answer.

In *Cessation and Contemplation* it says that *arhats* are like charcoal, *pratyekabuddhas* are like ashes, *bodhisattvas* are like a little left-over ash, and Buddhas are like the aeonic fire, where there is no charcoal and no ash.

As for this question, "Is *this* destroyed or not?" Foguo said, "From the beginning this monk didn't know the ultimate point of the words. Now to begin with, what is '*this*'?" Dasui said, "Destroyed." This saying goes contrary to the ordinary to merge with the Way—it is most difficult to chew on. The monk said, "If so, does everything go with it?" This monk is a laugh—he doesn't know how long it's been since he dropped the stirrups while holding on to the whip. Dasui said, "Yes, it all goes with that." I say, the monk goes along with Dasui, Dasui goes along with the monk.

Xuedou and Longji (Master of the Mountain Xiu) were contemporaries—he hadn't seen Longji's answer, later saying it isn't destroyed, because it is the same as the universe—he only eulogized Dasui's words: "In the light of the conflagration ending the age he poses a question; the monk is still lingering within the double barrier." Many people misunderstand this line and say that Dasui's saying "It is destroyed" is one barrier, and Longji's saying "It is not destroyed" is the second barrier. Didn't you see what I just said?—Xuedou only eulogized Dasui; he had not seen the collected sayings of Longji. Just the question "Is this destroyed or not" is already a double barrier. "How touching, for a single phrase 'going along with it' he plodded back and forth ten thousand miles alone." This eulogizes the monk who, not understanding what Dasui said, went right (from Siquan through Hunan province into Anhui) and asked Touzi, who said, "In Siquan there's an ancient Buddha appearing in the world—you should go back there right away." When the monk returned, Dasui had already died. The Tang monk Jingzun wrote a poem,

> Clearly there is no other truth;
> Only the Way sealed Huineng of the South.
> One saying—'it all goes along with the fire'
> Sends a monk running over a thousand mountains.

Xuedou used this association and said, to continue,

> A cold cricket cries in the surrounding leaves;
> On a silent night bowing to a lamp in a crypt,
> When his lament is finished in the moonlight at the solitary window
> He wanders back and forth, unable to overcome his regret.

When Tiantong eulogized these ancients he added the saying of Longji, "It isn't destroyed, because it's the same as the universe." One version says, "because it isn't the same as the universe." This story is most worthy of consideration; you can say "the same" or you can say "not the same"—adding error to error, none is right or wrong. Longji also said, "'Destroyed' and 'Not destroyed' both stop people dead." Wansong says, when Dasui said "It is destroyed," he had a way out, and when Longji said "It is not destroyed," he too had a way out. It's not entirely void of intelligent assessment, but you can't understand it just by feelings and cognition.

Haven't you seen how Chan Master Zhiche of Jiangxi asked the Sixth Patriarch about the meaning of permanence and impermanence in the Nirvana scripture? The Patriarch said, "What is impermanent is the Buddha nature, and what is permanent is the mind that discriminates all things good and bad." Zhiche said, "The scripture says the Buddha nature is permanent and yet you say it is impermanent. Good and bad things, even the thought of enlightenment, are impermanent, yet you say they are permanent. This is a contradiction, causing the student all the more doubt and confusion." The Patriarch said, "If the Buddha nature were permanent, then what good or bad or anything can you talk about anymore? I say it is impermanent—that is indeed the way of true permanence spoken of by the Buddha."

Nowadays beginners see Dasui's saying, "It is destroyed—everything goes along with it," and don't avoid confusion; by consulting the Sixth Patriarch besides they can be freed from doubt. Especially when Dasui was the grandson of Baizhang and Longji was the heir of Dizang—they transcended feelings and views and thoroughly aided people of the present. Xuedou before only eulogized one half—now with Tiantong it's finally complete.

Verse   *Destroyed, not destroyed,*
Going along with that, the billion world-universe.
In their phrases after all there's no hook-and-chain action—
Their feet are much obstructed by entangling vines;
Do you understand or not?
For a matter which is distinctly clear, punctiliousness is extreme.
Those who know the heart bring it forth, don't haggle—
You'll lose to me, buying and selling at the market.

Xuedou's verse was on this monk asking "Is *this* destroyed or not?" He said, "The monk still lingers within the double barrier." Tiantong's verse says at the outset, "Destroyed, not destroyed"—his meaning is not the same. He cites the two monks' questions and includes the answers of both teachers, bringing them out right before us. Just "going along with that, the billion worlds," referring to Dasui's words, puts out the hook and line of the two teachers and raps these two monks for chasing a clod. Yunju said to the assembly, "Speech must be like tongs, like pliers, like hooks, like chains—you must make them continuous, unbroken."

Now he versifies the two teachers' answers—they give it over right away, without getting too subtle—but what can be done—everybody's been tripped up by the entangling vines.

One day 'self-pointer' Zhen was staying as a guest at Zhangjiang monastery in Nanshang, in the congregation of Chan Master Zheng. One day he walked by slowly, holding his robes up, his legs bared. Zheng wondered about this and asked him; Zhen said, "In the front hallway and washroom are all-entangling vines—I'm just afraid of being tripped up." Zheng laughed heartily at this. Tiantong says, in effect, "I have produced it in verse so clearly—do you understand it or not? If you are an excellent student with long experience, you'll take charge of the market and buy and sell without seeking to haggle." Wansong today has just fooled 'em out of the house.

A monk asked Dasui, "When the fire at the end of an aeon rages through and the whole universe is destroyed, is this destroyed or not?"—Sad man, don't speak to the sad.

Destroyed—Already you wonder how that can be.

Then it goes along with that?—You can experience it right in front of your eyes.

Dasui said, "It goes along with that."—He doesn't run downhill, so he gives him another push.

A monk asked Longji the same question—Those with the same illness commiserate.

Longji said "not destroyed."—He tears up his ticket, pulls his nose around.

The monk asked, "why is it not destroyed?"—He goes on this way too.

Longji said, "Because it is the same as the universe."—Cast of raw iron.

Destroyed, not destroyed—Even the Buddha's hand can't pick them out.
Going along with that, the billion-world universe—Immeasurably great
people are turned about in the flow of words.

In the phrases after all there's no hook-and-chain action—There's not a little
sticking to the teeth too.

Their feet are much obstructed by entangling vines—Who told you to
produce branches and trail vines?

Do you understand or not?—When the mind is hurried, the hand rushes.

For a matter which is distinctly clear, punctiliousness is extreme—This is the
fault of the blind, not the fault of the sun and moon.

Those who know the heart bring it forth, don't haggle—The director of the
market sees the profiteer.

You'll lose to me, buying and selling at the market—Inside the house he sells
off the province of Yangzhou.

31 YUNMEN'S "PILLARS"

Introduction   The unique dynamic of transcendence—a crane soars into the sky. The unique road of direct confrontation with reality—a falcon passes the next country. Even if your eyes are like comets, you still don't avoid your mouth being (bent down) like a carrying pole. But tell me, what doctrine is this?

Case   Yunmen said, "The ancient Buddhas are merged with the open pillars—what level of activity is this?"
The assembly was speechless.
Yunmen himself said for them, "On South Mountain rising clouds, on North Mountain falling rain."

Commentary   According to the record, Yunmen asked a monk, "The ancient Buddhas and the pillars are merged—which level of activity is this?" The monk was speechless; Yunmen said, "You ask me and I'll tell you." So the monk asked; Yunmen said, "One belt, thirty cents." The monk said, "What is one belt for thirty cents?" Yunmen said, "Give." He himself answered the previous question by saying, "On South Mountain rising clouds, on North Mountain falling rain."
General Jing of the (latter) Tang and Song dynasties was good at drumming and singing; he had a saying, that 'on South Mountain rising clouds, on North Mountain falling rain' is borrowed for use, like (Yunmen's saying) "Avalokitesvara Bodhisattva comes with a penny to buy a sesame cake," letting down his hand, "actually it was a jelly doughnut instead." This is just like Muzhou's action point—"The saucer falls to the ground, the cup is in seven pieces"—how could it admit of explanations

137

and verbal understanding? Tiantong can add explanation where explanation can't reach, can verbally understand where verbal understanding can't reach.

Verse *One path of spiritual light*
Has never been concealed from the first;
Transcending perception and objects, it's so yet nothing's so;
Going beyond emotional assessment, it's meet yet nothing's meet.
The scattered flowers on the crag—in the bees' houses they make honey;
The richness of the wild grasses—in the musk deer they make perfume.
According to kind, three feet or ten and six:
Clearly, wherever you contact it is abundantly evident.

Commentary Yunmen said, "Everybody has a light, but when you look you don't see it—it's dark and obscure." He also said, "Space cannot fully contain it, earth cannot support it." According to the *Heroic March Scripture,* this perception and its objects are both the wondrously pure luminous body of enlightenment—how can there be affirmation or denial therein? In Sengzhao's treatise *Wisdom Has No Knowledge* he says, "If nothing is meet, nothing is not meet; if nothing is so, nothing is not so; because nothing is not so, it's so without being so; because nothing is not meet, it's meet without being meet." Therefore the scripture says, "Thoroughly see all things without seeing anything." This verse is clearly based on one scripture and one treatise, subtly pointing to transcendence of common-sense views and the merging of subject and object. Since the ancient buddhas and the pillars are merged, naturally clouds rise on the southern mountains, rain falls in the northern mountains; the bees collect from the flowers and produce honey, the musk deer eat the grass and make scent. High and low, mountains and gullies, together turn the fundamental wheel of truth, fish and animals great and small everywhere manifest the samadhi of the physical body. Elder Koshila saw three feet as unending, the 'bodhisattva with the boundless body' searched through the upper realms, yet there was still more. Nothing does not appear at once—nowhere is not pervaded; that is why he says, "Wherever you contact it is abundantly evident." But do you see? Blind!

Added Sayings /Case	**The ancient Buddhas merge with the pillars—what level is this?—** Already fallen into seven and eight. **On the south mountains rising clouds, on the north mountains falling rain**—Old man Chang drinks wine, old man Lee gets drunk.
Added Sayings /Verse	*One path of spiritual light*—It supports sky and earth. *Has never been concealed*—Clean and naked, washed bare. *Transcending perception and objects, it's so yet nothing's so*—Stop blinking your eyes in the flames of a fierce fire. *Going beyond emotional assessment, it's meet yet nothing's meet*—Beyond the points of the wheel of swords, don't turn your head back. *The scattered flowers on the crags become honey in the bees' houses*—The miraculous power is immense. *The richness of the wild grasses makes perfume in the musk deer*—Magical productions are boundless. *According to kind, three feet or ten and six*—Mount Chu is high, Mount An is low, the staff is long, the whisk is short. *Clearly, wherever you contact it is abundantly evident*—Having it thrust right in your face, there is no place to escape.

32 YANGSHAN'S "MIND AND ENVIRONMENT"

Introduction The ocean is the world of dragons—disappearing and appearing, they sport serenely. The sky is the home of cranes—they fly and call freely. Why does the exhausted fish stop in the shoals and a sluggish bird rest in the reeds? Is there any way to figure gain and loss?

Case Yangshan asked a monk, "Where are you from?"
The monk said, "From Yu province."
Yangshan said, "Do you think of that place?"
The monk said, "I always think of it."
Yangshan said, "The thinker is the mind and the thought-of is the environment. Therein are mountains, rivers, and the land mass, buildings, towers, halls and chambers, people, animals, and so forth; reverse your thought to think of the thinking mind—are there so many things there?"
The monk said, "When I get here, I don't see any existence at all."
Yangshan said, "This is right for the stage of faith, but not yet right for the stage of person."
The monk said, "Don't you have any other particular way of guidance?"
Yangshan said, "To say that I have anything particular or not would not be accurate. Based on your insight, you only get one mystery—you can take the seat and wear the robe. After this, see on your own."

Commentary Yangshan in the past once asked a monk, "Where do you come from?"
The monk said, "From Yu province." Yangshan said, "I'd like to hear

news of Yu province—what is the price of rice there?" The monk said, "When I came, I happened to go right through the market-place, and broke the bridge as I walked over it." Yangshan then stopped.

Yangshan was 'Little Shakyamuni'—he didn't have only one way of guiding people. This particular case is exactly the way a student enters the gate, where he goes to work and gains power. Yangshan asked the monk from Yu province, "Do you think of that place?" Suppose the monk had said "No"—then what? Yangshan certainly would have another strong point. But the monk instead said, "I think of it always." True words—he should repent. Yangshan said, "What thinks is the mind, what is thought of is the environment; in the environment there are a thousand differences—are there so many in the mind which thinks?" Yunmen once said, "Yangshan, because of his kindness and compassion, had a conversation in the weeds." After all the monk too was sharp; he said, "Here, I don't see any existence at all." Nowadays hardly one of ten thousand people reaches this state; if they do, then they point to themselves and carry a board, not knowing that by delighting in the road one ultimately fails to reach home. Yangshan had 'traveled the mountain path,' so he specially pointed out a living road.

In the past, as Yangshan was meditating in front of the monks' hall in the middle of night he didn't see the mountains, rivers, buildings, people, or even his own body—all was the same as space. The next morning he reported this to Guishan, who said, "I reached this state when I was at Baizhang's—this is just the achievement of melting illumination which dissolves illusions; later on, when you are teaching, there can be no one who surpasses this." I say, no one but Yangshan could realize this; no one but Guishan would recognize it.

The *Heroic March* Scripture says, "When stirring thoughts end and floating ideas vanish, this is like removing defilement from the mind of aware radiance; the whole course of life and death, from beginning to end, is completely illumined—this is called the ending of the cluster of conception. Such a person can transcend the defilement of afflictions. When you look into the basis, dissolving illusory conceptions is the fundamental." Here we also see Gui and Yang, father and son, wondrously according with the Buddha's mind.

Yangshan one day presenting his understanding said, "If you have me see for myself, at this point there is no state of completion, and nothing to cut off either." Guishan said, "According to your point of view, there are still phenomena, and you haven't yet got away from mind and objects." Yangshan said, "Since there is no complete state, where are there still mind and objects?" Guishan said, "Just now, didn't you make such an interpretation?" Yangshan said, "Yes." Guishan said, "If so, then this is completely mind and objects—how can you say there are none?" Yangshan saw that this monk still had this, and judged according to principle, saying, "This is all right for the stage of faith, but not yet for the stage of person." To cite the *Adamantine Concentration Scripture*, there is the stage of faith, the stage of contemplation, the stage of cultivation, the stage of practice, and the stage of relinquishment; now as he speaks of the stage of faith and the stage of person, they're not necessarily completely the same. Master Zhu-an Gui said, "In the opening and closing of the mouth you distinguish 'this side' and 'that side'—where there are words and no words you distinguish the stage of faith and the stage of person." This too is a particular interpretation.

Guishan questioned Yangshan, "Huiji, speak quickly, without going into the clusters and elements." Yangshan said, "I, Huiji, don't even set up faith." Guishan said, "Do you not set it up after having faith, or do you not set it up without having had faith?" Yangshan said, "I'm just Huiji—who else should I have faith in?" Guishan said, "If so, then you have a fixed disciple nature." Yangshan said, "I don't even see 'Buddha'."

Chan Master Haosheng of Qingju, in the ox-herding pictures, said at the sixth chapter, "The stage of faith is gradually matured, and one is generally aware of wrong states; although one distinguishes purity and defilement, it is like a sword cutting mud. One still retains the halter—one cannot yet rely on faith; therefore (the ox is) half white, half black." His verse says,

> Although long having herded in the fields,
> The hand leading the rope gradually loosens.
> Going along holding, not dark and muddled,
> Progressing in training, he doesn't follow close by.
> (The ox) sporting on clear ground,
> (The ox-herd) always keeps holding the long whip.

The fragrant grasses on the green mountains are slender;
With one flavor they daily satisfy hunger.

At the twelfth chapter, he says, "The state of person is fundamentally empty; body and mind are without attachment, gain and loss are cleared away. The hidden mysterious path is far beyond discrimination; as for the absolute word, attempt to discuss it and you fail." The verse says,

Falsely he creates toil, watching over the ox;
The ox is not, neither is the person.
Right in the middle forgetting conception,
Beyond there is a mysterious subtlety;
Fine dust rises in the ocean,
Snow flies in a huge furnace.
Meeting, seeking understanding,
It does not fall within the scope of your mental function.

I say, Yangshan doesn't even set up faith, Qingju says the state of person is originally empty: if you can pick them out within the sayings of these two teachers, the stage of faith and the stage of person are clearly visible; that is what is called retreating into oneself, not missing one out of ten thousand.

The monk said, "Don't you have any other particular way of guidance?" There are thorns in the soft mud. Yangshan said, "To say that I have anything particular or not would not be accurate." If there is, you add frost to snow; if not, you die at the phrase. Therefore he pointed out one mystery, telling him to see it on his own.

In the wellspring, emptiness is the seat, myriad practices are the robe. Some say the seat is quiet meditation, and the robe is the patchwork vestment covering the head. Some say the seat means opening the hall and ascending the high seat, and the robe means the Dharma vestments adorning the body. Each of these is reasonable. But tell me—'after this, see on your own'—see what? Ask of Tiantong; his verse says,

Verse **All-embracing, with no outside;**
Penetrating with no obstruction.
Gates and walls like cliffs,

Doors and locks redoubled.
When the wine is always sweet, it lays out the guests;
Though the meal is filling, it ruins the farmers.
Bursting out of the clear sky, the garuda takes wing on the wind;
Treading over the blue sea, thunder follows the roaming dragon.

Commentary   Tiantong first versifies "Think back on that which thinks—are there so many things there?" Yunmen said, "If you can understand, you engulf all before you—if you can't understand, you still engulf all before you." This is 'all-embracing, with no outside.' Mountains, rivers, towers, buildings, people, animals, and so forth—one and many do not impede each other, person and environment merge—this is 'penetrating with no obstruction.'

National Teacher Deshao said,

> *Crossing the summit of the mystic peak,*
> *It's not the human world;*
> *Outside of mind there are no things—*
> *Filling the eyes are blue montains.*

'Crossing the summit of the mystic peak' is the environment which is thought of; 'it is not the human world' is the mind which thinks. 'Outside of mind there are no things' is 'I don't see any existence at all.' 'Filling the eyes arc blue mountains'—just this one phrase separates this monk and National Teacher Deshao by the stage of faith, the stage of person, one mystery, three mysteries, so that 'Gates and walls are like cliffs, doors and locks are redoubled'—after all, it is difficult to see each other.

Also in the verse the monk's viewpoint is likened to a drunken guest or a ruined farmer, while Yangshan's instruction is like a garuda bird or a roving dragon. In the *Lotus Scripture* is the metaphor of someone who goes to the house of a close friend, gets drunk on wine and goes to sleep: at that time the friend has to go do some official business; he takes a priceless jewel and fastens it inside the other's clothing, while the man, being in a drunken sleep, is not aware of this at all. Zhaozhou said, "I've heard that once filled you forget a hundred hungers; today my body itself is this." Zhaozhou, once fulfilled, forgot a hundred hungers; he should receive the fine offerings of humans and gods. This monk, full of food, ruins the farmers; he can hardly digest even a drop of water. Clear-eyed people should discern.

Sanskirt *garuda* is called 'bird with beautiful wings' in our language; beating a wind, it parts the ocean, directly seizes a dragon and swallows it. When Confucius asked Laozi about rites, he said, "I see Laozi as like a dragon." A roaming dragon appears and disappears in the clouds and mist; it is not the same as one that hides away. This versifies "This is right for the stage of faith, but not for the stage of person. Based on your insight, you've just got a single mystery; after this see for yourself." Why make him shift his body and change his steps? 'As long as there is a road to ascend, there is also an eminent person to traverse it too.'

Added Sayings /Case

Yangshan asked a monk, "Where are you from?"—He shuts the door and digs for understanding.

The monk said, "From Yu province."—The public proof is clear.

Yangshan asked, "Do you think of that place?"—Just when he'd forgotten!

The monk said, "I always think of it."—A familiar place is hard to forget.

Yangshan said, "The thinker is the mind and the thought-of is the environment."—So actually he's even set up subject and object.

Therein are mountains, rivers, the land, buildings, towers, halls and chambers, people, animals, etc.—think back on the thinking mind; **are there so many things there?**—You yourself create the distinction, my good man.

Here, I don't see any existence at all—There's still this.

This is right for the stage of faith, but not yet right for the stage of person—The snow remaining in the garden, the sun will melt, but who will you have sweep out the red dust inside the room?

Don't you have any other particular way of guidance?—Now he comes on like this.

To say that I have anything particular or not would not be acccurate—He shoots through the double gate.

Based on your insight, you only get one mystery—There's already the moon in the boat.

After this, see on your own—He even adds wind to the sails.

All-embracing, with no outside—So big there's nothing it doesn't contain.

Penetrating without obstruction—So fine there's nothing it doesn't go into.

Gates and walls like cliffs—Better not grope.

Doors and locks redoubled—Not worth a snap of the fingers.

When the wine is always sweet, it lays out the guests—Wake them up and I'll strike.

While the meal is filling, it ruins the farmers—They're buried in the same pit.

Bursting out of the clear sky, the garuda takes wing on the wind—Piercing the blue sky.

Treading over the blue sea, thunder follows the roaming dragon—The early spring season when the insects are roused.

33 SANSHENG'S "GOLDEN FISH"

Introduction   Meeting the strong, be weak; meeting the soft, be hard. If both are hard and hit each other, there will surely be one damaged. But tell me, how do you interchange?

Case   Sansheng asked Xuefeng, "The golden fish that's passed through the net—what does it use for food?"
Xuefeng said, "When you come out of the net, then I'll tell you."
Sansheng said, "The teacher of fifteen hundred people, yet you don't even know a saying."
Xuefeng said, "My tasks as abbot are many."

Commentary   Master Changlu Qingliao of recent times was a fellow student with Tiantong; when he was teaching he had a congregation of seventeen hundred people. He ate gruel and passed the summer with Zhu-an Shigui, sharing quarters and allowing him private instruction. Xuefeng and Sansheng were of different generations but of the same way. Dagui Zhe said, "Sansheng can be said to be accustomed to having been a guest, at the ten-thousand-fathom Dragon Gate: Xuefeng is much like Meng Chang (who used to always have thousands of house guests)—when the gate opens, how could he fear an eminent guest?"
Sansheng, in posing this question, undeniably set out a bowl of glue in a forest of thorns. Xuefeng at first is thirty steps away, watching you looking in yourself and drawing out yourself; he said, "Wait till you come out of the net, then I'll tell you." Strange—it is just like a national champion playing chess first looking several moves ahead before he

147

makes his move. Sansheng, seeing that at this stage victory and defeat are not distinguished, went by a different route and said, "You're the teacher of fifteen hundred people, yet you don't even know a saying?" Using the tooth and nail of the cave of Dharma, he captured him alive. Xuefeng, honest and sincere, just said, "My tasks as abbot are many." Baofu said, "When contending, there's not enough; when conceding, there's extra." Xuedou said, "What a pity to let him go—he should be hit thirty times. This caning shouldn't be lessened by even a single blow, but it's just that it's rare to meet one who is capable." These two elders, one letting go and one holding fast, each has a way out.

Master Gaoyou Ding was asked by someone, "The golden fish that's passed through the net—what does it have for food?" He said, "Dry dung." My late teacher Xueyan heard this and said, "Thanks for the offering." This joy of Dharma and delight in meditation is not less than the ancients. What about on Tiantong's part? His verse says,

Verse   *When first ascending the tiers of waves, clouds and thunder accompany;*
Leaping up magnificently—look at the great function.
With a burnt tail, he clearly crosses the Gate of Yu;
The beautiful fish won't agree to be sunk in a pickle jar.
An old mature man does not startle the crowd;
Someone used to facing a great adversary has no fear from the start.
Floating, floating, just as light as five ounces;
Massive, massive—heavier than even a thousand tons.
Sansheng's exalted fame over the four seas—who again was his peer?
Xuefeng stands alone, the eight winds blowing do not move him.

Commentary   Dragon Gate Mountain in Jiang province was excavated by King Yu; it is also called Yu Gate, and it has three tiers. In the *Classic of the Waters* it says that the sturgeons come out of their holes and in the third month go up to cross Dragon Gate. Those who manage to cross become dragons; if not they fail and return. "When first ascending the tiers of waves" refers to the three-tiered gate. The *wenyan* wing of the *Book of Changes* says, "Clouds follow dragons, wind follows tigers." "Clouds and thunder accompany" means turning into a dragon. The two great heroes leaped with majestic splendor; Sansheng was like "first ascending the tiers of waves," Xuefeng was like "clouds and thunder accompany." Once Sansheng had crossed the Dragon Gate, would Xuefeng willingly be immersed in a pickle jar? When Linji saw off Luopu he said, "In the school of Linji there's a red-finned carp who wags his head, swishes his tail, and heads South—in whose house will it die immersed in a pickle jar?"

After this the verse finally eulogizes Xuefeng's "My tasks as abbot are many," and also eulogizes Sansheng's two questions as well: "An old mature man does not startle the crowd; someone used to facing a great adversary has no fear from the start." According to the *Annals of Emperor Guangwu*, Wang Xun and Wang Yi recruited a million soldiers and went forth and surrounded Kunyang. Guangwu himself acted as the general of the vanguard and slew dozens of men; all the generals rejoiced and said, "General Liu (Guangwu) usually is timid when seeing a lesser enemy— today, seeing a great adversary, he is brave; how strange!" At a glance hardly measuring up to five ounces, when you examine carefully there's a thousand tons on the scale, which cannot be budged. Later Xuefeng's lineage produced the two streams of Yunmen and Fayan; is this not a case of 'when the source is deep, the flow is long'?

Profit, decline, slander, fame, praise, censure, pain, and pleasure are the eight winds—for him, a genuine Chan master, they are like a breeze passing by his ear. Master Tantuo Xing said to Master Qingshou Kai, "If I call you a father, then how would it be?"

Added Sayings /Case

Sansheng asked Xuefeng, "What does the golden fish that's passed through the net have for food?"—Without waiting for the line to be put down, he rises to the hook himself.

Xuefeng said, "I'll tell you when you come out of the net."—When you meet someone, only say thirty percent for the time being.

Sansheng said, "The teacher of fifteen hundred, and you don't even know a saying."—The prophecy on Spiritual Mountain was not like today.

Xuefeng said, "My tasks as abbot are many."—You see jowls on his head from behind.

149

Added
Sayings
/Verse

When first ascending the tiers of waves, clouds and thunder accompany—He regrets heaven hasn't come.

Leaping up magnificently—look at the great function—Quickly bow thrice.

With a burnt tail, he clearly crosses the Gate of Yu—Look quickly!

The beautiful fish won't agree to be sunk in a pickle jar—There's an even worse scoundrel and thief.

An old mature man does not startle the crowd—Relaxed, tranquil, peaceful, accurate.

Someone used to facing a great adversary has no fear from the start—He accepts disgrace like glory and looks on death as he does on life.

Floating, as light as five ounces—Seeing at a distance is uncertain.

Massive, heavier than a thousand tons—When you look up close, it's clear.

His exalted fame over the four seas—who again was his peer?—He picks out the moon in the sky above.

He stands alone, the eight winds blowing do not move him—Just as if it never happened.

34 FENGXUE'S "SINGLE ATOM"

Introduction Bare-handed, empty-fisted, a thousand changes, ten thousand transformations—though this is making something out of nothing, what can you do—you employ the provisional to symbolize the real. But tell me, is there a fundamental basis or not?

Case Fengxue said, "If you set up a single atom, the nation flourishes. If you don't set up a single atom, the nation perishes."
Xuedou held up his staff and said, "Are there any mendicants who will die the same and live the same?"

Commentary When Xuedou held forth his staff, his meaning lay in the setting up of the atom; his verse said, "The peasants may not unfurrow their brows, but for now I hope the nation establishes a sturdy foundation. Crafty ministers, valiant generals—where are they now?" This versifies "are there any mendicants who will die the same and live the same?" "Ten thousand miles' pure wind, only I myself know."
"The old peasants do not unfurrow their brows"; this talk is not quoted completely—in the record, Fengxue ascended the hall and said,

> If a single atom is set up, the nation flourishes and the
> peasants frown; if you do not set up a single atom, the nation
> perishes and the peasants rest easy. If you can clearly under-
> stand here, you have no separate part—it's all this old monk,
> me; I am just you—you and I can enlighten everyone in the world,
> and can also delude everyone in the world. Do you want to know
> 'you'? (he slapped his left side) Here it is. Do you want to
> know 'me'? (he slapped his right side) Here it is.

151

Yunmen said, "'Here' is easy—'there' is hard." Langya Jiao said, "Casting a divining ladle, he listens to the empty sound." I say, Yunmen adds a point to the arrow; Langya pulls the shaft out from the back of the brain (taking it all the way through). This is also the elimination and setting up of an atom, the flourishing and perishing of the nation. Actually, when has the tree in the middle ever moved in the least? Xuedou does not discard anything in the gateway of buddha-work; Tiantong includes the principle of reality, which doesn't admit a single atom. Both laws are carried out equally—he brings them out together at once.

Verse   *As a greybeard rising from a hunt by the Wei River—*
How does that compare to those who starved in purity on Mount Shouyang?
It just lies in a single atom, distinguishing changing conditions;
Fame and accomplishment both are hard to efface.

Commentary   When Xi Bo was going to go out hunting, he cast an augury about it which said, "Your catch will not be a bear or a tiger—it will be the assistant of a ruler." As it turned out, he found Lu Shang on the north bank of the Wei river; as they talked together, he was overjoyed and said, "My former lord Taigong once said that there would be a sage who would go to Zhou; our Taigong hoped for you for a long time." Therefore he called him 'Taigong's Hope' and made him leader.

Boyi and Shuqi were Lord Guzhu's two sons; they gave up their country and both perished. When King Wu attacked King Chou, he beat his horse and remonstrated with King Chou, saying, "Your father is dead and you don't bury him; now you are taking up arms—can you call this filial piety? When the subject kills the lord, can this be called benevolence?" Those around wanted to attack him, but Taigong said, "This is a righteous man." He helped him and had him leave. King Wu brought down the Yin dynasty, and the whole land united under the Zhou dynasty. Boyi and Shuqi were shamed at this and wouldn't eat the grain of Zhou—collecting ferns on Mount Shouyang, they starved to death. Taigong destroying Yin and founding Zhou is the nation flourishing; Boyi and Shuqi abdicating their ranks and starving to death is the nation perishing.

National Teacher Xianshou just raised the diverse features in a single atom to explain an ocean of meaning in a hundred ways. 'Fame' refers to Boyi and Shuqi; 'accomplishment' refers to Taigong. Luopu said, "In front of the peasants' gates the affairs of court are not discussed." Therefore they farm peacefully and don't ever frown. Why? Uselessness becomes real usefulness; good conditions are bad conditions.

Added Sayings /Case

If you set up an atom, the nation flourishes—When you find this, it's originally there.

If you don't set up an atom, the nation perishes—When you lose this, it's originally nonexistent.

Are there any mendicants who will die the same and live the same?—I don't say there are none, just that they're few.

Added Sayings /Verse

As a greybeard rising from a hunt by the Wei River—Though old, he doesn't retire.

How does that compare to those who starved in purity on Shouyang?—Though young, they don't work hard.

It just lies in an atom, distinguishing changing conditions—Holding up the staff, I say, 'Look!'

Fame and accomplishment both are hard to efface—Throwing down the staff, I say, 'Xuedou is still around.'

35 LUOPU'S ACQUIESCENCE

Introduction   Quick action and swift intellect breaks the onslaught of outsiders and heavenly devils. Leaving convention and transcending sect indirectly helps those of superior faculties with sharp wisdom. If you suddenly meet someone who doesn't even turn his head when struck, then what?

Case   When Luopu called on Jiashan, without bowing he stood right in front of him.

Jiashan said, "A chicken roosting in a phoenix nest—it's not of the same species—go away."

Luopu said, "I've come from afar to find out your way, Teacher; I beg you for a reception."

Jiashan said, "Before my eyes there is no you, here there is no me."

Luopu then shouted.

Jiashan said, "Stop, stop, now don't be crude and careless. The moon in the clouds is the same, valleys and mountains are different. It's not that you don't cut off the tongues of everyone on earth, but how can you make a tongueless man speak?"

Luopu had nothing to say; Jiashan hit him. From this Luopu acquiesced.

Commentary   The various records of the Lamp of the Patriarchs all say that before Jiashan had seen the Boatman, he was already appearing in the world, residing at Zhulin monastery in Jingkou in Run province, without showing the name of the teacher to whose Dharma he succeeded. Only Foguo's *Measuring Tap* says, "Zhuanming first succeeded to Shilou."

That is Shilou of Fen province; Zhuanming is Jiashan's posthumous title. Chan Master Yunan of Luopu Montain in Li province studied under Linji for a long time and served as his attendant. Linji once said, "Who dares to stand up to the point of the arrow of the Linji school?" One day Luopu took leave of Linji, who said, "Where are you going?" Luopu said, "South." Linji drew a line with his staff and said, "If you can cross this, then go." Luopu immediately shouted; Linji hit him. Luopu bowed and left. He wandered around until finally he came to the summit of Mount Jia, where he built a shack and lived there for a year. Master Jiashan found out and sent an attendant monk with a letter for him. Luopu took the letter, then sat right down and extended his hands, in a gesture of seeking; the monk was speechless. Luopu then hit him and said, "Go back and recount this to the master."

The monk returned and told about this; Jiashan said, "If this monk reads the letter, he will surely come within three days; if he doesn't read the letter, he cannot be saved." Three days later Luopu came; without bowing he stood and faced Jiashan. Jiashan said, "A chicken roosting in a phoenix nest; they're not the same species—go away." Each bore the eye to push aside the weeds looking for the way. Luopu saw that in Jiashan's dismissal, dismissing was actually keeping him there; once he had come, how could he return for naught? He also saw that Jiashan's method was strict and hard, that each was unyielding, so he went easy and said to him, "I've come from afar to find out your way, Teacher; I beg you for a reception." Jiashan had a special forge and bellows; he said, "There is no one before me, and no me here." Jiashan knew that as a longtime meditator Luopu would surely carry out the true order of Linji and hence specially used the hammer and anvil that transcends sectarianism and goes beyond formalities. And after all Luopu did shout. Now you tell me, is it just this, or is there anything besides? Jiashan said, "Stop, stop, don't be crude and careless now." No need to be hurried. "The moon in the clouds is the same, valleys and mountains are different." The noodle depends on how people make it. "It's not that you don't cut off the tongues of everyone on earth,"—he just has the thousand-foot cold pine—"but how can you make a tongueless man speak?"—he also needs bamboo shoots.

Jiashan once discoursed on the establishment of method and the profound talk entering into principle: Luopu is the establishment of method, Jiashan is the profound talk entering into principle. Luopu, fondly gazing at the white waves, lost the rudder from his hands; after all he couldn't manage. Jiashan is all right—he after all takes the true order of Linji and puts the sticking key in the old lock for him. Luopu is used to vinegar; once he tastes it he knows how sour it is—at this he acquiesced.

Xinghua said, "Just know about fulfilling Buddhahood—what sentient beings would you worry about?" I say, what can be done about the fact that a single tree doesn't make a forest?

Xuedou said,

This monk is pitiful, lamentable—he bogs down Linji.

(I say, If an adopted son doesn't measure up to his father, the family declines in one generation.)

Since for him the moon in the clouds is the same, for me valleys and mountains are different.

(I say, the southern mountains and colors of autumn—in their splendor they exalt one another.)

What tongueless person speaking is he talking about?

(I say, this is still the spokesman.)

I'd whack him with a mat.

(I say, suppose he takes it and beats you twenty times, then what?)

Jiashan is a fellow who knows the way—he'll surely place him under the bright window.

(I say, that's not as good as restoring him to his original provisions.)

Wuzu Jie said, "Try to explain the principle more, then get out." I say, vipers and scorpions are born poisonous.

Dayang Yan said, "I still want the teacher's witness of enlightenment." I say, the essence of orchids, even when old, is fragrant to the end.

Furthermore, the school of Yaoshan is truly difficult to succeed to and uphold—when Yunyan swept the ground, the dust filled the skies; when Luopu submitted, the declaration of enmity was unceasing. Goodness is in being able to speak without a tongue, to use your fists without your hands. Even if the stick and the shout are employed together, this can only bring up a half on the side; to uphold this Path, it is entrusted to Tiantong:

Verse   *Wagging his head, shaking his tail, the red-tailed fish;*
         Independent through and through, he knows how to turn around.
         Even if he has the art to cut off tongues,
         Pulling his nose around subtly conveyed the spirit.
         Outside the screen of luminous jewels, wind and moon are like day;
         In front of the cliff of dead trees, flowers and plants are always in spring.
         Tongueless man, tongueless man,
         The true order's completely upheld in one knowing phrase.
         Walking alone in the kingdom, clear and comprehending,
         Let everyone in the land be happy and joyful.

Commentary When Luopu left Linji, Linji said, "In the school of Linji there's a
         red-tailed carp who wags his head, swishes his tail, and heads South."
         "Independent through and through, he knows how to turn around" is
         the work of the Linji school; it's not entirely the same as 'changing state
         and transforming achievement.'
         In the extensive record of Linji it says, "There is only the independent
         Wayfarer listening to the Dharma; this is the mother of the Buddhas.
         Therefore the Buddha is born of independence; if you realize indepen-
         dence, buddhahood too has no attainment. If one can see in this way, this
         is truly correct insight and understanding." I say, if Luopu couldn't 'turn
         around,' how could he be able to shout as Jiashan? If you say he managed
         to turn around, why was he speechless at the end? Try to see for sure.
         Tiantong admits he has eyes and has technique; Jiashan too does not deny
         he could cut off the tongue of everyone on earth. He was well able to go
         by the order. "But how can you make a tongueless man talk?"—Jiashan
         easily pulls back Luopu's heaven-challenging nose. Foguo, seeing Jiashan
         was as though reciting a spell, added the comment, "Where did you get
         this leftover?" I say, just this is it; Jiashan makes a tongueless man speak.
         Foguo doesn't have this leftover; he can only cut off everyone's tongue.
         Even if you have a special way to turn around and spew out breath, this
         is not necessarily the speech of a tongueless man.
         So tell me, what is this person's state like? The verse says, "Outside the
         screen of luminous jewels, wind and moon are like day; in front of the

cliff of dead trees, flowers and plants are always in spring." This is the experience of a tongueless man.

Emperor Ming of the Han dynasty built a Hall of Light; the blinds were made of pearls, the banisters were gold, the stairs jade—day or night, it was always light.

Tongan Cha said, "Before the dead tree cliff the divergent roads are many." Dongshan said, "You should seek some flowers on a withered tree."

This verse, at the stick and shout, is not without solitary strictness; once you've managed to reach the top of the hundred-foot pole, only then will a tongueless man be able to speak. By this we know that only the speech of a tongueless man is 'one knowing phrase upholding the true order.' Arriving here, the eye is high over the four seas, and one 'walks alone in the kingdom.' Later Luopu said, "Even if everybody is happy and joyful, I alone do not agree." Even if everyone gladly has their tongue cut off by him, Jiashan says, "Beyond there is still an opening." What is the opening beyond? When a tongueless man can talk, then he'll tell you.

Added Sayings /Case

When Luopu called on Jiashan, he stood right in front of him without bowing—When they don't dismount when meeting, it's because they each have their own way to go.

Jiashan said, "A chicken roosting in a phoenix nest—it's not of the same species—go away."—One hand pushes, one hand pulls.

Luopu said, "I've come from afar to find out your way; please give me a reception."—The probing pole is in his hands.

Jiashan said, "Before my eyes there is no you, here there is no me."—The shadowing grass is on him.

Luopu then shouted—Exhausting his strength, he cuts off his power.

Jiashan said, "Stop, stop, now don't be crude and careless."—Those who understand aren't hurried, those who are hurried don't understand.

Clouds and moon are the same, valleys and mountains are different—In side alleys on dark streets, the unfamiliar traveler gets lost.

It's not that you don't cut off the tongues of everyone on earth—He just sees the sharpness of the awl.

But how can you make a tongueless man speak?—He doesn't see the squareness of the chisel.

Luopu had nothing to say—Confronting the 'Long Snake' battle formation, his bow and lance crack to the ground.

Jiashan then hit him—Unexpectedly, Jiashan acts like Linji.

From this Luopu acquiesced—Artists get sick of having to perform.

Added Sayings / Verse

Wagging his head, shaking his tail, the red-tailed fish—His mouth coveting the fragrant bait, his body's caught up in the net.

Independent through and through, he knows how to turn around—Today he's dragged into a net.

Even if he has the art to cut off tongues—Just when you're going to sweep away snow you look for a pine branch.

Pulling his nose around subtly conveyed the spirit—I've already stuck out my stick and found some medicinal mushrooms.

Outside the screen of luminous jewels, wind and moon are like day—It doesn't use the energy of sun, moon, or stars.

In front of the cliff of dead trees, flowers and plants are always in spring—Inwardly digesting the accomplishment of uniformity.

Tongueless man, tongueless man—Answer through your nose.

The true order's completely upheld in one knowing phrase—He pulls out the sideways bone in the dark.

Walking alone in the kingdom, clear and comprehending—The true light doesn't shine.

Let everyone in the land be happy and joyful—The confusion I leave to them—what's it got to do with me?

159

36 MASTER MA IS UNWELL

Introduction Even investigating beyond mind, intellect, and consciousness, there is still *this*. Even studying in ordinary and holy paths, it's already too exalted. The red-hot furnace spurts out iron barbs. With tongue sword and lip spear, it's hard to open the mouth; without running afoul of the point, please try to bring it up.

Case **Master Ma was unwell. The monastery superintendent asked, "Master, how is your venerable state these days?" The Great Teacher said, "Sun face buddha, moon face buddha."**

Commentary When the ancients were ill they still did buddha-work. When the hindrance of illness suddenly arose in Master Huisi of Nanyue, he made an issue of the illness, inquiring, "Illness comes from doing, doing comes from illusion, illusion comes from mind; mind is fundamentally unborn—whence does illness come to be?" When he had formed this thought, suddenly he was well. I say, he attained peace and bliss from Tathagata Chan.

Chan Master Shen, imperial attendant of the western capital, had the strategy of the nun Congzhi (Bodhidharma's disciple); when he got sick he wrote a verse:

> When the breath ends, it cuts off emotions;
> Arousing the mind, there is no path of mind.
> Without even the strength to bat an eye,
> Never do I go out the door.

Although this is Patriarch Chan, it is much like the old crow in a cloth bag—'though alive, it seems as if dead.' Master Furong Daokai said, "This one verse alone naturally can continue my school." I say, although this is already too much, nevertheless there is something more.

Great Teacher Mazu is still otherwise; the monastery superintendent did not dare to directly ask about the improvement or deterioration of his sick body, but subtly took cover—"Master, how is your venerable state these days?" Now he didn't talk of Tathagata Chan or Patriarch Chan, but just said this: "Sun face buddha, moon face buddha." Tell me, what was his meaning? Foguo said, "Nowadays there are many who say that Great Teacher Mazu was leading the superintendent on; some glare and say, 'It's here! The left and right eyes are sun face buddha, moon face buddha!' Some say, 'Prepare some stomach medicine!' What grip have they got on it?"

Chan Master Shou said, "There is not a single name that doesn't broadcast an epithet of the Tathagata; there is not a single thing that doesn't reveal the form of Vairocana." I say, in the *Buddha Names Scripture* there are these two Buddha names (Sun Face Buddha, Moon Face Buddha)— after all, what was the great teacher's essential meaning? Haven't you heard it said that the horse in its prime tramples everyone on earth to death? Tianjiao's verse said,

> The horse of Shenfang was born with a ferocious spirit;
> He tramples on Vairocana's head as he goes.
> Now he suffers from spleen pains and headache;
> But even since falling sick he still has a clever sense.

I say, the basic nature is hard to change—it is easier to move mountains and rivers. This eulogizes Mazu still using the real thing to help people even while ill. We all are physically strong and healthy; just don't go against Mazu or be neglectful of Tiantong:

Verse Sun Face Buddha, Moon Face Buddha—
Stars fall, thunder rolls,
The mirror faces forms without subjectivity;
The pearl in a bowl rolls of itself.
Don't you see, before the hammer, gold refined a hundred times;
Under the scissors, silk from one loom.

Commentary These two buddhas, sun face and moon face, are like stars falling, thunder crashing—they do not admit any hesitation.

161

In ancient times in the palace in Qin was a mirror made of jade, which reflected all the officials so that their guts were all revealed. Also when foxes acted as humans, in the mirror only their original form showed. This is having no private secrets.

In the *Records of Sympathy of Species* it says that the harbor of Mount Langfeng produces pearls which roll by themselves when placed in a bowl—these are called 'running pearls.' This eulogizes Mazu's mind being like the ancient mirror, his functioning like a running pearl; he doesn't keep any traces of reflections.

Gold of a hundred refinings is a matter for the hammer and anvil of an adept; silk from one loom is a matter for the scissors and ruler of a tailor.

A monk asked Yunyan, "Are 'the one in charge' and 'that one' one or two?" Yunyan said, "Is the silk from one loom one piece or two?" Dongshan said in his behalf, "It's like a man holding onto a tree." This is the union of environment and mind, the merging of knowledge and principle, the same autumn for sky and water, the joining of the paths of ruler and subject. When the silk has scissors and ruler, then the cutting depends on the person; when gold has hammer and anvil, then the refinement depends on oneself. But tell me, on the part of a patchrobed mendicant, what aspect of the work does this accomplish? Sun face buddha, moon face buddha.

Added Sayings / Case	**Master Ma was unwell**—Not necessarily like Vimalakirti. **The monastery superintendent asked, "How is the Master's venerable state these days?"**—Everyday matters keep him so busy he seldom gets to inquire about someone's health. **The great teacher said, "Sun face buddha, moon face buddha."**—Isn't this getting a cramp and suffering heat sickness?
Added Sayings / Verse	*Sun Face Buddha, Moon Face Buddha*—If you look right at it you'll go blind. *Stars fall, thunder rolls*—Already gone past the neighboring country. *The mirror faces forms without subjectivity*—Can't fool it a bit. *The pearl in a bowl rolls of itself*—Even if you try to grab it, it won't hold still. *Don't you see, before the hammer, gold refined a hundred times*—Pitchers, bowls, hairpins, rings, coins, cups, dishes. *Under the scissors, silk from one loom*—Quilts, covers, clothing, hats, vests, collars, sleeves.

37 GUISHAN'S "ACTIVE CONSCIOUSNESS"

Introduction   Driving away the plowman's ox, pulling its nose around; taking away the hungry man's food, holding his throat tight. Is there anyone who can administer the poison?

Case   Guishan asked Yangshan, "If someone suddenly said, 'All sentient beings just have active consciousness, boundless and unclear, with no fundamental to rely on,' how would you prove it in experience?" Yangshan said, "If a monk comes, I call him, 'Hey, you!' If the monk turns his head, I say, 'What is it?' If he hesitates, I say, 'Not only is their active consciousness boundless and unclear, they have no fundamental to rely on.'"
Guishan said, "Good!"

Commentary   A monk asked Yunan, "The *Treatise on the Flower Ornament* says that the fundamental affliction of ignorance itself is the immutable knowledge of all Buddhas; this principle is most profound and mysterious in the extreme, difficult to comprehend." Yunan said, "This is most distinctly clear, easy to understand." At that moment a boy happened to be sweeping there; Yunan called to him, and the boy turned his head. Yunan pointed to him and said, "Is this not immutable knowledge?" When Yangshan calls a monk and the monk turns his head, that is precisely this situation. Yunan then asked the boy, "What is your buddha-nature?" The boy looked around, at a loss, and left; Yunan said, "Is this not fundamental affliction?" If you can comprehend this, then you become a buddha immediately. The boy's bewilderment and the monk's hesitation are no different; the fundamental affliction of ignorance and the boundless unclear active consciousness are also the same. When Yunan and Yangshan examined monks and tested people, they accomplished their aim in this way; as for me, my viewpoint is otherwise—the boy and the monk both had thoroughgoing immutable knowledge; Yunan and Yangshan had boundless active consciousness. Anyone who can discern will personally see Tiantong. His verse says,

Verse *One call and he turns his head—do you know the self or not?*
Vaguely, like the moon through ivy, a crescent at that.
The child of riches, as soon as he falls
On the boundless road of destitution, has such sorrow.

Commentary Baizhang went up into the hall: when the assembly had gathered, he drove them out all at once with his staff; then he called to the crowd, and when they turned their heads, he said, "What is it?" Everywhere this is called Baizhang's hall-leaving phrase—it too should be investigated thoroughly. Sir Wang Jing said, "I got a saying from Xuefeng and became prime minister." Someone insistently inquired further; Wang Jing said, "The old fellow always used to say to people, 'What is it?'" The first line of the verse is about calling the monk, turning his head, and "What is it?"

As for "Do you know the self or not?" Yangshan used an unrighteous means to strike a defenseless house; if the monk had gotten a glimpse in the light of a spark, he could be said to have recognized the emperor in a bustling marketplace; if he hesitated and didn't come forth, then it would be "vague, like the moon through ivy, a crescent at that."

Huangbo went up into the hall; just as the assembly had gathered he drove them all out at once with his staff, and then called to them—when the people turned their heads, Huangbo said, "The moon is like a drawn bow; there's little rain, much wind." The verse's intent uses this.

Yangshan and Shandao of the Stone Grotto were gazing at the moon when Yangshan asked, "When the moon is a crescent, where does the round shape go? And when it is full, where does the crescent shape go?" Shandao said, "When it's a crescent, the round shape is concealed; when it's full, the crescent shape remains."

Yunyan said, "When it's a crescent, the round shape remains; when it's full, the crescent shape does not exist."

Daowu said, "When it's a crescent, yet it's not a crescent; when it's full, it's still not round."

A poem by Lo Pinwang says, "Since it can be round as a mirror, why should it be bent like a hook?"

The Huayan school calls this the gate of secret concealment and revelation existing together. Also in the teachings it says that bodhisattvas of the tenth stage see nature like looking at the moon through a gauze net. To call (the vaguely seen moon) a 'gauze moon' is also all right, but a poem by Li Bo says, "There is the moon through the ivies crossing the mirror of morning, a wind in the pines strumming the harpstrings of night." So the sense of the word 'ivy' is stronger. Tiantong uses the vague, indistinct new moon, now hidden, now shining in the misty ivies, though not full and bright, already showing its tips, to versify how this monk is half light, half dark, seeming to be there, seeming to be absent. I am being much like a salt and iron official; it sure seems to me that Tiantong is deep and meticulous with needle and thread. If the thread's not cut, it would be hard to complete the brocade design.

As Dongshan and his spiritual uncle Mi were walking along, they saw a white rabbit pass by. Mi said, "How excellent!" Dongshan said, "How so?" Mi said, "It's like a commoner being appointed prime minister." Dongshan said, "So venerable and great, you talk like this?" Mi said, "How about you?" Dongshan said, "After generations of nobility, a temporary fall."

Sima Xiangru's *Elegy on Entering the Woods* says, "The child with a fortune in gold does not sit near the hall (afraid it will fall); the sage Yuanji always sits in a dilapidated cart—when he meets the end of the road, then he wails and turns back." I say, if you can return home on the road, then you can turn your body back to your father.

Haven't you heard it said, "If you can turn back the light in an instant of thought, it's the same as original realization"? Since it is so, why is the immutable knowledge of all Buddhas called boundless unclear active consciousness in sentient beings? If they had known the lamp was fire, the meal would have been cooked long ago.

<table>
<tr>
<td>Added Sayings /Case</td>
<td>

Suppose someone asked about "all sentient beings just have active consciousness, boundless and unclear, with no fundamental to rely on," how would you prove it in experience?—The horse is a government horse—it doesn't need a license.

If a monk comes, I call him—A knock on the back of the head—you don't know where it came from.

If the monk turns his head—He knocks three spirits off his head.

I say, "What is it?"—Following up on the oven-like heat, he strikes again.

If he hesitates, I say "Not only is their active consciousness boundless and unclear, they have no fundamental to rely on."—Captured alive.

Guishan said "Good!"—A bitter mouth produces kind words.

</td>
</tr>
<tr>
<td>Added Sayings /Verse</td>
<td>

One call and he turns his head—do you know the self?—A real pickpocket working in broad daylight—what is hard to see?

Vaguely, like the moon through ivy, a crescent at that—Hiding the body, revealing the shadow.

The child of riches, as soon as he falls—Though the wind screen is broken, the frame is still there.

On the boundless road of destitution, has such sorrow—A little vessel doesn't have a large measure.

</td>
</tr>
</table>

38 LINJI'S "TRUE MAN"

Introduction Taking a thief for one's son, taking the servant for the master. Can a broken wooden ladle be your ancestor's skull? A donkey-saddle rim is not your father's jawbone either. When breaking earth, separating reeds, how do you discern the master?

Case Linji said to the assembly, "There is a true man with no rank always going out and in through the portals of your face. Beginners who have not yet witnessed it, look! Look!"
Then a monk came forward and said, "What is the true man of no rank?"
Linji got down from the seat, grabbed and held him: the monk hesitated. Linji pushed him away and said, "The true man of no rank—what a piece of dry crap he is!"

Commentary In the extensive record of Linji's sayings it says, "In the field of the body of five clusters there is a true man of no rank, grandly revealed, without a hairsbreadth gap; why don't you recognize him? The reality of mind is formless and pervades all directions." Since it pervades all directions, it is not only in the physical field of five clusters, it is always going out and in the gates of your face; "Beginners who have not yet witnessed it, look, look!" I say, the true man of no rank looks at the monks, the monks look at the true man. At that point a monk asked, "What is the true man of no rank?" Everywhere they call this "conveying the matter along with the voice," but what can be done—the one riding the donkey doesn't see the assembly; Linji got down from his seat and grabbed him. Tell me—

167

where is the true man? He should give a slap. This monk hesitated; the true man is absent—what a pity! Linji pushed him away, saying, "The true man of no rank—what a piece of dry crap he is!" Though face to face, he's hidden away. Xuefeng said, "Linji is much like a thief who steals in broad daylight." I say, he's been busted. Xuedou said, "One who steals skillfully is unbeknownst to even ghosts and spirits; since he has been seen through by Xuefeng, Linji is not an expert." Xuedou also called to the assembly and said, "Today Xuedou has snatched your eyeballs. If you don't believe it, each of you go back to your rooms and try to find them." I say, Xuedou has lost his eyebrows as well. If you want to know how to be a thief in the hands of a thief, you must ask Tiantong.

Verse   *Delusion and enlightenment are opposite,*
Subtly communicated, with simplicity;
Spring opens the hundred flowers, in one puff,
Power pulls back nine bulls, in one yank.
It's hopeless— the mud and sand can't be cleared away;
Clearly blocking off the eye of the sweet spring,
If suddenly it burst forth, it would freely flow.

Commentary   The *Complete Enlightenment Scripture* says, "It's like someone who's lost, the four directions change places." In reality the directions don't move; when enlightened, it's just as before. The *Source Mirror* says, "Hitherto having been deluded about enlightenment, it resembles delusion; now being enlightened from delusion, still it's not enlightenment." This is 'subtly communicating with simplicity.' Given out, it's not squandered. If you can comprehend, then the mass of naked flesh is the true man of no rank; if you don't comprehend, as before he goes out and in the gates of your face. This monk had him too, but he couldn't bring him out; instead he transmitted a saying, conveying words as a servant of the true man, asking about the turns of events—he troubled Linji to descend from nobility to lowliness, confronting the essence with complete function. Since this monk couldn't manage to do anything, Linji too withdrew without looking back—seeing he couldn't scoop it up, he said, "The true man with no rank—what a piece of dry crap he is." This is the ability to let go and to gather in, able to call together and to disperse with a shout, never tying them up to die at a phrase, creating sickness in people's hearts.

Tiantai said, "Puff once—the world forms; shouting once, the world disintegrates." Furthermore, "At the moment of puffing, shout; at the moment of shouting, puff."

According to Liezi, Gong Yizi was famous for his strength: King Xuan of Zhou went to call on him with full ceremony, but when he got there, he found that Gong was a weakling. The king asked, "How strong are you?" He replied, "I can break the waist of a spring insect, I can bear the wing of an autumn cicada." The king flushed and said, "I'm strong enough to tear apart rhinoceros hide and drag nine oxen by the tail—yet I still lament my weakness. How can it be that you are so famous for strength?" He replied, "My fame is not for having such strength, it is for being able to use such strength." Here the verse eulogizes Linji's powerful action gathering in and letting go.

As Fayan was excavating a well, the spring's eye was blocked by sand; he asked a monk, "The spring's eye doesn't penetrate the sand blocking it; when the eye of the Way doesn't penetrate, what is it hindered by?" The monk had no reply; Fayan himself answered for him, "It is hindered by the eye." Now tell me, is it the monk blocking off the spring's eye, or is it Linji blocking off the spring's eye? When suddenly bursting forth, how is it? (Master Wansong took up his staff and got down from his seat—the assembly ran away all at once.)

Added Sayings / Case

Linji said, "There is a true man with no rank."—He's laid a foundation and set his feet.

Always going out and in through the portals of your face—What about that which is in back of you!!!

Beginners who have not yet witnessed it, look!—But do you have the eye?

A monk came forward and said, "What is the true man of no rank?"—Don't you know how to speak?

Linji got down from the seat, grabbed and held him—You still turn away.

The monk hesitated—He bogs down the true man.

Linji pushed him away and said, "The true man of no rank—what a piece of dry crap!"—He's much like holding his bowl and not getting anything.

Added Sayings / Verse

Delusion and enlightenment are opposite—Not a hairsbreadth apart.

He subtly communicates, with simplicity—Already into wind and smoke.

Spring opens the hundred flowers in one puff—The letting go is a bit dangerous.

Power pulls back nine bulls in one yank—The gathering in is too fast.

It's hopeless—the mud and sand can't be cleared away—One's own eyes are originally true.

Clearly blocking off the eye of the sweet spring—They go wrong because of teachers.

If suddenly it burst forth, it would freely flow—Even throwing over the meditation seat couldn't be considered strange.

Hongzhi also said, "Dangerous."—Throwing down the staff, Wansong said, "I let the first move go."

39 ZHAOZHOU'S "WASH YOUR BOWL"

Introduction When food comes you open your mouth; when sleep comes you close your eyes. As you wash your face you find your nose, when you take off your shoes you feel your feet. At that time, if you miss what's being said, take a torch and make a special search deep in the night. How can you attain union?

Case A monk asked Zhaozhou, "I have just entered the monastery: please give me some guidance."
Zhaozhou said, "Have you had breakfast yet?"
The monk said, "Yes, I've eaten."
Zhaozhou said, "Then go wash your bowl."

Commentary Catching a dragon with a straight hook is already being dull; three inches apart from the hook is already being taken over by the boatman and Jiashan. I do not say people of these times have no share, but generally they swallow the hook out of greed for the bait.
See how that Zhaozhou doesn't break the fishing pole, and doesn't kick over the boatman either: as he sits at leisure on the stone bridge, passing the time by the log crossing, naturally there are those who climb up the bank and fall into his hands.
The original record has it that this monk hereby attained enlightenment; one might say, 'you may sport with the line on the pole—without disturbing the clear waves the meaning is naturally distinct.' Zhaozhou and Mr. Ren (the whale catcher) got their wish before; Tiantong strikes the boat (to drive the fish into the net) afterwards:

Verse   *Breakfast over, the direction is to wash the bowl;*
        Opened up, the mind ground meets of itself.
        And now, a guest of the monastery, having studied to the full—
        But was there enlightenment in there or not?

Commentary   Lingyun awakened to the Way upon seeing peach blossoms; he presented a verse to Guishan, who said, "Those who enter by way of conditions never regress." Xuansha heard of this and said, "Lingyun's quite correct indeed, but I dare say the old brother's not through yet." Lingyun heard of this and said, "Are you through yet?" Xuansha said, "Now you've got it."

Tiantong eulogizes this monk's attaining enlightenment, the meeting of the mind ground. The monk, having just entered the monastery, is extolled for his great enlightenment and great penetration, a guest of the monastery who has studied to the full. "But is there enlightenment in there or not?" Here this is called a searching question. Xuedou said, "Fundamentally there's no delusion or enlightenment—such are numerous as flax seed; I admit only Lingyun as an adept." Xuansha said he was not through yet, Xuedou admits him alone as an adept—carrying a board across the shoulder, each sees only one side. But tell me—'wash your bowl'—did the monk have enlightenment or not? Peace is originally the accomplishment of the general, but the general is not allowed to see peace.

Added
Sayings
/Case

I've just entered the monastery, please guide me—The monastery isn't bad for you.
Have you had breakfast yet?—Unrefined gold, a jewel in the rough.
I've eaten—A long-experienced monk is not as good as this monk.
Go wash your bowl—Don't cast doubt.

Added
Sayings
/Verse

Breakfast over, the direction is to wash the bowl—The opportunity goes by so fast it is hard to meet.
Opened up, the mind ground meets of itself—It's not just today.
And now, a guest of the monastery, having studied to the full—As before, after eating gruel he washes his bowl.
But was there enlightenment in there?—One person transmits a falsehood, ten thousand transmit it as truth.

40 YUNMEN, HOUBAI AND HOUHEI

Introduction   Where the wheel of potential turns, even the eye of wisdom is confused; when the jewel mirror is opened, not so much as a mote of dust can get past. Opening the fist, not falling to the ground, dealing with beings in accord with the time, when two sword blades cross, how's the exchange?

Case   Yunmen asked Jianfeng, "An answer, please, teacher."
Jianfeng said, "Have you come to me yet?"
Yunmen said, "Then I'm late."
Jianfeng said, "Is that so? Is that so?"
Yunmen said, "I thought I was like Houbai the crook: you're like Houhei, even worse!"

Commentary   King Milinda asked Venerable Nagasena, "I am going to pose a question; can you answer?" Nagasena said, "Please ask your question." The king said, "I have already asked." Nagasena said, "I have already answered." The king said, "What did you answer?" Nagasena said, "What did you ask?" The king said, "I asked nothing." Nagasena said, "I answered nothing." This can still be investigated, but Yunmen's question is like crashing lightning in a clear sky; Jianfeng's answer is like rolling thunder on dry ground. When they both let go and both gather in, then you see there is a head, there is a tail; this is why none but a Chan monk would know, none but an adept could see. Master Tiantong has entered deeply into this gate; his verse says,

Verse   *Bowstring and arrow-notch interlock,*
Jewels in the net face each other:
Shooting one hundred percent bullseyes, no arrows are wasted;

Unifying all the various reflections, each light is without impediment.
Attaining total mastery of words and phrases,
Dwelling in the meditation of roaming at play:
Subtle is the interplay therein of relative and complete—
It is necessary to be like this, free in all ways.

Commentary   When the arrow is on the bowstring, it cannot but be shot; this eulogizes the active point in Yunmen's question, which cannot be touched. "Jewels in the net face each other" eulogizes Jianfeng's answer, wherein guest and host commingle—the question is in the answer, the answer is in the question. "Shooting one hundred percent bullseyes, no arrows are wasted" eulogizes Yunmen's "Then I'm late." Zhijiao said, "It's like someone shooting at the ground—there's no way he can't hit it."

Merging lights enmesh each other, phenomena do not hinder one another—here he eulogizes Jianfeng's "Is that so?" According to the commentary on the *Flower Ornament Scripture,* in the palace of Indra is a net made of jewels threaded together, their lights and reflections mutually reflecting, multiplying infinitely. This versifies the general meaning of the whole case; it's not necessarily arranged to correspond phrase by phrase, tuning the lute with the bridge glued down.

Yunmen said, "I thought I was Houbai; you're (bad as) Houhei!" In the Sui dynasty there was a Houbai, styled Junsu; he was a fast-talking liar. (The great general Yang Xiu knew of him; he wrote a book recording the unusual, very detailed on communication between humans and spirits, also worthy of respect.) In the Tang dynasty there was Li Bai, who was good at poetry; later there was a Li Zhi, who imitated him, but was not at all in the same class—people talked of him as a laugh. Here it says Houhei, and this is in the same category; some books say, "I'm already Houbai; you're even Houhei." What it means is 'even worse.'

There are three kinds of spells conferring total mastery: those with many syllables, those with one syllable, and those with none; they totally contain all the teachings. Meditation is right concentration. Tiantong's 'relative and complete' is like phenomena and inner reality. National Teacher Zhengguan said, "Inner reality is real, words are relative; when words are born, inner reality is lost." Tiantai's *Stopping and Seeing* says,

"The three dots of the (Sanskrit) letter *i* of reality is not like the vertical of marks on water or like the horizontal of a series of fires. Also, vertically going through the three times is called 'high,' horizontally extending throughout the ten directions is called 'wide'—therefore the *Lotus Scripture* says, "That chariot is high and wide.'" Tiantong comprehends the ocean of the teachings besides, clearly penetrating the sky of meaning. Yunmen and Jianfeng set up an unlettered tablet; Tiantong, singing a song, puts it in a wordless poem. Yang Xiu, seeing his young wife, in one look knew beauty.

Added Sayings /Case

Yunmen asked Jianfeng, "An answer, please, teacher."—His empty head has no top.
Jianfeng said, "Have you come to me yet?"—He's already answered you.
Then I'm late—Concede, and there's more than enough.
Is that so?—Just don't interpret so.
I thought I was Houbai; you're even Houhei, yet!—Among experts there's no expert.

Added Sayings /Verse

Bowstring and arrow-notch interlock—Responding universally, high and low.
Jewels in the net face each other—Meeting the source right and left.
Shooting one hundred percent bullseyes, no arrows are wasted—Responsive preaching has a standard.
Unifying all the various reflections, each light is without impediment—Shining alone, without partiality.
Attaining total mastery of words and phrases—When you speak a word, it becomes a chapter.
Dwelling in the meditation of roaming at play—All activities accord with the rhythm.
Subtle is the interplay therein of relative and complete—Like a jewel rolling in a bowl.
It is necessary to be like this, free in all ways—Observe when the order is in effect.

41 LUOPU ABOUT TO DIE

Introduction   Sometimes out of loyalty and sincerity denying oneself, the pain and cramp is hard to express. Sometimes calamity extends to other people but one doesn't take responsibility. When about to pass away, we are cut down cheaply; at the very end there is the most care, tears come from a painful gut, it is impossible to hide or escape any more. But is there anyone who has cool eyes?

Case   When Luopu was about to die, he said to the assembly, "I have one thing to ask you people. If *this* is so, this is adding a head on top of your head. If it is not so, this is cutting off your head seeking life."
At that time the head monk said, "The green mountain is always moving its feet; you don't hang a lamp in broad daylight."
Luopu said, "What time is this to make such a speech?"
A certain elder, Yancong, came forth and said, "Leaving these two paths, I request the teacher not to ask."
Luopu said, "Not yet—speak again."
Yancong said, "I don't care if you can say it all or not."
Yancong said, "I have no attendant to answer the teacher."

That evening he called elder Yancong: "Your answer today was most reasonable. You should experientially realize the saying of my late teacher, 'before the eyes there are no things—that meaning is before the eyes. That is not something before the eyes, not in reach of the ears and eyes.' Which phrases are guest, which phrases are host? If you can pick them out, I'll impart the robe and bowl to you."
Yancong said, "I don't understand."
Luopu said, "You should understand."

Yancong said, "I really don't."
Luopu shouted and said, "How miserable!"
A monk asked, "What is the teacher's meaning?"
Luopu said, "The boat of compassion is not rowed over pure waves: over precipitous straits it is wasted effort to set out a wooden goose."

Commentary When Luopu was about to die, he was too kind. The head monk bared his heart entirely, but was blamed for being untimely; Yancong didn't move his lips, but Luopu allowed as he should understand. (Luopu) could only sift and strain over and over—what a pity, just to sink into oblivion. Kepin was willingly fined the price of congee; the blind donkey purposely destroyed the eye of the true teaching.

Xuanjiao said, "Tell me, did elder Yancong really not understand? Or did he fear that the bowl would defile him?" Thus the records of the Chan transmission include Yancong among the successors to the Dharma.

Luopu once instructed the group, "You must directly realize the source outside of the teachings; don't grasp principle within words." A monk asked, "What is practice of the inconceivable like?" Luopu said, "The green mountain is always moving its feet; the bright sun doesn't shift its orb." When we use this to test them, the head monk and Yancong can be seen clearly. As for Luopu's part, is there after all anyone to take up after him? After a hundred years, after all there's Tiantong: his verse says,

Verse *The bait is clouds, the hook the moon, fishing in the clear harbor:*
Old in years, alone at heart, he hasn't got a fish yet.
One song "leaving the clamor," coming on back:
On the Milo river, the only sober man.

Commentary An ancient used a rainbow as a pole, the new moon as a hook, a piece of cloud for bait: in the clear waters one can thus pole the boat of compassion; in the precipitous straits one must first release a wooden goose.

In the instructions for sitting meditation written by Master Wuyun of Hangchow it says, "Follow the flow through the ravine straits; don't get stuck with the wooden goose." The water of ravine straits is steep and dangerous, flowing so fast that if two boats collide on it they would surely be smashed; therefore they first cut a piece of wood and float it downstream—this is called a wooden goose. The different explanations given in various places are hardly reliable; none is as good as these meditation instructions for evidence (of the meaning of 'wooden goose').

"Old in years, alone at heart, he hasn't got a fish yet"—those who do not know think this means that Luopu had no successors, but in all Luopu found eleven people, like Wuya, Qingfeng, and others, who were all white-browed old adepts.

A poem by Master Na of Momo hermitage says,

> The sharp famous wine of present and past—
> Those it intoxicated were all outstanding heroes:
> The emaciated man by the marsh's edge
> Is not worthy of being considered the only sober one.

Qu Yuan was styled Ping; he served King Huai of Chu as the chief of the royal families. Denounced by Geshang, he was demoted and sent to Changsha. He walked alone by the riverside; he told the fishermen, "All the world is drunk; I alone am sober. All the world is polluted; I alone am pure." He plunged into the Milo river and died. The river is in the Luo district of Tan province. The classic *Leaving the Clamor* included in the *Literary Selections* was composed by Qu Yuan.

When Luopu was about to die, Yancong tarried dully. Though Luopu went fishing, he didn't get a fraction of a cent; in direct confrontation, after all water and rice didn't mix. Do you understand? If one doesn't get enfeoffed as a baron, then one is free.

Added Sayings / Case

When Luopu was about to die, he said to the group, "I have one thing to ask you people."—He's still talking military strategy.

If this is so, this is adding a head to your head—This way won't do. If it's not so, this is cutting off your head seeking life—Not this way won't do either.

At that time the head monk said, "The green mountain is always moving its feet; you don't hang a lamp in broad daylight."—If it's spoken clearly, it's all the more difficult to get out.

Luopu said, "What time is this to make such a speech?"—He's lost his money and incurred punishment.

A certain elder Yancong came up and said, "Leaving these two paths, I request the teacher not to ask."—Easy to open is the mouth of end and beginning; hard to maintain is the heart of the dead of winter.

Luopu said, "Not yet—speak again."—Poems must be recited twice to see their worth.

I can't say it all—Not letting people see it makes it all the more charming.

I don't care if you can say it all or not—Letting a bottomless one come, he can't help not stopping.

I have no attendant to answer you—The shadowing grass is around him.

That evening Luopu called elder Yancong; "Your answer today was most reasonable."—He just practices sticking it on his head.

You should experientially realize the saying of my late teacher, "Before the eyes there are no things—the meaning is before the eyes."—If you cut down the cassia tree on the moon, the pure light must be even more.

That is not something before the eyes, not in reach of the ears and eyes—When the moon sets, come to see me.

Which phrases are guest, which phrases are host? If you can pick them out, I'll impart the robe and bowl to you—Holding a stick, he calls the dog.

Yancong said, "I don't understand."—He's going to make a high mountain.

I really don't—He doesn't bring a single load of earth.

Luopu shouted and said, "How miserable!"—He cheats ordinary people.

A monk asked, "What do you mean?"—Where the torch was lost, greasy char is found.

Luopu said, "The boat of compassion is not rowed over pure waves; over precipitous straits it is wasted effort to set out a wooden goose."—Flaunting skill, he becomes clumsy.

Added *The bait is clouds, the hook the moon, fishing in the clear harbor—If you*
Sayings *don't enter the frightening waves, you'll hardly find a fish that you want.*
/ Verse *Old in years, alone at heart, he hasn't got a fish yet—Why so hurried?*
One song leaving the clamor, coming on back—Where?
On the Milo river, the only sober man—Luopu's still around.

42 NANYANG'S "WATER PITCHER"

Introduction   Washing the bowl, adding water to the pitcher, are all aspects of the teaching, buddha-work; hauling firewood and carrying water are all miraculous powers of sublime functions. Why can't you emanate light and make the earth move?

Case   A monk asked National Teacher Zhong of Nanyang, "What is the Vairocana of one's own body?"
The national teacher said, "Bring me the pitcher of clean water."
The monk brought the pitcher: the national teacher said, "Put it back where it was before."
The monk again asked, "What is Vairocana in one's own body?"
The national teacher said, "The ancient buddha is long gone."

Commentary   Shishuang asked Daowu, "What is enlightenment that meets the eye?" Daowu called to a novice, who responded; Daowu said, "Add some water to the washbasin." After a while he asked Shishuang, "What did you just ask?" As Shishuang was about to repeat it, Daowu went back to his room; Shishuang thereupon had insight. Daowu first used a 'body-block' saying, then afterwards used a 'body-throw' gesture. As he didn't run afoul of the point and hurt his hand, Shishuang had an insight.
The National Teacher, because of his kindness and compassion, had a conversation that went down into the weeds; but those who appreciate his benevolence are few. Tiantong therefore gathers flowers and scoops water; his verse says,

Verse

Birds' coursing in the sky,
Fishes' being in the water:
In rivers and lakes forgetting,
In clouds and sky they get their will.
The doubting mind—a single thread:
Before the face, a thousand miles.
Knowing benevolence, requiting benevolence—
How many people do?

Commentary

The flight of birds in the sky, the fish in the water; their roosts are ever more peaceful, their life is ever more harmonious. Zhuangzi said, "When the spring is dry the fish together on the land puff at each other to moisten each other with wetness from their mouths—this does not compare to forgetting each other in rivers and lakes." Chan Master Tonghui Gui from Baichao said, "It is like flying birds in the sky—they don't know the sky is their home; the fish swimming in the water forget the water is their life." Guifeng said, "The fish are not conscious of water, people are not conscious of air, illusion is not conscious of reality, enlightenment is not conscious of emptiness."

Usually the personal Vairocana, complete pure awareness, manifests form in the human realm; as soon as it is questioned, suddenly a shadow appears—you forget the blessings you have received, turn away from your parents and go to strangers. Ultimately if he can get rid of the spiritual seat, only then can the son take up the father's work. But tell me, what is the father's work? When brought up, there's nothing that's not it. Don't doubt its use.

Added Sayings / Case

What is Vairocana in one's own body?—Have you changed your name?
Bring the water pitcher—Don't forget the story.
The monk brought the pitcher—Don't misapprehend.
Put it back where it was before—The teaching is reiterated.
Again, what is Vairocana in one's own body?—Where are you going and coming?
The ancient buddha is long gone—Not far from here.

181

Added
Sayings
/ Verse

Birds' coursing in the sky—Encountering it everywhere.
Fishes' being in the water—Using it right and left.
In rivers and lakes forgetting—This side, that side.
In clouds and sky they get their will—No right or wrong.
The doubting mind—*a single thread*—It's just on this mountain.
Before the face, a thousand miles—The clouds are so deep you don't know where you are.
Knowing benevolence, requiting benevolence—Think of this, stay with this.
How many people do?—One child has personally accomplished it.

43 LUOSHAN'S "ARISING AND VANISHING"

Introduction One touch of the philosophers' stone turns iron into gold; one word of the ultimate principle transforms an ordinary man into a sage. If you know that gold and iron are not two, that ordinary and sage are fundamentally the same, then after all you'll have no use for it; but tell me, what one touch is it?

Case Luoshan asked Yantou, "When arising and vanishing go on unceasingly, what then?"
Yantou shouted and said, "Whose arising and vanishing is it?"

Commentary Chan master Daojian of Luoshan in Shen province first asked Shishuang, "When arising and vanishing go on unceasingly, what then?" Sishuang said, "You must be cold ashes, a dead tree, one thought for ten thousand years, box and lid joining, pure and spotlessly clear." Luoshan didn't get it, so he went and asked Yantou; Yantou shouted and said, "Whose arising and vanishing is it?" At this Luoshan awakened. Generally, Yantou just esteemed clarity of insight; Shishuang set up a 'dead tree hall'—he demanded that one personally arrive once first.

Haven't you seen how Ruiyan asked Yantou, "What is the fundamentally constant principle?" Yantou said, "Moving." Ruiyan said, "How is it when moving?" Yantou said, "You don't see the fundamentally constant principle." Ruiyan stood there thinking; Yantou said, "If you agree, you've not yet escaped the senses; if you don't agree, you're forever sunk in birth and death," and Ruiyan too attained enlightenment.

Yantou was an outstanding spirit, beyond the ordinary; in awakening students, he accomplished his purpose with a sharpness that was no less

183

than Deshan's. Later he produced the Dharma-jewel of Luoshan—ice is colder than water. This is what Guishan meant by "I only value your insight; I don't ask about your activity."

Luoshan's question is a model for everyone; and beginners these days time and again make their living in here—like pushing down a gourd on water, they suppress afflictions. Zhijiao said, "Don't be a companion of mind; when mindless, the mind is naturally at rest. If you take mind as a partner, when moving you'll be fooled by mind—without it, there is no deluded mind. When the Patriarch came from the West, directly pointing to the human mind so they could see its nature and attain buddhahood, was he teaching you to be bandits escorting a thief, to recognize the servant as the master?" Luoshan's question missed the real and grasped the false; Yantou's scolding merged with the false as the real itself. If it were me, I would stop after shouting; there is still something beyond real and false.

In the *Heroic March Scripture* Ananda says, "The Realized One now is probing the whereabouts of the mind, and I am using the mind to investigate and seek it; therefore that which seeks is what I take to be mind." The Buddha said, "Tsk! Ananda, this is not your mind." Ananda, startled, got up from his seat, joined his palms and said to the Buddha, "If this is not my mind, what should it be called?" The Buddha said to Ananda, "This is an empty conception of form of sense data before you—it confuses your real nature. It is due to your having recognized a thief as your son since beginningless time, losing your fundamental constant thus you experience transmigration." This shout is like the diamond sword; Yantou's shout is like a lion crouching on the ground, the power of the great function of his full majesty, which cannot be fooled.

Layman Pang said, "One gang of six thieves, you fool people completely, life after life. Now I know you, and will not be your neighbors. If you don't submit to me, everywhere I go I'll inform people all about you, causing your road to be cut off. If you agree to submit to me, then I won't discriminate; I'll stay together with you, and together witness birthlessness and deathlessness."

Yantou's saying, "Whose arising and vanishing is it?" is the same approach as Yunyan's lifting the broom up and saying, "Which moon is this?" Tiantong esteems his ability to produce transformation, and again speaks a verse:

Verse   *Severing old entangling vines*
Opening up a fox lair
A leopard covers itself with fog to change its spots
A dragon rides the thunder to change its bones
Bah!
Arising and vanishing in profusion—what is it?

Commentary   Cutting off the words, slicing away the intent of the question, simultaneously illumining and functioning, taking away both person and environment—Yantou had the action that transcends the teacher.

Yangzi said, "A sage is distinct as a tiger—his markings are clearly outstanding. A superior man is distinct as a leopard—his markings are fine. An eloquent man is distinct as a fox—his markings are clumped together. A fox changes into a leopard, a leopard changes into a tiger."

The dark leopard of the south mountains, shrouded in fog, changes its spots. In the *Biographies of Women of the Ages* by Liu Xiang of Han it says, "Dao Dazi worked as a potter for three years; he didn't become famous, but the prosperity of his house increased threefold. His wife, embracing her child, cried; her mother-in-law was angry, considering that unlucky. The wife said, 'I have heard that in the South Mountains there is a dark leopard; it hides in the fog and doesn't eat for seven days, to give luster to its coat and form to its spots. As for dogs and pigs, they are not selective about food, therefore they get fat; because they're fat they incur calamity.' As it turned out, in a year's time Dao was executed."

According to the *Records of the Extraordinary* recounted by Ren Fang, in the summer of the seventh year of the reign of Emperor Hui of the Han dynasty thunder shook the south mountains, the woods blazed, and the earth was burnt to umber. After a violent rain they found dragon bones.

Luoshan, meeting up with a bandit who destroyed his household, made a declaration of his case; Yantou summoned him and settled it. But tell me, where was the summons and settlement? 'Tch! Arising and vanishing in profusion'—who else could it be?

Added Sayings /Case

When arising and vanishing go on unceasingly, what then?—Diamond rubbing a clay mannikin's back.

Yantou shouted and said—Stars fall, clouds scatter.

Whose arising and vanishing is it?—If you know, it's not inimical.

Added Sayings /Verse

Severing old entangling vines—Producing even more branches and creepers.

Opening up a fox lair—Spitting out more stupid slobber.

A leopard covers itself with fog to change its spots—It sheds its skin.

A dragon rides the thunder to change its bones—Especially changing the shell of its body.

Bah—At one shout myriad actions cease; for three days, both ears are deaf.

Arising and vanishing in profusion—what is it?—A good guest has no strange companions.

44 XINGYANG'S "GARUDA"

Introduction   A lion strikes an elephant, a garuda strikes a dragon. Flying and running, they still distinguish ruler and subject; a patchrobed monk should remember guest and host. But how can someone who brazenly affronts the authority of heaven be judged?

Case   A monk asked Master Xingyang Pou, "A dragon king comes out of the sea, sky and earth are tranquil—how is direct presentation?"
The master said, "The garuda, king of birds, takes command of the universe—who can stick his head out here?"
The monk said, "Suppose one suddenly appears, then what?"
Xingyang said, "It's like a falcon catching a pigeon. If you don't realize, check in front of the tower, then for the first time you'll know the real."
The monk said, "If so, then I'll fold my hands on my chest and retreat three paces."
Xingyang said, "You blind turtle under the seat of Mount Sumeru! Don't wait for another scarring from a rap on the head."

Commentary   Chan Master Qingpou of Xingyang Mountain in Ying province succeeded to Dayang Mingan. Mingan had fifteen successors, but all of them died before he did; later, through Fushan Yuanjian, he got Master Qing of Touzi. Xingyang was one of the fifteen—thus he was an elder brother of Master Qing.
This monk's question was like the contest of Lautacha and Shariputra at the time of the establishment of the Jetavana Grove: Lautacha made a

187

dragon appear, in order to harm Shariputra; Shariputra produced a garuda, which caught the dragon, rent it open and ate it. A dragon is the greatest of scaled creatures, but nonetheless the garuda eats nothing but dragons.

The lord of Ping Yuan, Zhao Sheng, served as minister for Kings Huiwen and Xiaocheng of the kingdom of Zhao: at his house he built a multi-storied tower which faced the homes of the populace. Among the people was a lame man; a handsome man laughed at him, and the lame one asked for the head of the handsome one: the lord agreed, but didn't act; half of his house guests left. The lord beheaded a convict instead, but the guests adamantly refused to come. So finally he cut off the head of the handsome man who had laughed at the lame man, and hung it in front of the tower, to prove it was real; after a year guests gathered.

This family style of the Dong succession does not esteem the personal application of beating and shouting; it calls for temporary use of a bystander to convey the message. This monk's crime was not repeated; only thus could he interchange.

But do you know? A (painless) cattail whip, showing disgrace, is most difficult to go against; a drawing of a jail made on the ground isn't capable of deceiving. Official law is like a furnace, mind is like iron. Tiantong henceforth uses his hammer and anvil:

Verse   *The imperial decree comes down,*
          The commanding order's distinct:
          Within the heartland, the emperor,
          Outside the borders, the general.
          Without awaiting the thunder to roust the insects,
          How could one know the wind stops the coursing clouds?
          A continuous weave under the loom—naturally there's a gold needle and jade thread:
          Before the seal is wide open emptiness—originally there's no writing.

Commentary The imperial decree extends throughout the land; the king doesn't travel around. In the *Black Robe* section of the *Book of Rites* it says, "When the king's words are like thread, their issue is like yarn; when the king's words are like yarn, their issue is like rope. Therefore a great man does not speak frivolous words."

The dragon leaves the ocean, the garuda is in command. Once the commanding order is distinct, lord and minister establish their positions. Feng Tang said, "In high antiquity when a king dispatched a general, he knelt down and pushed the chariot, saying, 'Inside the gate, I drive; outside the gate, the general drives.'" Wei Zhao said, "This is the gate of the walls of the capital city."

Thunder startles and rousts the insects—this part versifies how the monk went too far in searching: not awaiting the time in the second month when the insects are stirred up, he already rouses the dragon's head, not knowing that the floating clouds would go along following the dragon, and that they'd be utterly stopped by the awesome wind of the garuda's magnificent wings—unawares he bumped his head. Some say that (it means) "If not for the monk's verbal defeat, how could Xingyang's active point be revealed?"—but then the words "without awaiting" and "how could one know" don't easily follow at all. "A continuous weave under the loom"—this is not referring to the functioning of a sharp wit: it means that under a weaving of brocade there must be a skillful housewife's needle and thread. My late master Xueyan once cited, "As soon as the narrow-eyed golden needle shows its nose, the long-topped jade thread goes finely through the hole." This is the bloodline of the Dongshan succession; unless you are one within it, it is not easy to know.

Using a seal, you don't set it on the wind; if the seal stamps space, it doesn't show any mark. Cang Jie gazed at the round, curved form of a constellation of stars above, examined the markings of turtles and forms of bird tracks below—he collected myriad beauties from all over and put them together to make writing. Later two forms of writing were modeled on polliwogs. The historian Zhou of King Xuan of Zhou created the 'large script' writing and Li Si, prime minister of Qin, made the 'small script' writing; nowadays seal script is called 'square and dense.' Now tell me, did Xingyang carve or not? 'The pure jewel is originally flawless; carving a design ruins its superior quality.'

*Added
Sayings
/Case*

**A dragon king comes out of the sea, sky and earth are tranquil—how
is direct presentation?**—A curled prawn with scales, a mudfish with
horns.

**The garuda takes command of the universe—who can stick his head
out here?**—Unfolding his wings, dashing through the clouds of the six
compounds, beating the wind he stirs up the waters of the four oceans.

Suppose one suddenly appears, then what?—You may bust a gut.

**It's like a falcon catching a pigeon. If you don't realize, check in front
of the tower, then you'll know the real**—Though much exhorted, he
won't listen.

If so, then I'll fold my hands and retreat three paces—He still awaits
the second mallet blow.

**You blind turtle under the seat of Mount Sumeru! Don't wait for
another scarring from a (failing mark) on the forehead**—A second
offense is not permitted.

*Added
Sayings
/Verse*

The imperial decree comes down—Listen to the message of the sage.

The commanding order is distinct—Those who violate it are decapitated.

Within the heartland, the emperor—The lord faces a thousand countries.

Outside the borders, the general—He occupies one region alone.

Without awaiting the thunder to roust the insects—Even getting up before
dawn . . .

How could one know the wind stops the coursing clouds?—. . . there's already
someone who's been traveling by night.

A continuous weave under the loom—naturally there's a gold needle and jade
thread—It's hard to fool those with eyes.

Before the seal is wide open emptiness—originally there's no writing—The
meaning of the graphs is clear.

45 FOUR SECTIONS OF THE *ENLIGHTENMENT SCRIPTURE*

Introduction   The presently forming public case is just based on the immediate present: the fundamental family style does not aim beyond the fundamental. If you forcibly set up divisions and foolishly expend effort, it's all drawing eyebrows for chaos, putting a handle on a bowl. How can you become peaceful?

Case   The *Scripture of Perfect Enlightenment* says, "At all times do not produce delusive thoughts, also don't try to stop and annihilate deluded states of mind; in realms of false conception don't add knowledge, and don't find reality in no knowledge."

Commentary   Guifeng, classifying this section, called it "the deluded mind suddenly attaining realization" and also named it "forgetting mind, entering awakening." I add the word 'no' to each of the four clauses, meaning, "not producing, not annihilating, not knowing, not distinguishing." These four lines everywhere are considered illnesses; here they become medicines. Now as for what everywhere is considered illness, not producing delusive thoughts—is this not 'burnt sprouts, ruined seed'? Not annihilating deluded states of mind—is this not 'losing your life while taking care of illness'? Not applying knowledge—is this not 'being temporarily absent, like a dead man'? Not finding reality—is this not 'presuming upon the enlightened nature, enshrouding true thusness'? Now tell me, what are the four medicines? It is necessary for Tiantong to concoct them and bring them:

191

Verse   *Magnificent, clearly outstanding:*
Serene, at ease.
Clamor pierces the head;
Quiet is where to tread.
Underfoot, the thread breaks, and I am free:
The spot of mud on the nose is gone—you don't have to chop.
'Don't budge'—
On a thousand-year-old scrap of paper medicine's compounded.

Commentary   When Huangbo first called on Baizhang, Baizhang said, "Magnificent, clearly outstanding—what did you come for?" Huangbo said, "Magnificent, clearly outstanding—not for anything else." Magnificent, outstanding, serene, at ease—these are all characteristics of a great man. In a forest of shields and spears, freely going directly through, in a thicket of brambles, going right on with open hands; no five-colored string under the feet, no crossroad barrier on the tongue, no trace of mud on the nose, no gold dust in the eyes—is this not a peaceful, happy life? Try taking Tiantong's three words 'do not budge' and substitute them for my four 'no's and then you will see that the one-word teaching cannot be completely written down even with an ocean of ink.

Deshan said, "The whole canon is old paper for wiping filth"—this is because those who already comprehend fear to pierce oxhide; a prescription for compounding medicines on thousand-year-old paper is because those who don't yet understand unavoidably block their eyes. Cijiao said, "The *Scripture of Complete Enlightenment* and the *Heroic March Scripture* are my constant companions." From the World Honored One's demise up till 1220 has already been two thousand, one hundred and seventy years; is it just thousand-year-old paper?

According to the *Biographies of the Wizards,* Ge You carved a wooden ram and rode up Sui Mountain on it: later he met Fu Zhong, who said, "If the strings under your feet aren't cut off, you won't be free." This happens to accord with Yongjia's "Let go of the gross elements, don't grasp: within the nature of quiescence, drink and eat as you may. All activities are impermanent, all is empty; this is the great complete awakening of the realized ones." Even so, there is still lacking the chant of 'how can we transcend?'

Added Sayings /Case	**At all times don't produce delusive thoughts**—No. **Also don't try to annihilate deluded states of mind**—No. **In realms of false conceptions don't apply knowledge**—No. **Don't find reality in no knowledge**—No.
Added Sayings /Verse	*Magnificent, clearly outstanding*—If you go on investigating further, you'll have to say the words 'dull and inconspicuous.' *Serene, at ease*—Nose stuck up to the heavens. *Clamor pierces the head*—When the bed is narrow, lie down first. *Quiet is where to tread*—When the gruel is thin, sit down later. *Underfoot, the thread breaks, and I am free*—Walking freely to the land of the immortals. *The spot of mud on the nose is gone—you don't have to chop*—Both get a break. *'Don't budge'*—Already this is arbitrarily administering a disturbing measure. *On a thousand-year-old scrap of paper medicine's compounded*—There's great miraculous effect.

46 DESHAN'S "COMPLETION OF STUDY"

Introduction   The clear ground where there's not an inch of grass for ten thousand miles deludes people; the clear sky without a fleck of cloud in the eight directions fools you. Even though this is using a wedge to remove a wedge, it doesn't prevent taking space and hanging it in space. A single mallet on the back of the brain—particularly observe appropriate technique.

Case   **Great Master Yuanming of Deshan said to the assembly, "When you get to the ultimate end, you just find the buddhas of all times have their mouths 'hung on the wall.' There is still someone who laughs, ha! ha! If you know this one, your task of study is finished."**

Commentary   The ninth generation master at Deshan in Ding province was Great Master Yuanming; his initiatory name was Yuanmi. Among Yunmen's successors, only this master's lineage was most widespread. This master invented the 'three phrases'—'containing the universe,' 'cutting off all streams,' and 'following the waves'—those who nowadays transmit them as the three phrases of Yunmen are not careful in their research.

One day he addressed the assembly, "When you get to the ultimate end, you just find the buddhas of all times have their mouths 'hung on the wall.'" This says that the form of the universal eternal tongue cannot be comprehended by verbal understanding. "There is still someone who laughs, ha! ha!" But tell me, who is it, laughing at what? "If you know this one, your task of study is finished." But really there is still something more: Master Touzi Yiqing brought this up and said, "Completely concealing the moon in the sky of Chu, still retaining the stars over the land of Han." I say, the cart is gone—what oil can would you borrow? This should be said to one at the top of the pole stepping forward.

Master Baofeng Zhao said, "You must be like a man who has utterly died; having died, die again." A monk said, "Is this not returning to life from the midst of death?" The master said, "Just die, don't live. You just go hurry to defecate while you're eating; you haven't yet eaten, so why are you asking about defecating?" This values great cessation, great rest, personally arriving to realization on your own. Being able to explain ten feet is not as good as putting one foot into practice. But how can you explain what cannot be practiced? Ask of Tiantong; his verse says,

Verse *Gathering in,*
Holding closed the throat.
Wind polishes, clouds wipe.
The waters are chill, the weather is autumn.
Don't say brocade-colored fish lacks rich taste.
Fishing through the ocean waves, one hook of moon.

Commentary Without Yuanming's address to the assembly being digested, Tiantong adds the word 'gathering'—along with Yuanming he's stuffed inside a cloth bag. Huisi said, "The Buddhas of the past, present, and future have been completely swallowed in one gulp by me—where are there still sentient beings to save?" This is impervious to leaking water, the road of ordinary and holy being cut off. At this very moment, the completely empty cosmos is like an ancient mirror; you can use the raging wind that destroys the aeon to polish it, and use the clouds of the golden treasury that forms the aeon to wipe it: water and sky are one color, clouds of moon merge their light—all of these depict pure spotless clarity. Here words are bland and tasteless; it is like a crescent moon hook baited with clouds—the dragons and fish cannot swallow it. Cheng Tang (founder of the ancient Shang dynasty) prayed over his net (hoping all would enter it), going along with your will; Lu Wang let down his hook, believing his own cause. Haven't you heard the saying, "Husked millet from the

mountain fields, wild vegetables and thin yellow soup—you may eat if
you will; if you don't eat, you may go east or west."

<table>
<tr><td>Added
Sayings
/Case</td><td>When you get to the ultimate end—There's still this.
You just find the buddhas of all times have their mouths hung on the wall—Stop and have a meal.
There is still someone who laughs—Who is it?
If you know this one—What does he look like?
Your task of study is finished—Give him a cup of tea to drink.</td></tr>
</table>

<table>
<tr><td>Added
Sayings
/Verse</td><td>Gathering in—Where will you put it?
Holding closed the throat—Just the time to flip over and breathe out.
Wind polishes, clouds wipe—Even the finest dust must be removed.
The waters are chill, the weather is autumn—Forming one whole.
Don't say brocade fish lacks rich taste—The stink is not little.
Fishing through the ocean waves, one hook of moon—Without disturbing the clear waves, the meaning is of itself distinct.</td></tr>
</table>

47 ZHAOZHOU'S "CYPRESS TREE"

Introduction The cypress tree in the yard, the wind-blown flag on the pole—it's like one flower bespeaking a boundless spring, like one drop telling of the water of the ocean. The ancient Buddhas, born periodically, go far beyond the ordinary current, not falling into words and thought. How can you understand verbally?

Case **A monk asked Zhaozhou, "What is the living meaning of Chan Buddhism?**
Zhaozhou said, "The cypress tree in the yard."

Commentary One day Zhaozhou got up in the hall and said, "This matter clearly cannot be got out of, by immeasurably great men. When I went to Guishan, a monk asked what the living meaning of Chan is, and Guishan asked him to bring him a seat. If one would be a real teacher of the source, one must use the basic thing to deal with people." A monk then asked Zhaozhou what the living meaning of Chan Buddhism is; Zhaozhou said, "The cypress tree in the yard." The monk said, "Teacher, don't use an object to guide people." The master Zhaozhou said, "I'm not using an object to guide anyone." The monk said, "Then what's the meaning of Chan Buddhism?" Zhaozhou said, "The cypress tree in the yard."

Chan Master Huijiao went to Fayan's place; Fayan asked, "Where have you recently come from?" Huijiao said, "Zhaozhou." Fayan said, "I hear Zhaozhou has a saying, 'The cypress tree in the yard'—is it so?" Huijiao said, "No." Fayan said, "Everyone who's been around says a monk

197

asked him about the meaning of Chan and Zhaozhou said, 'The cypress tree in the yard'—how can you say no?" Huijiao said, "The late master really didn't say this; please don't slander him." Everywhere Huijiao was called Iron Beak Jiao. Master Shengmo used to have people go through this story first, to clear away their intellectual views; he once said, "The three mysteries and five ranks are all within it." Chan Master Zhenru Fang awakened to this story and went right into the abbot's room to see Chan Master Langya Guangzhao Jiao. Guangzhao asked, "How do you understand it?" Zhenru said, "All night the bed mat's warm—as soon as you awaken, dawn has come." Guangzhao approved. Zhenru's realization of this story was excellent; Tiantong's versification of this story is not bad either.

Verse   *The bank-eyebrows lined with snow,*
The river-eyes contain autumn;
The ocean-mouth drums waves,
The boat-tongue rides the current:
The ability to quell disorder,
The strategy for great peace—
Old Zhaozhou, old Zhaozhou:
Stirring up the monasteries, never yet stopping.
Uselessly expending effort, still the cart is made to fit the groove:
Originally without ability, still it fills the ravines and gullies.

Commentary   Over fourteen hundred months old, he's been through a lot of things; that's why his 'bank-eyebrows are lined with snow.' A man of ancient times represented eyebrows and eyes as crags and lightning; Tiantong, using 'river eyes' and 'ocean mouth,' makes a four-line verse—it is like seeing the living Zhaozhou pointing to the cypress tree. His eyebrows are like banks covered with white reed flowers; his eyes are like the blue of autumn water. An ancient verse says, "The rivers in the countryside are clearer than the blue of a monk's eye; the distant mountains are dark as the indigo of Buddha's head."

'The ocean-mouth drums waves, the boat-tongue rides the current'—waves can overturn a boat, a boat can ride the waves; one word can create a nation, one word can destroy a nation. Therefore next he uses a technique for quelling disorder and a formula for great peace. Zhaozhou once said, "Sometimes I take a blade of grass and use it as the sixteen-foot golden body; sometimes I take the sixteen-foot golden body and use it as a blade of grass." This saying originally solved someone's doubts, but now how many people have doubts about it! Did Zhaozhou want to stir up the monasteries?!

People see Zhaozhou's answer, responding immediately as the question is voiced, as if not needing effort—only Tiantong knows how he traveled for eighty years with the resolution to study from anyone who was better than him, even be it a three-year-old child; this was work done in free time, put to use in a busy time. Unless you're someone who has suffered hardship, you won't know that "The lying wheel has talent—it can cut off a hundred thoughts. Confronting situations, mind is not aroused; day by day enlightenment grows." The Sixth Patriarch said, "I have no talent, I don't cut off the hundred thoughts. Confronting situations, mind is repeatedly aroused—how can enlightenment grow?" When you look at it in this way, what about that which fills the ravines and gullies? Now it is thrown into West Lake. The clear wind of unburdening—to whom is it imparted?

Added Sayings /Case

A monk asked Zhaozhou, "What is the living meaning of Chan Buddhism?"—Much involvement in idle concern.
Zhaozhou said, "The cypress tree in the yard."—Fired brick strikes solid ice.

Added Sayings /Verse

The bank-eyebrows lined with snow—Eating salt as much as rice.
The river-eyes contain autumn—Hard to fool one bit.
The ocean-mouth drums waves—If there's a verbal expression, it's not the fundamental message.
The boat-tongue rides the current—Without words, cutting off holy and ordinary.
The ability to quell disorder—This is the cypress tree.

The strategy for great peace—This is the cypress tree too.
Old Zhaozhou, old Zhaozhou—Why don't you answer?
Stirring up the monasteries, never yet stopping—Tiantong is number two.
Uselessly expending effort, still the cart is made to fit the groove—Bringing it forth, he uses it fittingly.
Originally without ability, still it fills the ravines and gullies—Buying all the current fashions without putting down any money.

48 VIMALAKIRTI'S "NONDUALITY"

Introduction   Even if one's subtle function is universal, there's a place where one can't even begin to act. Even if one's eloquence is unhindered, there's a time when one can't open one's mouth. Longya was like a handless man boxing, Jiashan made a tongueless man able to speak. Who is it who can extricate oneself midway?

Case   **Vimalakirti asked Manjusri, "What is a Bodhisattva's method of entering nonduality?"**
Manjusri said, "According to my mind, in all things, no speech, no explanation, no direction and no representation, leaving behind all questions and answers—this is the method of entering nonduality."
Then Manjusri asked Vimalakirti, "We have each spoken. Now you should say, good man, what is a Bodhisattva's method of entry into nonduality?"
Vimalakirti was silent.

Commentary   The Sanskrit name Vimalakirti means Untainted Name, or Pure Name; his wife's name was Golden Lady, his son's name was Good Thought, and his daughter's name was Moonlike Beauty.
A monk asked Master Yunju Jian, "Vimalakirti was the Golden Grain Buddha—why did he listen to the teaching in the assembly of Shakyamuni Buddha?" Yunju said, "He didn't make a contest between others and self."
In the large version of the *Vimalakirti Scripture,* thirty-two thousand bodhisattvas each expounded methods of teaching nonduality; now there are only thirty-two bodhisattvas. At the end, Manjusri doesn't

have any ground to stick an awl into. Vimalakirti doesn't even have an awl.

Baofu Congzhan said, "Manjusri is like covering his ears stealing a bell, his strength exhausted on the Black River: Vimalakirti's silence is still not beyond a teaching method." I say, it is hard for people to get out of right and wrong. Baofu also said, "Even the great Vimalakirti, once seated by Manjusri, cannot get up even now." I say, if he wants to get up, what's the difficulty?—and I slap.

Langya Jiao said, "Manjusri's applauding in this way still is casting a divining ladle, listening to the empty sound. Vimalakirti remained silent—don't you folks go drilling tortoise shells or striking tiles (to 'augur')."

I say, the inept are not few—only Xuedou does not say after Manjusri's question that Vimalakirti remained silent at his seat; he just says, "What did Vimalakirti say?" He also says, "Seen through!" I say, not knowing how to be a ghost, he shows his body in broad daylight.

Tianyi Yihuai versified,

> Vimalakirti was not silent, did not pause;
> Argument that he remained seated turns out to be wrong.

Even now in various places when they see this matter brought up, they still say, "Remaining silent for a while, (so-and-so) said, . . ." A monk asked one teacher, "In the records it often says *liang jiu*, '(silent) for a good while'—who is *liang-jiu?*" The teacher said, "The younger brother of Liang Ba." This is told as a joke. Tianyi's last two lines are most outstanding—he said,

> The chill light of the hair-blown sword shines from in the scabbard;
> Heretics and heavenly devils are all beheaded.

I say, passing the magical point over in the dark, he doesn't feel pain or irritation.

Baiyun Shouduan's verse says,

> One, two, a hundred, a thousand, ten thousand:
> Though searching through the letters with bent fingers,
> the count is not completed.
> Stay for a while in front of the dark window—
> I'll figure and count with you again tomorrow.

I say, what leisure time is there?

In Tiantong's verse on the story of Mazu's saying "Zhizang's head is white, Huaihai's head is black," in the last line he says, "Grandly sitting, cutting off the road of the tongue; what a laugh, the old awl of Vaisali." Today Vimalakirti has come; face and honor don't matter.

Verse   *Manjusri inquires after the illness of the old Vaisalian;*

The gate of nonduality opens—Behold the adept.

Crude without, pure within—who appreciates it?

Forgetting 'before' and losing 'after', don't sigh.

Struggling to present the gem—the man with his feet cut off in the garden of Chu:

Repaying with a jewel, shining bright—the cut snake of Sui.

Stop checking—

There are absolutely no flaws:

Mundanity totally gone, that's still but a little.

Commentary   Manjusri's name means wonderful good fortune. Vaisali is the name of the city (where Vimalakirti lived) known as 'extensive adornment.' In Master Sengzhao's treatise *Nirvana Has No Name* it says, "Shakyamuni closed his room in Magadha, Vimalakirti shut his mouth in Vaisali; Subhuti extolled speechlessness to reveal the Way; Indra and Brahma, beyond hearing, showered flowers. These are all because the truth is mastered by spiritual knowledge, so the mouth is thereby silent. How could you say they had no eloquence? It is what eloquence cannot speak of."

A '*Yan* gem' is a semiprecious stone; it's the modern 'water-stone' of the Zhuo district; it's also called a jewel replacement stone. Although Vimalakirti outwardly seems dumb, his speechless eloquence is pure and genuine within—that is to say, the stone conceals the jewel.

As for "forgetting 'before' and losing 'after'," in Yongjia's collection on meditation, in the verses on cessation, the fourth says, "Now when I speak of knowing, you needn't know knowing; just know, that's all. Then before, you don't continue extinction, and after, you don't bring on production; the continuity of before and after broken, in between is solitary and alone." In the last part of the *Inexhaustible Lamp,* in the section on those whose Dharma succession is not clear, there is a Chan Master Guangzhi of Yimen Mountain in Kaifeng prefecture; his initiatory name was Bensong. There is no other record of his sayings, except this whole section is recorded. Elder Wen (compiler of the *Inexhaustible Lamp*) didn't know it comes from Yongjia's collection, so I have straightened it out here, so students will know. This "forgetting 'before' and losing 'after'" is exactly what the Third Chan Patriarch's *Seal of Faith in Mind* says—"The path of words and speech ends; it is not past, future, or present."

Hanzi relates that Bian He found a rough jewel in a valley of Mount Jing in the Kunlun Mountains; he presented it to King Li of Chu. The King said, "This is a stone," and dismissed him and had one of his feet cut off. When King Wu assumed the throne, Bian again presented it, but again one of his feet was cut off. Finally, when King Wen was enthroned, Bian held the jewel, and cried at the foot of Mount Jing—the king summoned him and asked about it: Bian He said, "I do not resent the amputation of my feet, but I do resent that a real jewel is taken to be an ordinary stone, that an act of loyalty is taken to be a deception." The king had the stone split and found it was a real jewel. King Wen grieved and said, "How lamentable, that the two former sovereigns found it easy to cut off a man's feet but found it hard to split a stone. Now it actually turns out to be a gem, and a treasure for the nation."

According to the *Historical Records,* as Shu Yuanzhang, Marquis of Sui, was going to a feast, he saw a snake that had been cut and was dying. He washed and rubbed it with water, then applied a wonder drug and left. Suddenly one night a light appeared in the yard; thinking it was a robber, he took a sword and looked—then he saw a snake holding a jewel in its mouth going along the ground. He realized it was the snake's recompense to him.

Vimalakirti lay himself down to help the crowd, but didn't avoid calamity coming from his own house—how was it worth Manjusri's check, already showing a flaw? Even though Tiantong says that he appears to live in the dust of the mundane world but has no air of mundanity, still this is covering his nose while stealing incense.

Added
Sayings
/Case

Vimalakirti asked Manjusri, "What is a bodhisattva's way of entering nonduality?"—How many times has the question been asked?

Manjusri said—Should give him a punch in the mouth.

"According to my mind—He's brewing it up.

In all things—That's even too few.

No speech, no explanation—Take a torch for illumination and look.

No direction and no representation—Is there or not?

Leaving behind all questions and answers—How thick is the skin on his face?

This is the way to enter nonduality."—What is duality?

Then Manjusri asked Vimalakirti, "We have each spoken—Those who can speak, speak quickly.

Now you should say, good man, what is a bodhisattva's way of entry into nonduality?"—Once he's surrounded and divested of everything, they don't count on a violent outburst.

Vimalakirti was silent—Where's he gone?

Added
Sayings
/Verse

Manjusri inquires after the illness of the old Vaisalian—In the path of humanity and righteousness.

The gate of nonduality opens—behold the adept—It's the lot of patchrobed mendicants.

Crude without, pure within—who appreciates it?—Those with great eloquence are as though dumb.

Forgetting before and losing after, don't sigh—Those with great wisdom are as though stupid.

Struggling to present the gem—the man with his feet cut off in the garden of Chu—Presenting the straight he gets the crooked.

Repaying with a jewel, shining bright—the cut snake of Sui—When a luminous jewel is thrown to someone, rare is the one who doesn't draw his sword.

Stop checking—Fortunately it is inherently complete of itself.

There are absolutely no flaws—Go ahead and try to point any out.

Mundanity totally gone, that's still but a little—Looking at people on the basis of appearances, this is lost much of the time.

49 DONGSHAN PRESENTS OFFERINGS BEFORE THE IMAGE

Introduction   It can't be depicted, can't be drawn—Puhua just turned a flip, Longya just showed half his body. Ultimately, who is in what state?

Case   **As Dongshan was presenting offerings before the image of Yunyan, he retold the story from before about depicting the reality. A monk came forward and said, "When Yunyan said, 'Just this is it,' what did he mean?"**
Dongshan said, "At that time I nearly misunderstood my late teacher's meaning."
The monk said, "Did Yunyan himself know it is or not?"
Dongshan said, "If he didn't know it is, how could he be able to say this? If he did know it is, how could he be willing to say this?"

Commentary   When Dongshan took leave of Yunyan, Dongshan asked, "After your death, if someone asks me if I can describe your reality, how shall I reply?" After a while Yunyan said, "Just this is it." Dongshan sank into thought. Yunyan said, "You are in charge of this great matter; you must be most thoroughgoing." Dongshan left without saying anything more; later, as he was crossing a river he saw his reflection and then for the first time was thoroughly enlightened. Thereupon he composed a verse:

> *Just don't seek from others, or you'll be far estranged from Self.*
> *I now go on alone; everywhere I meet It:*
> *It now is me; I now am not It.*
> *One must understand in this way to merge with thusness.*

When Dongshan was in the community setting offerings before the image of Yunyan, he retold the foregoing story about describing the reality of Yunyan; then a monk asked, "When Yunyan said, 'Just this is it,' what did he mean?" Dongshan said, "At that time I nearly misunderstood what my late teacher meant." If you go to the pause and 'just this is it' to understand the point, this is just conveying the matter by a different name. That is why he knew the form upon seeing the reflection, and became enlightened just as he crossed the river. The monk said, "Did Yunyan know it is or not?" If you say he absolutely knows it is, then he's an attendant—haven't you heard it said that 'only one who knows it can uphold it'? If you say he absolutely doesn't know it is, here there is gain and loss: there is completely not knowing it is, there is knowing it is then after all not knowing, and there is not knowing it is turning into knowing it is. Dongshan said, "If he didn't know it is, how could he be able to say so? If he did know it is, how could he be willing to say so?" The Huayan school says, "Inner reality is complete, words are partial; when words are born, inner reality is lost." This is 'mystery upon mystery, ever more wondrous,' 'integration and harmonious communion,' the impartial, non-leaking bloodline.

Dongshan first dwelt at Baiji temple on Mount Xinfeng in the latter part of the Dazhong era of the Tang dynasty (847–859); later he moved to Mount Dong at Gaoan in Yuzhang, where he was the first generation. As he was conducting a memorial service for Yunyan, a monk asked, "What instruction did you receive at your late teacher's place?" Dongshan said, "Although I was there, I didn't receive his instruction." The monk said, "Then why conduct a service for him?" Dongshan said, "Even so, how dare I turn my back on him?" The monk said, "You rose to prominence at Nanquan's—then why do you instead conduct a service for Yunyan?" Dongshan said, "I do not esteem my late teacher's virtues or his buddhist teaching; I only value the fact that he didn't explain everything for me." The monk said, "You succeeded to the late teacher; then do you agree with him or not?" Dongshan said, "I half agree, half don't agree." The monk said, "Why don't you completely agree?" Dongshan said, "If I completely agreed, then I would be unfaithful to my late teacher."

I say, Yunyan was with Baizhang for twenty years, yet succeeded to Yaoshan; Dongshan rose to prominence at Nanquan's yet succeeded to

Yunyan. Different sprouts of the same kind became luxuriant, making the spiritual roots dense and firm; with Furong the school was revived, with Tiantong its embellishment was finally complete. What is the full embellishment? The verse says,

Verse *How could he be able to say this?*
In the third watch the cock crows—Dawn for the forest of homes.
How could he be willing to say this?
The thousand-year crane grows old with the pine in the clouds.
The jewel mirror, clear and bright, shows absolute and relative:
The jade machine revolves—see them both show up at once.
The Way of the school is greatly influential, its regulated steps continuous
and fine:
Father and son change and pass through—oceanic is their fame.

Commentary Dongshan instructed Caoshan, "I was personally sealed with the *Jewel Mirror Samadhi* by my late teacher Yunyan; its content is extremely clear and to the point. Now I hand it on to you; keep and uphold it well." "The jewel mirror shows up absolute and relative"—is this not the cock crowing in the forest of houses, the crane growing old with the pine in the clouds, the test of absolute and relative? Although the mirror is clean, it has a back and a front; only the jade works spinning it weaves them together, both light, both dark, with the technique of simultaneous realization.

The elaboration of the *Book of Changes* says, "When the way comes to an end, then change—having changed, you pass through." Having long passed through, Dongshan's father and son guide their actions and regulate their steps: even now the school's style flourishes greatly—proof that when the source is deep the flow is long.

Added **As Dongshan was presenting offerings before an image of Yunyan—**
Sayings Who says it's artificial?
/Case **He retold the story about depicting reality**—Each time you bring it up it's new.

A monk came forward and said, "When Yunyan said 'Just this is it,' what did he mean?"—Happily he doesn't misapprehend.

Dongshan said, "At the time I nearly misunderstood my late teacher."—He judges others in terms of himself.

The monk said, "Did Yunyan himself know it is or not?"—He breaks a blade of grass to measure the sky.

Dongshan said, "If he didn't know it is, how could he be able to say so?"—When the sun comes out it ranges over the mountains.

'If he did know it is, how could he be willing to say so?'—The moon, full, is at the door.

Added Sayings / Verse

How could he be able to say this?—Pulling out a bone sideways in the dark.

In the third watch the cock crows—dawn for the forest of houses—The sun rises in the east.

How could he be willing to say this?—Demolishing a hundred tongues in the light.

The thousand-year crane grows old with the pine in the clouds—The moon sets in the West.

The jewel mirror, clear and bright, shows absolute and relative—Phenomena are comprehended accurately and essentially.

The jade machine revolves—see them both show up at once—Mixing darkness with light.

The Way of the school is greatly influential, its regulated steps continuous and fine—The order of India is strict.

Father and son change and get through—oceanic is their fame—When one's view goes beyond the teacher, then one can handle the transmission.

50 XUEFENG'S "WHAT?"

Introduction   At the last word you finally reach the impenetrable barrier. Yantou is so sure of himself that above, he doesn't agree with his own teacher, and below, he doesn't concede to his Dharma-brother. Do you think this is forcibly creating subdivisions, or then again is there a special operation?

Case   When Xuefeng was living in a hut, two monks came to pay respects to him. Xuefeng, seeing them coming, opened the door, popped out, and said, "What is it?"
A monk also said, "What is it?"
Xuefeng lowered his head and went back inside.
Later the monk came to Yantou. Yantou asked, "Where have you come from?"
The monk said, "South of the range."
Yantou said, "Did you ever go to Xuefeng?"
The monk said, "Yes."
Yantou asked, "What was said?"
The monk recounted the preceding story: Yantou asked, "What did he say?"
The monk said, "He didn't say anything—he just lowered his head and went back inside."
Yantou said, "Too bad I didn't tell him the last word before. If I had told him the last word, no one in the world could affect old Xuefeng."
At the end of the summer the monk again brought up the foregoing story and inquired further about it. Yantou said, "Why didn't you ask before?"

The monk said, "I didn't dare to take it easily."

Yantou said, "Though Xuefeng is born of the same lineage as me, he doesn't die of the same lineage as me. If you want to know the last word, 'just this' is it."

Commentary Yunyan consulted Daowu, Xuefeng consulted Yantou; a superior man is not ashamed to ask humbly. Now the ways of Yunyan and Xuefeng are flourishing greatly—this too is the superabundant blessing of withdrawing oneself and deferring to others.

Now Yantou was extraordinary by nature; putting down and upholding Deshan's way, he went freely under heaven, with no one daring to face him head-on. It's because his insight was clear and comprehensive and his development was complete that he could be like this.

Look at those two monks at Xuefeng's door, how their arrow-points meet—and this one is a pilgrim too; so why did he still have doubts about the last word, even at the end of the summer session? Just because his eyes were dull and he didn't know where his head was, missing what's right in front of him. Yantou explained so much reasoning for him—"Xuefeng and I are born of the same lineage, but we don't die of the same lineage." Though one reality has no differences, the views of the three men differed. This monk and Xuefeng said, "What is it?" at the same time, but when it came to discussing the last word, even though it's explained to him he doesn't know—is this not a case of 'a hairsbreadth of difference misses by ten thousand miles'? But tell me, did this monk really not understand, or did he want to let this saying be made? Guishan Zhe said, "Even the great Xuefeng and Yantou have been exposed by this monk." I say, an impartial view doesn't preclude the possibility of sympathy for Xuefeng and Yantou. Later on they also pointed out Deshan as not understanding the last word either, but he would hardly stand for it. Therefore Tiantong expressed it in verse twice.

Verse Cutting, carving, polishing, grinding.
Changing appearances, with mixed dialect.
The staff changed into a dragon in Lake Gebi,
The shuttle hibernating in the Tao house.

Born of the same lineage, there are numbers:
Dying of the same lineage, there is no multitude.
The last word—just this is it:
The wind boat, ferrying the moon, floats on the autumn waters.

Commentary The 'Depths of Qi' section of the *Classic of Poems* eulogizes the virtues of Lord Wu, that he was cultured and could listen to admonitions therefrom, and governed himself by the rites—therefore he was able to go into Zhou and be prime minister. This poem was written in his praise:

> *Gazing into the depths of the Qi river,*
> *The green bamboo are lush.*
> *There is that cultured gentleman,*
> *As though cut, carved, and polished.*

When working bone, it's called cutting; on ivory it's called carving, on jewels it's polishing, and on stones it's grinding. Deshan, Xuefeng, and Yantou brought to light the last word; even now this story is very popular—this is the power of cutting, polishing, and transformation.

Xuefeng is like a staff changed into a dragon, the monk is like a hibernating shuttle. What Yantou points out is even now unknown; that is why those who die of the same lineage are not many. Those who may say that Yantou is like a staff changed into a dragon and Xuefeng is like a hibernating shuttle, I ask you to please consider the foregoing story carefully. Xuedou and Foguo use 'both light and both dark' to eulogize this story—anyone who has not investigated fully would not know.

According to the biographies of scientists in the Eastern Han dynasty, Fei Changfang was a man of Runan; he once was a city bureaucrat, when he met (the alchemist known as) Mr Pot. Cutting a staff of green bamboo, they pretended that Changfang had been strangled in his house, but actually Changfang went together with Mr Pot deep into the mountains to study the Tao. Unsuccessful, Changfang took his leave to go back; Mr Pot gave him the bamboo staff and told him to ride it back home and throw it in Gebi lake. When Changfang threw the staff in the lake, it turned into a dragon and left.

Also, when Tao Kan of the Jin dynasty was young he netted a shuttle while fishing in Thunder Marsh; he hung the shuttle on his wall. Later he heard thunder and lightning—it had turned into a dragon and left. Xuefeng is like the staff, the monk is like the shuttle, Yantou is like a wind-boat carrying the moon. What am I like? A teapot from Gongxian.

Added Sayings /Case

When Xuefeng was living in a hut, two monks came to pay respects to him—They pursue the fragrance, following the air.

Seeing them coming, Xuefeng opened the door, popped out, and said, "What is it?"—This is still a position of throwing the body; what about the position of hiding the body?

A monk also said, "What is it?"—After all he actually doesn't know.

Xuefeng lowered his head and went back inside—Better not say he had no words.

Later the monk came to Yantou—Transmitting a message about what's going on.

Yantou asked, "Where have you come from?"—If you don't drill, no hole.

The monk said, "South of the Range"—here is north of the range.

Yantou said, "Did you go to Xuefeng?"—A familiar place is hard to forget.

The monk said, "Yes."—Can't avoid it any more.

Yantou said, "What was said?"—He doesn't stop until it's vinegar.

The monk recounted the preceding story—When even a single letter enters the gate of the public domain, eight oxen cannot pull it out.

Yantou said, "What did he say?"—After all, better lower your head and leave right away.

The monk said, "He didn't say anthing—he just lowered his head and went back in the hut."—If so, you never went to Xuefeng.

Yantou said, "Too bad I didn't tell him the last word before"—And now have you said it yet?

"If I had told him the last word, no one in the world could affect old Xue"—Why not say 'I am none other than old Xue'?

At the end of the summer the monk again brought up the foregoing story and inquired further about it—People sober up from good wine slowly.

Yantou said, "Why didn't you ask before?"—He likes to sleep.

The monk said, "I didn't dare take it easily."—He sure is used to the monasteries.

Yantou said, "Though Xuefeng is born of the same lineage as me, he doesn't die of the same lineage as me."—Those who seek to divide are the first to reach an impasse.

If you want to know the last word, "just this' is it."—He sells it as he steams it hot.

Added
Sayings
/Verse

Cutting, carving, polishing, grinding—Only by experience . . .

Changing appearances, with mixed dialect—. . . is knowledge developed.

The staff changed into a dragon in Lake Gebi—We already hear it's crossed the ocean and pierced the clouds.

The shuttle hibernating in the Tao house—Still we see it resting on the fence, hanging on the wall.

Born of the same lineage, there are numbers—Near by nature.

Dying of the same lineage, there is no multitude—Different by learning.

The last word—just this is it—I just believe a half.

The wind boat, ferrying the moon, floats on the autumn waters—Just don't get stuck.

51 FAYAN'S "BOAT OR LAND"

Introduction In mundane truth how many people have been enlightened, in Buddhist truth how many people have been deluded! If they suddenly become one, can you then define delusion or enlightenment?

Case Fayan asked Elder Jiao, "Did you come by boat or by land?"
Jiao said, "By boat."
Fayan said, "Where is the boat?"
Jiao said, "The boat is on the river."
After Jiao had withdrawn, Fayan turned and asked a monk standing by, "You tell me, did that monk just now have eyes or not?"

Commentary Once when Huanglong Huitang was questioning Huang Luzhi, just as he was really pressing him, someone came: Huitang asked him, "Who sent you?" The man said, "The scholar Ye from Dalin." Huitang said, "Is there a letter?" The man said, "Yes." Huitang asked, "Where is the letter?" The man reached back, took it from his sleeve, and presented the letter to Huitang. Huitang said, "Study of the Way should reach this man's state." Huang Luzhi blushed with shame.
Fayan asked Elder Jiao if he came by boat or by land, and Jiao said by boat. Fayan said, "Where is the boat?" Here ninety-nine out of a hundred would present a display of their abilities; but he was at ease with reality, even and poised—where does he engage spear and shield with you?— here he said, "The boat is on the river." The old teacher of Cizhou said, "It's like putting an eight-legged pot on the sand—it's no longer unsteady anywhere at all." Fayan then asked a monk beside him, "Tell me,

215

did that monk just now have eyes or not?" This one question is most baffling—if you say he has eyes, what is there special or mysterious? If you say he doesn't have eyes, what gap do you see? Try to have Tiantong settle for sure:

Verse   *Water doesn't wash water,*
Gold isn't changed for gold.
Find a horse without knowing its color,
Enjoy the lute without the strings.
Tying knots, drawing trigrams, when there are such things,
Completely lost is the true pure mind of original man.

Commentary   "Water doesn't wash water, gold isn't changed for gold"—Buddha doesn't seek Buddha, Dharma doesn't speak Dharma. This is talk of the wonder horse, omitting its dull pallor. Those who get the message of the lute forget its strings.

According to Huainanzi, Lord Mu of Chui ordered Bai Luo to raise a corral and look for a horse. After three months he returned and said, "I got a horse, in Shachiu; it is a yellow stallion." When the horse arrived, it was a black mare. The lord said to Bai Luo, "In the horse you found, you didn't even know the color of its coat or whether it is a male or female—what a failure!" Bai Luo sighed loudly and said, "So it has come to this? What you see in the corral is the opportunity of heaven: getting the essential, forget the gross; seeing the inside, forget the outside." As it turned out, it was an excellent steed.

Tao Xuan of the Jin dynasty was named Yuanming. He didn't know how to play the lute, but he kept an unused lute, which had no strings. He said, "If you just get the essence of the lute, why bother with the sound in the strings?"

The Book of Changes says, "In high antiquity, they tied knots for order: the wise people of later times changed this and used written notes." It also says, "In ancient times, when Fu Xi was king over the land, he looked up and saw the patterns of the heavens, looked down and saw the designs of the earth, and observed the harmony of the markings of the birds and animals with the earth: nearby, he found it in his body, afar he found it in things. From this he first drew the eight trigrams." I say, when the most ancient ancestor first divided sky and earth, already he created an opposition—to tie knots and draw trigrams more and more loses true innocence. Before Shakyamuni had appeared in the world, and Bodhidharma hadn't yet come from the West, were there also 'real truth' and 'conventional truth' or 'mundane reality' and 'enlightened reality'? Chan Master Jiju of Haihui in Shu province, after he had realized the truth, once went to Langya Jiao's place: Jiao asked him, "Elder, where have you just come from?" Jiju said, "From Chejiang." Jiao said, "Did you come by boat or by land?" Jiju said, "By boat." Jiao said, "Where is the boat?" Jiju said, "On the river." Jiao said, "Without referring to the journey, how can you speak a phrase?" Jiju said, "Incompetent abbots are plentiful as flax and millet," and immediately left. I say, his acts and words make a good story.

The first master of Dongshan asked a monk, "Where do you come from?" The monk said, "Ru province." Dongshan said, "How far is it from here?" The monk said, "Seven hundred." Dongshan said, "How many pairs of sandals did you wear out?" The monk said, "Three." Dongshan said, "Where did you get the money to buy them?" The monk said, "Making rainhats." Dongshan said, "Go to the hall." The monk said, "OK." I say, even hands and eyes throughout the body can't see through you. But tell me, where are the monk's eyes? Under his eyebrows.

Added Sayings /Case

Fayan asked Elder Jiao, "Did you come by boat or by land?"—It very much seems like there are two kinds.

Jiao said, "By boat."—He speaks deeply on the mark of reality and skillfully explains the essence of the teaching.

Fayan said, "Where is the boat?"—Perhaps he didn't tell the truth.

Jiao said, "The boat is on the river."—After all he has a landing place.

After Jiao had withdrawn, Fayan asked a monk standing by, "Did that monk have eyes or not?"—What a pity.

Added Sayings /Verse

Water doesn't wash water—Spotlessly pure.

Gold isn't changed for gold—Forge it into one lump.

Find a horse without knowing its color—It can't be found by appearances.

Enjoy the lute without the strings—It cannot be sought by way of sound.

Tying knots, drawing trigrams, when there are such things—When laws are issued, crime is born.
Completely lost is the true pure mind of original man—Playing clever, turning out clumsy.

52 CAOSHAN'S "REALITY BODY"

Introduction   Those who have wisdom can understand by means of metaphors. If you come to where there is no possibility of comparison or similitude, how can you explain it to them?

Case   Caoshan asked elder De, "'The buddha's true reality body is like space: it manifests form in response to beings, like the moon in the water'—how do you explain the principle of response?"
De said, "Like an ass looking in a well."
Caoshan said, "You said a lot indeed, but you only said eighty percent."
De said, "What about you, teacher?"
Caoshan said, "Like the well looking at the ass."

Commentary   Chan Master Benji of Caoshan in Fu province was also named Tanzhang—this must be an honorific title or a posthumous name. When he first left Dongshan, he went to Caoqi and paid reverence to the monument of the Sixth Patriarch. Then he went back to Jishui in Ji province. The people there respected his fame and eventually asked him to start teaching there: to emulate Caoqi, wherever he lived the master named the place Cao. The school of Dongshan became most flourishing with Caoshan; therefore it was called Cao-Dong.

Caoshan asked elder De, "'The true reality-body of buddhas is like space; it manifests form in response to beings, like the moon in the water'—how do you explain the principle of response?" These lines extolling the Buddha originally come from the old version of *Golden*

219

Light Scripture. Since it is like space, how does it respond to beings? Jiaofan, praising the venerable Kanadeva, said, "Manifesting according to circumstances, without falling into thought, he therefore put a needle into the bowl of water." Elder De said, "It is like an ass looking in a well." How can this be reached by intellectual judgments? Unless you have gone through long refinement and have the grip of a patchrobed monk, you can't reach this realm; someone of lesser ability, without the key of transcendence, would fully approve of this, but Caoshan said, "You said a lot indeed, but you only said eighty percent." It's like he weighed it and measured it. De said, "What about you?" This one challenge is the limit of words, the end of reason: one would dare say that Caoshan wouldn't be able to go beyond that saying "like an ass looking into a well," but Caoshan gently just turned it around; this could be called 'developing it in kind.' This is why he was called a source of the stream of the Cao-Dong school. Tiantong liked these two turning-words, and turns them over and produces them in verse at once:

Verse   *The ass looks at the well,*
The well looks at the ass.
Widsom is all-embracing,
Purity pervades, with abundance.
Behind the elbow who discerns the seal?
In the house no books are kept.
The loom threads aren't strung—the work of the shuttle:
The pattern going vertically and horizontally, the meaning is distinct of itself.

Commentary   'Wisdom has no knowledge,' but there is nothing it doesn't know; therefore "purity pervades, with abundance."
In the first year of the Yongshang era of Emperor Yuan of the Jin dynasty (322), Wang Dun, commander of Wushang, mobilized an army and attacked the imperial palace. Dao Xie urged the emperor to execute the entire Wang family. Wang Dao led his relations to the government office to await their execution. Zhou Yi was about to enter court; Wang Dao called to him and said, "Everyone is implicating you." Zhou Yi paid no

attention. When he went in, he spoke most highly of Wang Dao's loyalty and honesty, trying his best to save him. When he left, Wang Dao was still at the gate; again he called to him, but Zhou Yi didn't reply. Then he said, "This year I'll kill a brigand, take a golden seal as big as a ladle and fasten it behind my elbow." Finally he sent a petition to the emperor again, making it clear that Wang Dao was innocent. Wang Dao didn't know about this, and bore a bitter grudge against Zhou Yi. When Wang Dun's army came, he asked Wang Dao if Zhou Yi should be allowed to live; Wang Dao did not reply, and Wang Dun killed Zhou Yi. Later Wang Dao was looking through official documents and saw the petition of Zhou Yi trying to save him; he wept and said, "In the dark I have opposed such a good friend."

In the Chan monasteries there is also a 'talisman behind the elbow.' In the *Postscript to the Spring and Autumn*, Zhao Jianzi of Zhao said to his children, "On top of Mount Chang I have hidden a precious talisman for behind the elbow. The one who gets it first will be rewarded." Everyone rushed up the mountain looking for it, but none found it—only Wuxu returned and said, "I have gotten the talisman—the others cannot discern it." Jianzi asked him to present it; Wuxu said, "If you look down from the top of Mount Chang, a replacement can be gotten." Jianzi said, "Wuxu is wise," and made him the crown prince.

Yunyan said to his group, "There is a son of someone's house who can answer any question." Dongshan came forth and said, "How many books does he have in the house?" Yunyan said, "Not even a single letter." Dongshan said, "How can he be so knowledgeable?" Yunyan said, "Night and day he never sleeps." Dongshan said, "Can I ask about something?" Yunyan said, "If I could say, I wouldn't." "Behind the elbow, who discerns the seal?" The profound and self-realized Way is not discernable to others. "In the house no books are kept"—he is so knowledgeable; knowing it by birth is best, knowing it by learning is next.

As for this "The ass looks at the well, the well looks at the ass," does it admit of any understanding by dividing them, does it admit of transmission by learned understanding? Jiashan said, "Producing understanding from hearing, you color it in your intellect; although right before your eyes is fine, kept for a long time it becomes a sickness. The blue mountain and the white clouds never reach each other. The loom threads aren't

strung—the work of the shuttle: the pattern going vertically and horizontally, the meaning is distinct of itself. The knowledge of the wise is
far from the road of good omen—the lucky grass is rootless; the sages
don't esteem it." Tiantong at the end uses Jiashan's poem wholly to
clarify that in the story the embellishment is naturally complete without
falling into thought.

But tell me, with what meditation can one get to be like this? Just this,
with no grip, nothing can be done about.

<table>
<tr><td>Added
Sayings
/Case</td><td>

The Buddha's true reality body is like space—Officially not even a
needle is admitted.

It manifests form in response to beings, like the moon in the water—
Privately, even a horse and carriage are let through.

How do you explain the principle of response?—I'd fold my hands,
approach, and say 'Yes'.

Like an ass looking in a well—The falling flowers consciously go along
with the flowing stream.

You said a lot, but that's only eighty percent—If you want to see a
thousand miles further . . .

What about you, teacher?—. . . Climb a tier higher.

Like the well looking at the ass—The flowing stream mindlessly carries
the fallen flowers along.

</td></tr>
</table>

<table>
<tr><td>Added
Sayings
/Verse</td><td>

The ass looks at the well—Even getting up at dawn . . .

The well looks at the ass—. . . There's already someone going by night.

Wisdom is all-embracing—All the mendicants in the land cannot leap out.

Purity pervades, with abundance—None of the myriad forms can avoid
casting reflections of their substance.

Behind the elbow, who discerns the seal?—Even celestial eyes and dragon
eyes cannot see.

In the house no books are kept—A true writing doesn't sour.

The loom threads aren't strung—the work of the shuttle—The flowers aren't
damaged . . .

*The pattern going vertically and horizontally, the meaning is distinct of
itself*—. . . Yet honey can be made.

</td></tr>
</table>

53 HUANGBO'S "DREG-SLURPERS"

Introduction   Facing the situation, you don't see Buddha; great enlightenment doesn't keep a teacher. The sword that settles heaven and earth obliterates human sentiments, the ability to capture tigers and rhinos forgets holy understanding. But tell me, whose strategy is this?

Case   Huangbo said to the assembly, "You people are all slurpers of dregs. If you travel like this, where will you have *today*? Do you know that in all of China there are no teachers of Chan?"
At that point a monk came forward and said, "What about those who guide followers and lead groups in various places?"
Huangbo said, "I don't say there's no Chan, just that there are no teachers."

Commentary   This story is abbreviated: to bring up the whole of it, one day Huangbo went up in the hall and said, "What do you people want to look for?" And he chased them with his staff. The assembly didn't disperse, so he said, "You people are all dreg-slurpers." In Tang times they liked to rebuke people with the term 'dreg-slurper'. Once Lord Ji Heng was reading a book in a room: Lun Pian was planing a wheel outside the hall; Lun Pian put aside his mallet and chisel, came up and asked, "May I ask what you are reading, sir?" The lord said, "A book of the sages." Lun Pian said, "Are the sages alive?" The lord said, "They're already dead." Lun Pian said, "Then what you are reading is the dregs of the ancients." The lord said, "When a monarch reads a book, how can a wheelwright discuss it? If you have an explanation, all right; if not, then you die." Lun

223

Pian said, "I look upon this in light of my own work. When I plane a wheel, if I go slowly, it is easygoing and not firm; if I go quickly, it is hard and doesn't go in. Not going slowly or quickly, I find it in my hands and accord with it in my mind, but my mouth can't express it in words. There is an art to it, but I can't teach it to my son, and my son can't learn it from me. Therefore I have been at it for seventy years, grown old making wheels. The people of old and that which they couldn't transmit have died. Therefore what you are reading, sir, is the dregs of the ancients."

Huangbo also said, "If you travel on like this, you'll incur the laughter of others. You just see where there are eight hundred or a thousand people and immediately go there—but you shouldn't just seek the hubbub. When I was traveling, if I found there was someone at the roots of the grasses, I would stick him in the head and watch to see if he knew the feeling of pain; if he did, I could give him a cloth bag full of rice as an offering. Here if you're always taking it easy like this, where will you find Today's affair? Since you're called pilgrims, you should concentrate a bit. Do you know there are no teachers of Chan in all of China?"

Since Huangbo, Yantou and Luoshan liked to carry out this order. In recent times, Fori and Qingshou Yi never approved of anyone all their lives, and instead ended their succession with no one. Master Xin of Xiangshan and his spiritual uncle and descendants also carried out this order—those who didn't know thought it was conceit. Here, Huangbo wants someone who's aroused to come forth and take him up: it turned out there was a monk who came out and said, "The venerable adepts in all quarters are gathering people and teaching; why do you say there are no Chan teachers?" Huangbo said, "I don't say there is no Chan, just that there are no teachers." Guishan asked Yangshan, "What about it?" Yangshan said, "The king goose picks out milk from water—to begin with he's not a duck." Guishan said, "This is truly difficult to discern." Wuzu Jie spoke for the monk, "I thank the master for his fine explanation of the reason." I say, raw words, refined speech, cool lips, light tongue. Shimen Cong said, "Huangbo's instruction was undeniably marvelous, but the moment he is confronted by a monk he loses one eye." I say, he's snatched away both of that monk's eyes. Chengtian Zong said, "Wuzu Jie's eyes illumine all quarters. (I say, still this is just one eye.) It's still not enough to see Huangbo. (I say, so it turns out.) If you want to uphold the treasury of the eye of truth, you must be a master of the school of Huangbo." I say, he adds flowers to brocade. Cuiyan Zhen said, "Everywhere they judge and say Huangbo cut off this monk." I say, without knowing he supported the monk. Zhen also said, "When this monk came up to Huangbo, he just couldn't give an analysis;" I say, black and white are all the more distinctly clear—what about that? "Cuiyan thereupon gives rise to hesitation—the garuda bird is raised to be fierce, after all waiting to surprise people." I say, look five days later. Huangbo also said, "Don't you see that succeeding to Mazu were over eighty men who sat on a site of the Way and preached fluently, but those who attained the great master's true eye were only two or three? It was only Guizong who most of all amounted to something. Those who leave home should know something of the perennial matter; but even Great Master Rong of Ox Head Mountain, successor to the Fourth Patriarch, could speak horizontally and vertically but still didn't know the transcendental key. Only if you have this eye and brain can you discern false and true schools." I briefly quote thus far, to show the details of this speech; after this are still over a hundred and ten more words. These are the words he spoke to people when he first appeared in the world, so they circulated widely everywhere. Xuedou's eulogy and Foguo's exposition (in the *Blue Cliff Record*) are most thorough, but they still lack the true meaning of the address in the original record. Tiantong's rendition of it in verse is most complete:

Verse   *Paths divide, threads are dyed—too much trouble.*
Leaves in clusters, flowers in rows—ruins the ancestors.
Subtly wielding the guiding handle of creation;
Vessels of water and clouds are on the potter's wheel.
Clearing away tangles and chips,
Shaving off down:
The marked balance, the jeweler's mirror,
The jade ruler and gold knife:
Old Huangbo can perceive even an autumn hair;
Cutting off the spring wind, he doesn't allow exaltation.

Commentary In the *Shuofu* volume of *Liezi*, Yangzi's neighbor lost a sheep; he was already leading his friends, yet he also asked Yangzi's servant to go after it. Yangzi said, "Why are many people going after one sheep?" The neighbor said, "There are many forks in the road." When they returned, he asked, "Did you find the sheep?" He replied, "It's lost." "Why didn't you find it?" "There were forks in the forked roads."

According to Mozi, in the time of King Hui of Liang, a man of the way went out and saw white thread being dyed into other colors; saddened, he said, "People are deep and calm, essentially the same as the saints, but because of dwelling in an evil society, it stains them and becomes a burden."

"Paths divide, threads are dyed—too much trouble." As for "Leaves in clusters, flowers in rows," the verse of the First Patriarch, Bodhidharma, said,

> I originally came to this land
> To explain the true and rescue beings from delusion.
> One flower opens with five petals,
> Producing a fruit which matures on its own.

One flower with five petals is none other than "paths divide, threads are dyed." If there are no Chan teachers in all China, Bodhidharma too has no way to appear. According to the *Source Mirror Collection*, a guiding chariot is originally to direct those who are lost, and a mirror that reflects innards is to show up evil people. According to ancient and modern commentaries, when the Emperor of Yellow battled with Chiyou at Zhuolu, Chiyou created a tremendous fog, confusing the four directions: the emperor, in his chariot, pointed the way with his finger to give directions—his knights caught Chiyou and beheaded him. Afterwards it was called a guiding chariot.

As for the 'potter's wheel,' according to Chen Liu's *Record of Customs*, King Shun made pottery on a river bank; subsequently it became a trade, and they are surnamed Potter. This is molding myriad images in the mystic kiln, unifying myriad streams in the ocean of wisdom.

"Clearing away tangles and chips, shaving off down," is getting rid of the divergent forks in the path, cutting away the offshoots of the clustered leaves.

A balance scale is what is used to determine light and heavy; a mirror is used to differentiate beautiful and ugly.

As for the 'jade ruler,' according to the *Record of Collected Miscellany*, when King Yu was wandering around Dragon Gate, eight spirits searched out a jade bar and gave it to him: it was one foot two inches long, and with it he could measure the things in the world.

As for the 'gold knife,' in ancient times there were gold-adorned knives for money and gold-edged books.

These eulogize Huangbo grading everyone, with the balance and ruler in his hand. He also can clearly hear ants arguing and perceive the finest autumn hair. Nipping in the bud, he 'cuts off the spring wind', and 'doesn't allow exaltation'. As in the poem on bamboo shoots by Master Yi of Dashengan, as you are bringing down the axe on the root, avoid letting shoots regrow out of season.

Added Sayings / Case

Huangbo said to the assembly, "You people are all slurpers of dregs—Huangbo's disciples.

If you travel like this, where will you have Today?—Now is already not like the past; later and future will not be like now.

Do you know that in all China there are no Chan teachers?"—His eyes are high over the four seas.

Then a monk came forth and said, "What about those who guide followers and lead groups in various places?"—Huangbo himself is one of them.

Huangbo said, "I don't say there's no Chan, just that there are no teachers."—He's only saved a half.

Added Sayings / Verse

Paths divide, threads are dyed—too much trouble—When the things you're concerned with are few, your troubles are few.

Leaves in clusters, flowers in rows—ruins the ancestors—Where you know many people, there is much judgement of right and wrong.

Subtly wielding the guiding handle of creation—One day the authority is in your hands.

Vessels of water and clouds are on the potter's wheel—Observe when the order is in effect.

Clearing away tangles and chips—A great elephant does not walk a rabbit's path.

Shaving off down—Great enlightenment is not confined by small measures.

The marked balance, the jeweler's mirror—Not even the finest hair is unnoticed.

The jade ruler and gold knife—Measuring with profound clarity.

Old Huangbo can perceive even an autumn hair—Can't fool him one bit.

Cutting off the spring wind, he doesn't allow exaltation—He's prepared for trouble ahead of time.

54 YUNYAN'S "GREAT COMPASSION"

Introduction   Crystal clear on all sides, open and unobstructed in all directions, emanating light and making the earth tremble in all places, subtly exercising spiritual powers at all times—tell me, how is this manifested?

Case   Yunyan asked Daowu, "What does the Bodhisattva of Great Compassion do with so many hands and eyes?"
Daowu said, "It's like someone reaching back for the pillow at night."
Yunyan said, "I understand."
Daowu said, "How do you understand?"
Yunyan said, "All over the body is hands and eyes."
Daowu said, "You said a lot there, but you got only eighty percent."
Yunyan said, "What about you, elder brother?"
Daowu said, "Throughout the body is hands and eyes."

Commentary   Li Ao asked Ehu, "What does the Great Compassionate One use a thousand hands and eyes for?" Ehu said, "What does the emperor use public officials for?"
Once there was a mountain man who sold fortunes. After rain, on the muddy road, he would wear pure white shoes to go into the market. Someone asked, "You're blind—how come the mud doesn't soil your shoes?" The mountain man raised his staff and said, "There's an eye on the staff." The mountain man is proof—when reaching for a pillow at night, there's an eye in the hand; when eating there's an eye on the tongue, when recognizing people on hearing them speak there's an eye

229

in the ears. Su Zizhan, conversing with a deaf man, just wrote: then he laughed and said, "He and I are both strange people—I use my hand for a mouth, he uses his eyes for ears." The Buddha spoke of the interchanging function of the six senses—it is true, without a doubt.

In layman Wujin's *Record of the Hall of Great Compassion at Purple Cliff in Lu Province* he quotes the *Scripture of Great Compassion* and the *Heroic March Scripture* as most thorough and detailed. I have seen one story which says that the Bodhisattva of Great Compassion in ancient times became the princess Miaoshan; this was told to Precept Master Xuan by a celestial being. But then again the hundreds of millions of manifestation bodies of the thirty-two responses (of Great Compassion) are not the same, according to the vision—each goes by their explanation.

Tianjiao said, "'A thousand hands' illustrates the many-sidedness of guidance of the deluded and salvation of beings; 'a thousand eyes' illustrates the breadth of emanating light to illumine the darkness. If there were no sentient beings and no mundane turmoil, then not even a finger would remain, much less a thousand or ten thousand arms; not even an eyelid would be there, much less a thousand and or ten thousand eyes. All over the body, throughout the body, 'what's the necessity,' 'not necessarily'—there seems to be shallow and deep, but really there is no loss or gain."

Yunju said to his group, "Twenty years ago when I was living on Sanfeng Peak, Xinghua came and said, 'How about when a question is provisionally used as a screen?' At that time my mind and thought was slow and dull and I couldn't say. Because he had posed the question so marvelously I didn't dare oppose him: at the time he said, 'I think you can't answer this question, o hermit; better to bow and withdraw.' Now as I think of that time, it wasn't worth saying 'What's the necessity?'" I say, it's like letting it be gotten easily. Later, there was a preacher who came to Xinghua's place; Xinghua asked him, "When the master on the mountain Yunju was living in a hut on Sanfeng, I once asked him a question he couldn't answer; by now has he been able to speak yet or not?" After the preacher quoted the preceding story, Xinghua said, "In twenty years, Yunju has only been able to say 'What's the necessity?' I don't go along—how can that compare to saying 'not necessary'?" I say, he is arguing over the shortness or length of turtle-hairs. Sansheng said,

"Yunju's ability to speak after twenty years still only measures up to Xinghua's half-month journey." I say, he's disputing over the richness or paleness of flowers in the sky.

A monk asked Jiaofan, "Are there differences in the instructions of the old adepts?" Jiaofan said, "The Buddha had an inarticulate, dull monk repeat a broom-sweeping chant; one day he was greatly enlightened and attained great powers of intellect and eloquence. In this you should see the ancient worthies' intention of helping people." What about on Tiantong's part? His verse says,

Verse   One hole, emptiness pervading:
Crystal clear on all sides.
Formlessly, selflessly, spring enters the pipes:
Unstopped, unhindered, the moon traverses the sky.
Pure jewel eyes, arms of virtues:
All over the body—how does it compare to throughout the body being it?
The present hands and eyes reveal the whole works:
The great function works in all ways—what is taboo?

Commentary   Tiantong says, by one hole, emptiness pervading, all directions become crystal clear. It is like willow-grown banks and flower-grown walls on a warm day in a gentle breeze—where is the spring? What shape is it? Nevertheless it is able to accord with things and come with the time, unstopped, unhindered, like the moon in the sky, revolving naturally. I wonder—throughout the body, all over the body, reaching back for a pillow—who is it? Inside the puppet stage there must be someone pulling the strings.

The *Heroic March Scripture* speaks of eighty-four thousand pure clear jewel eyes, eighty-four thousand gesturing arms, and eighty-four thousand indestructible heads. A verse on Xinghua falling from a horse and breaking his arm says, "The Bodhisattva of Great Compassion has a thousand hands—what great man does not?" But tell me, which are the hands and eyes throughout the body? (Wansong drew open his eyes with his hands and said) 'Cat'.

Added Sayings / Case

Yunyan asked Daowu, "What does the Bodhisattva of Great Compassion do with so many hands and eyes?"—What is your aim in asking such a question?

Daowu said, "It's like someone reaching back for the pillow at night."—A miraculous power—it's not the same as the little kind.

Yunyan said, "I understand."—Don't pretend to be enlightened.

Daowu said, "How do you understand?"—After all he doesn't let him go.

Yunyan said, "All over the body is hands and eyes."—There's no gap.

Daowu said, "You said a lot there, but you got only eighty percent."—My tongue is short.

Yunyan said, "What about you, elder brother?"—When the reason is superior, then adhere to it.

Daowu said, "Throughout the body is hands and eyes."—No obstruction.

Added Sayings / Verse

One hole, emptiness pervading—Vertically, extending through past, present, and future.

Crystal clear on all sides—Horizontally, covering the ten directions.

Formlessly, selflessly, spring enters the pipes—Receiving blessings according to the season.

Unstopped, unhindered, the moon traverses the sky—It falls naturally into the valley ahead.

Pure jewel eyes, arms of virtues—Looking ahead and behind, picking up east and west.

All over the body—how does it compare to throughout the body being it?—Can't rationalize it.

The present hands and eyes reveal the whole works—The thief's loot is already exposed.

The great function works in all ways—what is taboo?—No right or wrong.

55 XUEFENG, THE RICE COOK

Introduction Ice is colder than water, blue comes from indigo: only when one's view goes beyond the teacher is one qualified for the transmission—if the son's upbringing is not as good as the father's, the family will decline in one generation. But tell me, who is it that steals his father's thunder?

Case When Xuefeng was at Deshan working as rice cook, one day the meal was late: Deshan came to the teaching hall holding his bowl. Xuefeng said, "Old man, the bell hasn't rung yet, the drum hasn't sounded—where are you going with your bowl?"
Deshan immediately returned to his room.
Xuefeng reported this to Yantou: Yantou said, "Even Deshan, so great, does not understand the last word."
Deshan had his attendant summon Yantou, and asked him, "You don't agree with me?"
Yantou then expressed what he meant. Deshan then stopped.
The next day when Deshan went up into the hall to speak, it was not the same as usual: Yantou clapped and laughed and said, "Happily the old guy understands the last word. Hereafter no one in the world will be able to have any effect on him."

Commentary Xuefeng lowered his head and returned to his hut, Deshan returned to his room. This really should be fully investigated. Yantou secretly revealed his intended meaning—tell me, what did he say? Deshan then stopped; we might say, 'meeting without bringing it up, as soon as you pay attention you know it exists.' When Deshan went to teach in the hall

233

the next day, after all it was not the same as usual. Yet this too is adding error to error. Yantou went out to the front of the monks' hall, and clapping and laughing said, "Happily the old guy understands the last word. Hereafter no one in the word will be able to affect him." Just don't cover up. "But even so," Yantou continued, "he still only has three years." As it turned out, Deshan passed away after three years. Tianjiao's verse goes,

> The sound of the bell and drum sinks away, he returns with his bowl.
> Yantou's one remark was like thunder.
> After all he only had three years of life;
> Did he not receive a prophecy from him?

I say, one knows the coverlet is worn when he has slept on the same bed. Mingzhao said in Deshan's place, "Tch, tch! Going nowhere, going nowhere." I say, his nose is in another's grip. Xuedou said, "I'd heard talk of this One-Eyed Dragon (Mingzhao)—it turns out he really has only one eye. What is hardly realized is that Deshan was a toothless tiger—if not for Yantou seeing through him, how could he be different tomorrow from yesterday? Do you people want to know the last word? 'I only admit the old barbarian knows—I don't admit the old barbarian understands.' Half blocking, half covering, he's let slip without even knowing it." Dagui Zhe said, "Yantou is like a high mountain crumbling into rocks; for a hundred miles tracks of running animals are obliterated. If not for Deshan's profound and clear capacity, how could he be different yesterday from tomorrow?" I say, the toothless tiger's claws are still there.

Whenever Luzu saw a monk coming he would immediately face the wall. Nanquan heard of this and said, "I usually tell them to attain realization before the empty aeon, to comprehend before the Buddha appeared in the world." If you know Nanquan, then you see Yantou, and even go arm in arm with Tiantong:

Verse *The last word—understand? No?*
Deshan the father and his sons are exceedingly indistinct.
In the assembly there also is a traveler from south of the river—
Don't sing of the partridges in front of people.

234

Commentary The last word is so hard to understand: even by those as steep and stolid as Deshan, sharp and keen as Yantou, even up till now it hasn't been distinguished clearly. Haven't you heard it said, "To get out still can be easy; expressing the whole thing must be hard."
A poem by Zeng Yu says,

> *The moonlit flowering balcony terrace is near the crossroads;*
> *A melody of clear song overturns the golden pot—*
> *In the audience there's also a guest from Hunan—*
> *Don't sing the partridges' song in the spring breeze.*

Tiantong uses the last two lines; it's not necessary to reiterate the underlying meaning. After it is brought up, then what? (Wansong got down from the seat and returned to his room.)

Added
Sayings
/ Case

When Xuefeng was at Deshan working as rice cook—If you don't work when young . . .
One day the meal was late; Deshan came to the teaching hall carrying his bowl—. . . you won't have peace of mind when old.
Xuefeng said, "Old man, the bell hasn't rung yet, the drum hasn't sounded—where are you going with your bowl?"—He makes the baby able to scold its mother.
Deshan immediately returned to his room—It's all in the not speaking.
Xuefeng reported this to Yantou—The family rebels, the home is disturbed.
Yantou said, "Even Deshan doesn't understand the last word."—The father is obscured by the son—the straight is therein.
Deshan had his attendant summon Yantou, and asked him, "You don't agree with me?"—He pours oil on the fire.
Yantou then expressed what he meant—Private words among people are heard as loud as thunder by the gods.
Deshan then stopped—After all he doesn't understand.
The next day when he went up in the hall, it was not the same as usual—He steers backwards along with the wind.
Yantou clapped and laughed and said, "Happily the old guy understands the last word—The shame of the house is exposed outside. **Hereafter no one in the world will be able to affect him."**—Why is his nose in my hands?

235

The last word—understand? No?—Here one can't understand; if you don't understand, you're snapped at the waist.

Deshan the father and his sons are exceedingly indistinct—Outside bright, you don't know inside the dark.

In the assembly there also is a traveler from south of the river—Don't say there are no people in north China.

Don't sing of the partridges in front of people—Can you stop?

56 SPIRITUAL UNCLE MI AND THE RABBIT

Introduction Better to be sunk forever than to seek the liberation of the saints. Devadatta experienced the bliss of the third meditation heaven while in uninterrupted hell; Udraka Ramaputra fell from the heaven of the summit of existence into the body of a flying wildcat. Tell me, where is the gain and loss?

Case As Dongshan and his spiritual Uncle Mi were walking along, they saw a white rabbit run by in front of them. Mi said, "Swift!"
Dongshan said, "How!"
Mi said, "It's like a commoner being made a prime minister."
Dongshan said, "Such a venerable old person still says such words!?"
Mi said, "Then what about you?"
Dongshan said, "Generations of nobility, temporarily fallen into poverty."

Commentary Dongshan and Chan Master Sengmi of Shenshan in Tan province were crossing a stream; Dongshan asked, "How is the event of crossing the stream?" Sengmi said, "Doesn't wet the feet." Dongshan said, "A venerable old person like you using such words!?" Mi said, "How about you?" Dongshan said, "The feet are not wet."
In the teachings there are two gates, natural and cultivated; in Dongshan's lineage this is called 'using the accomplishment to illustrate the state'. Usually we awaken by means of cultivation, entering sagehood from ordinariness—a commoner is directly appointed prime minister. If you're first enlightened and then cultivate afterwards, you enter ordinariness from sagehood—traditional nobility is originally honor-

237

able; though drifting destitute in myriad conditions, the basic constitution is still there. That is why it is said, "In the metaphor of the destitute son is illustrated the Path; in the verse on presenting the jewel is shown the net of salvation." You people, do you want to see the viewpoints of the two venerable adepts? See how Tiantong included their crimes on the same indictment:

Verse *Matching strength with snow and frost,*
Walking evenly through clouds and sleet.
Xiahui left the country,
Xiangru crossed the bridge.
Xiao and Cao's strategy was able to establish the Han,
Chao and Xu wanted to avoid Yao completely.
Favor and disgrace are disturbing—profoundly trust in yourself:
In the real state one mixes tracks with fishermen and woodcutters.

Commentary Reeds crave rain and dew, pine and cypress can stand wind and frost. When the year is cold you know the pine and cypress are the last to wither. This means not changing along with conditions. As for talk of nobility in poverty, great men of power can bear this—"walking evenly in the cloudy sky," directly transcending into the stage of enlightenment, is already too slow. What is hardly realized is that the traditional nobility is originally rich and honorable.

According to the *Analects*, Liu Xiahui was a criminal judge; three times he was dismissed from office. Someone said, "Shouldn't you leave?" He said, "If I serve the people honestly, where can I go and not be fired three times? If I serve the people crookedly, what need would there be to leave my native place?"

Sima Xiangru was nicknamed 'Doggie'. When he was young he lost his parents; at nine he took care of pigs for someone. He heard that Lian Xiangru became a minister, and he changed his own name to Xiangru, left the pigs and went to study. The owner of the pigs beat him. The schoolmaster questioned him and realized he was intelligent, and let him stay in a hut outside the gate. In ten years he had no more books to give him to read, and sent him away. As he crossed the 'bridge for ascending immortals,' he wrote on a pillar, "If I'm not riding a four-horse coach, I won't cross this bridge again." Later he composed the *Idylls of Zixu;* General Yang was pleased by it, and at night when he stayed in the palace he recited it. The emperor said, "I regret not having been a contemporary of the man who wrote this." The general said, "He is now living in Shu." The emperor ordered him to go summon him; together they rode on a four-horse coach across the bridge; he was appointed a councillor.

Xiao He and Cao Can made the work of Emperor Gao of the Han dynasty successful. Chao Fu refused King Yao and washed his ears; Xu You watered his ox (upstream to avoid the water in which Chao washed his ears). Laozi said, "Favor and disgrace are disturbing—when you get one you're disturbed, when you lose one you're disturbed." In each of the above four pairs, one phrase is old Mi, one phrase is Dongshan.

Wonderfully indeed, Guifeng brought up a metaphor, likening it to the royal family sinking into obscurity and poverty, becoming accustomed to it so that it becomes natural. Later when they are recognized and rescued, though restored to their original status, they still have to relearn and cultivate the 'three tips' (brush, sword, and tongue) and the six arts (ritual, music, archery, riding, writing, arithmetic) before their power and action will be complete. Even so, for Tiantong this still falls within stages; don't you see—"Favor and disgrace are disturbing—profoundly trust in yourself; in the real state one mixes tracks with fishermen and woodcutters."

Added Sayings / Case

Dongshan and Uncle Mi saw a white rabbit run by in front of them; Mi said, "Swift!"—What can be done about running in the weeds?

Dongshan said, "How?"—Wondering why you're so slow.

Mi said, "It's like a commoner being made a prime minister."—It is easy to ascend into the sky from the ground.

Dongshan said, "Such a venerable old person still says such words!?"—Nearly let him go.

Mi said, "What about you?"—If the man has no mind to harm the tiger, the tiger has no intention to injure the man.

Dongshan said, "Generations of nobility, temporarily fallen into poverty."—Descending from the sky is hard.

Added
Sayings
/ Verse
Matching strength with snow and frost—When poor, cultivate yourself well alone.

Walking evenly through clouds and sleet—When successful, help everyone on earth as well.

Xiahui left the country—A bitter gourd is bitter to the root.

Xiangru crossed the bridge—A sweet melon is sweet to the stem.

Xiao and Cao's strategy was able to establish the Han—Sunflowers turn to the sun.

Chao and Xu wanted to avoid Yao completely—Willow fuzz goes along with the wind.

Favor and disgrace are disturbing—profoundly trust in yourself—Enlightenment must be true enlightenment, study must be true study.

In the real state one mixes tracks with fishermen and woodcutters—This still hasn't escaped the sacred tortoise dragging its tail.

57 YANYANG'S "THING"

Introduction Playing with reflections, struggling for the form, you don't recognize that the form is the source of the reflection. Raising your voice to stop an echo, you don't know the voice is the root of the echo. If it's not riding an ox looking for an ox, then it's using a wedge to remove a wedge. How can you avoid these extremes?

Case Venerable Yanyang asked Zhaozhou, "When not a single thing is brought, then what?"
Zhaozhou said, "Put it down."
Yanyang said, "If I don't bring a single thing, what should I put down?"
Zhaozhou said, "Then carry it out."

Commentary Venerable Yanyang of Xinxing monastery in Wuning district of Hong province first went to Zhaozhou and asked, "When not a single thing is brought, then what?" This is the same as a monk asking Baoci, "'When feelings arise, wisdom is blocked; when characteristics change, the body differs'—how about when feelings haven't arisen?" Baoci said, "Blocked." The monk said, "If feelings haven't arisen, what can they block?" This is the same as "If I don't bring a single thing, what should I put down?" Brash fellows are much the same. Zhaozhou said, "If you can't put it down, then carry it out." At these words Yanyang was greatly enlightened.
In Foguo's sermons he quoted Huanglong's verse on this case, adding remarks (in parentheses):

241

Not bringing a single thing, both shoulders can't bear it up
(someone with clear eyes is hard to fool)
At the words he suddenly knows his error
(step back and you fall into a deep pit)
In his heart is boundless joy
(like a poor man finding a jewel)
Since from poisonous ill he forgot what was on his mind
(when beginningless past karma is exhausted, there's pure clarity)
Snakes and tigers have been his intimates
(different species equally understand)
Empty and still for a thousand years, the pure breeze still hasn't stopped
(who would not appreciate and look up to it?)

Where the master lived there was always a snake and a tiger who ate from his hand: therefore the Venerable Yanyang is referred to in the manner of one who had attained sainthood. Zhaozhou and Venerable Yanyang were men unfathomable to ordinary people or sages; when they uttered a single word or posed a single question, it was a guide for people of a thousand ages.

Tiantong saw that the monks of recent times were getting more and more coarse-minded, so he beat the grass to scare the snakes:

Verse   *Not prepared for meticulous action, he loses to the first to move—*
Realizing himself the coarseness of his mind, he's embarrassed at
bumping his head.
When the game is ended, the axe handle's rotted at his side:
Clean and purify the ordinary bones to play with the immortals.

Commentary   Old Wang Jie Fu, in his secret talk on playing Chinese chess, says, "The other doesn't dare advance, you don't dare advance—only this not daring to advance is why there is no contest; only if there is no contest do you enter into nondying and nonbirth. Chess is the method of contending over the lead; if you win, then you win an aggressive move—if you lose, you lose a confrontation." Before you have put down your piece, Zhaozhou already sees several moves ahead; Yanyang only flies around and leaps right over, moreover occupying how many columns—he doesn't realize that the axe handle has already rotted.

According to the *Annals of Spirits and Immortals,* in the Longan era of the Jin dynasty (397-401), Wang Shi of the Xinan district was gathering firewood, when he came to Dark Room Hill; in a stone grotto he saw four boys playing chess. They gave him some substance like a date; after he ate it he wasn't hungry. When the game was ended, the axe handle had rotted at his side and his clothes were flapping in the wind. When evening came he returned home—it had already been several decades!

As for Zhaozhou's two turning-words, "Put it down" and "Carry it out," pull out your tendons, extract your marrow, change your bones and wash your guts—then you can walk hand in hand with Zhaozhou. Some say "Pure tranquility is the real basis of the path; the unconcerned are little immortals." Even so, don't take unconcern for unconcern—"time and again concern is born of unconcern."

Added Sayings /Case

Yanyang asked Zhaozhou, "When not a single thing is brought, then what?"—This is still beyond him.

Zhaozhou said, "Put it down."—The robe and shirt sticking to the body—understand that you should shed them.

Yanyang said, "If I don't bring a single thing, what should I put down?"—People don't know their own faults, oxen don't know the magnitude of their strength.

Zhaozhou said, "Then carry it out."—When called he doesn't turn his head—what can you do?

Added Sayings /Verse

Not prepared for meticulous action, he loses to the first to move—Before black and white are yet distinguished is still the relative within the absolute.

Realizing himself the coarseness of his mind, he's embarrassed at bumping his head—He puts his child in the tiger's mouth.

When the game is ended, the axe handle's rotted at his side—Tell me, what time is it now?

Clean and purify the ordinary bones to play with the immortals—Head light, eyes clear.

58 THE *DIAMOND SCRIPTURE'S* "REVILEMENT"

Introduction Understanding the meaning based on the scriptures is the enemy of the Buddhas of all times; deviating one word from the scriptures is the same as devil talk. Does someone who is not included in cause or effect still experience the results of action or not?

Case **The Diamond-Cutter Scripture says, "If someone is reviled by others, this person has done wicked acts in previous ages and should fall into evil ways, but because of the scorn and revilement of people in the present age, the wicked deeds of past ages are dissolved."**

Commentary With seeing and hearing as seeds, those in the eight difficulties transcend the ranks of the ten stages; with understanding and practice in oneself, in one lifetime the fruit of vast aeons is perfected.

Guifeng, sectioning this scripture, called this 'transforming wrongdoing and becoming enlightened'. This is the nonduality of enlightenment and affliction, the nonduality of birth and death and nirvana. Prince Zhaoming of Liang, in sectioning this scripture, considered this the part able to clear away karmic obstructions.

Mahasattva Fu said in verse,

> *In a previous embodiment there were consequential hindrances;*
> *Today accepting and upholding the scripture,*
> *Temporarily slighted and scorned by people,*
> *It turns the serious back into light.*

This is truly understanding the meaning based on the scripture.
The last four clauses have the breath of a patchrobed monk, saying (in

effect) if you comprehend relativity, you can get rid of feelings based on mere thought construction; always relying on the insight of pure wisdom, why worry about it not being absolute reality? The first four clauses are the power of accomplishment and virtue, the latter four are the power of contemplation practice.

The oral transmission of the Sixth Patriarch says,

> *Buddha said that people who uphold the scripture should*
> *receive the respect and offerings of all people; (if)*
> *because of heavy karmic obstructions for many lives, though*
> *you uphold the scripture in this life you are always*
> *reviled by people and do not get respect or support, (yet)*
> *because you yourself uphold the scripture you do not produce*
> *images such as self and others, and always practice*
> *respect and honor without question of enemy or friend, not*
> *contending when offended against, always cultivating tran-*
> *scendent wisdom—so the burdensome faults of the ages will*
> *all vanish. Also, to speak in terms of inner reality, 'pre-*
> *vious ages' is the deluded mind of the preceding moment;*
> *'the present age' is the awake mind of the succeeding moment.*
> *The awake mind of the succeeding moment scorns the deluded*
> *mind of the previous moment; because the delusion cannot*
> *remain, therefore it is said that the wicked deeds of previous*
> *ages will thereby be dissolved. Once deluded thoughts die*
> *out, bad deeds aren't done, and one attains enlightenment.*

These two understandings, inner reality and phenomenal, both are reference to contemplative practice. A monk asked Yunju, "I understand in the teachings there's a saying, 'This person has done evil in previous existence and should fall into the evil ways; because in present life he is scorned and reviled by people, the bad karma of previous existence is thereby dissolved'—what does this mean?" Yunju said, "If he moves he should fall into the evil realms; if he's still he'll be reviled by people." Chongshou Zhou said, "If there's anything outside of mind, he should fall into the evil ways; if he keeps to himself he'll be reviled by people." I say, the two old fellows' mundanity is not yet gone. But tell me, what about Tiantong?

Verse *Continuous, merit and fault:*
Inextricable, cause and effect.
Outside of the mirror crazily ran Yajnadatta.
With the staff the oven-breaker struck—the oven fell;
The spirit came to celebrate,
Only to be told he'd been turning away from his self.

Commentary 'Merit' is upholding the scripture; 'fault' is former karma. Once you've established an illusory cause, you'll surely bring on an illusory result.

The *Heroic March Scripture* says, "Haven't you heard how in the city of Shravasti, Yajnadatta suddenly one morning went to a mirror to see his face; he wanted to be able to see his head, eyebrows and eyes in the mirror, and got mad that he couldn't see the face on his own head; thereby he became insane and ran crazily for no reason. What do you think? Why did this person run crazy?" Purna said, "This man was crazed—no other reason." This is missing the real and clinging to the illusory. When real wisdom appears, illusory karma vanishes, and unexcelled enlightenment is already inherent. This is the meaning of the true teaching; how about for a Chan monk?

About the oven-breaker monk: the mountain aborigines had a shrine with an oven in the hall where they made burnt sacrifices all the time. The Breaker had led some followers into the shrine, hit the oven three times with his staff and scolded it, "This oven is composed of mud and brick—where does the holiness come from, where does the spirit arise, that you burn living creatures?" And he hit it again three times, whereupon the oven collapsed. National Teacher An named him the Oven-Breaker. In a flash there was a man dressed in green, with a tall hat; he bowed and said, "I was originally the spirit of the shrine. For a long time I have been subject to consequences of karma; today, having heard your explanation of birthlessness, I am freed from this place and born in heaven. I came just to offer thanks." The master said, "It is your fundamental nature, not my insistence." The spirit bowed again and disappeared. Compounded of mud and brick—where does the holiness come from? No sign of self or others—this is true wisdom. Always having been turned away, today coming to celebrate—he burned many living beings, and had no benefit; three hits of the Chan ancient's staff and he's born in heaven. Tch! Demons, fearing evil men, can hardly open their hands; thieves relying on stolen goods can easily take the lead.

Added Sayings /Case

If someone is reviled by others—I am an insect in manure.
This person has done wicked acts in previous ages and should fall into evil ways—I'll go first of all.
But because of the scorn and revilement of people in the present age—Monastery donkeys and mules stomp on dragons and elephants.
The wicked deeds of past ages are dissolved—Where do they go?

Added Sayings /Verse

Continuous, merit and fault—Only excepting suddenly enlightened people.
Inextricable, cause and effect—They don't even go along with the Dharma.
Outside of the mirror crazily ran Yajnadatta—Smoke rises under his feet.
With the staff the oven-breaker struck—Smashing into a hundred fragments.
The oven fell—Whence is the spirit born, where does the holiness come from?
The spirit came to celebrate—I think he's fallen into disgrace.
Only to be told he'd been turning away from his self—Why didn't you say so before?

59 QINGLIN'S "DEAD SNAKE"

Introduction   Try to get rid of it and it stays; try to keep it and it leaves. Not leaving, not staying, it has no country—where will you meet it? Everywhere, every place—tell me, what thing can be so special?

Case   A monk asked Qinglin, "When the student goes by a short cut, then what?"
Qinglin said, "A dead snake lies across the great road: I urge you not to step on its head."
The monk said, "When one steps on its head, then what?"
Qinglin said, "You lose your life."
The monk said, "How about when one doesn't confront it?"
Qinglin said, "There's still nowhere to escape."
The monk said, "At just such a time, then what?"
Qinglin said, "It's lost."
The monk said, "Where has it gone?"
Qinglin said, "The grass is deep, there's no place to look for it."
The monk said, "You too should be on guard, teacher."
Qinglin clapped and said, "This one's equally poisonous."

Commentary   When Chan Master Qinglin Shijian, third generation abbot at Dongshan, first came from Jiashan to call on (Dongshan) Wuben, Wuben asked, "Where did you come from?" Qinglin said, "Wuling." Wuben said, "How does the way of teaching in Wuling compare to here?" Qinglin said, "In other lands bamboo sprouts in winter." Wuben said, "Cook fragrant rice in a special pot to offer to this man." Qinglin then

248

went out. Wuben said, "Later on this fellow will trample everyone on earth to death."

When Qinglin was at Dongshan Mountain planting pines, there was an old man Liu who asked for a verse from the master. Master Qinglin said,

> Point sharp—*three feet and more;*
> *Thick, dense, covering the wild weeds.*
> *I don't know in what generation*
> *People can see these old pines.*

The old man showed it to Wuben, who said, "I appreciate your joy, old man; this person will be the third generation at Dongshan."

Qinglin took leave of Wuben, and went to Qingcuo mountain in Shannanfu, where he lived in a hut for ten years. Suddenly he remembered Wuben's words and said, "I should help the ignorant; how could I be confined to a small measure?" Eventually he arrived in Sui province, where it happened that a community invited him, and he dwelt at Earth Gate Little Green Forest Sanctuary—that is why he is called Qinglin, 'Green Forest.'

He once said, "You people should investigate apart from mind, intellect, and cognition, go beyond the roads of ordinary and holy to learn: only then can you be in command. Otherwise, you are not my disciples."

A monk asked him, "How about when a student goes by a short cut?" This monk in the hall of great compassion wants to go to the central capital; he even boasts of his knowledge of the direct essential road. What he doesn't realize is that 'directly' is already too roundabout. Qinglin stopped him with a dead snake on the great road; the monk didn't fear danger or death and said, "When one steps on its head, then what?" He's already poisoned. Some ask why Qinglin didn't enforce the order with shout and cane, but did Qinglin ever let him go?—he said, "You lose your life." This monk had some sense of pain; looking for a way out, he said, "What about one who doesn't confront it?" Qinglin said, "Still there's nowhere to escape." Even Qinglin himself can't avoid it. This monk, using all his strength, said, "At just such a time, no one around can do anything; what would be right?" Qinglin said, "It's lost." The method of reviving people—at this point you see he can send away, he can summon; there is the ability to capture and to release. If applied to your body, there's no way to grasp hold; taken away for you, then there's a resting place. The monk said, "Where has it gone?" Qinglin said, "The grass is so deep there's no place to look." I don't say there's none, just that it can't be seen. This monk was unusual too; he said, "You too should be on guard, Teacher." Qinglin used a dead snake to roust out this monk; in the end, after all, it's stuck around his waist, wrapped around his legs. Finally he clapped his hands and exclaimed, "This one's equally poisonous!" I say, the poison permeates heaven and earth.

The *Inexhaustible Lamp* says, "Qinglin's mainspring was swift and sharp; this is not the light of only one time, it is also a standard for vast ages." I say, this is disturbing the spring wind unceasingly. Look further: Tiantong blows on the flowers and rustles the willows:

Verse	*The boatman turns the rudder in the dark,*
	The lone boat turns its bow in the night.
	Reed flowers—'snow' on both banks;
	Hazy water—autumn on one river.
	The power of the wind helps the sailboat go without rowing.
	The voice of the flute calls the moon down to the land of spring.

Commentary Chan Master Danxia Zichun's verse on this case says,

> *The long river clear to the depths reflects the moonlit flowers;*
> *The clear light filling the eyes is not yet home.*
> *I ask where the fishing boat has gone;*
> *Deep in the night, as of old it rests in the reed flowers.*

The two elders (Danxia and Tiantong) alike versify the still water of the clear source, on which still is rowed a lone boat. Danxia uses Xuedou's eulogy of Xuansha, which says,

> *Originally he was a traveler fishing on a boat;*
> *He happened to shave his hair and put on monastic robes.*
> *Even in the ranks of Buddhas and Patriarchs he didn't stay;*
> *By night, as before, he rests in the reed flowers.*

I say, one might have thought there was something else.

250

In *Talks about Poetry Past and Present* it says that in Shanxia a boatman is called an 'elder statesman'. A poem by Du Fu says,

> The salt of Shu, the flax of Wu—they have been traded for ages.
> The ten-thousand bushel boats sail like the wind.
> In the long song of the elder statesman,
> Pitching pennies in broad daylight in the towering billows.

This matter is like someone going in a boat: he doesn't land at either shore, doesn't stay in midstream. Danxia rests by night in the reed flowers, Tiantong pipes freely along with the wind. But tell me, how about when turning the rudder, turning the boat around? Deep in the night, not resting in the reedy shoals, going far beyond the middle and both sides.

Added Sayings /Case

A monk asked Qinglin, "How is it when a student goes by a short cut?"—Taking a step is already the long way around.

Qinglin said, "A dead snake lies across the great road; don't step on its head"—He's used to poisoning.

The monk said, "What about when one steps on its head, then what?"—You've got guts, all right.

Qinglin said, "You lose your life."—Of course.

The monk said, "What about if you don't run into it?"—How does it just depend on you?

Qinglin said, "There's still nowhere to escape."—You bump into it everywhere.

The monk said, "At just such a time, then what?"—Now don't be flustered!

Qinglin said, "It's lost."—Though it's a dead snake, if you can handle it, it's alive.

The monk said, "Where has it gone?"—If you don't believe, look in your breast pocket.

Qinglin said, "The grass is deep, there's no place to seek."—Above the head, boundless; below the feet, boundless.

The monk said, "You too should be on guard, teacher"—It's returned.

Qinglin clapped and said, "This one's equally poisonous!"—'I thought I was a crook, but here's an even worse scoundrel!'

Added
Sayings
/Verse

The boatman turns the rudder in the dark—He hides the boat in the valley by night.

The lone boat turns its bow in the night—Putting the oar in the clear source.

Reed flowers—'snow' on both banks—Self and other mysteriously combine.

Hazy water—autumn on one river—Above and below subtly merge.

The power of the wind helps the sailboat go without rowing—Finding the wonder along with the flow.

The voice of the flute calls the moon down to the land of spring—It falls into the valley ahead as it goes.

60 IRON GRINDER, THE COW

Introduction Nose high, each has a powerful appearance. Footsteps firm and solid, one may study 'old woman Chan'. When you penetrate the ungraspable dynamic, for the first time you see the method of a true master. But tell me, who is such a person?

Case Iron-Grinder Liu went to Guishan: Guishan said, "Old cow, you've come?"
The Iron-Grinder said, "Tomorrow on Taishan there's a big gathering and feast—are you going, teacher?"
Guishan lay down, sprawled out.
The Iron-Grinder immediately left.

Commentary Guishan called himself a water buffalo, he called Iron-Grinder Liu a cow—giving a name, an epithet of praise, it is a meeting of adepts. Though she was a nun, she had studied with Guishan for a long time. She had built a hut several miles away.
One day she called on Zihu, who asked, "Aren't you Iron-Grinder Liu?" She said, "I daren't presume so." Zihu said, "Do you turn to the left or to the right?" She said, "Don't tip over, Master." Zihu immediately hit her.
See her with Guishan: when letting go, they both let go; when gathering in, both gather in. Foguo called this a 'body-block' saying—the meaning is conveyed but the words intervene. Do you want to know the realization of the meaning and the phrase? Look ahead at how Tiantong produced the whole thing in verse:

253

Verse   *Success in a hundred battles accomplished, growing old in great peace:*
Serene and gentle, who is willing to trouble to contend?
The jade whip and golden horse are idle all day:
The bright moon and pure wind enrich a whole lifetime.

Commentary   Many young monks talk about Buddha; old generals don't talk about the army. If they don't yet discern whether the wheat in front of the mountain is green or yellow, and don't know the 'price of rice in Luling,' yet still go on talking about Buddhism, who has ever seen it even in a dream? The biography of Chen Fan of the Eastern Han dynasty says, "Fan was able to set up local education and establish his character and repute; he argued against ignorant customs, striving in the midst of danger and prejudice, and contended with convicts and eunuchs." In the meeting of Guishan and Iron-Grinder Liu, they didn't establish character or repute, didn't strive in danger and prejudice—they were relaxed and easygoing, seasoned and mature. Why is it that Tiantong can't finish praising them?

> *Upon attainment, calculations are naturally forgotten—*
> *When in action, no effort is wasted.*

Added Sayings /Case   Iron-Grinder Liu went to Guishan—Already they've met.
Guishan said, "Old cow, you've come?"—He picks off the bees and scrapes off the termites.
Liu said, "Tomorrow on Taishan there's a big gathering and feast—are you going?"—The poison is like smoky fire burning.
Guishan lay down sprawled out—He extricates himself midway.
Iron-Grinder Liu immediately left—One push and she turns.

Added Sayings /Verse   *Success in a hundred battles accomplished, growing old in peace*—At peace in one's house, enjoying one's work.
Serene and gentle, who is willing to trouble to contend?—Not contending with people is not stupidity.
The jade whip and golden horse are idle all day—Though they exist, it's like they didn't.
The bright moon and pure wind enrich a whole lifetime—Enjoyment of them is inexhaustible.

61 JIANFENG'S "ONE"

Introduction   A roundabout explanation is easy to understand—it imparts with one hand. A direct explanation is hard to understand—it opens up in all dimensions. I urge you not to use clear speech, for if speech is clear, getting out is all the more difficult. If you don't believe, let's try to bring this up:

Case   A monk asked Jianfeng, "'The Blessed Ones of the ten directions are on one road, the gate of *nirvana*'—where is that road?"
Jianfeng drew a line in the air with his staff and said, "It is here." The monk asked Yunmen the same question: Yunmen said, "The fan leaps up to the thirty-three heavens and hits the emperor of the gods on the nose. The carp of the eastern sea is hit once with the stick, and it rains buckets. Do you understand? Do you understand?"

Commentary   Chan Master Jianfeng of Yue province was asked by a monk, "All the Blessed Ones of the ten directions are on one road, the gate of *nirvana*—where is that road?" This question originally comes from the fifth part of the *Heroic March Scripture;* this is *abhidharma:* the Blessed Ones of the ten directions are on one road, the gate of *nirvana*—where is the entrance to the road? To interpret the meaning of this, according to the scripture, the Realized One is speaking on his own, to prepare the ground for 'complete pervasion.' After that Manjusri analyzes complete pervasion. As for patchrobed monks, Tiantong once said, "There are no walls in the ten directions—from the very beginning there is fundamentally no obstruction. There are no doors in the four quarters—just right here is the entry

255

way." That is why Jianfeng drew a line with his staff and said, "Here it is." Time and again those who don't know say that Jianfeng was pointing out the road to his monk; or else they say that he delineated it for the monk and didn't go anywhere else. It is definitely not these principles. Don't you see how Yunmen explained so profusely?

Huanglong Huinan said, "Jianfeng temporarily points out the road, indirectly helping beginners; Yunmen then went through his transformation, so to make people of later times be unwearied." I say, if the waves of Chan were alike, innumerable ordinary people would be bogged down.

Yunmen stayed a long time with Jianfeng, Caoshan, and Sushan; this monk thought surely he must know Jianfeng's methods, therefore he inquired further from Yunmen about Jianfeng's answer. If Yunmen had then used Jianfeng's needle and thread, it would be a donkey-tethering stake. Suddenly he brought out the antique rut-turning drill of Muzhou, and the cup fell to the ground, the saucer broke into seven pieces. This monk didn't understand Jianfeng's meaning; Yunmen gave him another way of living—it was much like pouring oil to stop a fire, like fanning to melt ice.

Zhu-an has already evaluated it thoroughly; his verse says,

> Jianfeng, don't direct the front;
> Yunmen, stop with the curios!
> By nature the carp of the eastern sea
> Whacks Indra on the nose.

Zhu-an is even more exceedingly compassionate than Yunmen, but people find it even harder to understand. It doesn't compare to Tiantong's cool eye, which nevertheless after all amounts to a little bit:

Verse *Starting in, it turns out he uses medicine for a dead horse:*
The reviving incense is about to cause you peril.
If all your life you squeeze out sweat through all your body,
Only then will you believe he didn't spare his eyebrows.

256

Commentary Jianfeng's medicine for a dead horse didn't work as medicine—this monk was a man who had already perished and lost his life; Yunmen gathered some reviving incense, to enable the dead to come back to life again.

In *Miscellaneous Lore* it says that in 84 AD, during the Han dynasty, an emissary came from the Yuezhi nation of the West with a gift of four ounces of incense, as big as sparrow eggs, colored like mulberry and cypress. Later, when there was a great plague in the capital city, the emperor took the incense and burned it; the dead revived within three days; the fragrance of the incense lasted for three months. The incense comes from the Man-bird Mountains on the Isle of Clustered Caves, where there are trees like maple whose fragrance can be sensed for miles. It is called the tree that returns the living spirit; the root is cut, and the sap is boiled to a black paste in a jade pot. One name is the vitalizer, a second name is the reviver, a third is sandalwood, a fourth is death-remover.

In an informal talk, Tiantong said, "Having sufficiently gathered revivifying incense, alike they come beat the poison drum." Yunmen's leftover, Tiantong says, is revivifying incense, but elsewhere they have made it into a poison drum. Just try to make them turn around and they can't breathe out; choke their throats and stop their noses, and still sweat will pour from all over their bodies.

Master Zhi said, "Suddenly realizing that fundamental nature is basically empty is like fever breaking in a sweat." Even so, how many strands of eyebrows do I have left?

Added Sayings / Case **A monk asked Jianfeng, "'The Blessed Ones of the ten directions are on one road, the gate of nirvana'—where is that road?"**—For a swift horse there's nothing like a hole to slow it up.

Jianfeng drew a line in the air with his staff and said, "It is here."—I believe a half for now.

The monk brought this up to Yunmen and asked him—If you doubt, seek elsewhere.

Yunmen said, "This fan leaps up to the thirty-three heavens and hits the emperor of the gods on the nose.—Please speak in our language.

The carp of the Eastern Sea is hit once with the stick, and it rains buckets.

Do you understand?"—When you understand this way, it's even harder to understand.

Added Sayings /Verse

Starting in, it turns out he uses medicine for a dead horse—The thunderous hand uses wolf and tiger medicine.

The reviving incense is about to cause you peril—Opening the coffin, rescuing from death, there is a special miraculous power.

If all your life you squeeze out sweat through all your body—If the medicine doesn't stun, the malady won't be cured.

Only then will you believe he didn't spare his eyebrows—Head and all has disappeared.

62 MI HU'S "ENLIGHTENMENT OR NOT?"

Introduction   Bodhidharma's highest truth, Emperor Wu's confusion; Vimalakirti's teaching of nonduality, Manjusri's verbal excess. Is there anyone who has the ability to enter in actively?

Case   Mi Hu had a monk ask Yangshan, "Do people these days need enlightenment or not?"
Yangshan said, "It's not that there is no enlightenment, but what can be done about falling into the secondary?"
The monk went back and reported this to Mi Hu. Hu deeply agreed with this.

Commentary   Chan Master Mi of the capital city was called Master Mi the Seventh, and also called Mi Hu, 'Mi the Foreigner'—he was the seventh child of his house in lay life, and he had a beautiful beard; hence the two names. According to *Jewels of the Eight Directions*, he succeeded to Xuefeng, but here, based on his being a fellow student with Yangshan, he succeeded to Guishan.
This monk had just asked, "Do the eminent sages since antiquity arrive at the real truth?" Mi Hu said, "Yes." The monk said, "If it's the real truth, how can it be arrived at?" This is not different from the situation of needing enlightenment. Mi Hu said, "At the time when Huo Guang sold a phony silver city and gave the receipt to the chief of a foreign tribe, whose doing was this?" Foguo extolled Mi Hu as a real man of knowledge—the name does not come down in vain. The monk said, "I can only shut my mouth and say nothing." Mi Hu said, "On even ground

259

you make people help out." Just as Mi Hu said, "Yes, they arrive," Yangshan said, "It's not that there is no enlightenment, but what can be done about falling into the secondary?" If we don't need to attain enlightenment, still it's said, "Only when you agree on your own will it be near."

Master Shengmo always used to say that Touzi's recitals of ancient stories are superbly beautiful within—whichever one comes up has no different value. He once recited this story and said, "Even though Yangshan was right in speaking this way, still can he avoid falling himself? If he can avoid it, there's still one who very much disagrees. If he can't avoid it, he also falls into the secondary. Although Mi Hu approved it, did he himself have a way to emerge? People, try to examine and see. If you can find it out, for both men the tiles crumble and the ice melts. If you can't find it out, don't be hasty now." His verse said,

> Atop the green peak he questions the man;
> Pointing out where the mountains end, he doesn't let him settle his body.
> Even though able to avoid the observance of autumn,
> How can that compare to the spiritual sprouts not invading spring?

I say, without the spring breeze the flowers don't bloom; and after they bloom, they also are blown away and fall.

National Teacher Zhong asked an imperial attendant monk, "What does 'buddha' mean?" The monk said, "It means 'enlightened.'" The National Teacher said, "Has a buddha ever been deluded?" He said, "No, never deluded." The National Teacher said, "Then what's the use of enlightenment?" The imperial attendant monk had no reply. This also has the meaning of fundamentally no delusion or enlightenment. I always liked Xuedou's saying, "'Fundamentally there is no delusion or enlightenment'—such are common as hemp and millet. I only approve Lingyun as an adept."

If enlightened, one falls into the secondary; if not, one can only agree oneself. What is right? Tiantong himself has a technique:

Verse *The secondary—distinguishing enlightenment, breaking up delusion:*
Quickly you should free your hands and relinquish net and trap.

Accomplishment, before it's exhausted, becomes an extra thumb:
Wisdom can hardly know, like you can't bite your own navel.
The full moon's icy disk weeps in the autumn dew:
The birds are cold in the jade tree, the dawn breeze is chill.
Brought forth, great Yang distinguishes real and false:
Completely without flaw, the white jade is esteemed.

commentary   "The secondary—distinguishing enlightenment, breaking up delusion."
When illumination comes, darkness disappears; when wisdom arises,
confusion dies out. All of these are things on the road.

According to the *Brief Sets* of the *Book of Changes*, a trap is how to get a
rabbit; when the rabbit is caught, the trap is forgotten. A net is how to
get a fish; when the fish is caught, the net is forgotten. So words are a trap
for images, images are nets for ideas: those who keep the words are not
those who get the image, those who keep the image are not those who
get the idea.

If you turn to the secondary and say that one must arrive at enlightenment once, what about the saying, "Even if you have marvelous enlightenment, you should spit it out too." Right away letting go, you
arrive home, without anything more; then for the first time you forget
the net and abandon the trap. Effort and knowledge, accomplishment
and wisdom, are both on the second level; when accomplishment ends
and wisdom cannot know, for the first time you attain a little unity.

In the outer chapters of *Zhuangzi,* chapter eight, on extra appendages, it
says webbing on the feet is useless flesh, an extra finger is an unnecessary
finger. A commentary says that on webbed feet the big toe is joined to
the second; and an extra finger is a sixth finger. If accomplishment isn't
exhausted it becomes an extra appendage, useless flesh.

In the *Spring and Autumn Annals,* King Wen of Chu, invading Shen,
passed through Deng. Marquis Qi of Deng said, "He is my nephew,"
and let him stay there as a guest. His other nephews Chui, Ran, and Yang
implored him to kill the one from Chu, but Marquis Qi wouldn't allow
it. The three nephews said, "The one who destroys Deng will certainly
be this man (Wen of Chu). If you don't plan ahead, later you'll bite your

navel." A footnote says (that 'bite the navel') means 'won't make it' (impossible to do anything about it). Where knowledge doesn't reach, wisdom cannot know.

'The aging rabbit' is (a literary term for) the full moon. Master Danxia Zichun said, "The water clear, the moon full, the wayfarer is sad; the icy disk weeps in the autumn dew." If you cling to it, that won't do.

According to the *Great Wilderness Scripture,* on the Kunlun Mountains there are jewel trees which bear fruit like pearls, and as small. In the *Seal Within the Mystery,* "The spiritual tree stands aloof but the phoenix doesn't rest on it." Together with "the crane doesn't stop its action," these do not allow clinging fondly and sitting there fixedly. The bird is cold and chilled but doesn't want to alight on its trunk, branches, or leaves.

According to the *Yang* section of the *Classic of Poetry,* the flaw on white jade can still be polished off; a problem inside the gem is called a defect—the substance is cleft; a problem outside is called a flaw—the color is impure. According to the verse, Yangshan esteems the clear white jade without flaw, he doesn't fall into the secondary. What is the primary? Only after you're greatly enlightened will you finally realize that's not it.

Added Sayings /Case

Mi Hu had a monk ask Yangshan, "Do people these days need enlightenment or not?"—Have they ever been deluded?

Yangshan said, "It's not that there is no enlightenment, but what can be done about falling into the secondary?"—How can you avoid it?

The monk went back and reported this to Mi Hu—Which number is this?

Mi Hu deeply agreed—It's not that there is no agreement, but how can you avoid the secondary?

Added Sayings /Verse

The secondary—distinguishing enlightenment, breaking up delusion—A man from bandit territory escorts a brigand.

Quickly you should free your hands and relinquish net and trap—Put it down.

Accomplishment, before it's exhausted, becomes an extra thumb—After all it is beyond one's lot.

Wisdom can hardly know, like you can't bite your navel—Where the power of King Yu doesn't reach, the sound of the river flows to the west.
The full moon's icy disk weeps in the autumn dew—If you're attached to it, that won't do.
Brought forth, great Yang distinguishes real and false—He can't be fooled a bit.
Completely without flaw, the white jade is esteemed—Just don't glom onto it.

63 ZHAOZHOU ASKS ABOUT DEATH

Introduction   Sansheng and Xuefeng were spring orchids, autumn chrysanthemums; Zhaozhou and Touzi were the gem of Bian, the gold of Yan. On a markless balance, both sides are even; in a bottomless boat they cross in one place. When the two meet, what then?

Case   **Zhaozhou asked Touzi, "When someone who has undergone the great death then returns to life, how is it?"**
Touzi said, "He can't go by night—he should arrive in daylight."

Commentary   Chan Master Datong of Touzi Mountain in Shu province first visited Chan Master Wuxue of Cuiwei. He happened to find him in the hall walking around; he immediately went forward to greet him with a bow and asked, "How does the master point out to people the esoteric meaning of Chan?" Cuiwei stopped walking and looked around at him; Touzi said, "Please direct me." Cuiwei said, "Do you want a second ladleful of foul water?" Touzi suddenly realized enlightenment; he bowed in thanks and withdrew. Cuiwei said, "Don't fall down." Touzi said, "When the time comes, the sprouts grow of themselves."
Another day Touzi casually asked, "What is the principle of buddhahood?" Cuiwei said, "Buddhahood is not a principle." Touzi said, "Doesn't that fall into emptiness?" Cuiwei said, "Real emptiness is not empty." On this occasion he presented a verse of prophecy which said,

> *When has the buddha principle ever been a principle?*
> *Real emptiness is not empty.*

Datong will dwell in an abode of silence,
Spreading the message of our teaching.

Touzi returned to Mount Touzi by Tongcheng, in his native region. Zhaozhou first met him at Tongcheng: Zhaozhou said, "Are you not the hermit of Touzi?" Touzi said, "Give me a coin for tea and salt." Zhaozhou went ahead up the mountain; Touzi arrived later, carrying a jar of oil. Zhaozhou said, "I have long heard of Touzi, but now that I've come here I only see an old man selling oil." Touzi said, "You only see an old man selling oil—you don't recognize Touzi." Zhaozhou said, "What is Touzi?" Touzi held up the oil jar and said, "Oil! Oil!"

Touzi set two places for tea and served Zhaozhou; he passed the cakes to Zhaozhou himself, but Zhaozhou paid no attention. Then Touzi had an attendant pass them; Zhaozhou bowed three times to the attendant. Now tell me, what was his meaning?

Chan Master Zhen of Yungguang temple in Su province said in a talk, "If the points of words miss, home is ten thousand miles away. You must let go your hold of the cliff, allowing yourself to accept, and after annihilation return to life again. I cannot fool you." Zhaozhou took this idea and asked about it; anyone but Touzi would after all have been helpless, but Touzi said, "One can't go by night—one should arrive in daylight." This seems to be the same in words and intent as an ordinary one who wants a white willow cane without stripping the bark, but when you get to the inner reality, it indeed accords with Zhaozhou's question. Zhaozhou said, "I am a thief to begin with—he has even robbed me!" Henceforth Touzi became famous on the Path, and a group gathered around him; they requested the emperor to name the temple Abode of Silence, in accordance with his prophecy.

Baiyun Shoudan's verse says,

Dying away, coming to life—his fangs are still showing.
One should arrive during the day—already he's gone ahead.
In the villa pond of whose house—
A pair of mandarin ducks—they cannot be depicted.

Try to see Tiantong's one stroke coloring:

Verse   *The seed castle, the aeon rock—subtly exhausting the beginning.*
       The living eye in the ring illumines vast emptiness.
       Can't go by night—arrive by the dawn's light.
       The sound of the family couldn't be entrusted to goose or fish.

Commentary According to the *Treatise on Transcendent Wisdom*, if there is a castle one-hundred-days'-march long on all sides filled with mustard seeds, and every year one seed is taken away, when the seeds are exhausted, the aeon is still not exhausted. As for the aeon rock, in Sanskrit an aeon is called a kalpa—here it is called a time span. According to the *Tower Ashes Scripture,* there is a huge boulder over ten miles square; every hundred years gods come and brush it with their gossamer sleeves: when the stone is worn away, the aeon is still not ended. When this seed castle and aeon rock are exhausted, this is exhausting the present, and reaching the time before the empty aeon, after which the eye comes alive.

As for "in the ring," according to Zhuangzi, "The pivot first finds its ring, whereby it can respond endlessly." This means that turning without limit is what has found its ring: the emptiness within the ring is the essence, turning is the inexhaustible function.

An emissary of the Western Han dynasty told a tribal chief, "The emperor shot a goose in the forest—on the goose's leg was tied a letter from a captive." Because of this the chief didn't dare deceive him. The daughter of Cai Bojie of Han was named Yan, and called 'Cultured Beauty.' She was the wife of Dong Si. As he followed the banks to keep order, Si rowed around; they were captured by border patrols, and she was made queen of the tribe. Longing for her home, she wrote a message, sealed it in a ball of wax, and tied it to a goose's neck. When the goose reached the land of Han, as it drank water the wax ball fell off and was swallowed by a fish. A fisherman cut open the fish and found the message, and knew where Yan was. This part of Tiantong's verse eulogizes "Don't travel by night—arrive in the daytime." Never has the disgrace of the family been shown outside, falsely transmitting a message. Even so, turning back to Tiantong, the attendant who just came gives thanks for the transmission of the Dharma.

Added
Sayings
/Case
Zhaozhou asked Touzi, "How is it when someone who has undergone the great death comes back to life?"—The probing pole is in his hand. **Touzi said, "He can't go by night—he should arrive in daylight."**—The shadowing grass is around him.

Added
Sayings
/Verse
The seed castle, the aeon rock—subtly exhausting the beginning—Consummating the present, then you can set up.
The living eye in the ring illumines vast emptiness—Coming back to life after annihilation, you can't be fooled.
Can't go by night—arrive by the dawn's light—Already on the way.
The sound of the family couldn't be entrusted to geese or fish—This is already wrongly transmitting the message.

64 ZIZHAO'S SUCCESSION

Introduction Yunmen personally saw Muzhou, but he offered incense for Xuefeng; Touzi received it personally from Yuanjian, yet he succeeded to the Dharma of Dayang. On the branches of the coral trees, jade flowers bloom; in the forest of sandalwood, golden fruits ripen. But tell me, how do you create?

Case Head monk Zizhao asked Fayan, "In opening a hall as a teacher, to whom do you succeed?"
Fayan said, "Dizang."
Zizhao said, "You're very much turning your back on our late teacher Changqing."
Fayan said, "I didn't understand one saying of Changqing's."
Zizhao said, "Why don't you ask?"
Fayan said, "'In myriad forms, a single body is revealed'—what is the meaning?"
Zizhao raised his whisk.
Fayan said, "This is learned at Changqing's place—what about on your own part, head monk?"
Zizhao had nothing to say.
Fayan said, "How about 'in myriad forms a single body is revealed'— is this effacing myriad forms or not effacing myriad forms?"
Zizhao said, "Not effacing."
Fayan said, "Two."
The students around all said, "Effacing."
Fayan said, "In myriad forms a single body's revealed!!!!!"

268

Commentary Fayan studied for a long time with Changqing Huileng, then succeeded
to Dizang. Changqing's senior monk Zizhao in the past used to discuss
and evaluate past and present stories of happenings with master Fayan,
and in his heart was irritated at him; so he led a group to go especially to
Fu province to interrogate him. The master, informed of this, went out
with a group to greet him; he was especially polite and observed the
statuses of guest and host; each held a whisk (as a teacher). During tea,
Zizhao suddenly flushed and raised his voice, saying, "Elder, in opening
a hall (as a teacher), to whom do you succeed?" The master said, "Dizang." Zizhao said, "Aren't you turning your back on our late teacher
Changqing? I was with you in his congregation for dozens of years,
discussing and evaluating past and present; there was never any difference
(between us)—why then did you succeed to Dizang instead?" This thing
is not a matter of many years, nor does it lie in long study—for example,
there were the 'Enlightened Overnight Guest' and Daoding Jian. How
can it be judged by outsiders? Zizhao was being factional and sectarian,
without thorough mastery of exegesis, and arbitrarily gave rise to slander and detraction. At that time Fayan deeply pitied this kind, who were
not complete adepts, and wrote *Treatise on Ten Guidelines for Chan Schools*
to educate them; students should not fail to read it. Human sentiments
and the power of the Way are as disparate as sky and earth. Therefore
Fayan used something basic to answer Zizhao, saying, "I didn't understand a saying." That is, the great master didn't explain, didn't argue, but
just took something they had thoroughly discussed before in Changqing's assembly as a test; Zizhao treated it as before, but as soon as he was
challenged, he fell apart—as he went along seeking rescue, all the more
he showed incompetence. We might say, 'a defeated army can't be swept
away with a broom.' Zizhao and his group were shamed and withdrew:
Fayan then had him stay, and said to him, "If you kill your parents, you
can still repent and reform, but if you repudiate great wisdom, it is
virtually impossible to repent and reform." After all Zizhao had no
reply; henceforth he studied with Fayan, discovered his own insight, and
didn't open a teaching hall any more.

The ancients would respond to the wicked with good, respond to the
angry with kindness; after that they would open them up and awaken
them, with equanimous buddha-wisdom. This senior Zizhao succeeded

to Fayan, but this was still not enough to requite Fayan's profound virtue or to purify his own beginner's mind.

Tiantong just used Zizhao's question and Fayan's final statement to versify this, naturally right from start to finish.

Verse   *Transcending thought to see Buddha,*
Breaking down an atom to produce a scripture.
The family law presently becoming—
Who establishes a school?
The moon follows the boat along the river's silken clarity;
Spring rises along with the grasses into the green in the burnt patches.
Effacing, not effacing:
Listen with care—
The three paths have become overgrown, but it's still possible to return:
The pine and chrysanthemums of yore are still aromatic and fragrant.

Commentary   The preface to the *Complete Enlightenment Scripture* says, "The mind is fundamentally enlightened—due to the arising of thoughts we float and sink. The bank doesn't really move—it rushes by because of the movement of the boat." The *Flower Garland Scripture* says, "There is a great scripture, equal in size to the universe, within an atom; the same is true of all atoms. Someone with clear eyes breaks open the atom and produces the scripture for the benefit and salvation of all people." Tiantong draws on these two great scriptures and joins them in a single verse.

As for "effacing myriad forms," whose myriad forms are the myriad forms? Whose single revelation is alone revealed? In this public case, presently becoming, the family law is always there—who still sets up a school and opens the door? According to the Flower Ornament school, "Three boats sport in the moon—it follows each boat; over the one route of the clear river it reflects alone for a thousand miles."

In a poem by Hui Song, "The river cuts through the hills and disappears; the spring enters the burned patches, green." In Xie Xuanhui's poem, "The remaining mists, dispersing, form patterns; the clear river is pure as silk." The moon follows the three boats, the spring follows the hundred grasses—the 'three boats' and 'hundred grasses' are the 'myriad forms,' the 'moon' and the 'spring' are the 'single revelation.' According to Tiantong's verse, seeing 'effacing' and 'not effacing' is extremely coarse-minded; here you should just be very attentive and careful, and exhaust the details.

Don't you see how Elder Zifang also came from Changqing's place and Fayan asked him about the same saying—Zifang also held up his whisk. Fayan said, "How can you understand in this way?" Zifang said, "What is your honorable opinion?" Fayan said, "What do you call myriad forms?" Zifang said, "The ancients didn't efface myriad forms." Fayan said, "In myriad forms a single body is revealed—why talk about effacing or not?" Zifang was suddenly enlightened. At the end of Fayan's previous discussion, he said, "In myriad forms a single body's revealed!!!!!"—at the end of this discussion he says, "In myriad forms a single body's revealed—why talk of effacing or not?" One might say, 'About to go, immediately returning, then realizing, when you sum up, the land is wretchedly little.' Mr Zizhao and Mr Zifang exhausted the subtlety and lost the source—this is the fault of the eddies of unclear knowledge. Dao Yuanming wrote in a poem on returning home, "The three paths are overgrown, but the pine and chrysanthemum still remain." Jiang Xiu, known as Yuanqing, wrote, "Opening three roads, only uncle Yang and uncle Qiu roam along together." This part of Tiantong's verse eulogizes Fayan understanding the source on hearing the words, and awakening the subtlety in the two teachers to not lose Changqing's essential message.

What is Changqing's message? In the myriad forms a single body is revealed.

Added Sayings /Case

Zizhao asked Fayan, "In opening a hall as a teacher, to whom do you succeed?"—If he had known before that today would produce an idle concern, he would regret not having used a good intention then.

Fayan said, "Dizang."—There's a place for the favor to be returned.

Zizhao said, "You are very much turning your back on our late teacher Changqing."—The elbow doesn't bend outwards.

Fayan said, "I didn't understand one saying of his."—He pretends not to know.

Zizhao said, "Why don't you ask?"—Bring in a wolf and it'll crap in the house.

Fayan said, "'In myriad forms a single body is revealed'—what is the meaning?"—He presents it right to his face.

Zizhao raised his whisk—A double case.

Fayan said, "This is learned at Changqing's place—what about on your own part?"—He breaks his arrows and takes away his net.

Zizhao had nothing to say—Just take a jump.

Fayan said, "How about 'in myriad forms a single body is revealed'—is this effacing myriad forms or not effacing myriad forms?"—He's been wrapped by the gourd from bottom to top with vines.

Zizhao said, "Not effacing."—The saying's become two pieces.

Fayan said, "Two."—Chan eyes are hard to fool.

The students around all said, "Effacing."—Even more unsuitability is shown.

Fayan said, "In myriad forms, a single body revealed!!!!!—Two faces, one die.

Added Sayings / Verse

Transcending thought to see Buddha—When the grass is withered, the falcon's eye is swift.

Breaking down an atom to produce a scripture—When the snow is gone, the horse's feet are light.

The family law presently becoming—Not too little, not too much.

Who establishes a school?—All flows from here.

The moon follows the boat along the river's silken clarity—One and many unobstructed, going and staying free.

Spring rises along with the grasses into the green in the burnt patches—Pick out Jiashan there.

Effacing, not effacing—Turning must go both ways.

Listen with care—Can't be too meticulous about things.

The three paths have become overgrown, but it's still possible to return—If you don't run downhill . . .

The pine and chrysanthemum of yore are still aromatic and fragrant—It's hard to catch a swift opportunity.

65 SHOUSHAN'S "NEW BRIDE"

Case   Tut, tut, pshaw, pshaw, stripping, removing; puff, puff, whoosh, whoosh, vague, confusing. Impossible to chew, hard to approach. Tell me, what story is this?

Introduction   **A monk asked Shoushan, "What is buddha?"**
Shoushan said, "A new bride rides a donkey, the mother-in-law leads it."

Commentary   (Shoushan was) Chan Master Xingnian of Baoying monastery in Ru province, a man from the province of Cai; his surname was Ti. He studied from Fengxue. Fengxue said to the assembly, "In ancient times the World Honored One looked at Kasyapa with his blue lotus eyes—what did he say then?" Shoushan immediately went out. Fengxue's attendant entered his room and asked further, saying, "Why didn't Xingnian answer you, master?" Fengxue said, "He understands." The next day, as Shoushan and the gardener Zhen had gone up to stand in attendance on Fengxue, Fengxue said, "What is the World Honored One's unspoken saying?" Zhen said, "The doves cry in the trees, their minds are in the hemp fields." Fengxue said, "Why are you making so much ignorant goodness? Why don't you investigate the spoken word thoroughly?" He asked again the same as before, to Shoushan—"What about you?" Shoushan said, "Activity expresses the ancient road, not falling into a somber, passive state." Fengxue said to Zhen, "Why don't you contemplate Xingnian's saying?"
Later on Shoushan appeared in the world. In the teaching hall he said, "If

273

you want to attain intimate understanding, just don't ask with a question. The question is in the answer, the answer is in the question. If you come with a question, I am under your feet. If you hestitate and deliberate, then all connection is lost."

One day he held up his bamboo stick and said, "If you call it a bamboo stick you are clinging; if you do not call it a bamboo stick you are opposing—what do you people call it?" Shexian Sheng grabbed it and broke it in two; throwing it at the bottom of the steps, he said back, "What is it?" Shoushan said, "Blind!" Shexian then bowed. Everywhere this is called the barrier of opposing and clinging.

There's a folk saying which goes, "It's backwards—a new bride rides a donkey, her mother-in-law leads it."

Foguo eulogized,

> Shoushan had a saying, transmitted past and present;
> Stop saying these words are a reverse—
> The new bride is drunk and rides on the donkey,
> The people then laugh and laugh at the mother-in-law leading.

He didn't versify it as delightfully as Tiantong did:

Verse
> The new bride rides the donkey, her mother-in-law leads it:
> Their appearance and style are indeed natural.
> How laughable, the neighbor girls imitating a frown:
> To other people it increases ugliness, does not make beauty.

Commentary Yuantong Xiu's *Verse on the Iron Wall* says,

> Why bother to comb the hair three times a day?
> If the roots are strong when pulled, then stop.
> Most lose to the fineness of her skin and features—
> Even without rouge she's still elegant.

Shoushan's answer doesn't use adornments; the old woman and the bride are naturally graceful.

When Xishi had a pain in her chest, she held her chest and grimaced. It made her even more beautiful. Homely girls imitating her only increased their ugliness. This is a criticism of study by mouth and ear, those who do not work for ineffable enlightenment. Wholeheartedly anticipating creating beauty, the four limbs and eight arteries standing by do not consent.

Added Sayings /Case **What is Buddha?**—How very fresh and new!
A new bride rides a donkey, the mother-in-law leads it—What principle is this?

Added Sayings /Verse *The new bride rides the donkey, her mother-in-law leads it*—The original doesn't need to be brought out.
Their appearance and style are indeed natural—Can't be depicted completely, can't be drawn exactly.
How laughable, the neighbor girls imitating a frown—Acting clever, turning out inept.
To other people it increases ugliness, does not make beauty—It fetches the laughter of bystanders.

66 JIUFENG'S "HEAD AND TAIL"

Introduction Even those who subtly exercise spiritual powers cannot set a foot down; even those who forget objects and end thought cannot raise a foot. As you might say, 'Sometimes running to death, sometimes sitting to death.' How can you attain proper timing?

Case A monk asked Jiufeng, "What is the head?"
Jiufeng said, "Opening the eyes and not being aware of the dawn."
The monk asked, "What is the tail?"
Jiufeng said, "Not sitting on a ten-thousand-year seat."
The monk said, "How is it when having a head but no tail?"
Jiufeng said, "After all it's not precious."
The monk said, "How about having a tail but no head?"
Jiufeng said, "Though full, no power."
The monk said, "How about when you get the head and tail in mutual harmony?"
Jiufeng said, "Descendants gain power, in the room it's unknown."

Commentary Chan Master Daojian of Jiufeng in Yun province was a man from Guanhai in Fukien; his lay surname was Liu. Though he was at many teaching centers, he received the seal from Shishuang. He first lived at Jiufeng; there his students in the mystery were most numerous. Later he moved to Letan in Hong province, where he died. By imperial decree he was given the posthumous title Dajiao, Great Enlightenment.
One day a monk asked him, "What is the head?" If your eye of the Way is not thoroughly clear, and your knowledge of differentiation is not complete, even though you may discuss this head and tail, before and

after, it won't be clear in your mind and you won't know what it comes down to. Jiufeng said, "Opening the eyes and not being aware of the dawn."

Once a monk asked, "Everybody speaks of asking for help—what do you use to save people, Teacher?" Jiufeng said, "You tell me—has a mountain ever lacked a bit of earth?" The monk said, "If so, what is everybody in the land searching for?" Jiufeng said, "Yajnadatta missed his head and in his mind went crazy by himself." The monk said, "Is there anyone who does not go crazy?" Jiufeng said, "There is." The monk said, "Who is the one not crazed?" Jiufeng said, "Dawn breaking on the road, the eyes are not open." This is the manifest form of 'opening the eyes and not being aware of the dawn.'

The monk here asked, "What is the tail?" Jiufeng said, "Not sitting on a ten-thousand-year seat." Also a monk asked, "What is before Dipankara Buddha?" Jiufeng said, "Working hard, not gaining strength." The monk said, "What about right at the time of Dipankara Buddha?" Jiufeng said, "If the head is big, the tail is small." The monk asked, "What is after Dipankara Buddha?" Jiufeng said, "Retiring from rank but not knowing leisure." This is the appearance of 'not sitting on a ten-thousand-year seat.'

The monk asked, "How about having a head but no tail?" Jiufeng said, "After all, it's not precious"—this is 'opening the eyes and not being aware of the dawn.' The monk said, "How about having the tail but no head?" Jiufeng said, "Though full, no power." This is 'retired, not knowing leisure.' The monk said, "How about when you get the head and tail in mutual harmony?" Jiufeng said, "Descendants gain power"— they're satisfied and have power, "in the room it's unknown"—after all it's precious.

The *Source Mirror Collection* says, "If you want to enter our school's source, first you must know it exists, and then uphold it." It also says, "The head and tail must accord with each other; principle and practice should not be lacking, mind and mouth should not be contradictory. If you enter the source mirror, principle and practice are both complete."

Shishuang was Jiufeng's teacher: he said to his community, "Beginners who have not yet got the great matter first should know the head, and the tail will come of itself." Sushan came forth and asked, "What is the

277

head?" Shishuang said, "You should know it exists." Sushan said, "What is the tail?" Shishuang said, "Fulfilling the present." Sushan said, "How is it when one has the head but not the tail?" Shishuang said, "What's the use of spitting out gold?" Sushan said, "What about when having the tail but not the head?" Shishuang said, "There is still dependence." Sushan said, "If the head and tail are in harmony, then how is it?" Shishuang said, "Even if he doesn't even entertain this understanding I still don't approve of him yet."

Therefore Jiufeng said, "When the ancients spoke of the head, it was just to let you know it exists; speaking of the tail is just to make you use the present time to the full. Because you have so many unharmonious things, they have you remove them and obliterate them, to make you accomplish realization and fulfillment today. If someone is essentially so, real and true, always thus, then you shouldn't speak this way anymore. Even so, you must be such a person before you realize this. Now, don't make the same sound in different mouths; you should work hard right away. Take care."

I have used public cases about Jiufeng to illustrate this case of Jiufeng; having commented and explained thoroughly, the remaining sense is entrusted to Tiantong—his verse says,

Verse   *Round in a compass, square in a ruler:*
Used, it acts; left, it's concealed.
Stationary, the birds resting on the reeds:
Going back and forth, the ram caught in the fence.
Eating others' food,
Sleeping in one's own bed.
Clouds spring up and make rain,
Dew forms and turns into frost.
The jade thread is pushed through the eye of the golden needle:
Silk floss unceasingly spits from the shuttle's guts.
The stone woman's loom stops—the color of night turns toward noon:
The wooden man's road turns—the shadows of the moonlight have
reached the center.

Commentary One who finds the marvel 'horizontally and vertically', who meets the source left and right—this is what Zhuangzi called 'The round is in the compass, the square in the ruler.'

Confucius said to Yan Yuan, "Use this and it goes along; neglect it and it hides; do you and I alone have it?" If you are not thus, you are tuning a lute with the sounding-bar glued down, notching the side of a boat to mark where something fell overboard.

In the *Jewel Treasury Treatise* it says, "In the start of progressive practice there are myriad roads; the weary fish rests in the shoals, a slow bird dwells in the reeds—these two do not know the great ocean or the forest; people proceeding on petty ways are the same."

In the *Book of Changes*, under the *Great Vigor* hexagram, under negative at the top, it says, "A ram caught in a fence can't go back, it can't go forward. There is no profit. Hardship is auspicious."

"Eating others' food, sleeping in one's own bed" is like saying eating public food and letting your own donkey free. Also it is said, one who can eat people's food with a cool mouth is hard to find—coming forth, he makes fog and rain; where he goes in, ice freezes, frost congeals. This means that suddenly going out and suddenly going in is not yet mastery—you must have the needle threaded through, the stitching fine, the pattern going every which way with the loom threads unstrung. Just when the stone woman's loom stops, already the wooden man's road turns: just as the night's color turns toward noon, the shadows of the moonlight have reached the center. The last two lines of the verse are just one line. These days Confucian scholars of literature call this a reply on the other side of the phrase. I separate the hard and join the different like this so as to meet with Tiantong. You people, don't turn your backs on Jiufeng.

Added Sayings /Case **A monk asked Jiufeng, "What is the head?"**—Loftily transcending before the prehistoric buddhas.

Jiufeng: "Opening the eyes and not being aware of dawn."—The light doesn't go beyond the door.

Monk: "What is the tail?"—Walking alone after the aeon of emptiness.

Jiufeng: "Not sitting on a ten-thousand-year seat."—A hole doesn't reside in a nest.

Monk: "How is it when having a head but no tail?"—The first to go doesn't arrive.

Jiufeng: "After all it's not precious."—The butler, seeing the maid, takes care.

Monk: "How about when having a tail but no head?"—In the end he goes too far.

Jiufeng: "Though full, no power."—What use is it?

Monk: "How about when you get the head and tail in harmony?"—The paths of ruler and subject meet, above and below harmonize.

Jiufeng: "Descendants gain power, in the room it's unknown."—Each rests in their place.

*Added
Sayings
/ Verse*

Round in a compass, square in a ruler—A bowl is round, a tray is square.

Used, it acts; left, it's concealed—Revolving in a basket, turning in a bushel.

Stationary, the birds resting on the reeds—But can they fly high and range afar?

Back and forth, the ram caught in the fence—Unable to walk alone on earth.

Eating others' food—Better spit it right out.

Sleeping in one's own bed—Avoid forming roots.

Clouds spring up and make rain—Sprouting in spring, growing in summer.

Dew forms and turns into frost—Harvesting in autumn, storing in winter.

The jade thread is pushed through the eye of the golden needle—Continuous, uninterrupted.

Silk floss spits unceasingly from the shuttle's guts—Over and over, pervading equally.

The stone woman's loom stops—the color of night turns toward noon—The pattern goes every which way, the meaning is distinct of itself.

The wooden man's road turns—the shadows of the moonlight have reached the middle—Knowing how to go, you don't touch on the road of the present.

67 THE *FLOWER ORNAMENT SCRIPTURE'S* "WISDOM"

Introduction   One atom contains myriad forms, one thought includes a billion worlds. What about a powerful man who wears the sky on his head and stands on the ground, a spiritually sharp fellow who knows the tail when the head is spoken of—doesn't he turn his back on his own spirit and bury away the family treasure?

Case   **The *Flower Ornament Scripture* says, "I now see all sentient beings everywhere fully possess the wisdom and virtues of the enlightened ones, but because of false conceptions and attachments they do not realize it."**

Commentary   Throughout his great commentary on the *Flower Ornament,* the great master Zhengguan of Qingliang, classifying this level of the scripture, calls it the opening up of the causal nature. In the commentary on the practice and vows of Samantabhadra he calls it opening up the source of the nature of beings. How does it open? The chapter on manifestation says, "O Children of Buddha, there is not a single sentient being who does not fully possess the wisdom of the enlightened ones; it is only because of false conceptions, error, and attachments that they do not realize it. (A note says, ordinary people conceive illusions; those of the lesser and provisional greater vehicles have attachments—there is error in both.) If they give up false conceptions, then omniscience, spontaneous knowledge, and unhindered wisdom can become manifest." Then it cites the metaphor of an atom containing a scripture as extensive as the universe. A previous verse, on the 'single body revealed in myriad forms,' saying, "Transcending thought to see Buddha, breaking down an atom to produce a scripture," is precisely this topic of the scripture.

It also says, "Then the Buddha observed all the beings of the cosmos with his pure unobstructed eye of wisdom and said, 'How wonderful! How is it that these beings all have the wisdom of the enlightened ones, yet in their folly and delusion do not know or see it? I should teach them the right path to make them abandon illusion and attachment forever, so that they can perceive the vast wisdom of the enlightened ones within their own bodies and be no different from the Buddhas.'" Qingliang's great commentary says, "Sentient beings contain natural virtues as their substance and have the ocean of knowledge as their source: but when forms change, the body differs; when feelings arise, knowledge is blocked. Now to bring about knowledge of mind and unity with the substance, arrival at the source and forgetting of feelings, I discuss this scripture, with illustrations and indications." The explanation says, "This includes the explanation of the source of beings' illusion about reality; it is like a man with appearance befitting one full of virtue and wisdom who sees himself as poor, sick, and suffering in a dream—this is the 'change of form'—he doesn't see his original body—this is the 'differing of the body.' He takes it to be his own body—this is 'feelings arise'; he does not believe his own body is handsome and blessed with good qualities—this is 'knowledge is blocked.'"

A monk asked Baoci, "'When feelings arise, knowledge is blocked; when forms change, the body differs'—how is it before feelings arise?" Boaci said, "Blocked." Nobody knows where this comes from; most think 'forms' are 'concepts' and understand it in those terms. Students should know how Yangshan criticized Xiangyan, "I grant you understand the Chan of the Buddhas, but you haven't even dreamed of the Chan of the ancestral teachers." But tell me, how far is it from the Buddhas' Chan? Try to see into the meaning of Tiantong's verse by means of the passage of the *Flower Ornament Scripture*:

Verse   *Sky covers, earth bears,*
Making a mass, making a clump.
Pervading the universe, without bound,
Breaking down subatomic particles, with no inside.

Getting to the end of the mysterious subtlety,
Who distinguishes turning towards and away?
Buddhas and patriarchs come to pay the debt for what they said.
Ask old teacher Wang of Nanquan
Each person just eats one stalk of vegetable.

Commentary   Yantou said, "Let it flow from your own heart to cover sky and earth for me." Now Tiantong says, "Sky covers, earth bears"—why so contrary? It's just that he says this in terms of human sense—human intellect says that sky and earth give birth to humans—they call this the basic three (sky, earth, human beings). Buddhism, on the other hand, says that humans create heaven and earth—thus 'the three realms are only mind, myriad things are only consciousness.' Here it makes a mass, forms a clump, encompassing the cosmos with nothing outside, no bounds.

In the *Heroic March Scripture* the Buddha tells Ananda, "Examine the nature of earth; in its gross form it is the gross element earth, in its fine form it is subtle atoms, down to subatomic particles, which are next to nothing; analyzing the most minute form of matter, it is composed of seven parts—when you go even further to break down subatomic particles, this is real emptiness." I often quote the *Poem on Faith in the Mind,* which says, "The smallest is the same as large—you forget limitation entirely; the largest is the same as small—you do not see its bounds." If someone asks what is the largest thing in the world, I would say it is real emptiness. Why? Because the largest is the same as small—you do not see its bounds. If someone asks what is the smallest thing in the world, we should say real emptiness. Why? Because the smallest is the same as large—you forget the objective sphere entirely. Ah, what kind of man was the Third Patriarch—he uttered a single saying which no monk in the world can leap out of.

A monk asked Zhaozhou, "What is the mystery within the mystery?" Zhaozhou said, "How long have you been mystified?" The monk said, "I have been into this mystery for a long time." Zhaozhou said, "Anyone but me might have been mystified to death." Dongshan's *Seal in the Mystery* says, "Do not take to the road; but if you return, you turn your back on your father." Since it fills the cosmos, making a single entity, is

283

there indeed a mysterious subtlety apart from and beyond the dust of the turmoil? Is there indeed any before and behind, turning toward or turning away? Even if buddhas do not appear in the world, this doesn't cause any lessening; even when buddhas appear in the world, explaining and illustrating, this doesn't cause any increase. The breadth of the ocean of fame, the brightness of the sun of pride, are not worth talking about—all is presumption, exaggeration.

As Nanquan and Shashan were working picking bracken for vegetables, Nanquan picked up a stalk and said, "This is a fine offering." Shashan said, "'He' wouldn't take notice of a feast of a hundred delicacies, let alone this." Nanquan said, "Even so, everyone should taste it before they'll realize."

Mingan of Dayang said, "don't go on the path of mind; don't sit in effortless nothingness. When detached from existence and nonexistence, heaven and earth are wide open, empty." That is why Nanquan said, "Everyone should eat a stalk of vegetable; if you try to get another stalk, you'll go to hell as fast as an arrow shot."

I say, today there are seven people.

Added Sayings /Case	**I now see all sentient beings everywhere fully possess the wisdom and virtues of the enlightened ones**—A bear turns a somersault, a donkey does a tribal dance. **But because of false conceptions and attachments they don't realize it**—False conceptions and attachments aren't bad, either.
Added Sayings /Verse	*Sky covers, earth bears*—Reaching above, penetrating below. *Making a mass, making a clump*—Even a sword or axe cannot cut it open. *Pervading the universe, without bound*—The ten directions are without walls. *Dividing subatomic particles, with no inside*—Even the Buddha's eye can't see in. *Getting to the end of the mysterious subtlety*—A good thing isn't as good as nothing. *Who distinguishes turning towards and away?*—Nowhere to escape. *Buddhas and Patriarchs come to pay the debt for what they said*—When the words are many they harm practice.

Ask of old teacher Wang of Nanquan—He avoids Shashan.
Each person just eat one stalk of vegetable—There's nothing more besides
to work on.

68 JIASHAN "SWINGING THE SWORD"

Introduction Inside the heartland, the emperor's command; outside the castle walls, the general's order. Sometimes empowered at the gate, sometimes honored in the room—tell me, who is this?

Case A monk asked Jiashan, "How is it when getting rid of the dust to see Buddha?"
Jiashan said, "You should directly swing the sword. If you don't swing the sword, the fisherman stays in a nest."
The monk brought it up to ask Shishuang, "How is it when getting rid of dust to see Buddha?"
Shishuang said, "He has no country—Where will you meet him?"
The monk returned and quoted this to Jiashan: Jiashan went up in the hall and said, "In the establishment of method and school, he does not compare to me: in profound talk entering the principle, I am still a hundred steps behind Shishuang."

Commentary Chan Master Shishuang Qingzhu of Tan province first was at Guishan, where he served as the rice maker. Just as he was sifting rice, Guishan said, "Gifts from donors should not be thrown away." Shishuang said, "I'm not throwing it away." Guishan picked up a grain of rice off the floor and said, "You said you aren't throwing it away—where did this come from?" Shishuang had no reply. Guishan said, "Don't take this one grain lightly—hundreds of thousands of grains come from this one grain." Shishuang said, "Then where does this one grain come from?" Guishan laughed and returned to his room; that evening he went up in the hall and said, "People, there's an insect in the rice!"

Later Shishuang studied with Daowu, and asked about enlightenment that meets the eyes; Daowu called to a novice to add water to the pitcher. The story has been recounted before. Shishuang was with Daowu for two summers, then he received the seal of enlightenment. During the danger of the Huishang era (845-847, when the Buddhist orders were persecuted), he mixed in with the potters in Linyang in Tan province. He wandered during the daytime and stayed in at night.

In the beginning of the Dazhong era (847) a monk came from Dongshan and quoted Master Dongshan's saying, "At the beginning of fall, the end of summer, you brethren may go east or west; you must go where there is not an inch of grass for ten thousand miles. (A pause) But if there isn't an inch of grass for ten thousand miles, how can you go?" Shishuang said, "Going out the gate, already it's grass." The monk then related this to Dongshan, who said, "These are words of a teacher of fifteen hundred people—how many could there be in all China?" For the first time he became known as an enlightened man; he emerged from anonymity, and he dwelt as abbot at Shishuang monastery; ultimately according with Dongshan's prophecy, for twenty years he had an oceanic congregation of over a thousand. Again and again they sat constantly without lying down, erect as tree stumps—the name of his 'dead tree hall' originated from this.

A monk asked about getting rid of the dust to see Buddha: the question is one; Jiashan said, "If you don't swing the sword, the fisherman stays in a nest." Shishuang said, "He has no country—where will you meet him?" I say, in profound talk of the principle, Shishuang is better; in setting up method, Jiashan is a hundred steps ahead. Is there no one with two faces on one die? What does Tiantong say?

Verse   *The star-brushing sword, the army-washing weather.*
Settling disorder, deferring the merit, who else is it?
One morning the haze of dust clears over the four seas:
Robes hanging down, the imperial rule is naturally effortless.

Commentary   The style of the Linji school—the diamond sword kills the buddhas and patriarchs; Jiashan cuts off the old vines and breaks up the fox nests.

According to the *Annals of the Jin Dynasty*, Lei Huan was good at astronomy and familiar with the signs of the heavens. As Zhang Hua was looking between the North star and the star Altair, there was always a strange phenomenon: he called Huan, and they went up into a tower at night to gaze above. Huan said, "I have been examining this for a long time: the energy of precious swords has gone up into the heavens. They are in the region of the Feng City district of Yuzhang." Hua then recommended Lei Huan to be the governor of Feng City. As he was having a foundation excavated while rebuilding a prison there, he found a pair of swords ensheathed in stone; they shone with exceeding lustre. He sent one to Hua and kept the other at his own belt. Hua was executed and lost his sword. After Lei Huan died, his son became a provincial functionary, and wore his father's sword. When he went by the Yanping bridge, the sword leaped into the water. He ordered someone to go in after it. The man who went into the water saw two dragons with markings and was so frightened he came back.

According to the *Garden of Talk*, as King Wu was going to attack the state of Zhou, he ran into rain. San Xuansheng said, "Isn't this a disaster?" The king said, "No. Heaven is washing the troops." This part of Tiantong's verse eulogizes "If you don't swing the sword, 'the fisherman stays in a nest.'"

The *Book of Changes* says, "Emperors Huang, Yao, and Shun ruled the land with their robes hanging down—their effortless rule was enforced without command." This part of the verse eulogizes no nest to stay in—"He has no country," no sword to wield—"where will you meet him?"

Chan Master Tongan Cha said, "The subtle essence fundamentally has no location—throughout the body, where else is the source of its traces?" I say, I grant that you meet Shishuang, but you're still a hundred steps behind Jiashan. Do you want to see Jiashan? It is because of inequity that the sword is drawn from its precious scabbard; it is to treat disease that medicine is taken from the golden jar.

*Added
Sayings
/Case*
How is it when getting rid of the dust to see Buddha?—What's the necessity?
You should directly swing the sword—Of course.

If you don't swing the sword, the fisherman stays in a nest—If you seat it, it's not Buddha.

How is it when getting rid of the dust to see Buddha?—If you see, you don't get rid of; if you get rid of, you don't see.

He has no country—where will you meet him?—If not seated, it's a buddha.

The monk returned and quoted this to Jiashan—Going and coming is not easy.

Jiashan went up in the hall and said, "In the establishment of method and school, he does not compare to me; in profound talk entering the principle, I am still one hundred steps behind Shishuang."—Each has one piece.

Added
Sayings
/ Verse *The star-brushing sword, the army-washing weather*—Peace is the doing of the general, . . .

Settling disorder, deferring the merit, who else is it?—. . . but the general is not allowed to see peace.

One morning the haze of dust clears over the four seas—Just end ordinary feelings.

Robes hanging down, the imperial rule is naturally effortless—There is no special holy understanding.

69 NANQUAN'S "COWS"

Introduction   Becoming a Buddha and being a Patriarch is disliked for wearing a
defiled name; wearing horns and fur is pushed to the superior position.
This is why 'the true light doesn't shine, great wisdom appears foolish.'
There is yet another who is deaf for convenience and pretends not to be
skillful—do we know who he is?

Case   Nanquan said to the assembly, "The buddhas of past present and
future do not know it is: cats and cows know it is."

Commentary   In Dharma Master Feishan's *Preceptual Jewels* he discussed the teaching of
the special transmission of mind and criticized Nanquan, saying, "Someone like Nanquan never devoted himself to study, and didn't know the
fundamental—he is not worthy to speak of the teachings of the Buddha."
Going by the collection appended to the *Inexhaustible Lamp*, it is plainly
stated that Nanquan first learned the *Vinaya*, rules of monastic conduct,
next he heard the *Flower Ornament* and *Entry into Lanka* scriptures expounded, and entered into the contemplation of the middle way and the
Hundred Gates. Hearing that Mazu was transmitting the path outside of
words, he repeatedly sought his essential meaning, then suddenly managed to 'forget the trap.' One day as Nanquan was serving gruel, Mazu
asked, "What is in the bucket?" Nanquan said, "Shut up, old man, if
you're going to talk like this." Like this, Nanquan didn't defer to Mazu
in facing the situation; later on he paid back his debt in the hands of
Zhaozhou.
Nanquan asked a lecturer, "What is the ultimate principle of the *Nirvana*

Scripture?" The lecturer said, "Thusness is the ultimate principle." Nanquan said, "As soon as you call it 'thus,' it has already changed. Monks in the present time should act in the midst of different kinds." Zhaozhou, in front of the monks' hall, asked, "I don't ask about 'different'—what about 'kind'?" Nanquan pushed on the ground with both hands; Zhaozhou kicked him, and Nanquan immediately fell over on the ground. Zhaozhou ran into the life-prolonging hall (infirmary) shouting, "Sorry! Sorry!" Nanquan had an attendant ask Zhaozhou, "Sorry about what?" Zhaozhou said, "Sorry I didn't kick him again."

Nanquan, up in the hall, said, "Since youth I have brought up a water buffalo: when I was herding it east of the valley, I didn't let it eat the water plants of that country; when I was herding it west of the valley, I didn't let it eat the water plants of that country. Now it takes in a little bit anywhere possible, without being seen at all."

One day Nanquan saw the bath steward heating the bath and said, "After lunch, invite the water buffalo to bathe." The bath steward went and invited him; Nanquan said, "Did you bring a rope?" Zhaozhou pulled Nanquan's nose with his hand. Nanquan said, "Right, but too rough." Zhaozhou asked, "Where does one who knows it is go?" Nanquan said, "To the house of a patron in front of the mountain, to be a water buffalo." Zhaozhou said, "Thanks for your directions." Nanquan said, "Last night in the third watch the moon came to the window."

When Nanquan was about to pass away, the head monk asked, "After you die, where will you go?" Nanquan said, "Down the mountain, to be a water buffalo." The monk said, "Can I follow you?" Nanquan said, "If you follow me, you must come with a blade of grass in your mouth."

This talk about "different kinds" was first spoken by Nanquan; Guishan joined in, Daowu and Yunyan transmitted it, and now it is Caoshan's "three falls."

When Daowu went to Nanquan, Nanquan asked, "What is your name?" Daowu said, "Zongzhi (Source Knowledge)." Nanquan said, "Where knowledge doesn't reach how can you take as source?" Daowu said, "Just don't speak of it." Nanquan said, "Clearly if you speak of it then horns grow on the head." Three days later, as Daowu and Yunyan were in the back room mending, Nanquan passed by and asked, "The other day we said, 'Where knowledge doesn't reach, just don't speak of; if you

speak of it, horns grow in the head'—how do you put it into practice?"
Daowu immediately got up and went into the meditation hall; Nanquan
then left. Yunyan asked Daowu, "Little brother, why didn't you answer
the teacher just then?" Daowu said, "You are so sharp." Yunyan didn't
get it, and instead went to ask Nanquan, "Why didn't Daowu answer
that issue just then?" Nanquan said, "He is acting within different kinds."
Yunyan said, "What is acting within different kinds?" Nanquan said,
"Haven't you been told, 'Where knowledge doesn't reach, just don't
speak of; if you speak of it, then horns grow on the head.' You must go
act within different kinds.'"
Yunyan still didn't understand. Daowu knew he didn't get it, so he said,
"This man's affinity is not here." So he went back together with Yunyan
to Yaoshan. Yunyan subsequently related the foregoing story to
Yaoshan, who said, "How did you understand this time there, that you
have come back?" Yunyan had no reply. Yaoshan then laughed. Yunyan
then asked, "What is acting within different kinds?" Yaoshan said, "I'm
tired today; come another time." Yunyan said, "I have come back especially for this." Yaoshan said, "Go away for now." So Yunyan then left.
Daowu was outside the abbot's room; hearing Yunyan's failure, unconsciously he bit his finger so hard it bled. He went down and asked his
elder brother about what he had asked the teacher about. Yunyan said,
"The teacher didn't explain it to me." Daowu hung his head.
When both men were standing in attendance, Yaoshan asked, "Where
knowledge doesn't reach, don't speak of; if you speak of it, then horns
grow on the head." Daowu immediately said good-bye and went out.
Yunyan then asked Yaoshan, "Why didn't little brother Daowu answer
you?" Yaoshan said, "Today my back is sore—he understands; you
should go ask him." Yunyan then asked Daowu, "Why didn't you
answer the teacher just then?" Daowu said, "I have a headache today—
go ask the teacher."
Later when Yunyan passed on, he sent someone with a letter of farewell
to Daowu. After Daowu read it he said, "Yunyan didn't know it is—too
bad I didn't tell him that time. Anyway, even so, actually he was nonetheless a successor of Yaoshan."
Xuanjiao said, "When this man of old spoke this way, did he himself

know it is or not? When Yunyan didn't understand back then, in what
way didn't he understand?"
Cuiyan Zhi said, "Daowu said, 'Yunyan didn't know it is—too bad I
didn't tell him that time'—in speaking thus, did he know it is or not?"
I say, Yunyan was the teacher of Dongshan, the source of the whole
branch—over and over, time and again, he didn't understand this matter:
I have thoroughly recorded this, to give people of later times one-half-
power help in looking into it from the side. Was it only Yunyan who
didn't know it is? Cuiyan Zhi said, "Did Daowu know or not?" I say, not
only Daowu—does Cuiyan himself know or not?
Have you not seen how a monk asked Changsha, "Why don't the
Buddhas of the past, present and future know it is?" Changsha said,
"Before entering the Deer Park, they still had realized a little." The monk
said, "Why do cats and cows know it is?" Changsha said, "What's so
strange about that?" At this point I can just look on from the side; even
the great Tiantong must praise:

Verse   **Limping and palsied,**
Tattered and disheveled.
A hundred can't be taken, one isn't worth it.
Silent, knowing himself the peace of his state:
Ebullient, who says in his guts he's a fool?
All throughout the universe, everything becomes food—
Nose hanging all the way down, one may freely seek to repletion.

Commentary   "Limping and palsied" describes clumsiness. As Yaoshan was reading a
scripture, Baiyan said, "You should stop making monkeys of people,
Teacher." Yaoshan rolled up the scripture and said, "What time of day is
it?" Baiyan said, "High noon." Yaoshan said, "There is still this pattern?"
Baiyan said, "I don't even have nothing." Yaoshan said, "You are too
brilliant." Baiyan said, "I am just thus; what is your meaning, Teacher?"
Yaoshan said, "I am limping and palsied, ungainly in a hundred ways,
clumsy in a thousand, and yet go on this way."

293

A verse of Master Xian of Guanxi said,

> *Many years of austerities—a worn patched robe.*
> *Frayed threadbare, half flying with the clouds,*
> *I take it and hang it on my shoulders—*
> *Still it is better than the brocade robes people wear today.*

"A hundred can't be taken, one isn't worth it." Being in the crowd as though incompetent in a hundred ways, you'll be at rest all your life. "Silent, knowing himself the peace of his state; ebullient, who says in his guts he's a fool?" When an ascetic wore footwear upside down, people said he was wrong; he said, "Better to stick in your eyes than to hide my feet." The ascetic Raja was an unusual man—these words were widely circulated among the people. He might be called a skin-lamp ball—light on the inside, dark on the outside.

The final lines eulogize having fully investigated to the point where on the ground of rotten antiques, on your eyebrows and eyelids is all grains of rice: one day you'll pop through your sick belly skin and vomit out all your guts.

Added Sayings /Case

The buddhas of past, present and future don't know it is—Just because they know it is.

Cats and cows do know it is—Just because they don't know it is.

Added Sayings /Verse

Limping and palsied—Not near, he gives up hurrying.

Tattered and disheveled—People don't like to look.

A hundred can't be taken, one isn't worth it—Opening the gate, still weak; banking embers, still wet.

Silent, knowing himself the peace of his state—He moves his toes inside his shoes.

Ebullient, who says in his guts he's a fool?—He plays tricks among idiots.

All throughout the universe, everything becomes food—Can't be spit out, can't be swallowed.

Nose hanging all the way down, one may freely seek to repletion—He casts away a half, throws out a half.

70 JINSHAN ASKS ABOUT NATURE

Introduction One who hears the scent-bearing elephant crossing the river has already gone with the flow; even one who knows that birth is unborn is stayed by birth. If you go on talking about before concentration and after concentration, making bamboo shoots and making bamboo rope, you will be marking the boat when the sword is long gone already. Kicking the wheel of potential into motion, how can you particularly travel on one road? Let's try to bring this up:

Case Master Jinshan asked Master Xiushan, "Clearly knowing the unborn nature of life, why are we stayed by life?"
Xiushan said, "Bamboo shoots will eventually become bamboo, but if you use them now for bamboo rope, can you make them serve the purpose?"
Jinshan said, "Later on you'll be enlightened on your own."
Xiushan said, "I am just this way—what is your meaning?"
Jinshan said, "This is the monastery superintendent's quarters, that is the cook's quarters."
Xiushan then bowed.

Commentary When Chan master Hongjin, master of Pure Valley Mountain in Rong province, was the senior monk under Master Guichen of Dizang, two monks both bowed to Dizang, and Dizang said, "Both wrong." Neither monk said anything; they went down and asked for help from the Master Xiushan, who said, "You yourselves are magnificent and outstanding, yet you bow to someone else—is that not wrong?" Hongjin, hearing of

295

this, didn't agree; he said, "You yourself are deluded and ignorant—how can you help others?" Xiushan, indignant, went up to the hall to ask Dizang. Dizang pointed to the hall and said, "The cook went down into the pantry." Xiushan then realized his error.

Hongjin one day asked Xiushan, "Clearly knowing the unborn nature of life, why are we stayed by life?" The girl Antisha was of Brahmin caste, daughter of the elder Parsini of Chanti village, about ten miles from the city of Sravasti. As there was a big gathering at her house, inviting the Buddha and the monks, there it was she got her good fame. The great being Manjusri asked, "Is there anyone who knows the unborn nature of life who is held back by life?" The girl said, "There is—the one who clearly sees yet whose strength is not yet sufficient is held back by life." Master Xiushan answered, "Bamboo shoots will eventually become bamboo, but can you use them now for bamboo rope?" Bamboo rope is made from the covering of bamboo, used to tie things up. Bamboo shoots are tender and have no strength. Green bamboo has strength, while the bamboo shoot's strength is not yet mature, and it cannot be used for rope.

In Jiaofan's eulogy of Guanyin, he says,

Pity that my mind is clear but my power is insufficient:
Time after time seeds produce manifest patterns;
Like a man gone crazy from wine,
No sooner sworn off drink than finding some fine liquor.

This too is talking about strength being insufficient. I confess the ancients were so familiar with the doctrinal vehicle that whenever they spoke out it was in accord with the scriptures.

Jinshan (Hongjin) wanted the saying picked up and turned over; that's why he didn't approve and said to Xiushan, "You'll be enlightened on your own later on." Xiushan said, "My view is just like this—what is your meaning?" Mr Xiu first sat still where it's level on all sides, full in all ways; Mr Jin, rousting him, must have another road of life—he finally pointed out, "This is the superintendent's quarters, that is the cook's quarters." But tell me, does Mr Jin understand the unborn nature of life or not? Is he stayed by life or not? Xiushan then bowed—he studied the living word, not the dead word. This is no different from "The cook has gone down into the pantry."

Everybody says that Fayan's school is of one flavor, equal reality, the mystery within the essence; please consider the foregoing story. Tiantong saw this story is extraordinary and special, so he produced it in verse with his whole heart:

Verse   *Empty and at ease, without dependence;*
Lofty and serene, untrammeled:
Home and country peaceful, those who arrive are rare.
A little bit of power divides ranks and grades:
The fluid, clear mind and body is beyond right and wrong.
Right and wrong ended,
Standing alone on earth, there is no beaten track.

Commentary This eulogizes Jinshan's "This is the superintendent's quarters, that is the cook's quarters." When you eliminate dependence, you're spontaneously empty and at ease; where you're untrammeled, you're naturally lofty and serene. How many arrive at the homeland of peace? There must be no afflictions to cut off, no path of meditation to investigate, and throughout the twenty-four hours of the day, only dressing and eating be points of casual mental application.

The sense of Master Jin's question also has a little bit of hook and line to call forth the ancient, test the present, discern the level and determine power. Yet his fluid, clear body and mind is fundamentally beyond right and wrong. And Master Xiu also undeniably understands the talk proper to assessment of equal reality—but what can he do about Baizhang's saying, "Understanding the meaning according to the scriptures is the enemy of the buddhas of all times"? Therefore he distinguishes extent of power a little, and provisionally sets up gradations, saying that bamboo sprouts are weak and have no strength for use, whereas bamboo rope can haul a thousand pounds. "The arising of the tracks of words is how 'right' and 'wrong' come to be." Mr Jin cuts away for him, separately pointing out a road of living potential—he certainly is not opening a door, making a rut, deceiving a companion on the way. Mr Xiu bowed to apologize for his dullness. But do you recognize the forge and bellows of the house of the two masters?

> *In the fire, you must forge finer yet;*
> *On the anvil, then you can pound again.*

Added Sayings /Case

Jinshan asked Xiushan, "Clearly knowing the unborn nature of life, why are we stayed by life?"—Watch for the nose pin.

Xiushan said, "Bamboo shoots will eventually become bamboo, but if you use them now for bamboo rope, can you make them work?"—His nose is in another's hands.

Jinshan said, "Later on you'll be enlightened on your own."—Supposedly so great, he despises the good as base.

Xiushan said, "I am just this way—what is your meaning?"—Having stabbed the head, he turns to the man's heart.

Jinshan said, "This is the superintendent's quarters, that is the cook's quarters—He hit the ball to another place.

Xiushan then bowed—For now he treats him goodheartedly.

Added Sayings /Verse

Empty and at ease, without dependence—Yanking out the donkey-tethering stake.

Lofty and serene, untrammeled—Pulling apart the golden chains.

Home and country peaceful, those who arrive are rare—Setting foot where it's peaceful.

A little bit of power divides ranks and grades—Forcibly creating subdivisions.

The fluid, clear mind and body is beyond right and wrong—If you see the strange as not strange, . . .

Right and wrong ended . . . the strangeness will dissolve of itself.

Standing alone on earth, there is no beaten track—Halcyon has no reservations—what place is not splendid?

71 CUIYAN'S EYEBROWS

Introduction   One who sips blood and spits it at others defiles his own mouth; from greed for a cupful one will be paying back a debt to others all one's life. If you sell any paper, for three years there's a lack of bills to offer the ghosts. In my further inquiries for you people, is there any accounting or not?

Case   Cuiyan, at the end of a summer retreat, said, "All summer I've been talking to you brethren: look—are Cuiyan's eyebrows still there?" Baofu said, "The thief's heart is cowardly." Changqing said, "They've grown." Yunmen said, "Barrier!"

Commentary   Great Master Yongming of Cuiyan in Ming province was named Lingcan; he was a man from Hu province. He received the parting prophecy of Xuefeng, and taught a large assembly.

One day he went up in the hall and said, "All summer I've been talking this way and speaking that way for you brethren; look—are my eyebrows still there?" Many people in various places say that he basically wanted to confess himself, unawares doubling the case. Then, seeing Baofu's saying, "The thief's heart is cowardly," they just say he stuck firewood on his back and hid his own fault of speech. Foguo said, "Many people misunderstand and say, 'Under the bright sun in the blue sky he spoke without reason, creating an issue where there is none, confessing his own error first, to avoid being checked by others.' Fortunately this has nothing to do with it."

299

Changqing said, "They've grown." I say, as before they're above the eyes.

Yunmen's word "Barrier," like "Universal" and others, is called 'one-word Chan'.

All three succeeded to Xuefeng: see how the people of the house speak no outside talk. They saw Cuiyan teaching the assembly in an extraordinary manner so they all chimed in. When the ancients uttered remarks, they didn't blunder in their gestures.

An abbot invited Cuiyan to a meal on the occasion of a lecture on the teachings of the *Flower Ornament Scripture*. Cuiyan said, "I have a question—if you can answer it, then I'll partake of the meal." Then he held up a sesame cake and said, "Does this contain the Body of Reality?" The abbot said, "Yes." Cuiyan said, "Then I eat the Body of Reality." The abbot had no reply. The monk who gave the lecture said in behalf of the abbot, "What fault is there in that?" Cuiyan didn't agree. Yunmen said instead, "I especially thank the master for putting down seriousness and empty the seat." Jiaofan called Yunmen a king among monks.

As we might expect, Tiantong has threaded it through on one thread and produced it in verse from the beginning:

Verse   *The heart to be a thief,*
The guts to excel others;
Clearly, in all directions responding to situations effectively:
Baofu and Yunmen—their noses hang down and fool their lips;
Cuiyan and Changqing—their long eyebrows reflect in their eyes.
What limit is there to inept Chan followers?
Insisting that meaning and expression are equally stripped away,
They bury themselves, swallowing breath and voice,
Dragging down their ancestors, facing a wall carrying a board.

Commentary   Xuedou said, "A good thief is unknown even to ghosts and spirits." Since he was seen through, spied out by Baofu and Tiantong, Cuiyan is not an expert. What is hardly realized is that even the great Yunmen and Changqing both had their noses pierced at once by Cuiyan, using a single eyebrow hair! If you hide your head yet reveal your shadow, what strong-arm tactics can you count on to coerce people? Therefore he was able to clearly deal with situations freely in all ways, responding effectively.

Baofu said, "The thief's heart is cowardly." Yunmen said, "Barrier!" These are both long noses for patchrobed monks; they already notice the stink of dry crap a thousand miles away, they even smell the odor of rotten melons in late winter.

When Cuiyan said, "Are my eyebrows still there?" Changqing said, "They've grown." This is the time where 'the eminent monk on the wall replies to a call,' and 'the goose raised in the bottle has already come out with the voice'—how could it be figured out by discrimination and feeling? This is why Tiantong said their long eyebrows reflect in their eyes—he looks at people coolly; you can't fool him a bit.

Some say, a whole summer of growing branches and sending out creepers from entangling vines, now he cuts the growth, getting rid of the roots, slashing them away equally all at once. What they hardly realize is that 'after thirty years this story will circulate widely in the world'—why hide under cover, withhold your energy and swallow your voice? This way, you'd face a wall and carry a board, dragging down your ancestors. Everywhere they say carrying a board lengthwise across your shoulders, you only see one side. In the *Shang Shu* it says if you don't study, it's like facing a wall; a commentary says that facing a wall means not seeing anything. Haven't you read, "On Spiritual Mountain Buddha emitted light from the white curl on his forehead, lighting up to view eighteen thousand worlds in the East."

Added Sayings /Case

Cuiyan, at the end of a summer retreat, said—He still thinks there's some lack.

"All summer I've been talking to your brethren—By himself he exposes the shame of his house.

Look—are my eyebrows still there?"—He isn't harmed by sand in his mouth.

Baofu said, "The thief's heart is cowardly."—He too is one of the group. **Changqing said, "They've grown."**—He adds frost to snow.

Yunmen said, "Barrier!"—Blocks the street and cuts off the alley.

Added
Sayings
/Verse

The heart to be a thief—The loot is already exposed.

The guts to excel others—As though there were no one beside.

Clearly, in all directions responding to situations effectively—Dipping in broad daylight—skillful stealing.

Baofu and Yunmen—their noses hang down, fooling their lips—Searching too much.

Cuiyan and Changqing—their long eyebrows reflect in their eyes—Pretending not to know.

What limit is there to inept Chan followers?—How is Tiantong's ineptitude comparable to mine?

Insisting that meaning and expression are equally stripped away—When you want to hide you show all the more.

They bury themselves, swallowing breath and voice—If one doesn't bring up one's child as well as one's father, . . .

Dragging down their ancestors, facing a wall carrying a board—. . . the family will decline in a generation.

72 ZHONGYI'S "MONKEY"

Introduction A battle of wits across a river—hiding the army, concealing the troops. Face to face, they hold each other up—the spear of reality, the sword of truth. That is why patchrobed monks esteem the great function of the whole potential. From relaxation into urgency, try to spit it out in the open.

Case Yangshan asked Zhongyi, "What is the meaning of buddha nature?" Zhongyi said, "I'll tell you a simile: it's like putting a monkey in a room with six windows—when someone outside calls it, 'Simian! Simian!' the monkey then responds. In this way, when called through all six windows it responds."
Yangshan said, "What about when the monkey is asleep?"
Zhongyi got right down from his seat, grabbed and held Yangshan and said, "Simian, Simian, you and I see each other."

Commentary Chan Master Hongen of Zhongyi in Liang province was one of the eighty-some great enlightened men produced by Mazu—he was the spiritual great-uncle of Yangshan.
Yangshan received the precepts in Jiangling, then went to give thanks for the precepts. Zhongyi saw that Yangshan was young, and used the monkey responding to the six windows to explain the buddha nature; it was like bobbing a big breast playing with an infant. Yangshan hides an army and picks a fight; he cannot restrain his acumen: after bowing in thanks, he said, "Now I have heard your simile, Teacher; nothing is unclear. But there is one more thing. What about when the monkey

inside is asleep when a monkey outside wants to meet with it—what then?" Wonderful! A true lion cub immediately bares the claws and fangs of the cave of Dharma.

Zhongyi, unselfconscious, got down from his meditation seat, took Yangshan by the hand and said, "Simian, simian! You and I see each other." Why didn't he explain this metaphor? Yunju Yi said, "If Zhongyi hadn't gotten this saying from Yangshan at that time, where would there be Zhongyi?"

My late teacher and my spiritual uncle Shengmo were regarded with respect and awe in Chan communities for over twenty years. Master Bao of Jeng province was famous throughout North China; when my late master was making visits all over, he went to see Master Bao. He said, "Brother, you are elder—I should call on you. Before I always concentrated on Buddhism with every thought." My late teacher leaned forward and ventured to say, "How about now?" Master Bao said, "It's like a stranger." My late teacher said, "If I didn't get these words, I might have inanely gone a thousand miles." Bao got down from his seat, grabbed my teacher by the hand and said, "An adept, huh!" After that my teacher stayed for a few days.

Jiashan said to Fori, "In the dead ashes a tiny bean bursts into flame." That's about what this means. Xuanjiao said, "How could anyone but Yangshan see Zhongyi? But tell me, where did Yangshan see Zhongyi?" I say, in the teaching hall of this monastery. Chongshou Zhou said, "Can anyone determine this principle? If you can't, you're just fooling around with your minds, hands, and feet. Where is the meaning of the buddha nature?" I say, discern it in the gestures of playing with the mind and body.

Fojian said, "Zhongyi was flirting, Yangshan played the fool. A charming manner sells folly, folly indulges a charming manner. Even if the monkey sleeps, nevertheless he's awake in his heart. Even if you close off the six windows, where is the monkey not met? Do you want to see the two ancients' problem? 'The skin on each one's face is three inches thick.'" I say, it's hard to find someone who knows shame and conscience; but Tiantong has gotten a little ways:

Verse　*Freezing sleep in a snowy room, the year about ended;*
The recondite ivy gate does not open at night.
Groves and forests withered in the cold—look at the changing conditions:
The spring wind's blowing stirs the ashes in the pipe.

Commentary　The *Biographies of Sages of Yore in Runan* says, "One time a great snow piled up over ten feet over the ground. The magistrate of Loyang personally came out to check around; he saw someone and dug him out of the snow—it was a beggar. When he got to Yuan An's house, there was no pathway, so he thought An had already died. He had the man shovel away the snow. He entered the door and saw An lying there. He asked him, 'Why don't you go out?' An said, 'In the great snow everyone is starving. It's not appropriate to deal with people.' The magistrate considered him wise, and recommended him for an honorary degree." This (freezing sleep in a snowy room) versifies Zhongyi speaking in a simile, talking in a doze—after all he is not wide awake. "The recondite ivy gate does not open at night"—suddenly rapped by Yangshan, Zhongyi then acts with his whole body, a barren tree in the autumn sky. "The spring wind's blowing stirs the ashes in the pipe"—among the seasonal duties described in the ancient *Book of Rites*, a bamboo tube is cut—this is called a 'pipe'—it is put in a closed room, its end filled with ashes made from reeds: when the breath of the moon comes it makes the ashes fly and empties the tube; then positive energy is born. That is life within death, like Zhongyi and Yangshan meeting like adepts. After meeting, then what? Don't bother to stand a long time.

Added　**Yangshan asked Zhongyi, "What is the meaning of buddha nature?"**—
Sayings　This professor is indeed capable of holding a discussion.
/Case　**Zhongyi said, "I'll tell you a simile**—It's appropriate provisionally, not appropriate in reality.
It's like setting a monkey in a room with six windows—Will it agree to rest quietly?
When someone outside calls it, 'Simian! Simian!' the monkey then responds—A second try isn't worth half a cent.

In this way, when called through all the six windows, it responds."— 'She just wants to have the master acknowledge her voice.'

Yangshan said, "What about when the monkey is asleep?"—Don't talk in your sleep.

Zhongyi got right down from the seat, grabbed and held him and said—Have you waken up yet?

"Simian, simian! You and I see each other."—Why didn't you say so before?

Added Sayings /Verse *Freezing sleep in a snowy room, the year about ended*—If the door of concealment does not open . . .

The recondite ivy gate does not open at night—The dragon has no dragonic statements.

Groves and forests withered in the cold—look at the changing conditions—Almost died entirely.

The spring wind's blowing stirs the ashes in the pipe—Luckily revived again.

73 CAOSHAN'S FULFILLMENT OF FILIAL PIETY

Introduction   Lurking in the grasses, sticking to the trees, one turns into a spirit. Being constrained and unjustly punished, one becomes a ghostly curse. When calling it, you burn paper money and present a horse; when repelling it, you curse water and write charms. How can you get peace in the family?

Case   A monk asked Caoshan, "How is it when the mourning clothes are not worn?"
Caoshan said, "Today Caoshan's filial duty is fulfilled."
The monk said, "How about after fulfillment of filial duty?"
Caoshan said, "Caoshan likes to get falling-down drunk."

Commentary   A monk asked Chan Master Tongan Wei, "How was it before Niutou saw the Fourth Patriarch?" Tongan said, "A spirit shrine beside the road—all who see it raise their fist." The monk asked, "How about after seeing the Fourth Patriarch?" Tongan said, "In the house there is no bier—the whole family is not pious."
This monk said, "How is it when the mourning clothes are not worn?" Dongshan Chu said, "Take off your sooty bandanna and stinking shirt and be a free and clear monk." Later a monk asked him, "What is Buddha?" He answered, "Three pounds of hemp." If you reach this point, you will understand how Caoshan fulfilled his filial duty. This monk is all right too—he wants to see how Caoshan acts today, asking, "How about after fulfillment of filial duty?" Caoshan said, "Caoshan loves to fall down drunk." Jiaofan said, "His mind is like a clear mirror, his mouth like a drunken man."

One day a monk asked, "I, Qingshui, am alone and poor; please help me." Caoshan called, "Qingshui!" and the monk responded, "Yes?" Caoshan said, "After three cups of finest wine, still you say it hasn't wet your lips."

Also a monk asked Jiufeng, "How is it when the golden cup is full of wine?" Jiufeng said, "I am helplessly drunk." Foguo brought this up and said, "In understanding the source when hearing words, comprehending the situation and responding universally, Jiufeng cannot be denied, but if you examine carefully, he's too indulgent. If someone asked me how it is when the golden cup is full of wine, I'd just answer, 'I am naturally disciplined.'"

Also a monk asked Caoshan, "How can one be in charge all the time?" Caoshan said, "Like passing through a village with poisoned wells—don't touch even a drop of water."

Caoshan is sometimes sober in the midst of intoxication, sometimes is sober yet can't tell day from night—it's because his dreams of yellow grain have ended, his personal feelings are forgotten.

Dongshan asked Yunju, "A great incorrigible kills his father and mother—where is the filial care?" Yunju said, "This for the first time fulfills filial care." This is a man whose filial duty is fulfilled and is falling-down drunk. Dongshan said, "In the wild forest that meets the eyes, free through the years." Tiantong is used to roaming there; his verse says,

Verse   *The pure household has no neighbors:*
For long years staying in sweeping, not admitting any dust.
Where the light turns tilts the moon remaining at dawn:
When the forms of the hexagrams are distinguished,
Then are established dawn and spring.
Having freshly fulfilled filial duty,
Then one meets the spring—
Walking drunk, singing crazily, turban hanging down,
Ambling with tousled hair, who cares—
In great peace, with no concerns, a man falling-down drunk.

Commentary   One whose eyes cannot get sand in them is too restricted. Caoshan said, "Crude mundane greed, anger, and folly may be difficult to cut off, yet they are still light—unconcern and nondoing purity is graver than anything." That is why Dongshan said, "In front of the hall of the bright moon it is always summertime." The ultimate way cannot be formally described: the ancients found it nearby in themselves, and found it afar in things, comparing origins and aligning kinds, to exemplify the ultimate way.

Baoce's verse eulogizing Longya's 'half body' says,

> *The sun rises across the mountains,*
> *The moon is full at the door;*
> *It's not that he has no body—*
> *He doesn't want to show it all.*

Both elders were descendants of Dongshan. Jiaofan said, "The style of that house in action esteems indirectness so as not to violate the absolute state; in speaking it avoids saying the whole thing, so as to avoid falling into the present." So Baoce's masterful mind alone spoke wonderfully, not losing the source—this is worthy of esteem. This "Where the light turns tilts the moon remaining at dawn" depicts fulfillment of filial duty and meeting spring.

In the second line of the *sky* hexagram of the *Book of Changes* it says, "Seeing a dragon in a field: it is profitable to see a great man." According to the commentary, "A positive line in the second place corresponds to the interval between the twelfth and first months of the lunar calendar—at this time the first sprouts come out of the ground. This is the appearance of the positive energy. The form of the *sky* hexagram should be so."

In Lao Du's *Drinking Songs of the Eight Immortals* it says that "They took off their hats and bared their heads in the presence of kings," and "Though called by the emperor, they didn't get on the boat." All of them forgot forms and slighted etiquette; they could not be bound by any limits.

Danxia Tianran one day was lying on the Tianqin bridge; the leader of the entourage of the lieutenant governor Cheng hollered at him. The master Tianran paid no attention; when he was questioned, he said casually, "I am a monk with no concerns." Cheng admired him and considered him unusual.

Once when Zuefeng's assembly gathered for evening congregation, Xuefeng was lying in the inner garden. Elder Taiyuan Fu said, "Within the domain of the five states, there is only this teacher who amounts to anything." Xuefeng immediately got up and left.

These were both unconcerned drunkards with bare chests and tousled hair.

How can Caoshan's fulfillment of filial duty be used? The four seasons are rich in spring, all things are beautiful with wine.

Added Sayings /Case
A monk asked Caoshan, "How is it when the mourning clothes are not worn?"—The cicada has shed its shell but still holds the cold twig. **Caoshan said, "Today my filial duty is fulfilled."**—He doesn't turn away from everyday life. **The monk said, "How about after fulfillment of filial duty?"**—Easygoing, he takes big strides. **Caoshan said, "I love to fall down drunk."**—What's not all right?

Added Sayings /Verse
The pure household has no neighbors—If you see his jowls from behind his head, don't travel with him.

For long years staying in sweeping, not admitting any dust—Even if there is a spot, there's no place for it to settle.

Where the light turns tilts the moon remaining at dawn—When negative reaches its limit, positive is born.

When the forms of the hexagrams are distinguished, then are established dawn and spring—Negative is merciless, positive is relaxed.

Having freshly fulfilled filial duty—The traces of the tears still aren't gone.

Then one meets the spring—Calling each other, playing on a swing.

Walking drunk, singing crazily, turban handing down—Those who know well do not lecture on etiquette.

Ambling with tousled hair, who cares—A thousand freedoms, a hundred liberties.

In great peace, with no concerns, a man falling-down drunk—In a seven-house village this fellow is lively.

74 FAYAN'S "SUBSTANCE AND NAME"

Introduction Plenty has myriad virtues; swept clear, there's not a mote of dust. Detached from all forms, identical to all things: taking a step atop a hundred foot pole, the universe in all directions is one's whole body—but tell me, where does it come from?

Case A monk asked Fayan, "I hear that in the teachings there is a saying, 'From a nonabiding basis are established all things'—what is the nonabiding basis?"
Fayan said, "'Form arises before substantiation, names arise from before naming.'"

Commentary Manjusri asked Vimalakirti, "What is the basis of the body?" Vimalakirti said, "Craving is the basis of the body." Manjusri asked, "What is the basis of craving?" Vimalakirti said, "False discrimination is the basis of craving." Manjusri asked, "What is the basis of false discrimination?" Vimalakirti said, "Erroneous conception is the basis of false discrimination." Manjusri asked, "What is the basis of erroneous conception?" Vimalakirti said, "Nonabiding is the basis." Manjusri asked, "What is the basis of nonabiding?" Vimalakirti said, "Nonabiding has no basis. Manjusri, all things are established from a nonabiding basis." Master Sengzhao's note says, "The mind is like water: when it's still, there is reflection; when disturbed, no mirror. Muddled by folly and craving, fanned by misleading influences, it surges and billows, never stopping for a moment. Looking at it this way, where can you go and not be mistaken! For example, it's like trying to look into a flowing spring to

311

see your own appearance—it never forms." He also said, "If you take the movement of mind as the basis, then existence is born, based on significations; when the reason completes its initial movement, there is no more basis. If you take nothingness as the basis, then existence is born based on nothingness; nothing is not based on nothing—there is no more basis." He also said, "Because of nonabiding, erroneous conceptions; because of erroneous conceptions, discrimination; because of discrimination, craving; because of craving, there is a body; since there is a body, then good and bad are both set forth; once good and bad are set forth, the myriad things arise." It goes on from here—the words are too numerous to go through all of them.

Master Sengzhao used the first moving thought, fundamental nescience, as the nonabiding basis. In the *Essence of Mind* spoken by National Teacher Qingliang in reply to the imperial crown prince, recorded in the *Transmission of the Lamp,* he says, "The ultimate way is based on the mind; the reality of mind is based on no abode; the essence of the nonabiding mind is spiritual knowledge undimmed."

National Teacher An brought up the *Diamond-Cutter Scripture,* saying, "'You should enliven the mind without dwelling on anything'—not dwelling on anything means not dwelling on form, not dwelling on sound, not dwelling on delusion, not dwelling on enlightenment, not dwelling on essence, not dwelling on function. Enlivening the mind means manifesting one mind in all places: if you enliven the mind dwelling on good, goodness appears; if you enliven the mind dwelling on evil, evil appears—the basic mind is concealed. If it doesn't dwell on anything, anywhere, the whole world is one mind."

The Sixth Patriarch asked Shenhui, "Friend, you have come from afar; that is quite a hardship. Did you bring the fundamental or not? If you have the fundamental then you should know its master. Try to speak of it." Shenhui said, "No abode is fundamental, seeing is the master." Shenhui's *Record of Revelation of the Source* says, "Since the demise of the World Honored One, the twenty-eight patriarchs in India all communicated the nondwelling mind." This nondwelling basis is called nonabiding because of its own nature. If you use the merging of reality and falsehood, in one there are many kinds, in two there is no duality.

Fayan's answer comes from the *Jewel Treasury Treatise:* "Form arises before substantiation, names arise from before naming. Once forms and names have appeared, floating mists disturb the clarity." Xuedou raised his staff and said, "Everyone, the staff is bringing up both form and name together. Form is formless, name is nameless. You're all a bunch of blind people, without any perception; you only recognize that which is formless and seamless and take it to be the ultimate principle: you turn away from Fayan."

Chan Master Yongming Yanshou's *Secret of Only Mind* says, "There is not a single name that does not broadcast an epithet of the Buddha; there is not a single thing that does not expose the form of the reality-body Buddha Vairocana."

There is also a kind who study alone and are poor in learning, who do not consent to investigate the inner principle with penetrating questioning, but just say, "Basically, what is there?" I say, already too much. They say, "How to avoid it?" I say, basically, what is lacking? Just understand in this way, and as you seek out Fayan, you will also see Tiantong.

Verse   *Without tracks,*
No news.
The white clouds are rootless—
What color is the pure breeze?
Spreading the canopy of the sky, mindless,
Holding the carriage of the earth, powerful;
Illumining the profound source of a thousand ages,
Making patterns for ten thousand forms.
Meetings for enlightenment in the atoms of all lands—in each place
is Samantabhadra:
The door of the tower opens—everywhere is Maitreya.

Commentary   When you look at it, it has no form; it extends throughout heaven and earth: when you listen for it, it has no sound; its full sound is uninterrupted. Although the clouds are rootless, the sky is marked by a fleck of cloud; though the wind has no color, the earth is supported by its atmosphere.

Lord Liu Yuduan asked Yunju, "Where does the rain come from?" Yunju said, "It comes from your question." The lord was delighted and thanked him. Yunju asked back, "Where does the question come from?" The lord said nothing.

As Xichan was sitting with an official, he asked, "What color is the wind?" The official said nothing. Xichan then asked a monk; the monk lifted up his patchrobe and said, "In a shop in the city." Xichan said, "How much cloth did it require?" The monk said, "No connection." Xichan said nothing. Yunmen said in his behalf, "Tch! This preacher is fallen in his words!" Xuedou joined them and made two verses:

> Where does the rain come from?
> What color is the wind?
> At ten-thousand-fathom Dragon Gate, who got the rap?

> What color is the wind?
> Where does the rain come from?
> Without needing to snap the fingers,
> The door of the tower opens:
> Wave after wave, crest upon crest—
> No return yet from the South.

Tiantong eulogizes the nonabiding basis—"The white clouds are rootless; what color is the pure breeze?" He eulogizes establishing all things— "Spreading the canopy of the sky, mindless; holding the carriage of the earth, with power."

Mahasattva Fu's poem Mind King says, "Observe the empty mind king: mysterious and subtle, hard to fathom. Without form, with no marks, it has great spiritual power." Guanzi says, "When water issues but doesn't flow away, it is called deep water; when it flows and the flow is long, it is called a source. Before high antiquity is the deep deep source of a thousand ages; myriad forms take shape from this."

In the Flower Ornament Scripture, in the book on the practice and vows of Samantabhadra, it says, "The Buddhas teach, the Bodhisattvas teach, the lands teach, the sentient beings teach, everything in the past, present, and future teaches." Also, Samantabhadra does not see Samantabhadra—seeing and not seeing are both Samantabhadra. During the book on entering the Dharma realm, Maitreya Bodhisattva first went to the tower and made a sound by snapping his fingers; the gate then opened. He told Sudhana to go in, and there Sudhana saw the ten billion continents of the worlds of the universe: in the heaven of happiness of each world was a Maitreya. Also there is a verse which says,

> Maitreya, real Maitreya—
> Ten trillion manifestation bodies
> Time to time you show to people,
> But no one recognizes you at the time.

These both stand for the establishment of all things.
But do you see Fayan?
'The place where I saw my guest off always reminds me of when we parted.'

Added Sayings /Case

A monk asked Fayan, "I hear that in the teachings there is a saying, 'From a non-abiding basis are established all things'—What is the nonabiding basis?"—Shut that dog's mouth.

Fayan said, "'Form arises before substantiation—Don't hallucinate. Names arise from before naming.'"—Ultimately what do you call it?

Added Sayings /Verse

Without tracks—The ram hangs up its horns.
No news—Having long turned away, no meeting.
The white clouds are rootless—The subtle essence fundamentally has no location.
What color is the pure breeze?—Throughout the body where is there any trace of where it came from?
Spreading the canopy of the sky, mindless—Still able to come out of the mountain caves.
Holding the carriage of the earth, with power—Not wasting mental power.
Illumining the profound source of a thousand ages—All flows forth from here.
Making patterns for ten thousand forms—Reflections of a single truth.
Meetings for enlightenment in the atoms of all lands—in each place is Samantabhadra—He blocks the streets and cuts off the alleys.
The door of the tower opens—everywhere is Maitreya—We bump into him everywhere.

75 RUIYAN'S "CONSTANT PRINCIPLE"

Introduction   Even as you call it 'thus,' it's already changed. Where knowledge doesn't reach, avoid speaking of it. Here, is there any investigating or not?

Case   **Ruiyan asked Yantou, "What is the fundamental constant principle?"**
Yantou said, "Moving."
Ruiyan said, "When moving, what then?"
Yantou said, "You don't see the fundamental constant principle."
Ruiyan stood there thinking.
Yantou said, "If you agree, you are not yet free of sense and matter: if you don't agree, you'll be forever sunk in birth and death."

Commentary   Chan Master Ruiyan Chican of Tai province was a man of Min; his surname was Xiu. He first questioned Yantou, setting up a name, first calling it the fundamental constant principle. Yantou sometimes let go; he just shone through it for him, saying, "Moving." Ruiyan was in a fine situation to get beaten thirty times—how was he so lucky as to escape it? He still didn't watch out for deadly peril—he said, "When moving, then what?" Yantou, half drunk, half sober, again let him go; he just shone through it for him, saying, "You don't see the fundamental constant principle." Masters of great skill admit beings in this way. Ruiyan then stood there thinking; here's where he reaches the place where the divergent roads before the dead tree cliff are many. Yantou already was heedless of his body and life, cutting off Ruiyan's pathway and opening up the public road to the capital right under the sun, saying, "If you agree, you are not yet free of senses and matter; if you don't agree, you're forever sunk in birth and death." Giushan called it the tooth and nail of the cave of Dharma. It captures alive, without any useless effort.

A monk from Jiashan's community went to Shishuang. As soon as he entered, he said, "How are you?" Shishuang said, "Don't need you." The monk said, "If so, then farewell." He also went to Yantou and did as before: Yantou then puffed twice; the monk said, "If so, then farewell." As he started to walk away, Yantou said, "Although he is of the younger generation, he can keep control." The monk returned to Jiashan and recounted these stories. Jiashan said, "Does everybody understand? If no one speaks, I will be heedless of my eyebrows and go on talking." Then he said, "Though Shishuang has the killing sword, he still lacks the life-giving sword. Yantou, though, has both the killing sword and the life-giving sword." In the Linji tradition this is called always having the seven pieces of equipment handy. Yantou saw Ruiyan was determined and sincere in questioning further; this was not a time for a test of wits, so he therefore met him as an eye of reality, extending kindness out of compassion for people. Ruiyan attained enlightenment following his words. Later he would call to himself, "Old Master, don't be fooled by others!" It was all because he had met a poison hand and could never forget it.

No one in the past or present has brought out this case; who but Tiantong could reflect appreciation of it?

Verse   *The round pearl has no hollows,*
The great raw gem isn't polished.
What is esteemed by people of the Way is having no edges.
Removing the road of agreement, senses and matter are empty:
The free body, resting on nothing, stands out unique and alive.

Commentary   According to *Annals of the Ages,* there were two friends who both had fine features, who were compared to the jewel of Bian Ho, clear and flawless, and the pearl of the Marquis of Sui, perfectly round, with no hollows. Shaving a bamboo cane round, removing purple felt, white jade is polished into an elephant-tusk comb, yellow gold is beaten into brass ore veins, twine is tied to a bowstring, a handle is affixed to a bowl. You try turning the light around and steadily introspect: who is not like this.

Baizhang said, "The spiritual light shines alone, far free from senses and objects." Since "When you agree, you are not free of senses and matter," when you "take away the road of agreement, sense and matter are empty of themselves." Since the six sense faculties and six fields of sense objects are empty, the six consciousnesses naturally return to the ocean of awareness.

In general, when things have edges, they cannot roll freely; if you want to be lively and frisky, without sticking to or depending on anything, just set your eyes on agreement-nonagreement—naturally you will not stay on this shore, nor on that shore, nor in midstream. This is why Dongshan said, "I half agree, half don't agree." This is why Shoushan said, "Agreement cannot be complete." Do you know such a person's plan to return?

> *The golden chains and hidden barrier cannot stop him;*
> *He travels in different paths, transmigrating for now.*

Added Sayings / Case

Ruiyan asked Yantou, "What is the fundamental constant principle?" —If there is a principle, it doesn't lie in a loud voice.

Yantou said, "Moving."—You should know the principle.

Ruiyan said, "When moving, what then?"—A second offense is not permitted.

Yantou said, "You don't see the fundamental constant principle."— Sizing up the item, he makes a price.

Ruiyan stood there thinking—Don't you know any shame?

Yantou said, "If you agree, you are not yet free of sense and matter;— Herein there is no way of agreement.

If you don't agree, then you'll be forever sunk in birth and death."— He doesn't sit right in the hall—how could he tend to dualistic action?

Added Sayings / Verse

The round pearl has no hollows—Where could you start to work on it?

The great raw gem isn't polished—Save your effort.

What is esteemed by people of the Way is having no edges—According to the principle, don't let the tip of the brush show when you write.

Removing the road of agreement, senses and matter are empty—Forget the shadows and echoes in the sense media.

The free body, resting on nothing, stands out unique and alive—Shedding pure light on the universe.

76 SHOUSHAN'S THREE PHRASES

Introduction One phrase illumines three phrases, three phrases illumine one phrase. One and three have nothing to do with each other—distinctly clear, the road going beyond. But tell me, which phrase is first?

Case Shoushan said to the assembly, "If you attain at the first phrase, you will be teacher of buddhas and patriarchs. If you attain at the second phrase, you will be teacher of humans and gods. If you attain at the third phrase, you cannot even save yourself."
A monk asked, "At which phrase did you attain?"
Shoushan said, "The moon sets; midnight, going through the marketplace."

Commentary The formulation of the three phrases began with Baizhang Huaihai, based on the *Diamond-Cutter Wisdom Scripture:* he said, "The words of the teachings all have three successive phases—the beginning, middle, and final good. At first one should just be taught to produce a good mind; in the middle, the good mind is dissolved; only the final good is really good. Thus 'A bodhisattva is not a bodhisattva; this is called a bodhisattva,' and 'The Dharma is not Dharma, nor is it not Dharma.' It's all like this. If you just expound one phrase, you cause sentient beings to go to hell; if all three phrases are expounded at once, sentient beings will go to hell by themselves. This is not the business of a teaching master. To explain that the present mirroring awareness is your own buddha is good in the beginning. Not to keep dwelling in the present mirror awareness is good in the middle. Not making an understanding of not dwelling is final good."
Yunmen once said, "Enclosing the universe in the heavens, judging grains and ounces at a glance, not involved in the conditions of spring— how do you attain to this?" He answered himself, "One arrow smashes

319

three barriers." Even though the idea was there, he never set it up as 'three phrases.' Later he had a successor known as Great Master Yuanming, whose initiatory name was Yuanmi, and who was the ninth-generation abbot of Deshan in Yan province; this master said, "Deshan has three phrases—one phrase encloses the universe, one phrase goes along with the waves, one phrase cuts off all streams." Later he had a successor, Chan Master Dao of Puanshan in Yan province, who made verses on the above three phrases:

1. Verse on containing the universe
   The universe and myriad forms,
   Hells and heavens;
   In everything reality is seen—
   It is used everywhere without harm.

2. Verse on cutting off all streams
   Piling in mountains, heaping in crags,
   Each is completely dust;
   If you still try to discuss mystery and marvel,
   The ice melts and tiles crumble.

3. Verse on following the waves
   An eloquent mouth and clever tongue question:
   High and low, responding without fail
   Is like medicine appropriate to the disease;
   Examination and diagnosis depend on the time.

Outside of the three phrases, if one brings it up, how can it include the three phrases? If someone asks about it, on Nanyue and Tiantai time and again they say these verses were made by Yunmen—none of them have read carefully. Yuanmi succeeded to Yunmen; though Yunmen had the saying about 'containing the skies' and 'one arrow smashes three barriers,' it was Yuanmi who brought them out, and Dao who put them in verse. After three generations of ancestral tradition, the three phrases were first clarified. These are much the same as Dayang's three phrases and the 'three mysteries' and 'three essentials.'

Shoushan said to the assembly, "If you attain at the first phrase, you will be teacher of buddhas and patriarchs." When Huangbo was head monk at Nanquan's place, one day he occupied Nanquan's seat. When Nanquan came, he asked, "Head monk, how many years have you been practicing the Way?" Huangbo said, "Since before the prehistoric buddhas." Nanquan said, "Then you're still my grandson—get down!" Huangbo then returned to his own place and sat there. Jingqing said that Vairocana has a teacher, the reality-body has a master. This is called someone who transcends buddhas and patriarchs. That is why it is said that if you attain realization at the first phrase you become a teacher of buddhas and patriarchs.

Lingshu left a letter in a box saying, "The head monk in the hall is the eye of humans and gods." The head monk was Yunmen. This is why it is said that if you attain realization at the second phrase you become a teacher of humans and gods. Hearing me speak this way, don't say then that Nanquan can be teacher of Buddhas and Patriarchs while Yunmen can only be teacher of humans and gods—we might say, 'Don't discuss a dream in front of fools.' I have just briefly brought up one and two as models. As for those who can't even save themselves, they do not enter the ranks of the patriarchs—how are they worth speaking of?

A monk then asked Shoushan, "At which phrase did you attain?" There are thorns in the soft mud. Shoushan said, "The moon sets—midnight, going through the marketplace." Thus 'the traveler is even beyond the blue mountains.'

Tiantong saw that no one dared to talk about this story, so where hands are examined and feet pierced, he concocted it in verse:

Verse   *The skulls of the buddhas and patriarchs are strung on one line:*
The water clock quietly moves its arrow minutely in the night.
The dynamic essential of humans and gods shoots ten tons:
Brigades of clouds shining, flashing, swiftly let fly with lightning.
People here, observe the changes:
Meeting the lowly, then noble; to the noble, lowly.
Getting the jewel through formlessness, the ultimate way is continuous:
Letting the cleaver play over the dead ox, the red heart is naked.

Commentary   "The skulls of the buddhas and patriarchs are strung on one line"—after that one can be a teacher of buddhas and patriarchs; this can be called "Penetrating through and out to travel on Vairocana's head, coming back to sit on the tongue of the transformation buddha."

"The water clock quietly moves its arrow minutely in the night." An ancient design for water clocks says, "You make three tiers of vessels, each round, a foot across: these are set above vessels on the ground; pouring out water from golden dragon mouths, successively pouring into the vessels in the four directions, the top is covered with gold molded into the shape of a timekeeper, complete with clothing and hat, holding an arrow with both hands." Also, "The secret order in the army—at night an arrow is passed along"—these refer to awakening before the distinction of indications, able to be a teacher of Buddhas and Patriarchs. As soon as you fall into the present, this is the secondary—for the time being you 'take a little rest on the road of humans and gods.'

The lightning samadhi in the *Scripture on Contemplation of the Mind Ground* is what patchrobed monks call 'glimpsing.' If you are such a person, sometimes you travel on the heads of the buddhas and patriarchs, sometimes you walk the road of humans and gods, or travel among different kinds, in a herd of water buffalo.

Mr Wang Qing's poem on watching actors says,

On the stages of the plays,
One is noble, one is lowly;
In their hearts they know they're originally equal,
So there is no delight or resentment.

According to Zhuangzi's volume *Sky and Earth*, the Yellow Emperor, roaming north of the Red River, climbed the Kunlun Mountains and gazed south to return, but lost his mystic jewel. He sent Knowledge to look for it, but he couldn't find it; he sent Free From Stupidity to go look, but he couldn't find it; he sent Eating Shame to look for it, but he couldn't find it. Then he sent Formless, who found it. The Emperor said, "How extraordinary! Only Formless could find it!"

In Zhuangzi's volume *Nurturing Life*, it says that Bao Ding, butchering an ox for Lord Wen Hui, said, "The joints have spaces, and the cleaver's edge has no thickness. With no thickness it enters where there's space; as the cleaver floats easily, there is always extra room. Thus, after using it for nineteen years, the cleaver is still as sharp as it was when it just came from the whetstone." Lord Wen Hui said, "Great! Having heard the words of Bao Ding, I've found how to nurture life therein."

These two things versify "The moon sets; midnight, going through the marketplace." The endless continuous stretch of the ultimate Way is like the water clock minutely moving the pointer; helping people with naked heart is like letting the cleaver play freely and leaving the finding of the jewel to Formless. People these days see Tiantong using Zhuangzi and immediately clamor that Laozi and Zhuangzi are the same as the ultimate Way. What they hardly realize is that the ancient borrowed a path for a shortcut; it is only a temporary scene. If someone should suddenly come forth and say, "How could Zhuangzi have not known Shoushan's course of action?" I would just say to him, "'The moon sets—midnight, going through the market place'—is this a core chapter or an appended chapter?"

Added Sayings /Case	**Shoushan said to the assembly, "If you attain at the first phrase, you'll be a teacher of Buddhas and Patriarchs**—You would still be Wansong's descendent.

If you attain at the second phrase, you'll be teacher of humans and gods—Corrupting people.

If you attain at the third phrase, you can't even save yourself."—The guy speaking these inanities.

A monk asked, "At which phrase did you attain?"—You try to figure it out.

Shoushan said, "The moon having set at midnight, going through the marketplace."—The three phrases can be distinguished; the arrow soars into space.

Added Sayings /Verse	*The skulls of the buddhas and patriarchs are strung on one line*—Let them leap as they may.

The water clock quietly moves its arrow minutely in the night—Doesn't allow people outside to know.

The dynamic essential of humans and gods shoots ten tons—Using the light to struggle with the heavy.

Brigades of clouds shining, flashing, swiftly let fly with lightning—In the blink of an eye you've missed it.

People here, observe the changes—Planning is done according to the time.

Meeting the lowly, then noble; to the noble, lowly—In their hearts they know they're basically inherently the same, that's why there's no delight or resentment.

Getting the jewel through formlessness, the ultimate way is continuous—A single thought unborn, the whole body manifests.

Letting the cleaver play over the dead ox, the red heart is naked—Tears come from a painful gut.

77 YANGSHAN'S "ENOUGH"

Introduction   Like a man writing on space, as soon as he sets his pen he's wrong—how can it bear creating a pattern? What is the use of making a likeness?
I have already revealed a loose end: if there's a rule, go by the rule; if no rule, go by the example.

Case   A monk asked Yangshan, "Do you know written characters?"
Yangshan said, "Enough."
The monk then circled him once to the right and said, "What character is this?"
Yangshan drew a cross on the ground.
The monk circled him once to the left and said, "What character is this?"
Yangshan changed the cross to the mystic infinity symbol of well-being.
The monk drew a circle and held it up with his hands like a titan holding the sun and moon, and said, "What character is this?"
Yangshan then drew a circle surrounding the mystic infinity.
The monk then posed like Rucika.
Yangshan said, "Right, so it is. You keep it well."

Commentary   A verse beginning Cijiao's exhortations to Xiaowen says,

> *Before the birth of father and mother,*
> *One solid circle;*
> *Even Shakyamuni didn't understand it—*
> *How could Kasyapa transmit it?*

The Fourteenth Patriarch Nagarjuna concealed his body on the teaching seat and manifested a circular form; Kanadeva said, "This is the Venerable One showing us the form of the body of a buddha."

Thus, the form of signless meditation is like the full moon; the meaning of buddha-nature is vast emptiness and illumination—(but) these are only metaphors.

The making of circular symbols in China began with National Teacher Huizhong: he passed them on to his attendant Danyuan, who, receiving his prophecy, transmitted them to Yangshan. So now it has come to be called the family style of the Gui-Yang school of Chan.

Master Liang of Wufeng in Ming province once compiled forty examples (of circular symbols): Mingjiao made a preface, extolling this. Liang said, "Circular symbols have six names in all: one, circles; two, ocean of meaning; three, meeting of minds; four, study of characters; five, ideas and words; six, silent discourse."

The tradition of the Gui-Yang school says that Danyuan said to Yangshan, "The National Teacher transmitted the ninety-seven circular symbols of the Sixth Patriarch: he said, 'Thirty years after my death there will be a novice in the South who will cause this path to flourish greatly when he arrives.' As I carefully examine this prophecy, I realize it refers to you." After Yangshan had gotten the symbols, he burned them up. One day Danyuan said to him, "The circular symbols which I transmitted to you before should be kept deeply hidden." Yanshan said, "I have already burned them." Danyuan said, "That's all right for you, but what about those yet to come?" Yangshan said, "If you want, I'll recompile the book." Then Yangshan recompiled the book of symbols and showed it to Danyuan—there was not a single error or omission.

One day Danyuan went up into the hall, and Yangshan came forth from the assembly, made a circle, and offered it up in his hands; then he stood there with his hands clasped at his chest. Danyuan interlocked his fists and showed this to him: Yangshan advanced three steps and curtsied; Danyuan nodded, and Yangshan bowed. Among the ninety-seven kinds of symbols, the clasped hands is called the *rakshasa samadhi,* the curtsy is called the *woman samadhi*. These are all manifestations of the universal gate which flows forth from the samadhi which is king of samadhis.

Also, there was an Indian monk who came to call on Yangshan:

Yangshan drew a half-moon on the ground. The monk came nearer and added to it, making a full circle; then he erased it with his foot. Yangshan extended both hands: the monk immediately left, saying, "I came to China to pay respects to Manjusri, but instead met a little Shakyamuni."

Also a monk came and bowed: Yangshan paid no attention to him. The monk said, "Master, do you know written characters?" Yangshan said, "Enough." The monk drew a circle and presented it: Yangshan erased it with his sleeve. The monk also drew a half-moon sign and presented it: Yangshan made a gesture of throwing it behind him with both hands. The monk looked directly at him: Yangshan lowered his head. The monk walked around the master once, whereupon Yangshan hit him; the monk finally left. Here Yangshan towers like a wall a mile high, no different from the sharp and severe actions of Deshan and Linji.

As Yangshan was sitting, another monk came and made a bow; Yangshan paid no attention. The monk asked, "Do you know written characters?" Yangshan said, "Enough." The monk circled him once to the right and said, "What character is this?" With this kind of device, if you wait to let there be discriminating feelings, what essential message would it amount to? Yet if there is no principle at all, the ordinary people and the sages of India and China are peers in study.

A monk from the assembly at Guanyin came to call on Yantou: with his hand he made a circle to the left, then made another circle on the right, and also made a circle in the middle: as he was about to finish, Yantou swept it all away with his hand. The monk had no reply; Yantou then ejected him with a shout. Just as the monk stepped over the threshold, Yantou called him back and asked, "Did you come from Guanyin in Hong province?" The monk said, "Yes." Yantou said, "The circle on the left which you drew just now—what about it?" The monk said, "It is the expression of existence." Yantou said, "And the circle on the right?" The monk said, "It's the expression of nonexistence." Yantou asked, "What about the circle in the middle?" The monk said, "It's the expression of neither existence nor nonexistence." Yantou said, "And what about my doing as I did?" The monk said, "Like drawing on water with a knife." Yantou hit him and drove him out. This monk didn't understand the essential meaning of the circular figures, and wrongly created forced interpretations; anyone but Yantou might have been confused.

When the monk in the present case saw Yangshan and asked, "Do you know characters?" and then circled him once to the right, his abilities were already used up: Yangshan's explanation, a cross-shaped character (which means 'ten,' the basic perfect number), had finished explaining it too—what was the need for so much gruel and rice-breath afterwards? Why wait for it to come to this? Right in the beginning, as soon as he asked, "Do you know characters?" I'd just say, "I've always been illiterate," to see what he would do.

Haven't you read how in ancient times there was a monk who always passed the time at leisure; another monk urged him, "Elder, you're getting old—you should beware of wasting even a moment of time." The monk said, "What would you have me do?" He exhorted him, "Why not read scriptures?" The monk said, "I don't know characters." He urged him, "Why not ask someone?" The monk said, "What character is this?" The monk who had been exhorting him had nothing to say. We might say, 'Not a dot is added to the writing, not a note added to the music.'

The monk in this case also circled Yangshan once to the left and said, "What character is this?" Is this the same as the usual crossing from east to west, west to east, slapping the left knee—'this is the meaning of the Teachings,' slapping the right knee—'this is the meaning of Chan'? Yangshan shifted the stars, changing the cross into a 'well-being' sign. The monk drew a circle and posed like a titan holding the sun and moon in his hands; among the ninety-seven symbols this is called the *titan samadhi*.

Rucika means 'Crying' in Sanskrit. When the thousand buddhas of the aeon of virtue were princes, Rucika was the last to receive the prophecy of buddhahood and will be the last to attain it. At the time of receiving the prophecy, he wept and said, "Why am I so unfortunate as to have been the last to get the prediction?" Then he suddenly laughed and said, "I will get all the adornments of skill in techniques of the nine hundred and ninety-nine buddhas!" At present Rucika is the thunderbolt-bearing deity who guards the Teaching. When the monk at the end posed like Rucika, his meaning should thus be known. Yangshan said, "Right, so it is. This is what all Buddhas attend to. You are thus, and I am thus; keep and maintain it well. Very good indeed. You'd better go now." After the monk bowed in thanks, he sprang into the air and departed.

At that time there was a wayfarer who saw this, and after five days came to ask Yangshan about it. Yangshan said, "Did you see?" The man said, "I actually saw him go out the gate and take off into the air." Yangshan said, "That was a saint from the West who came for the purpose of investigating my way." The wayfarer said, "Although I have seen various meditation states, I don't understand the principle of that." Yangshan said, "I'll explain to you in terms of meaning: this is eightfold concentration: the ocean of awareness turns into the ocean of meanings; the essence is the same, but in the meanings there is cause, there is effect, simultaneity and difference in time, totality and distinction. This is none other than body-concealment concentration."

Therefore it is said, "The heart of nirvana is easy to attain; the knowledge of differentiation is hard to clarify." Try to see how Tiantong goes to work; his verse says,

Verse　*The void of the circle of the Way is never filled,*
The letters on the seal of emptiness are still unformed.
Subtly carrying the globe of heaven and axis of earth,
Finely weaving the military warp and cultural woof,
Opening up, kneading together,
Standing alone, traveling everywhere:
The mind activates the mysterious pivot, thunder roars in the clear blue sky;
The eye takes in violet light, seeing stars in broad daylight.

Commentary　"The void of the circle of the Way is never filled." This is where 'neither the person nor the ox is seen.' This is right when the moon is bright. Cijiao said, "Who would have known that the final expression is after all before distinction!" As for the "circle of the Way," Zhuangzi said, "When the pivot first is fit into its circle, it thereby responds endlessly." Tiantong borrows this to versify the gesture of lifting up the circle.

"The letters on the seal of emptiness"—though the character 'ten' is changed to 'myriad,' its reality cannot be grasped by conventional written characters. Daofu said to Bodhidharma, "According to what I see, the function of the Way neither holds to written words nor abandons written words."

Meditation leader Guan of Daning went to Fachang and saw the master draw a circle with a double ten in it—Guan immediately went out to do chores. The next day when Fachang went up into the hall, in front of the teaching seat he said, "What about yesterday's public case?" Guan drew a circle with the character for 'ox' in it, and then erased it with his foot. Fachang said, "Meditation leader Guan, you didn't get that name for nothing." Finally he got up on the seat and said,

> Suddenly the roar of thunder in a clear sky:
> At the triple sluice of the Dragon Gate the waves are immense;
> How many outstanding ones have become dragons!
> Shrimps and crabs glare as before.

This verse has the same inspiration as Tiantong's "The mind activates the mysterious pivot, thunder roars in the clear blue sky."

The "globe of heaven" and "axis of earth," "military warp" and "cultural woof" are the blood line of the two circumambulations, to the left and right, and the characters 'ten' and 'infinity.' "Opening up, kneading together," "standing alone, traveling everywhere" eulogize the titan holding the sun in his palm and Rucika raising his fist, encircling the infinite well-being sign and praising.

In the introductory words to the *Spring and Autumn Annals* it says, "Heaven as the body encloses earth within it; sun, moon, and stars belong to it. So sky and earth have forms of high and low, the four seasons have patterns of rising and falling, sun and moon have degrees of movement, the stars have constant successions of positions. Even the revolving of the stars is bound in a pattern like a globe—therefore it is called the 'globe of heaven'." The *Pictorial of Rivers Wrapping the Earth* says, "Under the ground there are eight pillars, one hundred thousand miles wide: there are thirty-six hundred axles holding each other in place. The great mountains and rivers and crevasses pass through." According to the *House Sayings*, earth's east-west is called the 'warp,' south-north is called the 'woof.' Also, "Cultural skills go through the heavens, military skills circle the earth: without culture, there is no way to make friends with other nations; without the military, there is no way to control disorder."

Muzhou said to the assembly, "Breaking open is up to oneself, kneading together is up to oneself too." A monk asked, "What is breaking open?" Muzhou said, "Three times nine is twenty-seven. Enlightenment, extinction, suchness, liberation, mind is buddha—I speak thus; what about you?" The monk said, "I do not speak thus." Muzhou said, "The cup falls to the ground, the saucer breaks into seven pieces." The monk said, "What is kneading together?" Muzhou sat there with his hands folded. Laozi said, "Still and silent, standing alone unchanging, going everywhere without danger."

The activation of the pivotal working is like lightning, like a spark; when there is a spiritual light in the eyes, it is called 'mountain lightning.'

Seeing stars in broad daylight is like shadows of trees in the dark, like fish tracks in water—they cannot be seen by the physical eye.

Jiaofan wrote to Lingyuan, "Shadows of trees in the dark—the meaning of everyday life; tracks of fish in the water—activity after illness. I think of seeing that emaciated face, without attachment; leaning on the wisteria, at leisure I watch the evening clouds return."

But do you know Yangshan's sphere of action?

> The morning's raven rooster embroiders late at night;
> The thread is truly hard to put through in the dark.

Added
Sayings
/Case

A monk asked Yangshan, "Do you know characters?"—What characters? **Yangshan said, "Enough."**—Where benevolence is concerned, he doesn't defer.

The monk then circled him to the right and said, "What character is this?"—Already the right and left components are visible.

Yangshan drew the character 'ten' on the ground—He goes on to draw lines and dots.

The monk circled him once to the left and said, "What character is this?"—Half and full both are distinguished, ideo-phonographs and analogical characters.

Yangshan changed the cross-shaped character 'ten' to the infinite well-being symbol—Where the wheel of potential turns, even the eye of wisdom is confused.

The monk drew a circle and held it up with his hands like a titan

holding the sun and moon, and said, "What character is this?"—Watch carefully where you're going.

Yangshan then drew a circle around the symbol—No monk on earth can leap out.

The monk then posed like Rucika—The vajra-bearer outside the gate is laughing at you.

Yangshan said, "Right, so it is. You keep it well."—Shutting the void, locking off dreams, firmly take it into the palm of the hand.

Added Sayings / Verse

The void of the circle of the Way is never filled—Carrying snow to fill the river.

The letters on the seal of emptiness are still unformed—Just don't carve.

Subtly carrying the globe of heaven and axis of earth—The balance scale is in hand.

Finely weaving the military warp and cultural woof—The general and the minister fulfill their abilities.

Opening out, kneading together—Muzhou is still alive.

Standing alone, traveling everywhere—Laozi is reborn.

The mind activates the mysterious pivot, thunder roars in the clear blue sky—Can't quite get a hand on it.

The eye takes in violet light, seeing stars in broad daylight—Shines through all under the four heavens.

78 YUNMEN'S "SESAME CAKE"

Introduction Seeking the price throughout the heavens, paying it all over the earth: a hundred plans, traveling in search, is all an embarrassment. Is there anyone who knows when to advance and when to retreat, what is admissible and what is blameworthy?

Case **A monk asked Yunmen, "What is talk transcending the buddhas and patriarchs?"**
Yunmen said, "Sesame cake."

Commentary Yunmen went up in the hall and said, "As soon as a single word is brought up, the thousand differences are in the same groove, including the most minute particles: yet this is still an explanation of teaching method—if one is a patchrobe monk, how should he be? If you take the meaning of the patriarchs and the meaning of the buddhas and haggle here, the one road of Chan would sink away. Is there anyone who can speak? If you can speak, come forth." A monk asked, "What is speech that transcends the buddhas and goes beyond the patriarchs?" Yunmen said, "Sesame cake." The monk said, "What relation is there?" Yunmen said, "Clearly there is some relation," then he continued, "You shouldn't think you're done. When you hear someone talk about the meaning of the founding teachers, you immediately ask about the principle of talk that goes beyond buddhas and patriarchs. But what are you calling 'buddha,' what are you calling 'patriarch' that you speak of talk that goes beyond buddhas and patriarchs? Then you ask about this leaving the triple world: you take hold of the triple world—what perception and congnition is there hindering you? What sound, form, or phenomena can be understood by you? What can you assess?" Another monk also asked, "What is speech that transcends buddhas and patriarchs?" Yunmen said, "The saffron of Bu province, the wolfsbane of Yi province." He also said, "Come, come! I question you people further: with your staffs across your backs you say you are investigating Chan, studying the Way, then you immediately seek the principle that transcends the buddhas and patriarchs. I ask you, in the twenty-four hours of the day, walking, sitting, standing, lying down, defecating and urinating, even including the flies in the latrine and the counters in the market where sheep flesh is bought and sold, is there still any principle that transcends the buddhas and patriarchs?"

Yuanwu said, "Some draw a circle, adding mud to dirt, putting on fetters and wearing chains." I say, if you want the hammer that smashes off fetters and chains, ask of Tiantong's verses on the ancients.

Verse   *"Sesame cake," he says, in a talk transcending buddhas and patriarchs:*
In the phrase there is no flavor—how can it be investigated?
If patchrobe mendicants one day know repletion,
Then will they see Yunmen's face not ashamed.

Commentary   Master Dongshan Chu's verse pointing out pervasive ability says,

> *Dongshan's desolation—nothing at all can be there.*
> *Flavorless talk blocks off people's mouths.*
> *Even if you can skillfully prepare a thousand kinds of delicacies,*
> *What can you do?—a satisfied man doesn't care.*

If you're hungry ghosts gobbling, chewing this way and that, you'll be like a dog gnawing a dry bone. Just wait till you bite through your tongue, then cast it to one side, and you'll meet with Yunmen. How about after meeting? The skin on everyone's face is three inches thick.

Added Sayings /Case   **A monk asked Yunmen, "What is talk transcending the Buddhas and Patriarchs?"**—This question is too lofty.
Yunmen said, "Sesame cake."—The sole topic of the forty-nine years of Buddha's teaching.

333

Added Sayings /Verse

"Sesame cake" he says, in a talk transcending Buddhas and Patriarchs—The whole canon cannot explain it entirely.

In the phrase there is no flavor—how can it be investigated?—Where do you bite in?

If patchrobe mendicants one day know repletion—Then for the first time you will know the ambrosia and the poison of the cake.

Then will they see Yunmen's face not ashamed—Yunmen has no eyes to see others.

334

79 CHANGSHA ADVANCING A STEP

Introduction   The bodhisattva appearing as a maiden on the banks of golden sand was a special spirit. Stuffing pastries in a crystal jar, who would dare to roll it? Without going into the frightening waves, it's hard to find a suitable fish. How about one expression of walking relaxed with big strides?

Case   Changsha had a monk ask Master Hui, "How was it before you saw Nanquan?"
Hui remained silent. The monk said, "How about after seeing him?"
Hui said, "There couldn't be anything else."
The monk returned and related this to Changsha. Changsha said,

> The man sitting atop the hundred-foot pole:
> Though he's gained entry, this is not yet the real.
> Atop the hundred-foot pole, he should step forward:
> The universe in all directions is the whole body.

The monk said, "Atop the hundred-foot pole, how can you step forward?"
Changsha said, "The mountains of Lang, the rivers of Li."
The monk said, "I don't understand."
Changsha said, "The whole land is under the imperial sway."

Commentary   Great Master Chaoxian of Changsha in Hunan was named Jingcen. Jiaofan said, "This Chan master was a spiritual grandson of Mazu, son of Nanquan, brother of Zhaozhou. Among monks of the time, even an obdurate one like Yangshan still was humbled before him and called him Tiger Cen."

In the hall, Changsha said, "If I were to wholly bring up the Chan teaching, there'd be weeds ten feet deep in the teaching hall. I can't but tell you that the whole universe in all directions is the eye of a monk, the whole universe in all directions is the whole body of a monk, the whole universe in all directions is the light of the self, the whole universe in all directions is within one's own light. In all the universe in all directions, there is no one that is not oneself. I always tell you, the Buddhas of all times, along with the sentient beings of the universe, are the light of great transcendent knowledge. Before the light is emitted, where do you sentient beings comprehend? Before the light is emitted, there isn't even any news of Buddhas or sentient beings—where do you get mountains, rivers, and earth from?"

Changsha had a monk question hermit Hui; Hui was one of those who had secretly attained to hidden realization, a disciple of Nanquan who did not appear in the world. In the *Records of the Lamp* he is listed in the last section, as we have no acts or words attributed to him. However, this story exists; it should be his biography—that wouldn't be too much.

This monk acted as a messenger, going to see the hermit; transmitting the essence of Changsha's teaching, he said, "How was it before you saw Nanquan?" Hui was silent. The monk went on, "How about after seeing Nanquan?" Hui said, "There couldn't be anything else." I say, once dead, he didn't revive. The monk returned and told this to Changsha. Changsha said in verse,

> The man sitting atop the hundred-foot pole
> Thought he's gained entry, this is not yet the Real.

This and Yantou's saying to Xuefeng that "Deshan didn't know the last word" are troubled about the same thing. I always tell people that it's much like someone having taken their grandparents' house and business, and their relatives themselves, and sold them off on the same ticket, then put it in a crystal jar which you keep with you wherever you are, guarding it like your eyeballs. Don't let me see! I'd surely pick it up and smash it, making your hands free, folks joyfully alive with no taboos.

Shengmo said, "Letting go over the cliff, you divide your body among myriad forms." After that, "The mountains of Lang province, the rivers of Li, the four seas and five lakes, the whole land, is under the imperial sway." Only then can you send Tiantong's water buffalo to pull a plow. His verse says,

Verse   *The jade man's dream is shattered—one call from the rooster*
Looking around on life, all colors are equal.
Wind and thunder, with news of events, roust out the hibernating insects;
Peach trees, wordless, naturally make a path.
When the time and season comes, laboring at the plow,
Who fears the spring rows' knee-deep mud?

Commentary   Tiantong has attained a transcendent state: he goes briefly to where the hermit is holding the pole tight and doesn't dare move, and stirs him, saying, "If you only go on this way, the weeds will be ten feet deep in the hall."

A man with views attached to his bodily self came to the patriarch Upagupta and sought initiation. Upagupta said, "The rule of seeking initiation is that you believe in my words and don't disobey my instructions." The man said, "I have already come to take refuge with you, Master; I certainly will obey your command." Then Upagupta magically produced a precipitous cliff on a mountain soaring high with big trees on it, and made him climb up a tree, and under the tree also he produced a chasm a thousand cubits wide. Then Upagupta bade him let go his foothold. The man did as he was told, and let go; Upagupta bade him let go one hand, and he let go a hand. Finally Upagupta bade him let go the other hand; the man replied, "If I let go the other hand, I'll fall into the abyss and die." Upagupta said, "Before, you promised to do as I instructed—how can you disobey me?" At that moment that man's love for his body vanished; he let go his hands and fell—he didn't see tree or abyss anymore, whereupon he realized the fruition of the Path.

Changsha's "Mountains of Lang, rivers of Li" is called a phrase that skillfully uses a precipice. If not for the jade man's dream being shattered, and having a life beyond, how could the whole world be utterly new each day?

In the *Classic of Poetry*, it says, "Shoo-shoo, regularly the valley wind insists, awakening the hibernating creatures. After the springtime begins, thunder begins to sound."

In the *Books of the Han Dynasty*, in the biography of Li Guang, it says, "Peaches and plums, wordless—underneath them a path naturally forms." The *Source Mirror* says, "Once virtuous action is stored, you will be trusted without saying anything, like the peaches and plum trees naturally becoming the route of a path."

Also, the saying "The mountains of Lang, the rivers of Li" concerns trailing mud and dripping water.

When Sansheng was in the assembly, he asked Elder Xiu to ask Changsha, "When Nanquan passed on, where did he go?" Changsha said, "When Shitou was a novice he saw the Sixth Patriarch." Xiu said, "I didn't ask about Shitou seeing the Sixth Patriarch when he was a novice—where did Nanquan go when he passed away?" Changsha said, "The Sixth Patriarch told Shitou to seek out Xingsi." Xiu said, "Master, you only have a thousand-foot cold pine; you don't have bamboo sprouts sticking out." Changsha didn't reply. Xiu repeated this to Sansheng, who said, "If this is true, he's yet seven steps ahead of Linji." Sansheng personally went up to the abbot's room and said, "Master, your answer just now could be said to light up ahead and cut off behind." Changsha didn't speak. Sansheng said, "I had always doubted this fellow."

Foyin said in verse,

> *A guest sees Changsha on the same path;*
> *He bids someone investigate his family style, as promised.*
> *Sumeru's myriad heights are worn away past and present;*
> *Cutting grass to measure the sky is a waste of effort.*

Where the ancients held still, they could let go to advance a step from atop the pole; when they let go, they could hold still and stand like a thousand-foot wall. Why were they so free and independent? In the cities of Hunan the people are well nourished; rice is cheap, firewood is plentiful, all the neighbors have enough.

Changsha had a monk ask Master Hui, "How was it before you saw Nanquan?"—In the early morning there's gruel.

Hui remained silent—If you ask a question, there's an odor of crap.
The monk said, "How about after seeing him?"—He searches it out further for him.
Hui said, "There couldn't be anything else."—He just stumbles and falls in a pile of crap.
The monk returned and related this to Changsha—A fellow running off at the mouth accompanied by his tongue.
Changsha said, "The man sitting atop the hundred-foot pole—An embarrassment for the one at the bottom of the pole.
Though he's gained entry, this is not yet the real—When solitariness is not set up, then is the path lofty.
Atop the hundred-foot pole, he should step forward—At the extreme, it's very much like a cutting off and discarding.
The universe in all directions is the whole body."—For the first time one believes the sitting cushion isn't heaven.
The monk said, "Atop the hundred-foot pole, how can you step forward?"—After all there is still this.
Changsha said, "The mountains of Lang, the rivers of Li."—You bump into it everywhere.
The monk said, "I don't understand."—How very brilliant!
Changsha said, "The whole land is under the imperial sway."—You may leap all you want.

Added Sayings / Verse

The jade man's dream is shattered—one call from the rooster—Opening his eyes, he's not aware of the dawn.

Looking around on life, all colors are equal—In the inexhaustible treasury, using without end.

Wind and thunder, with news of events, roust out the hibernating insects—Seasons don't overlap.

Peach trees, wordless, naturally make a path—Where water goes a channel forms.

When the time and season comes, laboring at the plow—Shirkers don't work.

Who fears the spring rows' knee-deep mud?—Workers don't shirk.

80 LONGYA PASSES THE BRACE

Introduction The great sound is rarely voiced; a great vessel takes a long time to complete. In the midst of great hurry and turmoil, pretending to be an idiot, waiting a thousand years after passing away to take it easy—tell me, what kind of person is this?

Case Longya asked Cuiwei, "What is the meaning of the founding teacher's coming from the west?"
Cuiwei said, "Pass me the meditation brace."
Longya took the brace and gave it to Cuiwei: Cuiwei took it and hit him.
Longya said, "Hit me if you will, but there's no meaning to the founder's coming from the west."
Longya also asked Linji, "What is the meaning of the founding teacher's coming from the west?"
Linji said, "Pass me the cushion."
Longya took the cushion and gave it to Linji: Linji took it and hit him.
Longya said, "Hit me if you will, but there's no meaning to the founding teacher's coming from the west."
Later, when Longya was abbot of a monastery, a monk asked him, "Teacher, that time when you asked those two masters about the founder's meaning, did they clarify it or not?"
Longya said, "They clarified it all right, but there is no meaning to the founder's coming from the west."

Commentary Chan Master Judun of Longya Mountain in Hunan first called on Cuiwei and Linji, and later called on Dongshan and Deshan. One day he asked Dongshan about the meaning of the founder's coming from the west; Dongshan said, "When the water of the Dong river flows backwards, then I'll tell you." Longya was awakened at these words.

Yuanwu said, "At the time when Longya took the meditation brace, how could he have not known that it was to hit him?" After Longya was abbot of a monastery, a monk asked him, "When you saw those two old adepts, did you agree with them or not?" Longya said, "I agree, all right, but it's just that there is no meaning of the founder." Yuanwu said, "I am otherwise—I don't really agree, and there is no meaning of the Founder." Chan Master Fori Gao's verse said,

> *Zeqing did not bow to the Hunnish chief;*
> *From beginning to end he follows the etiquette of the Chinese emperor.*
> *After snow you know the hardiness of pine and cedar;*
> *When the task is hard, then you see a powerful man.*

Xuedou just put him down; Dagui Zhe said, "Cuiwei and Linji can be called real Chan masters; Longya is foremost in pulling out the weeds looking for the Way—he is a model and guide for later generations." Then, quoting the question of the monk after Longya had become an abbot, Dagui said, "Longya looks ahead and behind, giving medicine according to the disease. I am otherwise: when he asked at the beginning if the two old masters clarified it or not, I'd hit him right on the spine, not only supporting Cuiwei and Linji, but also not rejecting his question." I say, this is truly the hammer of the Linji succession—he can't let go. If you want to see the magical talisman under Longya's elbow, you need Tiantong's eye of the same branch.

Verse *The cushion and brace answer Longya:*
Why not be the master at the appropriate time?
He doesn't expect complete clarification on the spot:
He's afraid it would fall on the horizon of the sky.
How could a sword be hung in empty space?
The River of Stars, however, floats a raft.

The unsprouted grass can hide a musky elephant:
In the bottomless basket can be put a living snake.
Today's rivers and lakes—what obstructions?
At the universal ford there are boat and car.

Longya's cushion and brace—Cuiwei and Linji made him bring them in the presence of the assembly—why couldn't he use them?

After Baizhang had told the story of the wild fox, Huangbo asked, "An ancient gave a wrong answer and fell into a wild fox body for five hundred lives: if one is not mistaken time after time, what will become of him?" Baizhang said, "Come here and I'll tell you." Huangbo came close and gave Baizhang a slap first. Baizhang said, "I knew barbarians' beards were red—here's another red-bearded barbarian." This is truly being the master at the right moment. It's not that Longya is not an adept—he doesn't expect complete clarification on the spot; he doesn't want to take charge of the situation by thundering and flashing lightning, being strict and sharp for the time.

An ancient poem says, "The color of a thousand miles—the mid-autumn moon; the clamor of a hundred thousand troops—the tide at midnight." This is called cold beggary, not having anything stored up.

A monk asked Jingqing, "I have not yet reached the source—please give me an expedient method." Jingqing said, "If it is the source, how could it admit of expedients?" An attendant asked, "Just then, did this conclude it for him?" Jingqing said, "No." The attendant said, "What was your meaning?" Jingqing said, "One drop of ink in two places completes the dragon." Conclusion is like finishing or wrapping up—he was afraid of making an advertisement and disgracing the way of the school.

Dongshan, in his last instructions to Caoshan, said, "At my late teacher Yunyan's place I was personally sealed with the 'precious mirror meditation,' in which all matters are comprehended most clearly and essentially. Now I impart it to you; keep it well, and don't let it be cut off. Later, if you meet a true vessel of Dharma, only then should you pass it on. It should be kept hidden, not revealed in words—I think that if it's relegated to current conventions, it will be hard to contact people later."

A monk asked Dongan Cha, "What is having no shield or spear?"

Dongan said, "A sword is not hung in space; the moon isn't covered with scales."

It is said in the world that the River of Stars (Milky Way) and the ocean commune; on the seashore, every year in the eighth month there's a floating raft which comes and goes without fail. Zhang Jian, Marquis of Bowang, brought a lot of supplies, boarded the raft, and went off—rushing along, he wasn't aware of day or night; suddenly he came to a place, where he saw houses inside a city wall, with many women inside the houses weaving. There was just one man, leading an ox to the river bank. Without drinking, surprised, he said, "What man has come here?" Jian asked, "What place is this?" The man said, "You should go to Shu and ask Yan Junping." So Jian did as he said: Junping said, "In certain years the moon has a guest star, which gets into the ox constellation." Recorded as it is told, this appears in the *Book of Han;* that Zhang Jian searched out the source of the river refers to the great distances of his missions (as emissary of the Han imperial court to major nations of the regions west and north of the borders of the Chinese empire); really there's no mention of the River of Stars. Only the *Record of Many Things* says that someone brought provisions and boarded a raft and reached the River of the Sky (Milky Way), saw a man watering his ox, asked Junping about it, and was told an outside star entered the ox-constellation. This was the man. This eulogizes Longya letting go when it was time to act, and after letting go, separately being the master.

A monk asked Caoshan, "Why can the unsprouted grass hide a musky elephant?" Caoshan said, "Luckily you are an adept—why still ask me?" The unsprouted grass and bottomless basket are Longya's unused great function. Thus a wild elephant does not walk a donkey track, a live snake doesn't die under the phrase.

Longya taught the assembly, "Students of the Way must pass beyond buddhas and patriarchs before they'll attain. Dongshan, Master of Xinfeng, said, 'When the verbal teachings of buddhas and patriarchs are like born enemies, you then have some part in study.' If you can't pass beyond them, then you'll be fooled by the buddhas and patriarchs." A monk then asked, "Do the buddhas and patriarchs have any intention to fool people?" Longya said, "You tell me—do rivers and lakes have any intent to hinder people?" He went on, "Though rivers and lakes have no intention to obstruct people, because people at the time can't pass over them, rivers and lakes become obstructions to people—you can't say they don't hinder people. Longya went beyond the idea of the buddhas and patriarchs, like a natural enemy; that's why he said, "They clarified it all right, but there is still no meaning in the founding teacher's coming from the West."

A proverb says, "If one doesn't know how to float, one regrets that the river is wide." An old-timer said, "If one can't float, one laments that the pit is hot."

Added Sayings /Case

Longya asked Cuiwei, "What is the meaning of the founder's coming from the West?"—Each time you bring it up it is new.

Cuiwei said, "Pass me the meditation brace."—He invests his capital, hoping for profit.

Longya took the brace and gave it to Cuiwei—Staring unmoving.

Cuiwei took it and hit him—I knew he was right.

Longya said, "Hit me if you will, but there's no meaning of the founder's coming from the west."—Half agreeing, half disagreeing.

Longya also asked Linji, "What is the meaning of the founder's coming from the West?"—Hard skin, leprous flesh.

Linji said, "Pass me the cushion."—Good texts are mostly the same.

Longya took the cushion and gave it to Linji—He meets error with error.

Linji took it and hit him—He wields the mace freely.

Longya said, "You may hit me if you will, but there's no meaning to the founder's coming from the West."—He manages to be so soft and hard.

Later, when Longya was abbot of a monastery, a monk asked him, "Teacher, that time when you asked those two masters about the founder's meaning, did they clarify it or not?"—A poor man thinks about his old debts.

Longya said, "They clarified it all right, but there is no meaning to the founder's coming from the West."—Fired brick striking solid ice.

Added Sayings /Verse

The cushion and brace answer Longya—His plan settled, he's content to have his spine butchered.

Why not be the master at the appropriate time?—The dog who bites a man does not show its teeth.

He doesn't expect complete clarification on the spot—If people have no foresight . . .

He's afraid it would fall on the horizon of the sky—. . . there'll surely be trouble near at hand.

How could a sword be hung in space?—He doesn't use the business of the swordpoint.

The River of Stars, however, floats a raft—There is a road of transcendence beyond.

The unsprouted grass can hide a musky elephant—Even the buddha-eye can't see it.

In the bottomless basket can be put a living snake—Held up for everyone, given to you it's different.

Today's rivers and lakes—what obstructions?—In great peace there is no aversion.

At the universal ford there are boat and car—What place is not beautiful?

81 XUANSHA COMES TO THE DISTRICT

Introduction Move, and shadows appear; notice, and dust arises. Lifting up, distinctly clear; casting down, calm and peaceful. In a meeting of people of the Way, how do they talk?

Case When Xuansha came to Pudian district, they welcomed him with a hundred festivities. The next day, he asked Great Elder Xiaotang, "Where has all of yesterday's commotion gone?"
Xiaotang held up the corner of his vestment.
Xuansha said, "There's no connection, not by a long shot."

Commentary Great Master Zongyi of Xuansha in Fu province was named Shibei. With straw sandals, muslin clothing, and turnips for food, he was content. Xuefeng esteemed his asceticism and always called him "Ascetic Bei." According to tradition, Xuansha didn't leave the mountain, just as Baoshou didn't cross the river; as Xuansha stumbled and injured his toe, he lamented, "This body is not existent—where does the pain come from? This body, this pain, is ultimately without origin. Stop! Stop! Bodhidharma didn't come to China, the Second Patriarch didn't go to India." Then he went back (to Xuefeng). Also, as he read the *Heroic March Scripture,* he was illuminated, and therefore his response to people in situations was swift and keen, in accord with the scripture. And when it came to being tested by Xuefeng, he didn't back down when in the right. Xuefeng said, "Ascetic Bei is a reincarnation." The commander of Min, Wang Fanzhi, and the magistrate Wang Yanbin, both honored him as their teacher. His community usually numbered eight or nine hundred.

When Xuansha came to Pudian district, he was welcomed with many festivities. The next day he asked Great Elder Xiaotang, "Where has all yesterday's commotion gone?" Xiaotang lifted up a corner of his vestment. Xuansha said, "No connection—not by a long shot." Where is it that Xiaotang was out of touch? Did Xuansha approve or not?

Dagui Zhe said, "I would do otherwise—if someone asked me, I'd just snap my fingers. If a monk came forward and said, 'No connection,' then I'd agree with him. Why? For a powerful man to grab a tiger's whiskers is ordinary. But tell me, where is the gain and loss?" He also said, "Xuefeng holds the ultimate jewel hidden in his breast; when he meets another, it increases its shine: Xuansha's hammer of the fundamental strikes a blow, and the light flows for a thousand ages."

Fayan said as an alternative, "Yesterday how much commotion was there?" Fadeng said, "Today's an even better laugh." See how these two adepts, descendants of Xuansha's lineage, see through Xuansha's action, just loosely interposing a net outside, while inside arrows spontaneously hit each other.

Tiantong has the all-pervasive eye; seeing the shortcoming within the strength of that house, he produces it in verse, piercing the depths.

Verse *Hiding the boat in the night valley,*
Setting the oar on the clear source.
The dragon and fish don't know the water is their life:
Busting a gut, nevertheless it's just a little shake.
Master Xuansha, Elder Xiaotang:
Box and lid, arrowpoints;
Probing pole, shadowing grass.
Submerged, withdrawn, the old turtle nests in the lotuses;
Frolicking, the multi-colored fish plays in the water grasses.

Commentary Xuansha's question about yesterday's commotion is like the chapter on the great master in Zhuangzi: "Hiding a boat in a valley, hiding a mountain in a swamp, is considered sure, yet in the middle of night a strong man carries it off while the unseeing do not know. In hiding the small and the large, there is appropriateness, and still it's gone some-where; if you hide the world in the world, you can't find where it's gone. This is the constant general condition of things." Tiantong likens Xuansha's posing the question about yesterday and today to hiding a boat, carrying it secretly, to test Xiaotang, then coming back to the deep still water of the clear source, like rowing a lone boat. This is the seal within the mystery: wary of lingering in stagnant water, the eye in Xuansha's saying comes alive; he wants people to know the source of both movement and stillness.

Master Wolun Qiu said, "If you want to get the bare essence, it is the mountains, rivers, and earth that discover it for you; the thing is eternal and can comprehend the ultimate. If you enter by way of Manjusri's door, all conditioned things—earth, wood, tile, stone—help you awaken your potential. If you enter by Avalokitesvara's door, all sounds and echoes, even clams and spiders, help you discover your potential. If you enter by Samantabhadra's door, you arrive without moving a step. I use these three doors to provisionally direct you, like using a broken stick to stir the ocean, making the fish and dragons there know that water is their life." If you always know the source of motion, stillness, speech, silence, going and coming, already you're not wasting time. Here Tiantong eulogizes Xuansha's way of helping people; if you're an adept, with box and lid (joining), with arrowpoints (meeting), with probing pole and shadowing grass, you hold still and let go. Take a look at holding up the vestment and 'no connection'—look, what principle is it?

In the *Historical Records*, in the biography of Kui Ce, the great ambassador says, "I went to Jiangnan and watched what went on there. The turtle lives a thousand years, and sports on lotus leaves." This is 'no connection.' Pulling in his head and limbs and hiding in his shell doesn't hinder sporting, and sporting doesn't hinder hiding. Now a picture of fish in duckweed is drawn. Duckweed is a water plant; it drifts along with the waves, naturally forming patterns. Also, duckweed is the water plant with patterns—it appears in the *Analects of Confucius:* "Mountainous beams, duckweed columns."

> *Do you want to know the two elders?*
> *When there's spirit, add spirit; where there's no style is also stylish.*

Added
Sayings
/Case

"Where has all of yesterday's commotion gone?"—It's still noisy.
Xiaotang held up the corner of his vestment—As it turns out his hands are flustered and his feet flurried.

Xuansha said, "There's no connection."—Thanks for your testimony.

Added
Sayings
/Verse

Hiding the boat in the night valley—A renunciant is hard to fool.

Setting the oar on the clear source—Willing to fall into stagnant water?

The dragons and fish don't know the water is their life—The one playing the game is lost.

Busting a gut, nevertheless it's just a little shake—Beating the grass to frighten the snakes.

Master Xuansha, Elder Xiaotang—Their crimes are listed on one indictment.

Box and lid, arrowpoints—Easy to open is the mouth of beginnings and endings.

Probing pole, shadowing grass—Hard to maintain is the heart of dead winter.

Submerged, withdrawn, the old turtle nests in the lotuses—When you hide let there be no tracks.

Frolicking, the multi-colored fish plays in the water grasses—Where there are no tracks, do not hide.

82 YUNMEN'S "SOUND AND FORM"

Introduction   Not cutting off sound and form is falling wherever you are; searching by way of sound and looking by way of form, you don't see the Buddha. Isn't there anyone who can take to the road and return home?

Case   Yunmen said to the assembly, "Hearing sound, awaken to the way: seeing form, understand the mind. The Bodhisattva Avalokitesvara brings money to buy a sesame cake: when he lowers his hand, it turns out to be a jelly-doughnut."

Commentary   Tiantong brings up the story talking about the swift steed, omitting its color. In the original record, Yunmen said to the assembly, "Hearing sound, realize the Way; seeing form, understand the mind. How is this?" He raised his hand and said, "Avalokitesvara Bodhisattva brings money to buy a sesame cake; when he lowers his hand, actually it turns out to be a jelly-doughnut."

National Teacher Yuantong said, "We might say of Yunmen that as his tune became more lofty, those who harmonized became rarer. Right now he enters the universal net of meditation atop my whisk, enters concentration in the East and emerges from it in the West, and so on, including entering concentration in a male body and emerging in a female body. But do you understand? The colors of the meadows are not blocked by any more mountains—the moonlight and water directly penetrate each other." I say, seeking without finding in the sea, instead they meet on the shore.

Look further—where does Tiantong meet him? The verse says,

Verse   *Going out the gate, making the horse leap, sweeping away the comets—*
The smoke and dust of ten thousand countries is spontaneously clear.

The twelve media are free of useless images and echoes:
Pure light emanates in a billion worlds.

Commentary   "Hearing sound, awaken to the Way"—does the Way have any sound? "Seeing form, understand the mind"—does the mind have any form? Here rites, music, and military campaigns issue from the emperor; an army of humanity and righteousness has no enemies in all the world.

A comet is a bad omen; taking sound and form for image and echo represents their unreality. Image means the reflection in a mirror, the moon in the water; echo means reverberating sound in an empty valley—these are both like comets in the mind of the Way.

"Ten thousand countries" means myriad things; the "twelve media" means the six sense organs and six sense fields.

The light of the billion worlds shines through reflections and echoes, but getting rid of reflections and echoes, the light is released. Haven't you seen how Baizhang of old said, "The spiritual light shines alone, far transcending the senses." If suddenly each sense faculty and each sense field extended throughout the universe, what about that?

I thought it was a jelly-doughnut; after all it's a sesame cake.

Added   **Yunmen said to the assembly, "Hearing sound, awaken to the Way—A**
Sayings   **couple of pills are blocking the ears.**
/Case   **Seeing form, understand the mind—A pair of leaves are covering the eyes.**

Avalokitesvara brings money to buy a sesame cake; when he lowers his hand it turns out to be a jelly-doughnut."—He's also blown by the wind into a different tune.

Added   *Going out the gate, making the horse leap, sweeping away the comets—*
Sayings   Beyond the castle walls, it's the general's command.
/Verse   *The smoke and dust of ten thousand countries is of itself cleared*—Where the wind blows the grass bends down.

The twelve media are free of idle reflections and echoes—Together they make one house.

The billion worlds emanate pure light.—There is no second appearance besides.

351

83 DAOWU TENDS THE SICK

Introduction The whole body being sickness, Vimalakirti is hard to cure; the grass being useable for medicine, Manjusri uses it well. How can that compare to calling on a transcendent man and gaining peace and wellbeing?

Case Guishan asked Daowu, "Where are you coming from?"
Daowu said, "I've come from tending the sick."
Guishan said, "How many people were sick?"
Daowu said, "There were the sick and the not sick."
Guishan said, "Isn't the one not sick you, Ascetic Zhi?"
Daowu said, "Being sick and not being sick have nothing to do with *him* at all. Speak quickly! Speak quickly!"
Guishan said, "Even if I could say anything, it would have no relation."

Commentary Chan Master Lingyou of Guishan in Tan province called on Dazhi of Baizhang when he was twenty-three years old, and filled the post of chief cook for twenty years. By bringing out fire he awakened to the Way. Later he contended with Hualin in giving an answer to a water-jug, and won Mount Gui. The military commander Li Jingrang petitioned the emperor to grant the name Dongjing to the temple there, and the prime minister Pei Xiu came there to ask about the deep mystery.
One time the master, seeing a field fire, asked Daowu, "Do you see the fire?" Daowu said, "I see." Guishan said, "Where does it come from?" Daowu said, "Please ask another question, apart from walking, stand-

ing, sitting, and lying down." Guishan stopped. Fojian, bringing this up, said, "The flaming field fire, everyone sees; there's only Daowu who sees far beyond."

I say, it's all tending the sick—it's not as good as Daowu seeing through the heart, liver, and guts. Guishan was a master of appropriate technique; sizing up the audience to make his pronouncement, he said, "Even if I could say anything, it would have no relation." Only Tiantong says, "Where there is no relation—that is just right to say."

Verse　*When has the wonderful medicine ever passed his mouth?*
　　　　Even the miraculous physician can't hold his wrist.
　　　　As though existent, he is basically not nonexistent:
　　　　Utterly empty, he is basically not existent.
　　　　Not perishing, yet born,
　　　　Alive without dying:
　　　　Completely transcending before prehistoric buddhas,
　　　　Walking alone after the empty aeon.
　　　　Subsisting peacefully—sky covers, earth supports;
　　　　Moving on—the sun flies, the moon runs.

Commentary　The red-thread vessel broken, medicine and disease both gone, when taking medicine the mouth is forgotten, when taking a pulse the wrist is forgotten. This is what is called an incurable disease—doctors fold their hands and frown. If you say it exists, yet throughout the body there's not a shadow or reflection; if you say it doesn't exist, yet the whole world has never hidden it.

The priest Danluan of the Qi dynasty had a ten-volume scripture on immortality. Later he met Buddhist Canonical Master Bodhiruci and asked him, "In the Buddhist teachings, is there a method of eternal life without death that surpasses the methods of the wizards of China?" The master spat on the ground and said, "How can this country have a method of eternal life? Even if you could extend your years, once the reward is ended you fall." Then he took out a copy of the scripture on

353

Contemplation of the Buddha of Infinite Life and gave it to Danluan, saying, "This is the method of the Great Wizard, to eternally realize liberation and forever leave birth and death."

In the *Heroic March Scripture,* when the rewards of the ten wizards are exhausted, they come back into the various realms of being. Laozi said, "One who dies yet does not perish is long-lived." A poem presented to Foyin by Su Dongpo says, "Even living a long time, still there's no leisure to study; for the time being I'll study not dying."

"Completely transcending before prehistoric buddhas" means the primordial, not yet formed yet already complete. "Walking alone after the empty aeon" means the temporal, already destroyed yet not destroyed. "Subsisting peacefully—sky covers, earth supports; Moving on—sun flies, moon runs"—this is called the function of the whole body, returning the function to the substance. When still, being the root of heaven and earth; in action, harmonizing with the minds of sages and saints—do you understand this kind of talk?

'Opening up the wondrously pure, completely clear eye, recognize the lucky man at peace.'

Added Sayings /Case

Guishan asked Daowu, "Where are you coming from?"—Where he's coming from needs clarification.

Daowu said, "I've come from tending the sick."—The foremost of the fields of blessings is not lacking.

Guishan said, "How many people were sick?"—Yet demanding two kinds.

Daowu said, "There was the sick and the not sick."—It turns out you have a 'second moon'.

Guishan said, "Isn't the one not sick you, Ascetic Zhi?"—A pitfall for a tiger.

Daowu said, "Being sick and not being sick have nothing to do with him at all. Speak quickly!"—He's been wrapped head to foot with vines by the gourd.

Guishan said, "Even if I could say anything, it would have no relation."—Calamity does not enter the door of the careful.

Added
Sayings
/Verse

When has the wonderful medicine ever passed his mouth?—Can't be swallowed, can't be spit out.

Even the miraculous physician can't hold his wrist—There's no place to grasp.

As though existent, he *is basically not nonexistent*—It just says He's everywhere in the world.

Utterly empty, he *is basically not existent*—You don't see so much as a hair.

Not perishing, yet born—Empty as the spirit of valleys, always undying.

Alive without dying—The Way grew of itself prior to the emperor of images.

Completely transcending before prehistoric buddhas—Rolled out, doesn't reach the beginning.

Walking alone after the empty aeon—Rolled up, doesn't reach the end.

Subsisting peacefully—sky covers, earth supports—Holding heaven and earth still.

Moving on—the sun flies, the moon runs—Action and creation.

84 JUDI'S "ONE FINGER"

Introduction   A thousand awakenings at one hearing, at one understanding a thousand follow. The highest people comprehend all with one determination; the middling and lesser hear much but disbelieve much. Let's try and bring out the direct, simple point.

Case   **Whenever Master Judi was asked a question, he would just raise one finger.**

Commentary   Chan Master Judi of Jinhua mountain in Wu province first lived in a hut on Mount Tiantai. There was a nun named Shiji ('Reality') who arrived with a rain hat on her head and a staff in her hand. She circled Judi three times and asked, "If you can speak, I'll take off my hat." Three times she asked, but Judi had no reply at all: Shiji went away. Judi said, "It's getting late; just stay for the night." She said, "If you can speak, I'll stay." Again Judi had no reply. After Shiji had left, Judi lamented to himself, "Though I'm in the body of a man, I don't have the spirit of a man." He was about to abandon his hut to go traveling to study, but that night the spirit of the mountain told him, "You don't need to leave this mountain. There will be a great bodhisattva who will come explain the Dharma for you." As it turned out, after ten days Master Tianlong arrived: Judi welcomed him, bowing to him in all sincerity, and recounted the foregoing events to him in detail. Tianlong raised his finger and pointed at him; Judi was greatly enlightened on the spot.

After this, whenever a monk came, Judi would just raise a finger, with no other explanation. The servant boy at his place was asked by people on the outside, "What does your master teach?" The boy held up a finger.

When he returned, he reported this to Judi, and Judi cut off that finger with a knife. The boy ran out screaming: Judi called to him, whereat the boy turned his head; Judi then held up one finger—the boy suddenly attained enlightenment.

As Judi was about to die, he said to the people, "I attained Tianlong's 'one-finger' Chan, and used it all my life without exhausting it." When he finished speaking he passed away. I say, the finger should be cut off for him. Changqing said instead, "Fine food is not for a satisfied man to eat." I say, not greedy for the taste of fragrant food, he can be called a dragon in a blue pond. Xuansha said, "If I had seen him at the time, I would have broken off his finger." I say, that would not only clear up the grudge for the boy, it would also give a breath of energy to people of later times. Xuanjiao said, "Tell me, what did Xuansha mean in speaking that way?" I say, after all he doubts. Yunju Yi said, "When Xuansha spoke that way, was he agreeing with Judi or not? If he agreed, why did he say he'd break off his finger? If not, where was Judi's fault?" I say, the fault lies in agreeing and disagreeing. The former Caoshan said, "Judi's understanding was crude—he only recognized one state, one perspective. Everyone claps their hands, but Nanyuan is extraordinary." I say, to pick milk out of water you must be a king goose. Xuanjiao also said, "Tell me, was Judi enlightened or not? If he was enlightened, why say his understanding was crude? If he wasn't enlightened, yet he said he used his 'one-finger' Chan all his life without exhausting it. Then tell me, where does the essence of Caoshan's meaning lie?" I say, when the tone is high, there are few who harmonize—you need to meet a connoisseur.

Later Chan Master Jiashan Lai was living at Tianning, west of Zhenfu, when someone asked, "Where is Master Iron Ox's tomb?" Jiashan pointed with his finger; the man was suddenly awakened, and made a verse saying,

> Iron Ox, Iron Ox!
> Don't seek elsewhere anymore.
> If someone asks me,
> I'd raise a finger.

I say, though the understanding is crude, still it doesn't depend on coming from the side.

Haven't you seen how the 'One-Eyed Dragon' Mingzhao asked Guo Tai Shen, "An ancient said that Judi just recited a three-line spell and gained a reputation surpassing all—how can you quote the three-line spell?" Guo Tai held up a finger. Mingzhao said, "If not for today, how could I have known this traveler from melon-land?" I say, even if the conditions of the afflictions are different, first you should cure the root.

The *Merging of Difference and Unity* says, "Hearing words, understand the source; don't set up your own rules." This might be called finding the road you came by deep in the night, immediately going out through the pass without waiting for dawn.

Foguo's verse said,

> How could the operative circumstances of question and answer
> > be easy to reply to?
> Without money it's hard to be really stylish.
> In his heart there's something, but he can't say it;
> He just holds up his finger in the midst of hurry.

If you want to be stylish and say what's in the heart, call on Tiantong today:

Verse *Old Judi's finger-tip Chan—*
Thirty years he used it without wearing it out.
Truly he has the unconventional technique of a man of the Way—
Ultimately there are no mundane things before his eyes to see.
His realization most simple,
The device the more broad.
An ocean of billions of worlds is drunk in the tip of a hair:
Fish and dragons, limitless—into whose hands do they fall?
Take care, Mr Ren, holding the fishing pole!

Tiantong then also raised a finger and said, "Look!"

Commentary The eternal void of a thousand ages; one morning's wind and moon—is it only thirty years of use without exhausting it? In *Zhuangzi*, in the chapter on the great master of the source, Confucius says, "He travels outside convention, I travel within convention." Without technique beyond convention, how could the mundane and transmundane all be on his single fingertip, seeing through to the root source? An ancient poem says, "Before the eyes there's no mundane thing; with many illnesses the body is still light." Tiantong apprehends it in his body near at hand, just using one finger, the simple, easy way, essential, not complicated. According to Vimalakirti, a hair engulfs the ocean—his teaching is called the small inconceivable scripture; according to the *Flower Ornament Scripture,* an atom contains the universe—it's called the great inconceivable scripture. According to the *Heroic March Scripture,* a single hairtip can contain the lands of the ten directions. It also says that on a hairtip is manifest the land of the jewel king, sitting on an atomic particle, turning the wheel of the great Dharma.

According to *Zhuangzi,* Mr Ren made a huge hook and stout cord, baited the hook with fifty calves, and cast it into the Eastern sea every morning. For a year there was no fish. Then an enormous fish ate the bait; he yanked the hook, it went down, and the fish, startled, came up shaking its head; foaming waves towered like mountains, the ocean waters were agitated, roaring like demons, flashing for a thousand miles. Once Mr Ren landed the fish, he cut it up and dried it. East of the Zhiche river, north of the Cangwu wilderness, there was none who didn't get their fill of this fish.

What it means is when the fishing poles are all broken he again plants bamboo, without figuring how long it'll take to succeed. When he makes a catch, he stops. Later he succeeded in enlightening a boy with a severed finger.

Guo Tai Shen met on a separate peak, Jiashan Lai mistakenly enters Peach Spring. Today, at the conclusion of Tiantong's verse, he too raised a finger and said, "Look!" Master Boshan Dayin said, "The great Tiantong runs following another's footsteps."

Master Wuzu Fayan quoted a monk asking Touzi, "What is the ten-body controller?" Touzi got down from the meditation seat and stood there. Wuzu said, "If a monk asked me, I'd also get down off the seat and stand there. Why draw a cat according to a model? Wait till my assessment is complete, then I'll tell you."

So we know that with Judi's finger, each time you drink water, each time it reaches your throat. What direction would you have me take besides? (throwing down the whisk) Let everyone check.

Added
Sayings
/Case **Whenever Judi was asked a question, he would just raise one finger— Why expend so much energy?**

Added
Sayings
/Verse *Old Judi's finger-tip Chan*—Retract the donkey legs.

Thirty years he used it without wearing it out—Even up to now his disturbing hand is indiscriminately applied.

Truly he has the unconventional technique of a man of the Way—Here it can't be used.

Ultimately there are no mundane things before his eyes to see—There's still a complaint of lack.

His realization most simple—It fills up heaven and earth.

The device the more broad—It's not worth a pinch.

An ocean of billions of worlds is drunk in the tip of a hair—Doesn't leave a drop.

Fish and dragons, limitless—into whose hands do they fall?—Tiantong is still there.

Take care, Mr Ren, holding the fishing pole—Undeniably startling method.

85 THE APPEARANCE OF THE NATIONAL TEACHER'S MONUMENT

Introduction When you have the mallet to smash space and the ability to rend a mountain, then for the first time you arrive at where there are originally no seams or gaps, where you don't see any flaws or scars. But who is such a person?

Case Emperor Suzong asked National Teacher Zhong, "After passing away, what will you need?"

The teacher said, "Make me a seamless monument."

The emperor said, "Please tell me the monument's appearance."

The teacher, after a silence, said, "Understand?"

The emperor said, "I don't understand."

The teacher said, "I have a disciple to whom I have transmitted the teaching, named Danyuan: he knows about this matter."

Later the emperor summoned Danyuan and asked him about the meaning of this.

Danyuán said,

South of Xiang, north of Tan:

Therein is gold filling the whole country.

Under the shadowless tree, the communal ferryboat:

In the crystal palace, no one who knows.

Commentary National Teacher Huizhong, after receiving the mind seal, lived in Tangzi Valley on White Cliff Mountain of Nanyang, never going down out the mountain gate for over forty years. His practice of the Way was heard of in the imperial city, and in 761 an emissary was sent by Emperor

361

Suzong to summon him to the capital, where he treated Huizhong with respect as a teacher. The national teacher first lived in Xichan cloister of Jianfu monastery; then when Daizong assumed the throne, Huizhong was again invited to stay, this time at the Guangto sanctuary. For sixteen years he talked about the Teaching according to the occasion. In 776, on the nineteenth day of the twelfth month, he lay on his right side and passed away forever. He was posthumously entitled Chan Master of Great Realization.

Foguo said, "There are many who say that the national teacher's silence is itself the appearance of the monument. If you understand in this way, the whole Chan school would be wiped off the face of the earth, and the mute would understand Chan."

In ancient times there were two monks living in huts: when they didn't see each other for ten days, one hermit asked, "I haven't seen you for many days—where have you been?" The other hermit said, "I've been in my hut making a seamless monument." The former hermit said, "I want to make one too—can I borrow the pattern?" The latter said, "Why didn't you ask before! I just lent it out to someone."

Fayan said, "Tell me, did he lend him the pattern or not?"

I say, the national teacher said nothing; why did the latter then explain the principle by way of a support?

Xuedou said, "Leaving aside the matter of Suzong not understanding, did Danyuan understand? It only takes one 'Please tell me the monument's appearance' and all the ancestral teachers of India and China, confronted with this, couldn't avoid making North out of South. If there are any bystanders who don't agree, come forth; I want to ask you what is the seamless monument."

I say, if this isn't it, I'll tell you.

Chan Master Zhenying of Danyuan Mountain in Ji province was initiated by Mazu, and was attendant to National Teacher Huizhong. After the national teacher passed on, the emperor summoned Danyuan into the palace, and brought up this story about the seamless monument and asked him about it. Danyuan also was silent for a while, then said, "Do you understand?" The emperor said, "No." Danyuan then spoke a verse:

South of Xiang, north of Tan:
Therein is gold filling the whole country.

Under the shadowless tree, the communal ferryboat;
In the crystal palace, no one knows.

Fushan Yuan made it "South of Ox-head, north of Horse-head." Just get the essence and forget the trap—nothing will not work. When Xuedou said that they will not avoid making South of North, this is just what he means.

A monk asked Daling of Korea, "What is purity in all places?" Daling said, "Breaking a branch of jewel, every inch is precious; cutting sandalwood, each bit is fragrant."

Master Danxia Zichun's verse says, "All heaven and earth is the country of gold; Myriad beings completely manifest the pure subtle body." Danyuan's gold fills the country; Danxia's country is gold—this is even more like the one continuous path.

"Under the shadowless tree, the communal ferryboat." The *Brief Sets* of the *Book of Changes* says, "You're crosssing over in the same boat, so why worry that different people are there." As in the third and fourth lines in the hexagram *gradual,* "Different bodies harmonizing well; no one can intervene; going along in mutual support, like being on the same boat—upper and lower are different physically, as though segregated, their keenness in action wards off bandits—why worry about different kinds?" This means that with the same body, a common life, benefit and injury are shared.

Chan Master Fazhen Yi asked, "This is Maitreya's place, where there is no gate at which there is no Sudhana—why does he say that in the crystal palace there is no one who knows?" I say, excavate the palace, then you'll see; after that, watch Tiantong bring it up to your very nose:

Verse   *Solitary and transcendent,*
Round and full:
Where the power of the eye ends, it towers high.
The moon descends, the pond is empty, the color of night is deep.
When the clouds recede, the mountain is lean, the faces of autumn many.
The positions of the eight trigrams right,
The energies of the five elements harmonize.
The body is in there before—have you seen it?

Nanyang, father and son, seem to know it exists;
The buddhas and patriarchs of India can't do aught about it.

Verse Xuedou said, "Layer upon layer, shadows upon shadows." This one phrase is an appropriate statement: Tiantong's saying "Solitary and transcendent, round and full" is a ten-thousand-year donkey-tethering stake. "Where the power of the eye ends, it towers high"—the buddhas of past, present, and future keep it in the invisible mark on the top of their heads. Xuedou, in eulogizing "Heaven and earth have the same root, myriad things are one body," and Nanquan pointing to a flower, saying, "It's like a dream," also said, "Seeing, hearing, awareness, and knowing, are not individual; mountains and rivers are not seen in a mirror. The frosty sky's moon sets, the night nearly half over; with whom will it cast a shadow, cold in the clear pool?" Compare this to Tiantong's "The moon descends, the pond is empty, the color of night is deep." The ancients sure were effective.

Later Fojian elucidated it thoroughly with a verse saying,

The seamless monument—it's not a shadow;
Vastly empty, at once enter the realm of true suchness.
The diamond eye's lightning courses;
Vague and dark, the mark on the head isn't seen.

This too is "Where the power of the eye ends, it towers high." Tiantong, eulogizing needle and thread penetrating, said, "The craggy green mountains, touched by autumn, thin; hair falls out, the appearance is old." This is also "When the clouds recede, the mountain is lean, the faces of autumn many." We might say, 'Having shed my skin completely, there is only one true reality.' At this point, as "The positions of the eight trigrams right, the energies of the five elements harmonize," in all actions and constructive undertakings, nothing is avoided. Why bother to go to the market place and ask about Sun Pin (the legendary warrior, source of traditional military methods)? Is a body first inside seen coming? Chan Master Tianyi Yihuai went to be abbot at Shashan at the request of the community there: entering the monastery, he went up in the hall and said, "For twenty years I've looked up to this mountain; today has happily arrived, circumstances are meet. Before I arrived on this mountain, my body had already come to the mountain; when I came, Shashan was inside my body."

"Nanyang, father and son, seem to know it exists." He doesn't presume to say that they are, just that they seem like ones who know. Why doesn't he approve them completely? He fears going against that National Teacher and his successor. Why is it that "The buddhas and patriarchs of India can't do aught about it"? Setting up golden mile-markers on the road, at lunchtime iron buns are brought out.

Added Sayings /Case — **Emperor Suzong asked National Teacher Zhong, "After passing away, what will you need?"**—Right now he doesn't lack anything.

The teacher said, "Make me a seamless monument."—Where do you start?

The emperor said, "What would its appearance be like?"—It can't be fully depicted, can't be completely drawn.

After a silence, the teacher said, "Understand?"—Here you can't understand; though not understanding, don't seek elsewhere.

The emperor said, "I don't understand."—Now he's getting somewhere.

The national teacher said, "I have a disciple to whom I have transmitted the Teaching, named Danyuan; he knows about this matter."—If the ancestors don't finish, the trouble reaches the descendants.

Later the emperor summoned Danyuan and asked him about the meaning of this.—An adept ruler doesn't forget last instructions.

Danyuan said, "South of Xiang, north of Tan—The sky is high, earth is wide, the sun is to the left, the moon is to the right.

Therein is gold filling the nation—It fills all of space.

Under the shadowless tree, the communal ferryboat—So dense and fine even a golden knife can't cut it open.

In the crystal palace, no one who knows."—Silent and still, the screen hanging down, he doesn't show this face.

Added Sayings /Verse — *Solitary and transcendent*—Not being companion of myriad things.

Round and full—No lack, no excess.

Where the power of the eye ends, it towers high—Shading the eyes to look, still the gaze can't reach.

The moon descends, the pond is empty, the color of night is deep—All worlds in the ten directions are like a point of ink.

When the clouds recede, the mountain is lean, the faces of autumn many—The body exposed in the golden wind.

The positions of the eight trigrams right—Heaven and earth join their virtues.

The energies of the five elements harmonize—Sun and moon join their light.

The body is in there before—*have you seen it?*—Where you reach you don't check.

Nanyang, father and son, seem to know it exists—I believe a half for now.

The buddhas and patriarchs of India can't do aught about it—The thousand sages have always stood downwind.

86 LINJI'S GREAT ENLIGHTENMENT

Introduction   Even with a head of bronze, a forehead of iron, the eyes of a god, the pupils of a dragon, the beak of an eagle, the jowls of a fish, the heart of a bear, and the guts of a leopard, under the diamond sword planning isn't admitted—you can't manage a single strategem. Why is it so?

Case   Linji asked Huangbo, "What is the true essential great meaning of the Buddha's teaching?" Huangbo immediately hit him.
This happened three times: then Linji left Huangbo and visited Dayu.
Dayu asked, "Where have you come from?"
Linji said, "From Huangbo."
Dayu said, "What did Huangbo say?"
Linji said, "Three times I asked about the truly essential great meaning of the buddhist teaching, and three times I was beaten with a stick. I do not know if I had any fault or not."
Dayu said, "Huangbo was so kind, he did his utmost for you, and still you come and ask if there was any fault or not!?"
Linji was greatly enlightened at these words.

Commentary   Chan Master Huizhao of Linji cloister in Zhen province had the initiatory name Yixuan. He was a man from Nanhua in Cao province; his surname was Xing. At first he studied the scriptures and treatises, and realized it wasn't the essential shortcut; so he went to Huangbo. There he went along with the assembly for three years, never calling on Huangbo himself to ask any questions; he just modestly kept to his place in silence.

367

The head monk considered him unusual, different from the crowd, and urged him to call on Huangbo to learn. The explanation in the *Inexhaustible Lamp* is incorrect; it seems to me that Huangbo could hardly have allowed people not to ask about things, yet Linji was there for three years, and he was allowed (not to ask any questions). Such as Linji's capacity and perception were, he couldn't ask one question, but had to await the instruction of the head monk before he was able to ask. I once saw a eulogy of Linji by Yang Wuwei which said, "The treasury of the eye of the true teaching perished in the blind donkey; Huangbo was too kind, Dayu was too talkative." I've also seen a eulogy of that head monk, Muzhou, by Yuanwu:

> *Bitter and harsh, biting like a dog,*
> *He opened up Linji of the north and made him a great tree;*
> *He pushed Yunmen over a precipitous cliff.*
> *His words were like dry firewood, his reason cannot be systematized.*

He is the one who was called 'Straw Sandal Chen.'

In the original record, immediately after Linji was enlightened he said, "Basically there's nothing much to Buddhism." Dayu said, "You bedwetting devil! You just asked if you had any error or not, and now you say there's not much to Buddhism? How much is this?" Dayu grabbed and held Linji, saying, "Speak! Speak!" Linji knocked Dayu three times in the side with his fist. Dayu let him go and said, "Your teacher is Huangbo—it has nothing to do with me." Linji returned to Huangbo, who asked, "Coming and going over and over—when will it ever end?" Linji said, "It's just because you are so kind." Then he told the story of what happened; Huangbo said, "That old fellow Dayu is too talkative—wait 'till I see him; I'll give him a beating!" Linji said, "Why talk about waiting to see him? Hit right now!" Then he gave Huangbo a slap. Huangbo laughed, "Ha, ha! This lunatic comes to grab the tiger's whiskers!" Linji then hollered. Huangbo said, "Attendant, take this madman into the meditation hall."

Guishan asked Yangshan, "Did Linji get Dayu's power or Huangbo's power?" Yangshan said, "He not only took the tiger's whiskers, he also knew how to sit on the tiger's head."

Linji later said to the assembly, "At my late teacher's place I asked about the ultimate meaning of buddhism three times, and three times I was beaten—it was like being brushed with a branch of mugwort. Right now I'm thinking of another beating—who can do it for me?" At that point a certain monk came forth and said, "I'll do it." Linji held up his cane to hand it to him; as the monk was going to take it, Linji hit him. Xuedou said, "Linji's letting go was a bit dangerous; he gathers in exceedingly fast."

Tiantong saw how that father and son were extraordinary, beyond the crowd; Huangbo's function was transmitted through Linji, Tiantong picks out the most urgent point to produce it in verse:

Verse **A nine-colored Phoenix,**
A thousand-mile colt:
The wind of reality crosses the pipes,
The spiritual works goes into action.
Coming on directly, the flying lightning is swift:
When the clouds of illusion break, the sun is alone.
He grabs the tiger's whiskers—
Do you see or not?
This is a brave and powerful man of great stature.

Commentary This praises Linji: like Xie Chaozong, he truly has phoenix feathers. In the past Huangbo had once slapped Baizhang—today he runs into that Linji's poison hand; a true dragon spawns a dragon's son, a phoenix raises a phoenix fledgling.

The *Pictorial of Auspicious Signs* says that phoenixes have nine features: one is that it gives back its life; two, that its mind accords with balance—balance means the balance of nature; three, that its ears hear well; four, its tongue is curled when extended; five, it has lustrous color; six, it's red; seven, it has sharp talons; eight, it has a loud cry; nine, it has a door in its abdomen.

Jiu Fangyan sized up a horse for Lord Mu of Qin, and it turned out to be a thousand-mile horse—this is a metaphor for Linji's spiritual swiftness, going a thousand miles in a day—as soon as he was enlightened, he could handle the great function of real potential. There's a couplet circulating everywhere which says,

> On Huangbo's jaw, a thunderous slap—
> On Dayu's ribs, three thumps of the fist.
> Truly it's because the real wind crossed the pipes
> That he got life's activities to function freely.

The first two lines are the inheritance of a teacher's bequest; the latter two are one's own communion with the source.

Laozi said, "(The space) between heaven and earth is like a bagpipe." The bag is a bottomless pouch, it's also a leather bellows; the pipe has three holes. Bajiao Che said, "It's like the lute and the dulcimer—though they have a wonderful sound, without excellent fingering it can't come out." It originally comes from the *Heroic March Scripture*.

"Coming on directly, the flying lightning is swift" refers to the severity of action and swiftness of wit of Linji; "When the clouds of illusion break, the sun is alone" bespeaks the clarity of his enlightenment.

As for "He grabs the tiger's whiskers," Zhuangzi said, "Confucius saw a robber—he retreated and said, 'This is what I call giving oneself moxa burns without having any sickness.' Running quickly to grab the tiger's head and braid its whiskers, he barely escapes its mouth!"

As for "Do you see or not?"—Tiantong is pointing it out to people, demanding that people involved in study experientially apprehend the great function of the whole potential, and not hold back in doing what is proper. This is called the grip of a patchrobe mendicant.

The layman Wujin wrote a continuation of the history of Mount Qingliang, after a request which he answered immediately; later he heard tell of how Chan Master Jieto hit Manjusri, and spontaneously eulogized him as "a brave and powerful man of great stature." But do you see Linji's enlightenment?

> Shaming to death the new bride of Hoyang,
> Startling back to life the old-woman chan of Muta.

Added Sayings /Case **Linji asked Huangbo, "What is the true essential great meaning of Buddhism?"**—Killing people can be forgiven, but emotional reasoning is hard to countenance.

Huangbo immediately hit him.—At every hit of the stick you see blood.

This happened three times; then Linji left and visited Dayu.—He takes advantage of the heavy, not the light.

Dayu said, "Where are you coming from?"—Dangerous—watch out!

Linji said, "From Huanbgo."—The scars of his staff are still there.

Dayu said, "What did Huangbo say?"—Here's where he should get his revenge.

Linji said, "Three times I asked about the essential meaning of buddhism and three times I was beaten with a stick. I do not know if I had any error or not."—He's still sixty strokes short.

Dayu said, "Huangbo was so kind, he did his utmost for you, and still you come and ask if there was any error or not!"—A second offense is not permitted.

Linji was greatly enlightened at these words.—For the first time he knows pain and itch.

Added Sayings /Verse

A nine colored pheonix—Feathers and wings already mature.

A thousand mile colt—A miraculous steed is also provided.

The wind of reality crosses the pipes—One hole penetrates with emptiness.

The spiritual works goes into action—One push and it turns.

Coming on directly, the flying lightning is swift—It doesn't allow hesitation.

When the clouds of illusion break, the sun is alone—The light rays of yore.

He grabs the tiger's whiskers—Who in my school dares?

Do you see or not?—Look quickly!

This is a brave and powerful man of great stature—What about the doting kindness?

87 SUSHAN'S "EXISTENCE AND NONEXISTENCE"

Introduction When the door is about to close, with one push it opens; when the boat is about to sink, one stroke of the oar and it turns. The canyon enters the valley—there's no way of return. The peaks cross the sky—there is a gateway. Tell me, where does it go?

Case When Sushan came to Guishan, he immediately asked, "I hear you have a saying, 'expression and no expression are like vines clinging to a tree.' If suddenly the tree falls and the vines die, where does the expression return?"
Guishan laughed out loud. Sushan said, "I came a thousand miles, selling cloth mats—how can you play with me?"
Guishan called to an attendant, "Get some money to repay this elder."
Finally Guishan told him, "Later on there will be a one-eyed dragon who will point it out to you."

Later Sushan came to Mingzhao. He told the preceding story.
Mingzhao said, "Guishan could be right to be straight and true from beginning to end, only he didn't meet one who knows."
Sushan also asked again, "When the tree falls and the vines die, where does the expression return?"
Mingzhao said, "Renewing Guishan's laughter again."
At these words Sushan had an awakening. Then he said, "Guishan actually had a sword in his laughter."

Chan Master Guangren of Sushan in Fukien called on Dongshan and asked, "Please teach me the word that doesn't yet exist." Dongshan said, "When you don't consent, no one agrees." Sushan said, "Should one take care of it?" Dongshan said, "Can you take care of it now?" Sushan said, "If not, there's no place to avoid."

Later he was in the assembly of Xiangyan. A monk asked Xiangyan, "How is it when not looking up to the sages and not esteeming one's own spirit?" Xiangyan said, "Myriad impulses cease; even the sages don't accompany you." Sushan, in the assembly, made a spitting sound and said, "What kind of talk is this!" Xiangyan asked, "Who are you?" Sushan told him his name. Xiangyan said, "You don't agree with me?" Sushan came forth from the assembly and said, "That's right." Xiangyan said, "Can you speak?" Sushan said, "Yes." Xiangyan said, "Try to say it." Sushan said, "If you would have me speak, you must take the role of student." Xiangyan then got down from the seat and bowed to Sushan, then pursued the preceding question. Sushan said, "Why not say 'Consent and agreement can't be complete'?" Xiangyan said, "Agree to what? Consent with whom?" Sushan said, "Agree with the sages, consent with oneself." Xiangyan said, "Even granting you this, still you'll be vomiting for thirty years; even if you live on a mountain, you won't have any firewood to burn, and even if you live by a river you won't have any water to drink. Remember this clearly."

Later he lived on Sushan, Mount Su, and it turned out as Xiangyan had predicted. After twenty-seven years his illness disappeared; he said to himself, "Xiangyan predicted that I'd vomit for thirty years. Now I'm three years short." After every meal he'd stick his finger down his throat and vomit, to accord with Xiangyan's prediction.

Sushan later asked Chan Master Qingjing Daofu, "Agreement can't be complete—how do you understand?" Quingjing said, "It goes back completely to agreement." Sushan said, "What about 'can't be complete'?" Qingjing said, "Here there is no way of agreement." Sushan said, "You've finally got this sick monk's idea."

Lazy An of Guishan was one of the three 'Lazy's of Chan'; he was also called Chan Master Changqing Daan. He taught the assembly, "Expression and no expression are like vines clinging to a tree." Sushan didn't consider a thousand miles too far, and made his way to Guishan by selling mats to go question him. He found Guishan, Lazy An, plastering a wall, and promptly asked, "Expression and nonexpression are like vines clinging to a tree—isn't this your saying?" Guishan said, "It is." Sushan said, "How about when the tree falls and the vines die?" Guishan threw down his trowel, laughed, and went back to his room. Sushan followed him, saying, "I traveled over a thousand miles selling mats just to come here—how can you play around with me?" Guishan told an attendant to get some money for this monk in return for his mats. Then he predicted, "Later on there will be a one-eyed dragon who will point it out to you." Later it turned out he was enlightened by Mingzhao, who was known as the One-Eyed Dragon.

Sushan sold cushions for a thousand miles and more just for this saying; these days, those who travel on foot to neighboring houses should also keep their minds on the fundamental matter, but they just set themselves up everywhere and praise and elevate one another—that couldn't be as good as Sushan making spitting noises in the assembly.

I'm not saying he didn't have a particular strong point besides, but he broke the precepts, broke up the turning of the wheel of Teaching, and broke the harmony of the community; this had to evoke manifest results: Xiangyan's prophecy and Sushan's forced vomiting to accord with the prophecy were both making examples for people of later times.

Sushan was also an unfathomable man of high spiritual rank. When Sushan was dealing with people, he would hold a wooden snake in his hand. A monk asked, "What is it in your hand?" Sushan held up the snake and said, "A girl of the Cao family."

Xuefeng went into the mountains and found a stick shaped like a snake. On the back he wrote, "The original from nature, without any carving." He gave it to Guishan Daan, who said, "A genuine mountain dweller—it has no mark of blade or hatchet." Since Sushan had seen Guishan about the saying (in this case), he too used a wooden snake; whether it was personally transmitted or whether Sushan was emulating Guishan, cannot be known.

Mingzhao also asked Sushan, "A tiger produces seven cubs—which one has no tail?" Sushan said, "The seventh one has no tail."

Yunmen and National Teacher Zhao also called on Sushan, so the name of the dwarf Chan Master Sushan came to cap past and present.

Tiantong just uses Guishan's laughter, Sushan's seeing through, and Mingzhao's bringing it up, and produces a verse by shortcut:

Verse *The vines die, the tree falls—he asks Guishan.*
Big laughter, ha! ha!—is it indeed casual?
In the laugh there is a sword—he sees through it.
Word and thought have no road—gone are all machinations.

Commentary The outsiders set up *AU* as an auspicious symbol—this is the word at the beginning of their scriptures. The letter *A* means nonexistence, the letter *U* means existence. That is why the brahmin asked Buddha, "I do not ask about the spoken or the unspoken"—this is a whale swallowing the ocean: the World Honored One was silent—this is revealing a branch of coral. The brahmin bowed and lauded the Buddha, "The World Honored One, with great compassion and great kindness, has opened up my clouds of delusion and allowed me to gain entry into the truth."

Xiangyan Rui said, "Speech is slander, silence is deceit; there's still a road beyond speech and silence." Guishan borrowed this to teach the assembly. Sushan, seeing him say, "It's like vines clinging to a tree," immediately asked, "When the tree falls and the vines die, where does the expression return?" How could he not make Guishan laugh? For Guishan, 'words do not express the event, speech doesn't accord with the situation.' For Sushan, 'one who accepts words perishes, one who sticks to phrases is lost.'

If he had asked me then, I'd just say, "Heavens, heavens!" Haven't you heard the saying, 'The winter ceremonies are carried out in spring.'

Added Sayings /Case **When Sushan came to Guishan, he immediately asked, "I hear you have a saying, 'Expression and no expression are like vines clinging to a tree.'**—Hangs on people's lips.

If suddenly the tree falls and the vines die, where does the expression return?"—Those who accept words perish, those who linger over phrases are lost.

Guishan laughed—Where the power of Yu doesn't reach, the sound of the river goes towards the West.

Sushan said, "I came over a thousand miles, selling cloth mats—how can you play around with me?"—Have you returned the money spent on sandals yet?

Guishan called to an attendant, "Get some money to reimburse this elder."—'Unjust wealth is like floating clouds to me.'

Eventually Guishan told him, "Later on there will be a one-eyed dragon who will point it out to you."—There's another thousand miles.

Later Sushan came to Mingzhao. He told the preceding story—One guest troubles two hosts.

Mingzhao said, "Guishan could be right to be straight and true from beginning to end, only he didn't meet one who knows."—It's just that the rope itself is short—it has nothing to do with the depth of the well.

Sushan also asked again, "When the tree falls and the vines die, where does the expression return?"—Again he comes on this way.

Mingzhao said, "Renewing Guishan's laughter."—With another man's fist he draws on the ground.

At these words Sushan had an awakening—He's paid back for the mats.

Then he said, "Guishan actually had a sword in his laugh."—For the first time he's aware of his skin breaking and seeing blood.

Added Sayings /Verse

The vines die, the tree falls—he asks Guishan—Walking to where the water ends, sitting watching when the clouds rise.

Big laughter, ha, ha!—is it indeed casual?—He damn near understood it as making fun.

In the laugh there is a sword—he spies it out—He thought there was something besides.

Word and thought have no road—gone are all machinations—A thousand miles of ground have fooled me.

88 THE *SURANGAMA'S* NOT SEEING

Introduction When there is seeing and there is not seeing, this is lighting a lamp at midday; when there is no seeing and no not seeing, this is pouring ink at midnight. If you believe seeing and hearing are like illusion-creating cataracts, then you will know that sound and form are like flowers in the sky. But tell me, in the Teachings, is there talk of patchrobe monks?

Case The *Surangama* scripture says, "When I don't see, why don't you see my not seeing? If you see my not seeing, that is naturally not the characteristic of not seeing. If you don't see my not seeing, it's naturally not a thing—how could it not be you?"

Commentary Tiantong saw that Xuedou quoted the scripture in brief, and he too brought up the eye of the teaching in a general way. Though this quotation is abbreviated, his verse is most detailed.

In the second book of the *Surangama*, or *Heroic March Scripture*, it first explains that something that is not seeing is the present object, and seeing that is not a thing is real nature. Here the next section is quoted entirely— it is this that is this public case. The scripture says, "If seeing were a thing, then you could also see my seeing. If we see the same, that is called seeing my seeing. When I don't see, why don't you see my not seeing? If you don't see my not seeing, naturally it's not a thing—how could it not be you?"

The commentary of Master Rui of Changshui says, "The meaning of this passage, progressively developing then returning to a conclusion, consists of five layers; the words of the scripture keep three and conceal two meanings. To discuss it thoroughly, one should say, 'If you don't see my not seeing, then you don't see my seeing either. Since you don't see my sight, my seeing is naturally not a thing. If my seeing is not a thing, your seeing is not a thing either. Since your seeing is not a thing, how could it not be your true seeing?'"

Foguo brought out Ananda's intent—"The phenomena in the world all have names and forms: what is the basis of the essence of vision? Please show me." The Buddha said, in effect, "When I see the incense stand, what about you?" Ananda said, "I too see the incense stand—this is seeing what the Buddha sees." The Buddha said, "When I see the incense stand, that can be known; how about when I don't see the stand?" Ananda said, "I don't see the stand either—this is seeing the Buddha's not seeing." Buddha said, "You say you don't see—this you know by yourself. How can you know what another doesn't see?"

When the ancients got here they could only know for themselves—to others, they couldn't explain. Xuedou put forth the eye of the teaching and solely eulogized seeing Buddha; Tiantong profoundly grasps the meaning of the scripture and eulogizes true seeing:

Verse *The ocean dries up,*
Space is filled:
A patchrobe monk's nose is long,
The ancient Buddha's tongue is short.
The thread of the jewel passes nine bends,
The jade loom barely turns once.
Meeting directly, who knows him?
For the first time you believe this person cannot be accompanied.

Commentary Xuedou said, "The rock of ages may be worn away; the depth of the ocean must dry up where he stands." After that space is filled.

A successor of Foyan, Master Zhu-an Gui, enjoyed the *Surangama* scripture together with his uncle, the layman Zhiyi. Zhu-an said, "If there is a discriminating nature apart from present objects, this indeed is the root of birth and death." The layman, startled, said, "Did the Buddha speak wrongly?" Zhu-an said, "The Buddha sure wasn't wrong, but for the moment I'm speaking in terms of your present state of mind, closely questioning face to face. After all, where is it?" The layman sighed and said, "The Buddha spoke of emptiness of ultimate reality, calling it the lion's roar. Go—don't tarry around here."

Zhu-an later said in a lecture, "'When seeing sight, seeing is not sight; since seeing is apart from sight, seeing cannot reach it.' The falling flowers consciously go along with the stream; the stream has no sense of carrying the fallen flowers. All that is to be returned naturally isn't you; that which you don't return, who is it if not you? Always regretting spring's return has no place to seek, unawares turning and entering in here"; shouting once, he said, "Thirty years later, don't say Shakyamuni Buddha taught people wrongly." I just take the first three phrases to explain the case: Xuedou directly eulogizes seeing Buddha, Foguo brings up solely the place where Buddha can't see, that can be only known for oneself, Tiantong's verse says the ocean is dried up, space is filled. Zhu-an directly shows that seeing that is not a thing is also the root of birth and death. This is the length of a patchrobe monk's nose—they all went beyond the meaning in the teachings and produced another eye; (so) "The ancient Buddha's tongue was short." I say, the Buddha of old met the situation and went along with others' ideas; his words were reaching down for the sake of lower potentials, and thus he expounded the half-word teaching. Patchrobe monks just bring up the true order in its entirety; that is why there is a path of special transmission.

Chan Master Shangfang Yu-an of the Temple of the Auspicious Deer in Yun province, while punctuating the *Surangama* scripture, read in broken phrases, "When knowledge and views are established, knowing is the root of ignorance. When knowledge and views do not exist, seeing itself is nirvana," and suddenly had insight. People said, "Master, you're speaking in broken phrases." He said, "This is my understanding," and never changed it. In his time he was called 'Surangama An.' I say, he too hit upon truth by way of error.

"The thread of the jewel passes nine bends"—in legend, when Confucius was in danger in Chen, he had to thread a jewel with nine curves in its bore; he met a girl in the mulberries who gave him the secret formula: "*Secret!* Think of this—think of this, *secretly*." Confucius subsequently realized what it meant; he fixed a thread to an ant and induced it through the hole with honey (whose written character and spoken sound resemble those of the word *secret*). In the preface of Tiantong's verses on the ancients, written by Master Zong of Puzhao in Si province, it says, "Passing through the intricate curves, good as the ant who threaded the jewel." Pei Hui added, "Like a cloud dragon spreading rain."

In Fushan's *Nine Orbits* collection, there is the orbit of complex dealings; the overall sense is illustrating detailed actions for the present time.

"The jade loom barely turns once"—it's like one pass of the shuttle on a precious loom, not yet forming a pattern. Tiantong quoted Dongshan's saying (about going where there's not a blade of grass for a thousand miles) at the beginning of autumn, after the summer retreat; then said, "Going out the gate is grass—walking in it, thick and deep, when the leaves fall you know it's autumn, and descend into a dark, blue place. To get here you must experience where the loom is in motion but a pattern hasn't yet formed." After a while he said, "The water bright, after the oysters have been impregnated, when the clouds are heavy and the dragons are leaving their bones, directly meeting then, who recognizes *him?* Finally you'll believe this person cannot be accompanied." Jiashan said, "Cutting off the old master, you must know there's someone who cannot be accompanied." I say, coming alone, one would have thought no one would know him; in the midst of the hubbub he suddenly meets an old acquaintance.

Added Sayings /Case

When I don't see, why don't you see my not seeing?—What kind of mental excursion is this?

If you see my not seeing, that is naturally not the characteristic of not seeing—If you know it yourself, that'll do.

If you don't see my not seeing, it is naturally not a thing—how could it not be you?—Mind in a flurry, hands in a hurry, pushing out and enfolding in.

Added Sayings /Verse

The ocean dries up—As before the white waves flood the skies.

Space is filled—I don't see so much as a hair or wisp of thread.

A patchrobe monk's nose is long—Cold pines over a thousand miles pass on a subtle fragrance.

The ancient Buddha's tongue is short—Even one true word cannot be spoken fully.
The thread of the jewel passes nine bends—A waste of mental power.
The jade loom barely turns once—The pattern goes every which way, the intent is of itself distinct.
Meeting directly, who knows him?—What kind of face does he have?
For the first time you believe this person cannot be accompanied—Banished into solitary hell.

89 DONGSHAN'S "NO GRASS"

Introduction   Move, and you bury your body ten thousand feet deep; don't move, and sprouts grow right where you are. You must cast off both sides and let the middle go; then you must buy some sandals and travel some more before you'll really attain realization.

Case   Dongshan said to the assembly, "It's the beginning of autumn, the end of summer, and you brethren will go, some to the east, some west: you must go where there's not an inch of grass for ten thousand miles."
He also said, "But where there's not an inch of grass for ten thousand miles, how can you go?"
Shishuang said, "Going out the gate, immediately there's grass."
Dayang said, "I'd say, even not going out the gate, still the grass is boundless."

Commentary   During the changes of the Huishang era (845–847, when Buddhism was persecuted by the Chinese government), Shishuang lived among potters in Changsha, garbed in peasant clothing. In 847, the beginning of the Dazhong era, a monk came who had spent the summer retreat at Dongshan. Shishuang asked him where he was coming from, and he said, Dongshan. Shishuang asked what Master Dongshan was saying to the disciples; the monk said, "Recently, when he was disbanding the summer retreat, the master went up in the hall and said to the assembly, 'It's the beginning of autumn, the end of summer, and you brethren will go, some east, some west; you must go where there's not an inch of grass for ten thousand miles.' After a pause he added, 'But where there's not an inch of grass for ten thousand miles, how can you go?'" Shishuang said, "Going out the gate, immediately there's grass." The monk reported this to Donghsan, who said, "This is a saying of a teacher of fifteen hundred people—but how many could there be in all of China?" Once his excellence was exposed, the fragrance of ripeness floated on the air; the buddhist community asked him to be a monk again, and dwell at Shishuang, 'Stone Frost' monastery. After all he accorded with Dongshan's prediction (of being a teacher of fifteen hundred). By this public case Shishuang's way went throughout the land.

Later Chan Master Dayang Yan said, "Right now I'd just say, 'Even not going out the gate, still the grass is boundless.'" So tell me, where do you go to put it into practice? (silence) 'Don't stay by the green of the unusual plants on the cold cliff; if you keep sitting in the clouds, the source is not marvelous.'

National Teacher Shan of Yantong said, "Tell me, how can you express where you are right now? If you say there's not an inch of grass for ten thousand miles, you may see Dongshan; if you say upon going out the gate immediately there's grass, you may see Shishuang; if you say even not going out the gate there's boundless grass, you may see Dayang. If you can't speak at all, you may see me. Why? There is only a good wind coming over the assembly; there are no more useless words falling into human society." I say, if you want to be able to say all three phrases, you must also see Tiantong: his verse says,

Verse   *Grass boundless;*
Inside the gate, outside the gate, you see by yourself.
To set foot in the forest of thorns is easy,
To turn the body outside the luminous screen is hard.
Look! Look!
How many kinds?
For the while going along with the old tree, with the same emaciation
    in the cold,
About to follow the spring wind into the scars of the burning.

383

Commentary Dayang said, "Even not going outside the gate, the grass is boundless." Tiantong says then, "Grass boundless; inside the gate, outside the gate, you see by yourself." It is like talk, not trying consciously, roaming playfully between them. Going out the gate there's grass—this is easily known to everyone—it's also easy to shift around. Not going out the gate there's also grass—this is hard for people to know, and it's hard to turn the body around. This you must each see by yourselves; no one can substitute for you. He also says, "How many?" Yuantong makes four, Wansong makes five. On examination, it doesn't go beyond the final two lines: do you want to know how Tiantong manages the rear? When a tiger's thin, his boldness is still there; when a man is poor, his spirit remains.

Added Sayings /Case **Dongshan said to the assembly, "It's the beginning of autumn, the end of summer, and you will go, some east, some west; you must go where there's not an inch of grass for ten thousand miles."**—He's luring cats into a dry well.

He also said, "But where there's not an inch of grass for ten thousand miles, how can you go?"—Once a word is uttered, a team of horses can't overtake it.

Shishuang said, "Going out the gate, immediately there's grass."—Watch where you're going yourself.

Dayang said, "I'd say, even not going out the gate, still the grass is boundless."—There's no place for you to escape.

Added Sayings /Verse *Grass boundless*—Below, no bottom; to the sides, no borders.

Inside the gate, outside the gate, you see by yourself—Beware of being tripped up.

To set foot in the forest of thorns is easy—Picking plants in a wild field.

To turn the body outside the luminous screen is hard—The clear ground fools people.

Look, look—Tasks can't be done too carefully.

How many kinds?—Before the withered tree cliff, the diverging paths are many.

For the while going along with the old tree, with the same emaciation in the cold—Just keep today's determination. . . .

About to follow the spring wind into the scars of the burning—And you'll surely have a time of fulfillment.

90 YANGSHAN'S DECLARATION

Introduction 'I alone am sober'—this is drunkenness indeed. Yangshan speaks of a dream just like when awake. But say, as I say this and you hear it, tell me. is this wakefulness or is this a dream?

Case **Yangshan dreamed he went to Maitreya's place, where he occupied the second seat. A venerable one said, "Today it's up to the one in the second seat to preach." Yangshan rose, struck the gavel, and said, "The teaching of the Great Vehicle is beyond all predication."**

Commentary When Yangshan was seven years old he went into a trance and saw himself along with the Buddha, Kasyapa, and the twenty-seven patriarchs, all assembled together in a sanctuary. The hall of the sanctuary was in space, with no pillars or stones; the color of the floor was emerald. He was aware of himself with the patriarchs, with the same pure features, wearing a golden sleeved robe and with bare feet. He was in the eighth place. One of the blessed ones, most advanced in years, called, "Gautama! Today I'm responsible for the teaching." Yangshan then got down from his seat, went to the sounding board, and said to the assembly, "Let the great assembly clear their minds; the Great Vehicle teaching is beyond all predication." When he had spoken, he went to his seat, and the assembly of monks all discussed this, just interpreting the meaning. Yangshan also said himself that in a dream he went to Maitreya's place and was seated in the third place. In the *Collection of the Essentials* it also says the third seat, same as in the record of Yangshan. One of the blessed ones hit the signal board with the gavel and said, "Now the one in the third seat will teach." Yangshan then got up, hit the board with the gavel and said, "The teaching of the Great Vehicle is beyond all predication. Listen clearly." The Great Vehicle means the great vehicle of Buddhism. Predication means predication in terms of existence or nonexistence or logical permutations thereof.

Dagui Xiu said, "It's not that he doesn't understand the meaning according to the words, but if there were an adept in Maitreya's assembly, as soon as he saw Yangshan say, "The teaching of the Great Vehicle," he'd immediately tell him to shut up, not only stopping Yangshan's sleep talk, but also avoiding making people later on talk of a dream in a dream." I say, if Dagui could turn the light around and reflect back, even I would have no place to rest this body. Isn't there anyone who has clarity in the midst of a dream, who is sober in the midst of intoxication?

Verse   *In a dream, wrapped in his patchwork robe, he calls on the elders;*
The ranks of the saints serene, he sits to their right.
Responsible for humanity, he doesn't defer—the sounding board rings;
Expounding the teaching without fear, the lion roars,
Mind as peaceful as the ocean,
Heart as big as a bushel.
Fish eyes shed tears,
Clam guts open in pearls.
Much talk—who knows it leaks one's potential?
Shaggy eyebrows—laughable, they reveal the family disgrace.
Beyond all predication:
Mazu, father and sons, in sickness stopped doctoring.

Commentary   In the Northeast there's a land where they're always awake and never dream. In the center there's a land where they always dream and wake each half the time—they consider their doings in dreams to be unreal, and consider their doings on wakening to be real. In the Southeast there's a land where they're always dreaming, waking once in fifty days; they consider the waking state unreal and consider dreaming real. The unreality or reality of waking or dreaming is not easy to know. A verse by Longya said,

In a dream how can you know the dream is unreal?
Only when you've awakened do you realize what was in the
*   dream is nonexistent.*
When deluded, you're like a knight in a dream;
After enlightenment, like a peasant rising from sleep.

In the teachings dreams are said to be mental consciousness alone, viewing scenes which are only reflections or images. Since Yangshan had long been free from deluded dream thoughts, how could he act this way? The *Lotus Scripture* says "Always dreaming this good dream." And according to the *Golden Light Scripture*, ten kinds of good dreams of bodhisattvas of the tenth state are told of; there are good omens in dreams.

Great Master Quan of Daming monastery in Si province liked to compose poetry and to talk and laugh; Master Heng of Renshan instructed an attendant to keep him under control. The great master said, "Human life is one dream. Enjoying a lifetime is a good dream; keeping a life under wraps is a bad dream. I would rather have a good dream." The next day the attendant left his place.

Yangshan, even though in a dream, still sported with the Great Vehicle teaching; this is also the instinct of all saints.

Striking the sounding board is not necessarily just referring to the sounding board—it could be the bell or the wooden fish, etc., to alert the community. It is translated as 'sounding.'

"The lion roars"—in the *Scripture of Realizing the Way* it says that the lion roar speaks fearlessly; its mind is peaceful as the ocean. The *Lotus Scripture* says, "His mind is peaceful as the ocean; hearing him, my net of doubts is broken."

According to the *Annals of Shu*, the ministry president and generalissimo Qiangwei Boyue was popularly referred to as 'Qiangwei with a heart as big as a bushel.' Tiantong doesn't seem to have a single word that has no history.

In Fen Fang's *Records of Tales of Oddities*, it says that there was a mermaid in the South Seas who lived in the water like a fish; she wove ceaselessly, and the tears she shed became pearls.

In the *Continued Tales of the Unusual*, it says that once when Emperor Wu of the Han dynasty went to Gourd River, there was a man there, a little over a foot tall, who presented to him a pearl from a cave. Dong Fang Shuo said, "On the bottom of the rivers there are caverns hundreds of fathoms deep where there are red clams which produce these pearls. They are an inch in diameter and lustrous beyond anything in the world." Yangshan only knew tears come from a painful gut, but didn't realize his tongue was outside his mouth. The wine had driven his real nature and in a dream his natural potential leaked—he spewed out all predications of logic all at once.

Monks asked Mazu and his disciples about going beyond all predication; the former monk asked Mazu in terms of a question about the coming of Bodhidharma from the West. Yangshan added the footnote about the Great Vehicle; Yangshan was also a second-generation descendant of Mazu—why were the medicine and disease not the same? 'Getting out may still be easy, but expressing the whole thing must be hard.'

Added Sayings /Case

Yangshan dreamed he went to Maitreya Buddha's place, where he occupied the second seat—Tell me, who's in the first seat?
A venerable one said, "Today it's up to the one in the second seat to preach."—One who comes speaking softly of right and wrong.
Yangshan rose, struck the gavel, and said—Clearly behold the Dharma of the king of Dharma; the Dharma of the king of Dharma is thus.
"The teaching of the Great Vehicle is beyond all predication."—The words are pure, the action defiles.

Added Sayings /Verse

In a dream, wrapped in his patchwork robe, he calls on the elders—A familiar realm is hard to forget.
The ranks of the saints serene, he sits to their right—A dog carries the writ of amnesty in its mouth, all the barons get off the road.
Responsible for humanity, he doesn't defer—the sounding board rings—If one doesn't go against people in one's mind . . .
Expounding the teaching without fear, the lion roars— . . . there will be no color of shame on the face.
Mind as peaceful as the ocean—It swallows the hundred rivers.
Heart as big as a bushel—As though there were no one around.
Fish eyes shed tears—Each drop is blood.
Clam guts open in pearls—The naked heart beating.

Much talk—who knows it leaks one's potential?—His hands and feet are both showing.
Shaggy eyebrows—laughable, they reveal the family disgrace—By whom is it done?
Beyond all predication—Yet these words are still in our ears.
Mazu, father and sons, in sickness stopped doctoring—Sending aches and pains, spirits and ghosts cannot understand.

91 NANQUAN'S "PEONY"

Introduction Yangshan takes a dream for reality, Nanquan points to wakefulness as
unreal. If one knows that wakefulness and dreaming are fundamentally
nonexistent, for the first time one will believe unreality and reality are
absolute. But tell me, what eye does this person have?

Case Officer Lu Geng said to Nanquan, "Teaching Master Zhao was quite
extraordinary: he was able to say, 'Heaven and earth have the same
root, myriad things are one body.'"
Nanquan pointed to a peony in the garden and said, "People today
see this flower as in a dream."

Commentary Lu Geng of the Tang dynasty was styled Jingshan; he was a man of Wu
prefecture. In his official career he reached the post of inspector of
Shexuan, and also was a member of the supreme court. He first asked
Nanquan, "I've raised a goose in a bottle, and it gradually grew too big
to get out; now, without damaging the bottle or injuring the goose, how
would you get it out?" Nanquan called to him, "Sir!" Lu Geng responded, "Yes?" Nanquan said, "It's out." Lu Geng was awakened at
this.
Lu Geng concentrated on the nature of inner reality; perusing the treatises
of Sengzhao, when he came to the seventh section of the treatise *Nirvana
Has No Name,* on wondrous existence, (where it says,) "The mysterious
Way is in ineffable enlightenment, enlightenment is in merging with
reality, merging with reality involves seeing existence and nonexistence
as equal, and when you see them equally, then others and self are not
two. Therefore, heaven, earth, and I have the same root; the myriad

things and I are one body. Being the same as me, they're no longer existent or nonexistent; if they were different from me, that would oppose communication. Therefore, neither going out nor being within, the Way subsists in between." Lu Geng quoted these two lines as being wonderful; he hardly realized that this indeed is talking about a dream.

Even so, even someone as great as Master Shitou was vastly awakened to the Way while reading the treatises of Sengzhao, when he reached the seventeenth section, on penetrating the ages: "The ultimate man is empty and hollow; he has no form, yet of the myriad things there is none that is not his own making. Who can understand myriad things as oneself? Only a sage." Then Shitou said, "A sage has no self, yet there is nothing that is not himself." Then he wrote the *Merging of Difference and Sameness*.

If you say the meaning of the Teachings is the ultimate principle, why did Buddha still hold up the flower? Why did the patriarch Bodhidharma still come from the West? Nanquan's answer used the grip of a patchrobe monk; he brought out the sickness for him and broke up his nest; pointing to a flower in the garden, he called the attention of the officer to it and said, "People these days see this flower like in a dream." It was like leading him to a hundred-thousand-foot-high cliff and giving him a push, causing his root of life to break off. If he just pushed him over on level ground, he wouldn't even understand by the time the future Buddha Maitreya is born on earth.

National Teacher Shan of Yuantong held up his whisk and said, "All compounded things are like dreams, illusions, bubbles, reflections." Tiantong just goes into the dream and produces a dreamland;

Verse   *Shining through detachment and subtlety, the root of creation:*
Appearing and disappearing in profusion, you see the gate.
Letting the spirit roam outside of time, what question could there be?
Setting eyes before the body, you know ineffable being.
When the tiger roars, blowing on the cliff starts, moaning;
When the dragon howls, moving clouds o'er the caves are dark.
Nanquan breaks up the dream of people of the time,
Wanting knowledge of the magnificent Honored-One-to-Be.

Commentary In Master Zhao's *Jewel Treasury Treatise,* in the section on the wonder of the body of subject and object, it says, "Its emergence is subtle, its entry unattached. Knowing the nonattachment of entry, outside objects have nothing to rely on; knowing the subtlety of emergence, the inner mind doesn't do anything. When there are no doings in the mind, views cannot move it; as outside objects have no basis, myriad existences cannot bind."

Tiantong eulogizes Nanquan penetratingly illumining subject and object, the root of creation; appearing and disappearing in profusion, the gate is seen. The double gate, of the subtlety of emerging and the nonattachment of entry, is seen; just one gate divides inside and outside. In reality, there are no walls in the ten directions, no gates in the four quarters.

"Letting the spirit roam outside of time, what question could there be?" Heaven and earth have the same root. "Setting eyes before the body, you know ineffable being." The myriad things are one body. The root and the body produce the myriad things in heaven and earth, like mist arising when the dragon howls, like wind stirring when the tiger roars. When there is some effect there must be response. Therefore the bunch of flowers in the garden shows the flowers of the spring in the sky everywhere.

I have talked of a dream: first there is someone who doesn't sleep; then there is sleep. Because of not awakening from sleep there are dreams: by dreams scenes are seen; based on these scenes you see the existence of another body applying discernment within the scenes. If you know the one who never sleeps, so many complications would be erased at a stroke.

Do you want to know the compassionate Honored-One-to Be? If you don't search out the root source this time, wait till the future and ask Maitreya.

Added Sayings /Case **Officer Lu Geng said to Nanquan, "Teaching master Zhao was quite extraordinary**—It's another white boar from Korea.
He was able to say, 'Heaven and earth have the same root, myriad things are one body'."—I hold up two fingers.

Nanquan pointed to a peony in the garden and said, "People today see this flower as in a dream."—He conveys the statement from the other side of the wall.

Added Sayings / Verse

Shining through detachment and subtlety, the root of creation—'Walking, I come to where the stream ends;

Appearing and disappearing in profusion, you see the gate—Sitting, I watch when the clouds rise.'

Letting the spirit roam outside of time, what question could there be?—'Outside of mind there are no things;

Setting eyes before the body, you know ineffable being—Blue mountains fill the eyes.'

When the tiger roars, blowing on the cliff begins, moaning—Seeking fire, you find it with smoke.

When the dragon howls, moving clouds over the caves are dark—Drawing from the spring, you return with the moon.

Nanquan breaks up the dream of people of the time—Just when it would be good to sleeptalk.

Wanting knowledge of the magnificent Honored-One-to-Be—This place, this the Compassionate One.

92 YUNMEN'S "JEWEL"

Introduction   Attaining the great trance of freely exercising miraculous powers, mastering the spell of the languages of sentient beings, he turns Muzhou's antique drill and sports Xuefeng's South Mountain turtle-nosed snake. But do you know this man?

Case   **Great Master Yunmen said, "'Within heaven and earth, in space and time, there is a jewel, hidden in the mountain of form,' holding up the lamp, heading into the buddha shrine, bringing the triple gate on the lamp."**

Commentary   Great Master Yunmen liked to act like this; making a ruckus, he extricates himself halfway along. One day he taught the assembly, quoting Master Zhao's *Jewel Treasury Treatise;* to quote the whole passage, it would go, "Within heaven and earth, in space and time, there is a jewel, hidden in the mountain of form; it cognizes things, emptily shining, empty inside and out, alone and still, invisible; its function is a dark mystery."

Xuedou brought this up and said, "Within heaven and earth, in space and time, there is a jewel; hung on a wall, for nine years Bodhidharma did not dare to look right at it. Now if a patchrobe monk wants to see it, I'll hit him."

National Teacher Yuantong said, "He was unmistakably a descendant of Deshan. In the record it says, 'Bring the triple gate on the lamp'—how about it?" He also said, "Thunder starts, clouds appear."

Foguo said, "Kumarajiva was the teacher from whom Master Zhao received instruction; Buddhabhadra of Waguan monastery, whose name means enlightened sage, was the teacher from whom he inherited the Dharma." In the *Inexhaustible Lamp* he is listed among the successors of Buddhabhadra. Buddhabhadra succeeded to Buddhasena of India; Buddhasena and Bodhidharma both studied from the Twenty-Seventh Patriarch Prajnatara. When Seng Zhao was about to be executed, he asked for seven days' reprieve, during which he wrote the *Jewel Treasury Treatise*.

When Yunmen brings it up to the people, he can't be interpreting meanings and principles for you like a lecturer. He just wants you to add a comment. "Holding up the lamp, heading into the buddha shrine" can be fathomed by common sense, but how about "bringing the triple gate on the lamp"—can it be fathomed by common sense? Genuine teachers of the source never tie people up with anything as real. That is why Xuedou said, "There's a jewel inside; hung on the wall." If not for Tiantong borrowing it and putting it to use, it might have become leftover merchandise. The verse says,

Verse   *Wrapping up excess concerns, he dislikes fanciness in things.*
Returning, where is life?
To the woodcutter with the rotten axe handle it seems there is no road;
Mr Pot in the cassia tree cleverly has a home.
On the golden waves of the night water floats the reflection of the moon;
The autumn wind and arrays of clouds surround the reed flowers.
The cold fish on the bottom don't eat the bait;
The party ended, a clear song turns the raft around.

Commentary   Waters return to the ocean, the waves are still; when the clouds reach the wilderness, the atmospheric signs are idle. That is why it is said, 'When we're reviling each other, you may lock jaws with me; when we're spitting at one another, you may spew slobber.' Here Yunmen 'wraps up excess cares, disliking fanciness.' The word 'flower,' used to mean 'fanciness,' has two functions—one is that you discard the flower and take the fruit; the second is referring to disliking the flowery profusion of many affairs.

"Returning, where is life?" The former line is referring to the *Jewel Treasury Treatise;* the latter is referring to Yunmen's added words. Where do you search? If you then halt your activity and stop to think, ten thousand years in one thought, even if the 'axe handle rots at your side,' this is still dawdling over chess, slow to go. In a previous verse, on the story of Yanyang seeing Zhaozhou, there already was the story of the woodcutter whose axe rotted at his side while he watched a chess game for decades.

Also in a previous verse, on Xuefeng's final word, there is the story of the man who lived in a pot hanging in a tree: Fei Changfang saw Mr Pot sold medicines all at the same price. There was a pot hung up in a tree; suddenly he bounded up into the pot. Changfang saw him up in a tower and knew he wasn't an ordinary man; then he said he'd sweep for him and provide food. Mr Pot didn't refuse; after a long time he knew he was sincere and faithful, and told him to come in the evening when no one was around; Changfang did so, and he told Changfang to jump into the pot after him. Changfang obeyed and also jumped into the pot: he saw there was a pavilion, with five-colored multiple gateways, and dozens of attendants right and left.

The first line of the verse had eulogized the *Jewel Treasury Treatise,* the second line eulogized Yunmen's added words: as for the next two lines, the first eulogizes clarity, the second eulogizes plainness. Though the meaning of the discourse of the treatise is clear and plain, how many people succeed in realizing it? Yunmen completed the transformation and pointed out a living road. "The cold fish on the bottom don't eat the bait"—this uses the Boatman's "The night quiet, the water cold, the fish are not nibbling; the moon on the golden ripples fills the boat with light." Tiantong said, "When clear light shines in the eyes, it's as if one has lost the way home." Zhaozhou said, "I am not within clarity." That is why "The party ended, a clear song turns the raft around." But tell me, where does it go?

> *Deep in the night, not resting on the reedy banks;*
> *Going far beyond the middle as well as both sides.*

Added Sayings /Case

Yunmen said, "'Within heaven and earth—See that which contains heaven and earth!

Through space and time—See that which establishes space and time!

There is a jewel—If you don't believe, look under your vest.

Hidden in the mountain of form'—The mountain of form is the jewel.

Holding up a lamp, heading for the buddha shrine—Already this is the ass looking at the well.

Bringing the triple gate on the lamp."—Also the well is looking at the ass.

Added Sayings /Verse

Wrapping up excess concerns, he dislikes fanciness—When the water is deep, the waves are quiet; when one's learning is broad, one's voice is soft.

Returning, where is life?—So old and mature, yet you don't know where you live?

To the woodcutter with the rotten axe handle it seems there is no road—Where sun and moon do not reach,

Mr. Pot in the tree cleverly has a home—This is a separate universe.

On the golden waves of the night water floats the reflection of the moon—Reaching above, penetrating below.

The autumn wind and arrays of clouds surround the reed flowers—Great and small are clear.

The cold fish on the bottom don't eat the bait—It's a waste of effort to lower a hook.

The party ended, a clear song turns the raft around—Again blown by the wind into a different key.

93 LUZU'S NOT UNDERSTANDING

Introduction A precious gem hits a magpie, a rat bites a gold piece—they don't know they are treasures, and can't put them to use. Is there anyone who suddenly notices the jewel hidden in his clothes?

Case Luzu asked Nanquan, "'The wish-fulfilling jewel, people don't know—it is personally obtained from the mine of realization of thusness'. What is the mine?"
Nanquan said, "That in me which comes and goes with you is it."
Luzu said, "What about that which doesn't come and go?"
Nanquan said, "It's also the mine."
Luzu said, "What is the jewel?"
Nanquan called him by name: Luzu responded, "Yes?"
Nanquan said, "Go—you don't understand my words."

Commentary Chan Master Shizu of Yunji on Zhongnanshan succeeded in the Teaching to Nanquan; Tiantong erroneously has it as Luzu. Here I distinguish them for students to know. As for Chan Master Baoyun of Luzushan, he succeeded to Mazu, and so was Nanquan's elder brother in the Teaching. Indeed, here Nanquan calls Shizu by name, and he was enlightened by this case, so we know he was Nanquan's disciple, without a doubt.
He first asked Nanquan, "'The wish-fulfilling jewel, people don't know—it is personally obtained from the mine of realization of thusness.'" This saying originally comes from Chan Master Yongjia's *Song of Enlightenment*. Master Qi of Fantian noted, "The Sanskrit word for 'wish-fulfilling' means 'as one wishes,' also 'undefiled light,' also 'increase'." The *Lankavatara Scripture* says, "The peaceful and unimpas-

sioned is called *one mind;* one mind is called the mine of realization of thusness." 'Mine' contains three meanings: one, the meaning of concealment, because it covers and hides away buddhahood; two, the meaning of containing, because it contains the lands of all sentient beings; three, the meaning of producing, because it produces the practices of human and divine paths with untainted causes and effects. The first refers to before enlightenment, the last to after enlightenment, and the one in between is strictly the essence.

Also, in the scripture on Queen Shrimala's lion roar, there are said to be two kinds of the mine of realization of thusness: one is the empty mine, which is free of all afflictions; the second is the nonempty mine, which contains innumerable inconceivable aspects of buddhahood.

When Chan Master Shizu was first with Nanquan, he said, "The wish-fulfilling jewel, people don't know"; he asked about the mine and also about the jewel. Nanquan said, "Go—you don't understand my words." Shizu experienced true initiation from this.

National Teacher Yuantong said, "Right now is there still anybody who truly enters? If so, 'when Wang Xiang arrives, light sparkles'—if not, 'where Li Lou walks waves flood the skies.'"

Xuedou said as an alternative, "Peril! Acting clever on top of a hundred-foot pole is not what an expert does. If you can set an eye here, and guest and host interchange, then you can enter deeply into the tiger's cave. If not, even though Shizu was enlightened, still he had a dragon's head but a snake's tail."

Do you want to see the head and tail complete? What we need is Tiantong; his verse says,

Verse   *Distinguishing right and wrong, clarifying gain and loss.*
Responding to it in the mind, pointing to it in the palm.
Coming and going, not coming and going—
It's just this—both are the mine.
A universal monarch rewards it to those who have merit;
The Emperor of Yellow got it from Wang Xiang.
Turning the pivotal works, capably skilled,
A clear-eyed mendicant has no crudity.

Commentary The *Song of the Mind Jewel,* the *Ode on the Jewel,* and other such works, mostly talked about this jewel as the wish-fulfilling jewel; few speak of the mine of realization of thusness. Only the 'Enlightened Overnight Guest' Yongjia "personally obtained it in the mine of realization of thusness: its six kinds of spiritual powers are empty yet not empty; the light of the gem's orb is colored, but not color." What is the mine? What is the jewel? That which comes and goes is, that which doesn't come or go is too. Here he wants you to distinguish right and wrong and clearly understand gain and loss.

'Responding to it in the mind, getting it in the hand, pointing to it in the palm' originally comes from the *Analects of Confucius:* Nanquan points to the mine and points to the jewel like putting them in your palm and pointing them out to you. Since coming and going, give and take, and not coming or going, no give and take, are the mine, responding to a call and not responding to a call are both the jewel. What doubt can there be?

But tell me, does the mine come from the jewel or does the jewel come from the mine? Do you make them into one or divide them into two?

In the *Lotus Scripture* the Buddha says to Manjusri, "It is like when a monarch sees one of great accomplishment and merit among his armies, and his mind is most delighted; he takes this jewel, which is hardly believed in, kept in his topknot and not given to anyone, and now bestows it."

The Emperor of Yellow made Wang Xiang ('No Form') search out a jewel—this story is already explained in the commentary to a previous verse, on Shoushan's three phrases.

When the wheel of activity turns, even the eye of wisdom is deluded; if he were not able to use abilities in the midst of inability, Nanquan couldn't have said, "Go—you don't understand my words." Shizu was thereupon enlightened. Dongshan said, "It's not that there is no joy; it is like finding a lustrous jewel in a heap of trash." I say, I am not like the beggar-king of Dongshan, seeing a small profit; rejoicing is not rejoicing—it's like smashing a clear jewel in the mine of realization of thusness.

Added Sayings /Case Luzu asked Nanquan, "'The wish-fulfilling jewel, people don't know—it is personally obtained from the mine of realization of thusness'—Don't brag so much.

What is the mine?"—In front of the teaching hall, behind the buddha shrine.

Nanquan said, "That in me which comes and goes with you is it."—What's the big rush?

Luzu said, "What about that which doesn't come and go?"—Say the head, and he knows the tail; speak of going, and he knows coming.

Nanquan said, "It's also the mine."—One living made twice.

Luzu said, "What is the jewel?"—Getting one, he looks for two.

Nanquan called to him by name—It's not that I'm not setting it out.

Luzu responded, "Yes?"—It's not that you're not pulling it forth.

Nanquan said, "Go—you don't understand my words."—He spills his guts.

Added Sayings / Verse

Distinguishing right and wrong, clarifying gain and loss—There's power in the eye.

Responding to it in the mind, pointing to it in the palm—The insight penetrating, when in use it's clear.

Coming and going, not coming and going—Has nothing to do with him.

It's just this—both are the mine—So and not so are both ok.

A universal monarch rewards it to those who have merit—The modest don't take it, the covetous are not given it.

The Emperor of Yellow got it from Wang Xiang—Already using mind power.

Turning the pivotal works, capably skilled—Not at all comparable to you.

A clear-eyed mendicant has no crudity—Can't be too careful in doing tasks.

94 DONGSHAN IS UNWELL

Introduction The lower do not discuss the higher, the base do not move the noble. Even if you can control yourself and follow others, you still cannot toil at the heavy by means of the light. When the physical elements are out of tune, how does one attend and nurture?

Case When Dongshan was unwell, a monk asked, "You are ill, teacher, but is there anyone who does not get ill?"
Dongshan said, "There is."
The monk said, "Does the one who is not ill look after you?"
Dongshan said, "I have the opportunity to look after him."
The monk said, "How is it when you look after him?"
Dongshan said, "Then I don't see that he has any illness."

Commentary When the ancients were about to go, they frolicked in the realm of old age, sickness, and death; among them, Dongshan is unusual. Once he manifested a slight illness, everyone came to look in on him. One monk asked, "You are ill, teacher, but is there anyone who does not get ill?" This monk had an echo in his words; he was presenting his capability in his statement, and he also wanted to see if the sick man had eyes. Dongshan said, "There is." Scratch the itch and the sickness fully remits. The monk said, "Does the one who is not ill look after you?" He carries out this order in reverse, wanting people to know it isn't so. Dongshan said, "I have the opportunity to look after him." If you figure it by conventional feelings, the one who isn't sick should look after the one who's sick; Dongshan says, on the other hand, "I have the opportunity to watch over him"—is this the principle of inquiring after someone's health in the human sense? This monk wanted to see all the way through; he asked further, "How is it when you watch over him?" Here it's necessary that you should always serve and honor at all times, going to sleep late at night and getting up early to ask how they are; only then is it known that you are someone who knows to be grateful and obeys filially. Dongshan said, "When I watch over him, I do not see that he has any illness." This is where everyday practice empowers you when you're dying.

Dongshan also asked a monk, "When I leave this leaking husk, where will you go to meet me?" The monk had no reply. Dongshan said in verse,

> Though the students are many, not one is enlightened:
> The mistake lies in pursuing the paths of others' tongues.
> If you want to be able to forget physical form and obliterate tracks,
> Work hard to diligently walk in the void.

When he finished the verse, he shaved his head and sounded the bell: sitting in the hall, he bade farewell to the assembly and appeared to die. They wailed with grief. Dongshan opened his eyes, had a meal for stupidity prepared, and extended his life for seven days, after which he again bade farewell to the community and passed away as he sat there.

According to the Continued Lamp Record of the Dading era (1161-1170), during the eleven hundred forties in Xianping district's Dajiao monastery there was a Chan Master Faqing, who succeeded to Chan Master Foguo Bai. At one time he was a scribe; he was first abbot at Puzhao temple in Si province, and later moved to Shaolin on Songshan. When the Bian river was broken through by invaders from the North, he was taken captive and worked as an oxherd in the North. A lecturing monk recognized him, and subsequently he came to live in the eastern capital. As his attendant was reading the record of Dongshan, about the meal for stupidity, the attendant said, "That man of old was quite extraordinary!" The Chan master said, "After I die, you can call to me; if I can return, this will be because of having the power of the Way." Later he knew beforehand the time had come, so he composed a verse saying,

> *This year, in the first week of the fifth month,*
> *The four gross elements will leave their host:*
> *Let the white bones be exposed to the wind,*
> *And spare finding a plot from a donor.*

His clothing and things he left all to his attendant, to be sold to feed the monks. When he first heard the sound of the night bell, he sat and passed away. His attendant said, "According to our old pact, you'd have me call you." So he called to the master three times. The Chan master responded to him, saying, "What?" The attendant said, "Why are you going naked and barefoot?" The master said, "What did I have when I came?" The attendant tried to clothe him, but the master said, "Stop! Leave it to later people." The attendant said, "What about at just such a time as this?" The master said, "Still it's just thus." And he composed another verse saying,

> *Seventy-three years, like a lightning flash—*
> *About to go, for you I put a thread through.*
> *The iron ox leaps past Korea—*
> *Bumping into the void, smashes it into seven or eight pieces.*

Then he solemnly passed away. He was seventy-three years old; this was the fifth day of the fifth month, 1143.

Dongshan knew the one who isn't ill, Faqing knew the one who doesn't die. Therefore those two elders came and went freely. Tiantong, bringing this up, said, "Able to stay or go, able to go or stay; I can look after him, but he can't look after me—at this moment, how can you totally comprehend?" After a pause he said, "The perennial mist is still thick on the invisible crown; the spring wind is always in the unbudding branches." Tiantong brings up and illustrates the whole potential of what underlies it, and has already explained it as above. In the verse see the exertion of the ancients—how about that?

Verse *Taking off the smelly skin bag,*
> *Casting away the mass of red flesh;*
> *Directly, the nose is straight,*
> *Immediately, the skull is dry.*
> *The old doctor doesn't see the indigestion from before—*

The little one looks in on him, but it's hard to approach.
When the meadow streams are thin, the autumn ponds recede;
Where the white clouds end, the old mountains are cold.
You must cut off absolutely,
Don't be big-headed.
Evolving to the utmost effortlessness, he attains to the state;
The lone stand-out is not in the same class as you.

Commentary Master Shitou said, "If you want to know the man in the hut who doesn't die, how could he be apart from this skin bag now?" Tiantong says instead to slough off this skin bag. Tiantong and Dongshan were both descendants of Shitou, yet differ so—how can they be reconciled?

Linji also said, "In the mass of red flesh there's a true man of no rank." Tiantong instead has us remove the mass of red flesh. Tell me—where does the true man of no rank rest his body and establish his life? Master Fori said, "Before I came, the noses of the people of Peking weren't straight—I came especially to straighten them out." I say, Fori's nose fell into the hands of the people of Peking.

A monk asked Xiangyan, "What is the Path?" Xiangyan said, "A dragon howling in a dead tree." The monk said, "I don't understand." Xiangyan said, "Eyeballs in a dry skull." Later a monk asked Shishuang, "What is a dragon howling inside a dead tree?" Shishuang said, "Still having joy." The monk said, "What are eyeballs in a dry skull?" Shishuang said, "Still having consciousness." Also a monk asked Caoshan, and Caoshan expressed in verse:

The dragon howling in a dead tree really sees the Path;
When consciousness is exhausted in the skull, the eyes are
    finally clear.
When joy and consciousness are exhausted, happenings end;
How can that person distinguish the pure within the clouded?

The monk asked again, "What is a dragon howling in a dead tree?" Caoshan said, "The bloodline is not cut off." The monk asked, "What are eyeballs in a dry skull?" Caoshan said, "Not entirely dry." The *Corral of Facts about the Gardens of the Founders* has it "dried up." If you go by

405

Tiantong's *Eulogies with Preface,* where it says, "The red mass of flesh, alone, reveals true eternity; the skull has dripped dry of consciousness," then "dried up" isn't wrong either.

There's a proverb which says, "An old doctor seldom divines." It means that when a doctor is old he becomes clear and perceptive; he divines rarely, so he is skillful. Thus Dongshan, an old expert, doesn't see that there is any sickness: the young ones trying to come near to look in on him have a hard time because when they try to face him they are turning away from him. The cold pine's sick branches are even more outstanding for their sickness. Vimalakirti was emaciated but not worn out; by sickness, he waned day by day for the sake of the Way.

A verse by Chan Master Shen of Fengshen in the western capital, on recovery from illness, says,

> *Vitality ended, ended all feelings and sense:*
> *Trying to arouse my mind, there is no way for mind.*
> *No strength even to blink my eyes,*
> *For long years I never went out the door.*

Master Furong Daokai said, "This one verse alone naturally succeeds to me." This is the 'streams thinning, the pond receding, the clouds ending, the mountains cold.' "You must cut off absolutely, don't be big-headed." The sickness must be eradicated at the root; the doctor seeks not to have to use medicine.

"Evolving to the utmost effortlessness, he attains to the state; the lone standout is not in the same class as you." But do you know? 'One speck of gold in the sparkling water, flowing sand can't mix up.'

Added Sayings / Case When Dongshan was unwell, a monk asked, "You are ill, teacher, but is there anyone who does not get ill?"—Go ahead and explain away.

Dongshan said, "There is."—He emphatically makes a point of it.

The monk said, "Does the one who is not ill look after you?"—Current worldly convention.

Dongshan said, "I have the opportunity to look after him."—A meeting of the fundamental lot.

The monk said, "How is it when you look after him?"—What eye has he to see?

Dongshan said, "Then I don't see that he has any illness."—It's just that he doesn't agree to investigate the temporary.

Added
Sayings
/Verse *Taking off the smelly skin bag*—When the grass is withered the falcon's eye is swift.

Casting away the mass of red flesh—Where the snow is gone the horse's hoofs are light.

Directly, the nose is straight—Still it should be set in action.

Immediately, the skull is dry—Beware of seeing ghosts.

The old doctor doesn't see the indigestion from before—When the technique succeeds, the disease is removed.

The little one looks in on him, but it's hard to approach—He has no country—where can you meet him?

When the meadow streams are thin, the autumn ponds recede—Dragons go along the old way.

Where the white clouds end, the old mountains are cold—This is truly impossible to annihilate.

You must cut off absolutely—One word to a superior man. . . .

Don't be big-headed—Light the lamp, eat the meal.

Evolving to the utmost effortlessness, he attains to the state—Leaves fall and return to the root.

The lone stand-out is not in the same class with you—'When I came I had no mouth.'

95 LINJI'S ONE STROKE

Introduction   When a buddha comes, he strikes, when a devil comes, he strikes; if they have a reason, thirty blows, if they've no reason, thirty blows. Is this misapprehending enemies, or is it not distinguishing the good? Try to say.

Case   Linji asked the temple superintendent, "Where are you coming from?"
He said, "From selling rice in the city."
Linji said, "Did you sell it all?"
He said, "Sold it all."
Linji drew a stroke with his staff and said, "Did you sell this one?"
The superintendent immediately shouted: Linji thereupon hit him.
Subsequently the cook came and brought up the preceding story and said to Linji, "The superintendent didn't understand your meaning."
Linji said, "And how about you?"
The cook immediately bowed. Linji hit him too.

Commentary   In the original record there is no cook; he also asks the superintendent of offerings, "Where have you been?" The latter replied, "I've come back from selling rice in the city." Linji said, "Did you sell it all?" The superintendent said, "Yes." Linji also drew a stroke with his staff and said, "Did you sell this one?" The superintendent then bowed. Linji said, "Something's still lacking."
I say, what's wrong? The temple superintendent was hit—reward does

not bypass enemies. The superintendent of offerings was treated benevo-
lently—punishment does not exempt friends. Tiantong acts according
to the entire order, he wants to see the great function of the whole
potential. His verse says,

Verse   *Linji's whole dynamic—the character and tone are high:*
On the staff is an eye which can distinguish the finest hair.
Sweeping out the foxes and rabbits, the family manner is strict,
Transforming fish to dragons, lightning fire burns.
The life-giving sword, the death-dealing sword:
Leaning against the sky, shining on the snow, sharp enough to sever
a hair blown against it,
Equally the order's carried out, but tasting differs—
Where it's totally painful, who is it that experiences it?

Commentary   Sometimes Linji takes away the person but not the world, sometimes
both person and world are taken away at once. If he met someone in the
middle of that, he would act with his whole body; this was the high
character and tone of Linji—'when it comes up in the hand, deal with it
in the hand; when it comes up in the eye, deal with it in the eye; when it
comes up in all directions, deal with it like a whirlwind.'
Li Lou was a man of the time of the Emperor of Yellow, thousands of
years ago, who could see the tip of a strand of autumn down hair from
thirty miles away. 'There is an eye on the staff as bright as sun and moon.'
Not even a half-speck is admitted. It not only sweeps away the fox and
rabbits, it can also change fish into dragons. Fish leap the three tiers of
the Gate of Yu, whereupon it thunders and lightning burns their tails and
they become dragons. The swift activity in spiritual action of the stick
and shout are like this. Seven things accompany him—he has the sword
to kill and the sword to give life.
Fushan Yanjian set sixteen topics for his pupil Touzi Yiqing to make
verses on; among them too was the killing sword and the life-giving
sword. Xuedou, in eulogizing the 'blown-hair sword,' so sharp that a
hair blown against it is severed, wrote, "When it's necessary to even the

409

uneven, a great adept seems inept; sometimes on the finger, sometimes in the palm—leaning against the sky, it shines on the snow." In the *Great Words Ode* of Sung Yu, "The cornered earth the cart, the round heavens its canopy, with bent bow shooting at the sun-tree, long sword leaning on the edge of the sky."

A monk asked Linji, "What is the blown-hair sword?" Linji said, "Disaster, disaster!" Haven't you heard it said, "One taste of Deshan's vinegar and you know it's sour."

Linji's function came forth out of Huangbo's transmission, and didn't weaken. Zhu-an said, "Three punches in the face, seven slaps across the jaw, and no one in the world notices the pain." There is just one who notices the pain and still is taking medicine. Didn't you read how Linji said, 'It was like being brushed with a plant'?

<table>
<tr><td>Added
Sayings
/Case</td><td>

Linji asked the temple superintendent, "Where are you coming from?"—Slapping, I'd say, 'From here'.

He said, "From selling rice in the city."—It turns out he's truthful.

Linji said, "Did you sell it all?"—He goes into the weeds looking for the man.

He said, "Sold it all."—Though hit twice, he doesn't turn his head.

Linji drew a stroke with his staff and said, "Did you sell this one?"—What's the rush?

The superintendent immediately shouted—A clam howl.

Linji thereupon hit him—Hidden in his hand is a flail.

Subsequently the cook came and brought up the preceding story—Don't brag so much.

The cook said, "The superintendent didn't understand the teacher's meaning."—The mouth is the door of calamity.

Linji said, "And how about you?"—He climbs on him.

The cook immediately bowed—More and more we see he's not fit.

Linji hit him too—His follow-up is fast.

</td></tr>
</table>

<table>
<tr><td>Added
Sayings
/Verse</td><td>

Linji's whole dynamic—the character and tone are high—He too should be given a beating.

On the staff is an eye which can distinguish the finest hair—Can't be fooled one bit.

</td></tr>
</table>

Sweeping out the foxes and rabbits, the family manner is strict—The whole power of the lion.

Transforming fish to dragons, lightning fire burns—Quite a miraculous power.

The life-giving sword—Still is just a little bit.

The death-dealing sword—This tub of black lacquer!

Leaning against the sky, shining on the snow, sharp enough to cut a hair blown against it—Who dares to look at it straight on?

Equally the order's carried out, but tasting differs—This wine is very rich indeed.

Where it's completely painful, who is it that experiences it?—Striking, I say, 'It's you, it's you!'

96 JIUFENG'S DISAGREEMENT

Introduction   Yunju didn't rely on relics, the jewels of discipline; Jiufeng didn't admire sitting or standing death. Niutou didn't need the birds to bring flowers, Huangbo didn't envy sailing on a winecup across a river. But tell me, what is their strong point?

Case   Jiufeng worked as an attendant of Shishuang. When Shishuang passed away, the community wanted to invite the first-ranked monk in the hall to succeed to the abbacy. Jiufeng did not agree; he said, "Wait until I have questioned him—if he understands our late teacher's meaning, I'll serve him like our late teacher." Then he asked the chief monk, "The late teacher said, 'Cease, desist; spend ten thousand years in one thought; be cold ashes, dead trees; be a censer in an ancient shrine, be a strip of pure white silk.' Now tell me, which side does this illustrate?"
The chief monk said, "It illustrates the side of uniformity."
Jiufeng said, "Then you still don't understand the late teacher's meaning."
The chief monk said, "You don't agree with me? Set up some incense." The chief monk then lit the incense and said, "If I don't understand the late teacher's meaning, then I won't be able to pass away while this incense is still burning." So saying, he sat down and died.
Jiufeng then patted him on the back and said, "As far as dying seated or standing is concerned, you're not lacking, but as for our late teacher's meaning, you still haven't even dreamed of seeing it."

Commentary   Chan Master Daojian of Jiufeng in Chun province personally transmitted Shishuang's way. He got the staff that kills and gives life, and had the technique of a patchrobe monk. The chief monk was carrying a board— he only saw one side. If at the time Jiufeng said to him, "Then you still don't understand our late teacher's meaning," if he had simply said, "I am not as good as you," he then would have given Jiufeng no room to fit his body, and would have made him submit with all his heart. Haven't you heard it said, "When you contend, there's not enough; when you defer, there's extra."

Nowadays students just say that the ancients died sitting or standing, while people in present times are in turmoil and confusion when they're passing away. Also we see how Mr. Ouyang Wenzhong saw the old monk of Songshan: the monk said to him, "People these days are in a state of confusion every moment—how can they be steady when they're about to die?" And this time he attentively searched out momentary birth and disappearance. Jiaofan versified,

> *At the time of death, when you should be finished, then you should end.*
> *Dying sitting, passing away standing—boastful little kids!*
> *Butter comes from milk—there is no separate reality;*
> *Why bother to want to know the time of death beforehand?*

Two courtiers asked Master Baofeng Zhao, "People of old faced death free to go or stay—by what way was this accomplished?" Baofeng said, "In the future I will strangle myself to death." When he was about to die, the community of monks asked Baofeng for his final instruction; he wrote several lines of bad words and died. If the chief monk at Shishuang had come to this place, he would have escaped being pressed by Jiufeng into dying.

In a sermon to Dahui, Foguo said, "Ah, I see a stream of families of wild foxes with their hands over their eyes, who themselves had never seen the founder even in a dream, yet transmit to people the 'womb breath' and falsely attribute it to Bodhidharma, calling this transmitting the Dharma to save deluded beings. They even cite the most long-lived Chan masters since antiquity, like National Teacher An and Zhaozhou, and say they all practiced this breath energy. Also they boast of the First Patriarch with one shoe (returning to India after supposedly having died) and Puhua's empty coffin: they all say that this is the effect of this art; it can even effect complete disappearance of the body at death—they call this the twin sublimation of body and spirit. People love this body and fear the terror of the last day of life; they vie in transmitting teachings of 'returning to reality.' Looking at a shadow on the night before winter, they call it the host: then they 'divine sun and moon,' 'listen to the tower drum,' examine the 'jade pond,' look into the light of the eyes, and consider these the methods for shedding birth and death. Really they are fooling people, fabricating artificial nests, leaving to posterity the derision of eminent people. There's also a kind who make use of the story of the 'womb breath' of the First Patriarch, claiming that in Zhaozhou's individual songs of the twelve hours of the day and Layman Pang's 'turning the river cart' verse each divulge it, secretly transmitting its practice and maintenance, in hopes of long life and total disappearance of the body, wishing for three or five hundred years of life. They still don't know that this 'reality' is an illusion, an impassioned view." I say, nowadays many of those who look down on everyone else do so because they want others to see them dying, to enjoy putting make-up on a sore—what is there to delight in?

All his life Shishuang set up a 'dead tree hall' and settled a 'dead tree congregation.' Time and again they would sit without lying down, and among them, those who died sitting or standing were very many. Jiufeng alone did not approve of the head monk. As for those in the present who like dying sitting or standing, why don't you investigate Jiufeng's disagreement. And tell me, what function did Jiufeng have? Ask Tiantong; his verse says,

Verse   *The school of Shishuang*
Was personally transmitted to Jiufeng.
Passing away in incense smoke,
The true bloodline cannot go through.
The crane nesting on the moon has a thousand-year dream;
The man in the snowy room is deluded by the achievement of uniformity.
Cutting off the ten directions still gets a failing mark:
Quietly move a step and behold a flying dragon.

Commentary For Tiantong, "Humanity and righteousness first are cut off in poor places; worldly feelings only go to the moneyed families." I say, in terms of setting up methods of teaching, he doesn't compare to Jiufeng; as for profound talk entering into the principle, he's still a hundred steps behind the chief monk.

A poem in the *History of Poetry in Chan Gardens* by Master Shengmo says,

> *The chief monk uselessly died within the burning of a stick of incense;*
> *Jiufeng did not demean an eminent sage.*
> *If you take uniformity as the succession,*
> *You turn against the late teacher's nonreliance on conditions.*

In one of Shishuang's addresses to the assembly he said, "Never forgetting shining illumination is still called outer succession, the lineage of ministers; it's also called dependence. If you're born without a hair of obstruction, like a prince being born, then you can succeed to the great throne—this is called inner succession, called the royal lineage, and called statement without dependence. Dependence is only the matter of the state of uniformity, or 'one color'; unavoidably helping people according to the circumstances is carried hidden at the side."

The 'failing mark' and the 'flying dragon' also refer to the Dragon Gate of Yu, and also to the hexagram *Heaven* in the Zhou *Book of Changes*, positive in the fifth place: "The flying dragon is in the sky," a symbol of gaining rank. How can it be compared to the dream of the crane dwelling on the moon or the delusion of the man dwelling in a snowy room? Do you know what Shishuang transmitted to Jiufeng?

> *Pulling apart the incense bag, perfuming the whole nation;*
> *Pulling open the aperture of the sky, letting the real wind howl.*

Added Sayings / Case **When Shishuang died, the community wanted to invite the first ranked monk in the hall to succeed to the abbacy**—Then he should emulate Huineng, having no cleverness, he shouldn't be like Shenxiu sweeping dust.

Jiufeng didn't agree; he said, "Wait till I've questioned him—if he understands our late teacher's meaning, I'll serve him like our late teacher."—If you see iniquity on the road. . . .

Then he asked the chief monk, "The late teacher said, 'Cease, desist—

What are you doing wasting effort?

Spend ten thousand years in one thought—The fellow's forgotten before and lost after.

Be cold ashes, dead trees—What breath is there?

Be a strip of pure white silk'—Beware of even a spot soiling it.

Now tell me, which side does this illustrate?"—He just wants there to be no matter.

The chief monk said, "It illustrates the side of uniformity."—He's interpreted it dualistically.

Jiufeng said, "Then you still don't understand what the late teacher meant."—One day the authority is in your hands.

The chief monk said, "You don't agree with me? Set up some incense."—After all he doesn't understand.

The chief monk then lit the incense and said, "If I don't understand the late teacher's meaning, then I won't be able to pass away while this incense smoke is still rising."—Hurry is fatal.

So saying, he sat down and died.—What place is this to go like that?

Jiufeng then patted him on the back and said, "As far as dying seated or standing is concerned, you're not lacking—Personal liberation is relatively easy.

But as for our late teacher's meaning, you still haven't even dreamed of seeing it."—To express the whole thing must be hard.

Added Sayings /Verse

The school of Shishuang—Clustered like bees, gathered like ants.

Was personally transmitted to Jiufeng—Ice melts, tiles crumble.

Passing away in incense smoke—It's not that he has no freedom in birth and death.

The true bloodline cannot go through—But he hasn't seen the late teacher's meaning even in a dream.

The crane nesting on the moon has a thousand-year dream—Even though the tree falls over, it doesn't fly.

The man in the snowy room is deluded by the achievement of uniformity—After the sun comes out, an embarrassment.

Cutting off the ten directions still gets a failing mark—Beware of growing roots.

Quietly move a step and behold a flying dragon—Another kind of creation.

97 EMPEROR TONGGUANG'S HAT

Introduction Bodhidharma visited the court of Wu of Liang originally to communicate the mind. Yanguan recognized that Dazhong undeniably had the eye. The land's at peace, long live the king—he doesn't violate the majesty of heaven: sun and moon rest their beams, the four seasons harmonize—there's illumination of education. When a king of men and a king of Dharma meet, what should they discuss?

Case Emperor Tongguang asked Xinghua, "I've got the jewel of the Central Plain, but there is no one who can pay the price."
Xinghua said, "Lend me your majesty's jewel for a look."
The emperor pulled down his hat straps.
Xinghua said, "Who could presume to meet the price of the sovereign's jewel?"

Commentary Chan Master Cunjiang of Xinghua in Weifu first was with Linji; after Linji died, he was chief monk for Sansheng, and later he saw Dajiao. When he opened a teaching hall, in offering incense he said, "This one stick of incense—part is for my teacher and elder brother Sansheng, who was too austere with me; one part is for my teacher and elder brother Dajiao, who was too indulgent with me. These do not compare to offering to my late teacher Linji."
A monk asked, "When it comes from all directions at once, what then?"
Xinghua said, "Hit the one in the middle." The monk bowed. Xinghua said, "Everyone, yesterday I was going to a meal in the village, but halfway along I ran into a violent wind and fierce rain, and wound up in a spirit shrine avoiding it."

417

When Emperor Tongguang of the latter Tang dynasty went to Hebei, a monk asked Xinghua, "How is it when the journey of the king has a limit?" Xinghua said, "Galloping on five hundred mounts a day." As the emperor was returning, he stopped at the transient palace in Weifu, and summoned Xinghua to come there. After he gave him a seat and tea, he asked, "I've got the jewel of the Central Plain, but there's no one who can pay the price." Xinghua said, "Let me have a look at your jewel." The emperor pulled down his hatstrings. Xinghua said, "Who could presume to pay the price of your majesty's jewel?" The emperor was delighted and gave him a purple robe and a "Master" title. Xinghua didn't accept either of them. The emperor also gave him a horse to ride. I say, first let's get to know the sovereign; then we must know he is in the Central Plain; after that I want to ask where your jewel is.

Xuanjiao Cheng said, "Did Xinghua agree with the emperor or not? If he did, where are Xinghua's eyes? If not, where is the emperor's error?" I say, Subhuti did not understand the diamond teaching; he questioned till his doubting mind filled the world.

Xuedou said, "What the Most Honored One has obtained can only be observed from the side; if it were anyone but Xinghua the adept, time after time it would be sold off at a high price." I say, it seems like he hasn't purified himself.

Suiyan Zhi said, "Xinghua's play at the time could be called extreme; how can it be settled now?" I say, decide the case after having been hit by the cane.

Yunfeng Yue said,. "The real doesn't cover the false, the crooked doesn't hide the straight. Those who have eyes discern." I say, ask of this blind fellow.

Huanglong Xin said, "Xinghua for a time saw the opportunity and acted—what could be done?—he buried away that emperor of the court. At that time, if he had just told him that an oyster pearl, even if you get it, has no use, and taught him to have a separate life thereafter, they'd have avoided hindering each other. Right now if someone questions, again how do you price it?" I say, seven times nine equals sixty-three takes it.

In this group of old fellows there's not one who can presume to set a price: there is only Tiantong who sizes up the article and sets a price so there's no loss on either side.

Verse   *The sovereign's underlying meaning, he speaks to a connoisseur.*
All in the land incline to sincerity, hearts like sunflowers.
Bringing out the priceless jewel of the Central Plain,
It's not the same as the gem of Zhao or the gold of Yan.
The jewel of the Central Plain is shown to Xinghua:
One beam of light, it's hard to appraise.
The emperor's action can be teacher of ten thousand generations:
The light of the golden wheel shines all over the world.

Commentary   Tongguang is an era name, like the Dazhong (era) emperor was Xuan-zong. Emperor Zhuangzong of the latter Tang dynasty occupied the throne for three years; he made 923 the first year of the new era Tongguang. He calls it 'the jewel of the Central Plain,' but this is already a forced name. Ultimately what do you call it? Even Tiantong, who is supposed to be so great, can only say this—"The sovereign's underlying meaning, he speaks to a connoisseur."

See how that Zhuangzong carried out military operations: he got Zhen-ding district to follow, conquered Ding province and took Yun province and the Daming prefecture in Wei; then he galloped his horses across the Yangtse River, and the kingdom of Liang fell; he directed one division to the West, and Jianke couldn't hold out. Therefore he himself extolled, "I've gotten the jewel of the Central Plain, but there's no one who can pay the price." This is because he never met one who knows on the part of a patchrobe monk; if he hadn't met someone different, he'd never have opened his fist. But Xinghua was totally sincere, and didn't dare turn away from the great jewel of the celestial city, like a sunflower leaning towards the sun, yet keeping its base. Therefore if his feet are cut off, a man isn't as good as a sunflower.

"Bringing out the priceless jewel of the Central Plain"—this eulogizes pulling down the hatstrings; the jewel in the topknot of a monarch is not to be lightly imparted. Of all the wit in reply of all the emperors of ancient and recent times, none has yet been comparable to Zhuangzong's skillful use of time and situation; buddha-work and human sense were thoroughly satisfied at one time.

An official went to see Chan Master Guizong; Guizong lifted up his hatstrings, showing him, and said, "Do you understand?" The official said, "No." Guizong said, "I have a cold in the head—pardon me if I don't take off my hat." The official had no words. I say, Han Xin's merit is so high, who can be the same as him? Turning his body about, his tears open the bridge of clouds.

In the state of Zhao there was a famous jade. King Zhao of the state of Yan built a platform and put a thousand pieces of gold on it to invite the knights of the land; therefore it's called the platform of gold.

The verse also says that the unique beam of light of the jewel of the Central Plain shines on the heavens and mirrors the earth. Nanquan said, "It's not expensive or cheap—how can you buy it?" Thus it's hard to price.

A Gold Wheel King rules four lands, a silver wheel king rules three lands: copper, two, and iron, one. Though a gold wheel king has seven treasures, they can only illumine four lands—this is not as priceless as the one jewel of the Central Plain—all the worlds of the universe are its light.

Xinghua easily said, "Let's have a look at your jewel." Zhuangzong was the emperor of a dynasty; with great generosity he gave it to him. It might be said that an adept emperor naturally still has it.

I always laugh at Sanjiao, who instructed the assembly, "Whenever you speak of the Teaching, it must accord with the time and season"—then when he was living in a hermitage, he met a brigand wielding a sword who asked him, "Do you have any treasure, monk?" Sanjiao said, "The treasure of monks is not suitable for you." The brigand asked, "What is the treasure?" Sanjiao shouted. The brigand didn't understand, and cut him with the blade. Fayun said in verse,

> Tying thatch on the absolute peak, living on Sanjiao:
> His family treasure could not be deeply hidden away:
> Carelessly he opened the bag and fooled the man looking in;
> Bien He had his feet cut off—who could say it was a mistake?
> The mistake is giving courtesy and entertainment when meeting villains.

This is not like Xinghua and Zhuangzong not hurting the spirit of harmony.

A monk asked 'Iron Wall Xiu,' Master Fayun Yuantong, "I know the master has long kept a jewel in a pouch; today, at this assembly, let us have a look at it." The 'Iron Wall' said, "Nobles love wealth, but there is a proper way to get it." Don't say Fayun didn't bring it out; you should know Xinghua dared to assess.

Added Sayings /Case

Emperor Zhuangzong asked Xinghua, "I've got the jewel of the Central Plain—Don't brag so much.

But there's no one who can pay the price."—Even if you bankrupted the whole country, you still couldn't get it in exchange.

Xinghua said, "Let's have a look at your majesty's jewel."—He takes the opportunity to receive the authority.

The emperor pulled down his hatstrings—Lucky to meet the appropriate person.

Xinghua said, "Who could presume to meet the price of the sovereign's jewel?"—At once both are satisfied, with no particular lack.

Added Sayings /Verse

The sovereign's underlying meaning, he speaks to a connoisseur—Once good words are uttered . . .

All in the land incline to sincerity, hearts like sunflowers—. . . Blessings respond for a thousand miles.

Bringing out the priceless jewel of the Central Plain—Imparting it with both hands.

It's not the same as the gem of Zhao or the gold of Yan—This is a special family jewel.

The jewel of the Central Plain is shown to Xinghua—The imparting takes place obviously.

One beam of light, it's hard to appraise—He sells and buys it himself.

The emperor's action can be teacher of ten thousand generations—Past and present are torn open.

The light of the golden wheel shines all over the world—There is still civilization.

98 DONGSHAN'S "ALWAYS CLOSE"

Introduction Jiufeng, cutting off his tongue, made a sequel to Shishuang; Caoshan, cutting off his head, didn't turn away from Dongshan. The ancients' sayings were so subtle—where is the technique to help people?

Case **A monk asked Dongshan, "Among the three buddha-bodies, which one does not fall into any category?"**
Dongshan said, "I am always close to this."

Commentary In the original record, the question is "Among the three bodies, which one expounds the Dharma?" Dongshan said, "I am always close to this."
Chan Master Sushan Ren first asked Dongshan, "Please teach me a word which doesn't yet exist." Dongshan said, "No. No one would agree." Sushan said, "Then can it be approached or not?" Dongshan said, "Can you approach it right now?" Sushan said, "If not, still there's no way to avoid it." Dongshan agreed with him.
Later a monk asked Caoshan, "What is the meaning of the late teacher's saying, 'I am always close to this'?" Caoshan said, "If you want my head, cut it off and take it." The monk also asked Xuefeng; Xuefeng hit him with his staff and said, "I too have been to Dongshan." Chengtian Zong said, "In one turning-word 'the ocean is calm, the rivers are clear,' in one turning-word 'the wind is high, the moon is cold'; one turning-word rides a robber's horse chasing the robber. Please try to distinguish them. If a monk suddenly comes forth and says it's not this way at all, he too I grant has one eye."

To begin with, Yaoshan's descendants brought it up indirectly, protecting taboo. 'Good roots have much in common.' Haven't you heard how when a monk asked Shishuang about the meaning of the founder's coming from the West, Shishuang gnashed his teeth to show him. The monk didn't understand, and after Shishuang's death asked Jiufeng what the late master meant by gnashing his teeth; Jiufeng said, "I'd rather bite off my tongue than violate the nation's taboo." The monk also asked Yungai, who said, "What enmity is there between me and the late master?"

The verse of Chan Master Baoning Yong on this case says,

> This closeness is heartrending if you search outside;
> Why does ultimate familiarity seem like enmity?
> From beginning to end, the whole face has no color or shape,
> Still your head is asked for by Caoshan.

This is good, all right, but it gets too far into the wind and smoke. Look—see in how many ways Tiantong is thoroughgoing:

Verse   *Not entering the world,*
Not following conditions;
In the emptiness of the pot of ages there's a family tradition.
White duckweeds, breeze gentle—evening on an autumn river;
An ancient embankment, the boat returns—a single stretch of haze.

Commentary   "Not entering the world, not following conditions"—if you see his jowls behind his head, don't travel with him. "In the emptiness of the pot of ages there's a family tradition." Dongshan sings in this way, Caoshan harmonizes in this way, Xuefeng plays the interlude music this way. In sum, the Yellow River is muddy from its source.

Duckweed is a floating plant; regarding 'white duckweed,' a poem by Yang Hui says,

> Gathering white duckweed on the tranquil lake,
> The day turns to dusk in the South China spring.
> On the River Dong there's a returning traveler;
> He meets an old acquaintance on the Suxiang.

Later people named that place 'the duckweed bank.' As for "breeze gentle—evening on an autumn river," in Song Yu's *Ode to the Wind* it says, "A breeze rises on the tips of the blue duckweeds, gradually invading the valley; encircling the countryside of Taishan, it dances in the pines and cedars." This is called white duckweed because its sprouts are green but its flowers are white. I dare ask, "An ancient embankment, the boat returns"—to where? Who would have known that in the distant misty waves there is another, better realm of thought?

Added Sayings / Case

Among the three bodies, which one does not fall into any categories?—In front, three by three; in back, three by three.

Dongshan said, "I am always close to this."—He puts people in a deadly rush.

Added Sayings / Verse

Not entering the world—Freeing the body outside of things.

Not following conditions—Diminishing deep feelings, making a home.

In the emptiness of the pot of ages there's a family tradition—A cat pisses in the house.

White duckweeds, breeze gentle—evening on an autumn river—Pure, empty, cool, plain.

An ancient embankment, the boat returns—a single stretch of haze—The eye stops on the horizon of the sky.

99 YUNMEN'S "BOWL AND BUCKET"

Introduction There's a particular knowledge for chess, a particular stomach for wine. The three holes of a crafty rabbit, the myriad raids of a wily fox. There is still another uninhibited one—tell me, who is it?

Case **A monk asked Yunmen, "What is every-atom *Samadhi*?"**
Yunmen said, "Rice in the bowl, water in the bucket."

Commentary The *Flower Ornament Scripture* speaks of entering right samadhi on one atom and rising from right samadhi on all atoms. It also says, "Every atom is *thus*, every thing is *thus*." The monk's question just wanted Yunmen to bring it out right to his face: Yunmen said, "Rice in the bowl, water in the bucket." But tell me, did he bring it out or not? Some immediately grasp it and present some thing as it's voiced, and present their abilities in a phrase. Some say, "Each grain of rice in the bowl is round, each drop of water in the bucket is wet." Then there is yet another kind in such a rush they say, "In the bowl there is rice, in the bucket there is water." Foguo said, "Wash your mouth out for three years!" Just for you folks, Xuedou said, "The talkative teacher can't open his mouth." Actually he hasn't much guts. You look how Tiantong breaks open the skin on the face; his verse says,

Verse *Rice in the bowl, water in the bucket:*
Opening his mouth, he shows his guts, seeking one who knows himself.
Try to think and you fall into second and third impulses,
Face to face suddenly becomes ten-million miles.

> *Master Yunmen realized a little bit:*
> *The metal-cutting meaning—who is the same?*
> *The mind firmer than rock alone can be like this.*

Commentary   A monk asked National Teacher Huizhong, "What is the great meaning of Buddhism?" The national teacher said, "Ten-thousand bodhisattvas in the Manjusri hall." The monk said, "I don't understand." The teacher said, "Great Compassion, with a thousand hands and eyes."
Fojian said in verse on this case,

> *At this time of the year vegetables are cheap;*
> *The land is filled with turnips:*
> *One penny buys one;*
> *Those who get them snore with contentment.*

Here we see how Tiantong and Yunmen have put forth a single hand to hold up a broken-legged pot. In the Zhou *Book of Changes,* in the elaboration it says, "The way of a superior man is that he sometimes appears and sometimes stays put, sometimes is silent, sometimes speaks. When two people are of the same mind, its sharpness can cut through metal; words of one of like mind are as fragrant as orchids." A note says, "Metal is hard, yet it can cut metal; this expresses its sharpness."
A verse in the *Classic of Poetry* says, "My heart is not a stone, it cannot be turned; my heart is not a mat, it cannot be rolled up." In the notes it says, "A stone is hard but it can be rolled over; a mat, though even, can still be rolled up. It refers to the heart's determination being harder than a rock, more even than a mat." But tell me: National Teacher Huizhong, Fojian, Yunmen, and Tiantong—what were they doing in such a hurry? They were utterly sincere, but few are those who know: though it's heaped before their faces, few people look.

Added   **What is every-atom samadhi?**—I have a vow not to scatter sand.
Sayings   **Rice in the bowl, water in the bucket** —It bumps the head, knocks the
/Case   forehead, strikes the jowls and hits the face; it's everywhere.

Added
Sayings
/ Verse

Rice in the bowl, water in the bucket—The bowl is filled, the dipper ladles.

Opening his mouth, he shows his guts, seeking one who knows himself—
Simply by extreme clarity, paradoxically he makes the attainment belated.

Try to think and you fall into second and third impulses—Tiantong's is the
fourth.

Face to face suddenly becomes ten million miles—This must be an early
return journey.

Master Yunmen realized a little bit—I still don't dare guarantee it.

The metal-cutting meaning—who is the same?—If one does not turn
against people in the heart . . .

The mind firmer than rock alone can be like this— . . . there will be no color
of shame on the face.

100 LANGYA'S "MOUNTAINS AND RIVERS"

Introduction   One word can cause a nation to flourish, one word can cause a nation to perish. This drug can kill people and can bring people to life too. The benevolent, seeing this, call it benevolence; the wise, seeing this, call it wisdom. But tell me, where does the benefit or harm lie?

Case   **A monk asked Master Langya Jiao, "Purity is originally so—how does it suddenly produce mountains, rivers, and the great earth?" Langya said, "Purity is originally so—how does it suddenly produce mountains, rivers, and the great earth?"**

Commentary   Chan Master Wude Shanzhao of Fenyang stopped the night gathering because of the bitter cold up north there: an Indian monk arrived there flying on the clouds and exhorted him not to miss the time; "Though this congregation is not large, six of them are great vessels, and their path will give shelter to humans and divines." The next day Fenyang went up into the hall and said, "The light of the golden ring-staff of a foreign monk came to Fenyang for the sake of the Teaching. Six men will become great vessels; he asked me to preach for your sakes." At that time Dayu Zhi, Ciming Yuan, Langya Jiao, Fahua Zhu, Tiansheng Tai, and Shishuang Yong were among those in the assembly.

Chan Master Kaihua Guangzhao of Mount Langya in Chu province was named Huijiao. A man from Loyang, his father was governor of Hengyang: when his father died, he carried the casket back to Loyang. As he was passing through Li province on the way, he climbed up to the ancient monastery on Yaoshan to behold it and pay respect: as he looked where he was going, it was just like it had been a former abode of his.

Because of this he left home and became a monk. He got the teaching from Fenyang, and responded to conditions (to teach) on the Chu river. He and Xuedou Mingjiao expounded the Way at the same time, and everywhere in the land they were regarded as the 'Two Gates of Ambrosia.' Even now his remaining influence in south China is as of old.

Master Zhilin of Hunan, as soon as he saw a monk come, would immediately say, "A demon's coming, a demon's coming!"—he'd brandish a wooden sword at the monk, and secretly enter the abbot quarters. He did like this for twelve years, after which he put his sword down and said nothing. A monk asked, "For twelve years before why did you vanquish demons?" Zhilin said, "A robber doesn't strike a poor man's house." The monk said, "After years why didn't you vanquish demons anymore?" Zhilin said, "A robber doesn't strike a poor man's house." This is called the meaning of dividing the body with one sword.

In the fourth part of the *Heroic March Scripture,* Puruna asks, "If all the faculties and sense data in the world, the life clusters, the sense media, and elements of sense and consciousness and so forth, are all the 'mine of realization of thusness', pure in its original state, why does it suddenly produce mountains, rivers, earth, and all compounded characteristics which gradually change and flux, end, and then begin again?" The explainer says, "If you understand, you already know the essence of enlightenment is fundamentally immaculate; ignorance is fundamentally empty. The mountains, rivers, and earth are like features of flowers in the sky. If you are deluded, subject and object are falsely distinguished. Powerful awareness suddenly appears, and the three subtleties make the world, the four spheres make the elemental realm." Langya says, "I do not concur; if purity is originally so, how does it suddenly produce mountains, rivers, and earth?" This is called mounting the bandit's horse to chase the bandit, taking away the bandit's lance to kill the bandit.

Jianfu Xin said, "At first he didn't arrive; at the end he went too far." I say, carrying a board on a shoulder, each sees one side. If you want to get rid of the leaking of views, you must see Tiantong:

Verse *Seeing existence without considering it existent—*
Turning the hand over and back.

> *The man on Mount Langya*
> *Does not fall behind Gautama.*

Commentary Seeing existence, don't take it as existent, and the existence will disintegrate of itself. Seeing something strange, don't consider it strange, and the strangeness will disappear of itself.

The *Treatise on the Great Vehicle* was written by the Fourteenth Patriarch Nagarjuna: It says, "All things must exist because of all causes and conditions; all things must not exist because of all causes and conditions." This is "Turning the hand over and back."

Langya said, "Seeing, hearing, discernment and cognition are all the cause of birth and death; seeing, hearing, discernment and cognition are all the root of liberation. It's like a lion springing: south, north, east, west, without stopping in a fixed place. If you people don't understand, then don't turn against old Shakyamuni. Hum!" This is why he doesn't fall behind Gautama (Buddha). Gautama is Sanskrit, and it means 'Supreme on Earth,' because he was the greatest of people on earth. Right now it is the second millenium after his death; the age of that sage is distant, and many people are lazy—how can you avoid falling behind? Tear open past and present.

Added Sayings / Case A monk asked Master Langya, "Purity is originally so—how does it suddenly produce mountains, rivers, and earth?"—When deluded, the world exists.

Langya said, "Purity is originally so—how does it suddenly produce mountains, rivers, and earth?"—After enlightenment, everywhere is void.

Added Sayings / Verse *Seeing existence without considering it existent*—All noodles . . . .
Turning the hand over and back—. . . are made by people.
The man on Mt. Langya—Clasping my hands, I say, 'Huijiao!'
Does not fall behind Gautama—One word wounds people, a thousand swords shake the belly.

NOTES

1 The World Honored One Ascends the Seat, p 3

Manjusri   a transhistorical bodhisattva (enlightening being), particularly representing wisdom. Manjusri is called the teacher of the seven (prehistorical) Buddhas. The image of Manjusri is traditionally found in Chan/Zen meditation halls, referred to as the 'holy monk.'

Dharma   teaching, law, norm, truth, thing, state

ten epithets of Buddhas   1. One Who has come from Thusness (or gone to thusness, realized thusness) 2. Worthy of Offerings 3. Prefectly Enlightened 4. Complete in Knowledge and Action 5. One Who Has Gone The Right Way 6. Knower of the World 7. The Unexcelled 8. The Human-Tamer 9. Teacher of Humans and Divines 10. Enlightened One, Honored by the World

thus   suchness, being as is, reality unobscured by mental projections, conceptualization or imagination

repository consciousness   the underlying consciousness (much of which is in Western terms subconscious and preconscious) which contains all impressions and the seeds of all images

when Kasyapa struck a gavel, a billion Manjusris appeared   according to an old story, Manjusri once spent a summer retreat in places forbidden to monastics, like wineshops and brothels; Kasyapa, an ascetic, wanted to drive him out of the community, but when he tried to do so a billion Manjusris appeared

Yin and Yang   negative and positive energies, both necessary to the formation and operation of the universe, corresponding to natural oppositional complements and natural cycles

3 The Invitation of the Patriarch to Eastern India, p 11

Mahasthamaprapta a transhistorical bodhisattva, traditionally the guardian of Amitabha Buddha's wisdom, as Avalokitesvara is the guardian of Amitabha Buddha's compassion. Wisdom and compassion are the two wings or wheels of enlightenment, so the guardians of wisdom and compassion represent the eternal potential of complete enlightenment.

Avalokitesvara transhistorical bodhisattva, particularly representing compassion; especially associated with Amitabha (Amitayus) Buddha, which also represents infinite compassion, infinite life, and infinite light.

Fenggan talks too much Lu Qiuche invited Fenggan to be abbot of a certain monastery, but Fenggan didn't consent. Lu then asked who he should honor as a teacher; Fenggan told him that Hanshan and Shide (two famous eccentrics) were manifestations of the eternal enlightening beings Manjusri and Samantabhadra. Lu therefore went and bowed to them; when they asked why, he related to them what Fenggan had said. They laughed and said, "Fenggan talks too much—why don't you go bow to him—don't you know he is Amitabha Buddha? "

this side, that side the immanent and the transcendent; conventional reality and ultimate reality; the world of forms and emptiness

4 The World Honored One Points to the Ground, p 17

sixteen-foot body of gold refers to the physical body of buddha, hence, by definition, the whole world and universe, seen as the absolute within the relative.

5 Qingyuan and the Price of Rice, p 20

Shun and *Yao* sage kings of ancient China

6 Mazu's "White and Black," p 23

Huairang polished a tile and beat an ox Mazu sat in meditation all day: Huairang came and asked what he was doing. Mazu said he ws trying to become a buddha. Huairang picked up a tile shard and began to grind it with a stone. Mazu asked him what he was doing; Huairang said, "Polishing a tile to make a mirror." Mazu said, "How can polishing a tile make a mirror?" Huairang said, "How can sitting make a buddha?" Then Huairang told Mazu, "If you want to get an ox cart going, beat the ox, not the cart. "

the meaning of living Buddhism   the living meaning of Zen, actual enlightened life, beyond mere transmission of doctrine

four in the morning, three at night   according to Zhuangzi, some monkeys were told they'd be given three nuts in the morning and four at night by their keeper; they were dissatisfied and so the keeper gave them four in the morning and three at night, which satisfied them

black and white   black symbolizes the absolute, emptiness, nondifferentiation; white symbolizes the relative, form, differentiation

7   Yaoshan Ascends the Seat, p 28

bodhisattvas   enlightening beings, enlightening others as they enlighten themselves

8   Baizhang's "Fox," p 32

karma   doings, producing resulting states of being and forces of habit

10   The Woman of Taishan, p 42

Wuzho and Manjusri on Taishan   Manjusri asked Wuzho, "Where have you just come from?" Wuzho said, "The South." Manjusri said, "How is the Buddhist teaching being carried on in the South?" Wuzho said, "Monks of the last age have little regard for the precepts." Manjusri said, "How numerous are the congregations?" Wuzho said, "Some three hundred, some five hundred." Then Wuzho asked Manjusri, "How is it being carried on hereabouts?" Manjusri said, "Ordinary people and sages dwell in the same place; dragons and snakes intermingle." Wuzho said, "How numerous are the congregations?" Manjusri said, "Three by three in front, three by three in back."
As they drank tea, Manjusri held up a crystal bowl and asked, "Do they also have this in the South?" Wuzho said "No." Manjusri said, "What do they usually use to drink tea?"

11   Yunmen's "Two Sicknesses," p 46

Dharma body   the reality body of buddhahood; thusness as is; also refers to the pure clear mind. Being struck in the sphere of the Dharma body involves failing to develop the experience and manisfestation bodies of buddhahood, through which insight into and experience of the Dharma body is actually realized and carried out in the world. It can therefore refer to remaining fixed in a meditational state or trance of clarity.

12 Dizang Planting the Fields, p 51

the nine branches this refers to the preparatory Buddhist teachings, dealing primarily with cultivation of sainthood and self-enlightenment, taming oneself

13 Linji's "Blind Ass," p 56

the secret transmission on Mount Huangmei The fifth patriarch of Zen in China secretly handed on the robe emblematic of spiritual successorship to Huineng, an illiterate woodcutter, while everyone thought it would go to the eminent monk Shenxiu. The followers of the latter became known as the northern school of Zen, those of the former, the southern school.

16 Magu Shakes His Staff, p 66

Caoqi the place where the great sixth patriarch of Zen, Huineng, taught; symbolic of Zen

four meditations classic description of four stages of meditation. With the first stage comes emptiness, light, stability, knowledge, good will, gentleness, joy, bliss, and conformity to the environment; it is supported by five branches, of contemplation, reasoning, joy, bliss, and singlemindedness. The second stage has four branches, of inner purity, joy, bliss, and single-mindedness. The third stage has the branches of indifference, recollection, discernment, bliss, and singlemindedness. The fourth stage has the branches of neither pain nor pleasure, relinquishment, and singlemindedness.

four immeasurables immeasurable kindness, immeasurable compassion, immeasurable joy, immeasurable impartiality. These are specially cultivated by bodhisattvas.

four formless states absorption in infinity of space, infinity of consciousness, nothing at all, and neither perception nor nonperception. These and the four meditations are specially practiced by arhats, saints, and pratyekabuddhas, those enlightened enough for one, but they are also included in the training of the bodhisattvas.

20   Dizang's "Nearness," p 86

five ranks of absolute and relative   the relative within the absolute, the absolute within the relative, coming from the absolute, arriving in the relative, simultaneous realization of both.

garuda bird   a dragon-eating bird, symbolizing a highly discerning and able teacher 'picking out' a capable disciple, and also liberating the disciple from the most subtle attachments to states of realization

Pindola brushing his eyebrows with both hands   Pindola was an arhat (saint) with white hair and long eyebrows: King Prasenajit once asked him, "I've heard that you personally saw the Buddha; is that true?" Pindola showed him by holding up his eyebrows with his hands.

23   Luzu Faces The Wall, p 100

Dao Yuanming   A famous poet, Taoist, and drinker

24   Xuefeng's "Look out for the Snake," p 104

he bore witness on his father for stealing a sheep   This refers to an old story illustrating honesty above personal sentiments

25   Yanguan's "Rhinoceros Fan," p 108

Ajatashatru   a king who was a parricide, a classic paragon of evil

28   Huguo's "Three Embarrassments," p 120

naked heretic/burnt-faced ghost king   represent extremist asceticism or negativity

born in the four ways   by way of egg, womb, moisture, transformation

six dispositions   animals, hells, hungry ghosts, humans, gods, antigods. These represent mundane life and psychological states.

29 Fengxue's "Iron Ox," p 125

vairocana the 'illuminator'—name of the reality-body buddha in its pure clear aspect

30 Dasui's "Aeonic Fire," p 131

arhats, pratyekabuddhas, bodhisattvas these are the so-called 'three vehicles.' Arhats and pratyekabuddhas generally speaking are those who manage to transcend the world, but whose enlightenment remains separate from the world, so to speak, and is not translated into social action except as examples for individual liberation. The bodhisattvas practice both detachment and union, striving to go on the middle way, in which there is transcendence in the midst of ordinary life, and individual liberation and universal liberation are mutually dedicated and returned to each other. See notes on case 16.

31 Yunmen's "Pillars," p 137

samadhi concentration, absorption, mental focus; also used in Zen for a state of being, a state of mind, a point or focus of action or attention

32 Yangshan's "Mind and Environment," p 140

Shakyamuni 'Sage of the Shakyas' was a name of Gautama Buddha, the 'historical Buddha' who lived around 1000BC or 500BC.

clusters and elements physical form, sensation, perception, patterning, and consciousness are known as the five clusters which comprise the human being; the eighteen elements are the six senses (seeing hearing tasting smelling feeling perceiving) along with their associated consciousnesses and fields of data

fixed disciple nature this means someone whose nature in a given life, combined with prevailing conditions, is disposed toward or suited for individual liberation by following the teaching for saints. Disciple is a term for disciples of the Buddha, later became used as a somewhat derogatory term for literalists of those attached to certain forms or practices after their prime usefulness is outlived.

34 Fengxue's "Single Atom," p 151

Xianshou's ocean of meaning this refers to a treatise by Xianshou (Fazang, the third founder of Huayan Buddhism in China) in which he expounds ten aspects of each of ten aspects of universal relativity. The basis is the observation that each depends on all, all depends on each, each depends on each, all depend on all.

35   Luopu's Acquiescence, p 154

under the bright window   this has the meaning of the rank of chief monk, also refers to advanced Zen practice dealing with the 'knowledge of differentiation' after the realization of the 'heart of nirvana.' Differentiation is often symbolized by light, as the light of day where all various forms are visible.

36   Master Ma Is Unwell, p 160

Tathagata Chan and Patriarch Chan   the essence and function of enlightenment; the pure mind and transcendent action

40   Yunmen, Houbai, and Houhei, p 173

Houbai and Houhei   these were two frauds and scoundrels; the name of Houbai was infamous for trickery and deceit, but one day in the very midst of one of Houbai's capers he was fleeced by Houhei, yet another interloper with the cunning to rob even Houbai.

three dots of the Sanskrit i   refers to a symbol based on a letter of an Indian alphabet to represent the interdependence of emptiness, conditional existence, and the middle way in between. This is a classical formulation of Tiantai Buddhism.

41   Luopu About To Die, p 176

Kepin was willingly fined the price of congee   Xinghua said to Kepin, who was at that time working as an administrator at the monastery where Xinghua taught, "Before long you will be a teacher of the Way." Kepin said, "I won't enter that company." Xinghua said, "Do you not enter having understood, or do you not enter not having understood?" Kepin said, "Not this way at all." Xinghua hit him and said, "Duty-distributor Kepin has failed to win a Dharma battle; the fine is five strings of cash—provide congee for the whole assembly." The next day Xinghua went into the hall, struck the sounding board and said, "Kepin the duty-distributor did not win in Dharma battle; he is not allowed to partake of the meal." Kepin left right then and there; later he appeared in the world as a teacher, living on Daxingshan mountain, succeeding to Xinghua.

43 Luoshan's "Arising and Vanishing," p 183

Dharma Jewel of Luoshan Dharma Jewel is a translation of the name Fabao, name of the Zen Master of Luoshan.

44 Xingyang's "Garuda," p 187

when the king's words are like thread, their issue is like yarn . . .—a proverbial saying from the Chinese classics, likening the king's word going through the ministers and people to thread, yarn, and rope; in the context of Zen, it illustrates how impulses in the inner mind intitiate and sustain actions occupying sense faculties, the perceived world, and the consciousnesses, faculties, and world of other beings.

45 Four Sections of the *Enlightenment Scripture*, p 191

eyebrows for chaos according to Zhuangzi, Choas had no eyes, ears, nose, etc.; some well-meaning acquaintances made apertures in Chaos' face so that Chaos could be 'normal,' but Chaos died as a result. The world for chaos means prior to distinction.

47 Zhaozhou's "Cypress Tree," p 197

the blue of a monk's eyes in the early centuries A.D. some Buddhist monks who came to China from central Asia had blue eyes; as blue eyes were something quite remarkable to the Chinese, this particular association stuck. Bodhidharma, the Indian founder of Zen in China, is sometimes referred to as the blue-eyed foreign monk.

48 Vimalakirti's "Nonduality," p 201

divining ladles, drilling tortoise shells, striking tiles these are all ways of divination or fortune telling; using set ideas and conceptions to try to assess reality is likened to employing a superstitious divining system, accepting a random manipulation of its inventory of items for some kind of explanation.

Liang Jiu, Liang Ba Jiu (for a long time) sounds like jiu (nine); ba means eight: therefore 'Liang Jiu,' 'the ninth son of the Liang family' is the younger brother of

Liang Ba, the eighth son of the Liang family. A play on words. Liang-jiu, 'for a good long time' refers to a pause of silence, which precedes many answers in Zen lore.

offerings to images ceremonial offerings are placed before graven images of deceased spiritual ancestors; the word for image in this particular sense also means reality, so the offering is made to the reality. The ceremony of presenting offerings before the image, acknowledging the embodiment of truth and reflection of reality, is here made an occasion for bringing up the matter of the reality which cannot be fully described, cannot be wholly depicted.

52 Caoshan's "Reality Body," p 219

Kanadeva put a needle in the bowl of water Kanadeva was the fifteenth patriarch of Buddhism; when he first came to the fourteenth patriarch Nagarjuna, the latter presented to him a bowl full of water; then Kanadeva put a needle on the surface of the water. This story symbolizes ultimate and conditional reality both realized, essence and wisdom and function.

54 Yunyan's "Great Compassion," p 229

thirty-two responses of Great Compassion The bodhisattva Great Compassion is Avalokitesvara, which appears in many forms, according to the minds and states of the beings who need to be liberated. The *Lotus of true teaching* scripture mentions thirty-two forms, including different religious and social accommodations.

the little kind of miraculous power this refers to the various extraordinary powers of saints, such as telepathy and psychic travel; these are called 'little' because they are byproducts of individual liberation (which is called the 'little' or lesser vehicle in Buddhism). The great miracle is everywhere.

58 The *Diamond Scripture's* "Revilement," p 244

eight difficulties eight situations in which it is difficult to see a buddha and hear the teaching: hellish torment; insatiable craving; brute stupidity; earthly paradise; heavens of long life in the worlds of pure form and formlessness; being deaf, blind, and mute; being bright in terms of worldly wisdom; living in a time when no buddha is appearing in the world and there is nowhere the way of buddhahood is being taught.

Yajnadatta lost his head   Yajnadatta looked at the back of a mirror by mistake and thought he had lost his head. He went crazy until someone took a mirror and showed him his head was where it had always been. It is a simile for humankind forgetting its real nature, then pursuing all sorts of things and assuming all sorts of identities in an continuous unsuccessful attempt to relieve the persistent sense of loss and longing that accompanies estrangement. Finding one's head means being complete, with nothing added, nothing lacking.

karma   meaning deeds, doing, it also means ceremony, what is done in the performance of a ceremony. See the story of the spirit in the oven which the oven-breaker broke.

60   Iron Grinder, the Cow, p 253

draw a line   a single horizontal stroke, or short line, is used as a Chinese character to mean 'one' 'all' 'whole.' The text does not specify it as being used as a 'one,' (whereas it could easily be specified), so any interpretations connected with the use of the line as a Chinese character cannot be ruled in or out. The interpretation of the line as a line and as a character can of course be led into one another or drawn out of one another by the perception of the Huayan principle 'all in one, one in all.'

61   Jianfeng's "One," p 255

sparing eyebrows   sparing eyebrows means not talking much; not sparing eyebrows means talking or divulging much. One interpretation of the image is that, as the saying goes, talk is a way of calamity, and especially is one claims to, or seems to, convey the whole truth in words, one will 'lose face' so much that one's eyebrows and hair will fall out.

62   Mi Hu's "Enlightenment or Not?" p 259

I only approve of Lingyun   Lingyun was a famous monk who after thirty years of meditation was suddenly enlightened on seeing peach blossoms

64   Zizhao's Succession, p 268

Yunmen offered incense for Xuefeng   in the ceremony of opening a teaching hall, the teacher offers incense to the teacher to whom he succeeded

66 Jiufeng's "Head and Tail," p 276

Dipankara Buddha according to legend, the ancient Buddha in whose presence Shakyamuni Buddha originally vowed to realize complete enlightenment. Dipankara, whose name means 'burning lamp,' is used as a symbol of fundamental awareness. In Chinese, the character for 'burning' is often replaced by a similar substitute which also conveys the sense 'lamp of thusness.'

70 Jinshan Asks About Nature, p 295

marking the boat when the sword is gone a sword is dropped off a moving boat; a fool notches the side of the boat to mark the spot where the sword fell. Like this, it is a human tendency to hold to a limited frame of reference which was shortsighted to begin with, even after the extent of what original or immediate relevance it had is already gone. To sum up the matter, as Nanquan said, "Even as you call it 'thus,' it's already changing."

73 Caoshan's Fulfillment of Filial Piety, p 307

robe of mourning refers to nirvana, or the absolute state (in the narrow sense), involving death of human passions. The bodhisattva does not wear the robe of mourning in the sense of not remaining in the absolute state of individual liberation, not making extinction the final realization. See notes to cases 30, 16.

summertime this can also refer to the three months' retreat of monks and nuns in summertime. For three months in winter and three months in summer Buddhist monks and nuns stay in one place rather than travel, and practice special concentration. Summer is also the time of growing and maturing, before the harvest.

74 Fayan's "Substance and Name," p 311

Samantabhadra a universal transhistorical bodhisattva, traditionally administering the principles, meditations, and practices of buddhahood; associated with Samantabhadra, whose name means universally virtuous, is objective reality and action in accord with reality. Samantabhadra is a principle figure in the Huayan, or Flower Ornament or Garland scripture.

Maitreya the future buddha to succeed Shakyamuni Buddha as the guide of the world; now living in the heaven of satisfaction and happiness, in the highest state of bodhisattvahood, a 'Cloud of Dharma,' raining the enlightening teaching on countless beings, Maitreya is also an important figure in the Huayan scripture.

Sudhana another important figure in the Huayan scripture (in the section known in Sanskrit was the Gandhavyuha), Sudhana is a youth whose pilgrimage for enlightenment, visiting many teachers, is recounted in the scripture. Sent on his journey south by Manjusri, Sudhana at last comes to Maitreya, who shows him into a tower inside of which are myriad towers—myriad universes within the universe—in which he sees all that he has learned and practice in total perspective. Maitreya then finally sends Sudhana back to Manjusri.

South refers to traveling to call on teachers, also to Zen study in general.

76 Shoushan's "Three Phases," p 319

three phrases of Baizhang basically, not grasping, then not dwelling on detachment, then not entertaining any understanding of not dwelling.

teacher of buddhas and patriarchs 'patriarchs' is a term used for founding teachers and adepts. Buddhas and patriarchs means enlightened people in general, without regard to matters such as nationality or gender. If distinction were made in terms of common images, for example, buddhas represent the stillness of enlightenment while the patriarchs or founders represent the activity of enlightenment. This term, then, unambiguously encompasses both for the record. Past adepts were called ancestors because they handed on the way as though through a bloodline, and also left examples for later generations. If buddhahood or masterhood is looked for as an attainment, then nongrasping is properly the 'teacher of buddhas'.

transformation buddhas forms assumed by enlightened teachers in order to communicate with the variety of beings and mentalities. The world itself can be thought of as one or many transformation buddhas, teaching sentient beings in accord with their capacity to perceive and understand.

teacher of the human and the divine the awake being in the world, not clinging to anything greedily yet not dwelling on detachment either.

those who can't save themselves completely great enlightening beings who are identified with all beings; also refers to realization of infinity of life and finiteness of lifetime

80 Logyan Passes the Brace, p 340

a drop of ink in two places completes the dragon dotting the eyes of a picture of a dragon, representing the pupils, finishes the drawing

81   Xuansha Comes to the District, p 346

Baoshou didn't cross the river   going to visit a certain Zen teaching center, Baoshou was suddenly awakened when he saw the bannerpole of the monastery from across the river; so he turned right around and didn't cross the river, no longer needing to go to the monastery.

box and lid, arrowpoints   these terms represent phenomena, which are interdependent and the principle of equality in interdependence: the simile of box and lid for codependent phenomena is obvious; the simile of arrowpoints meeting contains an allusion, and represents the indefinable point of contact and separation of things-forces of equal valence (in the sense of not overriding one another, at once being dependent on others and supporting others). Both refer to relativity; the first refers to the face of existence, the second to the face of emptiness. These terms are also used in Zen for the meeting of teacher and apprentice and the fulfillment of their task together.

82   Yunmen's "Sound and Form," p 350

talking about the swift steed, omitting its color   just getting the essential, not worrying about outward form.

84   Judi's "One Finger," p 356

everyone claps their hands, but Nanyuan is outstanding   when someone saw master Nanyuan doing some menial chore, he asked the master why he didn't have someone do it for him; in reply Nanyuan clapped the ground with his hand three times.

peach (blossom) spring   a mythical never-never land where people of ancient times supposedly went to escape the woes of the world; in Buddhism, symbolic of the 'pure land' of selflessness, unaffected by mundane joy and sorrow.

ten-body controller   controller means the same thing as the human-tamer, an epithet of buddhas; ten bodies of a buddha according to the Garland scripture are: the body of sentient beings, the body of lands, the body of results of actions, the body of disciples, the body of self-enlightened ones, the body of enlightening beings, the body of those who realize complete enlightenment, the body of wisdom, the body of verities, the body of space; also, the bodies of the body of those who realize complete enlightenment include the body of enlightenment, the body of vows, the incarnate body, the body of practical application, the body of power, the body of virtues, the body of knowledge, the body of nonattachment, the body of nirvana, the body of universe, the mind body, the body of meditation, the body of fundamental nature, the body of reality.

88 The *Surangama's* "Not Seeing," p 377

talk of patchrobe monks   the living meaning of Zen

96 Jiufeng's Disagreement, p 412

womb breath   a Taoist term, a type of breathing exercise

sun and moon, tower drum, jade pond   anatomical terms from Taoist hygiene, in which the body is seen as a miniature cosmos

98 Dongshan's "Always Close," p 422

three buddha bodies   the body of reality, the body of enjoyment, and the body of manifestation; these correspond to essence, wisdom, and action; the body of reality has no beginning or end, the body of enjoyment has a beginning but no end, the body of manifestation has a beginning and an end. Thr corporeal being of a human buddha is the body of manifestation; the inner experience of the buddha's enlightenment is the body of enjoyment; the reality underlying all appearance and experience is the reality body.

100 Langya's "Mountain's and Rivers," p 428

three subtleties   three subtle mental events; stirring of the mind, the sense of perceiver, the sense of perceived. Following these three subtleties are six coarser events which consolidate the sense of the perceived, or objective world, and reinforce the sense of the perceiver as the subject. These terms refer to the division of subject and object based on mental disturbance which is identical to fundamental ignorance, loss of essential unity. The first subtle aspect is called fundamental ignorance, and it is also called karmic consciousness—striving, fabricating consciousness.

four spheres   wind, water, metal, space; the first three refer to spheres created by the actions of beings

things exist and don't exist because of causes and conditions   basic buddhist logic;

because things are conditional, coming into being due to causes and conditioning factors, nothing has any independent being, everything is dependent and relative to everything else; this is why things don't exist because they're conditional. Yet as things are empty because they are conditional, to be empty or nonexistent they must necessarily be relatively or conditionally existent, because there can be no relativity (without which there is no emptiness) without conditional existence. See note to case 40 ont he three dots of the Sanskrit i. This is also the integration of the absolute and relative.

Shakyamuni   Shakyamuni Buddha is the teacher of the scripture in the case.

GLOSSARY

A

absolute Emptiness; in the Buddhist sense, emptiness means the lack of inherent individual reality in conditional, relative things. Caoshan said, "The absolute state is the realm of emptiness where there is fundamentally not a single thing; the relative state is the realm of material form, where there are myriad forms and shapes. . . . . Mutual integration subtly responds to myriad conditions without attachment to any existence." Also, mind itself is sometimes equated with the absolute (inasmuch as it is formless and ungraspable; ungraspability is another definition of emptiness). In the small or individual vehicle of elementary Buddhism, the absolute state refers to nirvana, the state of dispassion, the extinction of egoism and suffering.

accepting and upholding, reading and writing This injunction found in most if not all greater vehicle Buddhist scriptures refers to faithfully putting into practice and propagating the teachings in the scriptures.

adamantine Indestructible, able to cut through anything without itself being broken; a symbol of transcendent wisdom. The 'adamantine eye' sees through all things without being disturbed.

aeon A long period of time; a 'great aeon' consists of aeons of formation, subsistence, decay, and nonexistence (of a world or world-system).

afflictions Human delusions, problems; there are lists of four and six major afflictions usually found to some degree in the ordinary human being: the idea of self, self-delusion, self-conceit, self-love, greed, hostility, ignorance, pride, opinions, and doubt.

after the skin bag The 'skin bag' refers to the human body; 'after the skin bag' means 'after death,' although this 'death' may not necessarily be physical death, and may refer to the death of egotism, the death of attachment to one's person and life.

alchemy A metaphor for the process of spiritual transmutation from the 'base metal' of ordinary being into the 'gold' of enlightenment.' Taoists also practiced alchemical chemistry seeking the 'philosopher's stone' to produce gold, and the 'elixir of immortality' to prolong life.

animals Domestic animals are used to symbolize ignorance, or the animal human being. Wolves symbolize hostility, foxes symbolize cleverness, deceit, and compulsive doubt. Tigers, leopards, and lions, on the other hand, represent sages and enlightened people; mythical animals such as unicorns can represent high meditators or enlightened beings. Jackals are teachings, people, and persuasions that have attachments.

ancient buddhas Refers to the timeless essence of enlightenment, also to extinct buddhas who have returned to the essence, also to great Zen teachers.

appearing in the world Being a teacher and guide, directing a community.

arhat A 'worthy' or 'saint' who has escaped the bonds of self and delusion, has conquered passion, and abides in nirvana, the 'coolness' of the dispassionate state.

autumn Poetically used to represent transcience, passing away, dying, detachment, and transcendence.

B

Baofu's four deceptions Cf. *Blue Cliff Record*, case 44, commentary.

before the empty aeon Before the formation of the world, before conception.

before the womb Before conception, before location, before stirring of potential before existence. In general, 'before the beginning' type expressions refer to prajna, signless transcendent wisdom, also to the beginningless and inconceivable absolute, and also to the mind before producing conceptions.

billion world universe A system of a thousand systems of a thousand systems of a thousand worlds each. There are infinitely many such universes in the cosmos of space, but generally 'the billion world universe' is used in the same sense as 'the universe,' meaning this universe, or this world, which itself contains myriad worlds.

black Symbolizes the absolute, nondifferentiation, nondiscrimination, nirvana, also the formless realm (a meditation state, not the true absolute); also sometimes used to symbolize ignorance. A (black) lacquer tub means a closed mind, an ignorant mind. Black and white symbolize emptiness and form, sameness and differentiation, nirvana and birth–and–death.

blind Can mean unseeing, heedless, ignorant; also can mean equanimous, non-discriminatory, unconcerned with petty distinctions.

blind turtle under the seat of Mt. Sumeru This refers to a meditator lingering in the formless realm, or one who only has the 'heart of nirvana' and lacks the 'clarity of differentiating knowledge.'

bodhisattva An enlightening being, enlightening self and others; the ten main channels of transcendence of bodhisattvas are generosity, morality, tolerance, effort, meditation, wisdom, knowledge, liberative methodology, power, and vows.

boring through paper, piercing a window Refers to attaining enlightenment by way of scriptures. In an old Zen hstory, an enlightened Zen student likens his old former teacher reading without illumination to a fly or bee trying to get out through a paper window, only succeeding in buzzing at the paper. Boring through paper also has the suggestion of getting through the written teachings to the essence behind them; it is also said in this regard that the eye to read the scriptures must be so penetrating that it can 'even pierce oxhide.' The 'window,' as part of the old story or in the form of proverbial sayings, also carries the natural connotation of the passage of light.

bow mistaken for a snake In an old story someone at a banquet saw a reflection of a bow in his winecup and thought it was a snake; having drunk the wine and no longer seeing the 'snake,' he thought he had swallowed it, and he became ill as a result of the suggestion. He didn't recover until he saw it had only been a reflection of a bow hung on the wall above. This represents self-delusion, mistaking a reflection for reality, and the fact that human malaise actually stems from misapprehension to begin with, taking illusion for reality. It also illustrates the appropriate expression 'to worry oneself sick.'

Brahma A Hindu god, responsible for creation. Also refers to several classes of heavens and celestial beings; in Buddhism, also used as a name referring to the 'pure abodes' of immeasurable kindness, compassion, joy, and impartiality. Also used in Buddhism as a symbol of the mind, as it creates an order of 'mind' and 'world' from primordial chaos of pure sense.

breath This can mean life, energy, or it can mean disturbance. Bodhidharma's teaching 'no whispering in the mind' uses a word for 'whispering' which also means heavy or hard breathing, and is used as such in meditation texts in dealing with mind-breath attunement procedures. 'What breath is there?' refers to thinking oneself clear and calm (which is itself 'raising waves where there's no wind'); then again, it can mean there's no life—both are sicknesses of meditation.

buddha-nature   This is enlightened nature, the nature of enlightenment, inherent in all beings, identical to all being; it is sometimes said to refer to the pure mind itself. In the Buddhist teachings there are said to be two, three, and five aspects of buddha-nature: of two, one is principle, meaning the unborn, undying essence of reality; the second is practice, meaning practices which are seeds of the knowledges or wisdoms of buddhahood (round mirrorlike knowledge, knowledge of essential equality, analytical knowledge, and practical knowledge). Of three, one is the inherent buddha-nature, the 'principle' of true thusness which of its own nature always remains unchanged inherent in all beings; second is the evoked buddha-nature, meaning that the inherent buddha-nature can only be brought out in people by cultivating the powers of wisdom, meditation, and concentration; the third is the realized result buddha-nature, the clear manifestation of the inherent buddha-nature as a result of accomplishment of practices to evoke it. Of five, one is the true basis buddha-nature, meaning reality, thusness; second is the basis of comprehension, meaning wisdom, true knowledge; third is the conditional basis, meaning the practices which invoke true wisdom; fourth is the result, meaning the realization of enlightenment; fifth is the result of the result, meaning great nirvana. The *Flower Ornament scripture* says, "The buddha-nature is the most profound real nature of things. It is silent and formless, like space." The *Great Demise scripture* says, "Buddha-nature is ultimate emptiness."

Buddhism, Buddha Dharma   This refers to teachings for enlightenment, or their meaning and practice. Also it can mean specifically 'Buddhism,' its forms and/or meaning.

busted   This means caught, arrested, defeated.

C

(the) Capital   Reality, true nature; can refer to enlightenment, also to nirvana, and to thusness as is. "The great way goes to the capital." The name Changan is also used for this term.

carved wood seat   Emblematic of the rank of abbot; teachership, authority.

cessation and contemplation   Ceasing habitual thought trains and fixedly contemplating essential verities. These are the two basic aspects of meditation, and may also be rendered as 'stopping and seeing,' meaning to end delusion and awaken to reality. The various schools of Buddhism each specialize in different, though related, techniques for accomplishing this. See below, under *counting*, etc.

Chang drinks wine, Lee gets drunk "When the mind is empty, all things are empty." Also, people see things according to their own disposition or state of mind.

change state and transform achievement This refers to transcending a state of realization, transcending a practice when its effect has been consummated, developing from a practice into a state of awareness, then developing from that state into a more advanced realm or level of practice; also, it means to return to the world after transcending it.

chariot Buddhism is likened to a vehicle, like a chariot with two wheels of wisdom and compassion; wisdom transcends life and death, compassion transcends nirvana. "That chariot is high and wide" refers to the 'One Vehicle' of buddhahood, or complete universal enlightenment, being coextensive with the universe.

Chu An ancient kingdom and region of southern China. It is well known for poetic, romantic, and aesthetic associations, though such associations may not be used in a Zen text.

claws and fangs Methodology, skills, ability, specifically for enlightened, liberated, or enlightening and liberating activity.

communion with the source Actual realization of enlightenment, direct experience of reality.

cold Symbolic of impermanence, death, dispassion, detachment, nirvana.

Confucianism The focus of Confucianism is on the ordering of culture, state, society, family, persons, and common morality. Confucian studies included manners and ritual, music, poetry, history, and social and moral philosophy.

counting, following, stopping, contemplating, returning, purification Meditation exercises: counting the breaths until the mind is calm and collected, then following the breath silently until the mind is one-pointed and thought stops; then leaving the mind stopped until utmost quiescence and peace is realized, then willfully contemplating the relativity of experiencer, experience, and medium; then turning from the object of contemplating to the contemplating mind itself, until the nongraspability of mind becomes the total experience; then there is no more seer and seen, everything is in its original pure state, with no more subjectivity—"As the mind is pure, so is the land pure." These practices are treated in detail in the 'adaptable' and 'complete and immediate' treatises on 'cessation and contemplation' (qv) by the founder of Tiantai Buddhism.

cut off this refers to the essence of stopping or cessation; to stop thinking of, stop being concerned or involved with, stop doing, stop continuing.

D

Devadatta A former disciple of Gautama Buddha who became infamous for opposing the Buddha.

digesting This referes to digesting teachings, comprehending them and putting them into practice, making them part of one's being; digesting offerings means being truly worthy of offerings, fulfilling the purpose of offerings by putting the enlightening teaching into practice.

doctor A Buddha is likened to a skillful physician who diagnoses illnesses and prescribes appropriate medicines.

Dongshan progression The living Zen lineage descended from the ninth century master Dongshan Liangjie. Also known as the Cao-Dong school, it was one of the 'five houses' of classical Zen in Tang-Song dynasty China.

donkey-tethering stake A 'hangup,' an object of attachment or clinging; it is also used in the sense of something to concentrate on.

drool Talk, drivel.

dusts Sense data, objects, the material world; 'wind and dust' is a classical Chinese metaphor for society, the world of striving and competition.

E

elephantine emperor A mythical sovereign of remote antiquity, used to represent existence as a colossus. Also translatable as 'emperor of images.' 'Before the elephantine emperor' or 'before the emperor of images' means before 'time,' before forms are characterized, before images are conceived, the original state.

Erya An ancient Chinese lexicon.

excellent cause The basis of an excellent result; the enlightening teaching.

eyes Perceptivity, vision, insight, enlightenment. 'Three eyes' symbolize insight into emptiness, conditional existence, and the mean; the 'third eye' or the 'eye on the forehead' symbolizes the insight which is beyond the duality of emptiness and existence. 'One eye' is often used to refer to insight into emptiness, but it can also refer to nonduality.

F

fall at the pinnacle Attachment to the stage at which illusions of thought and views are ended and the merging or interchange of the functions of the senses is experienced.

false cause, no cause False cause means false attribution of cause, and no cause means denial of causality.

father Symbolizes the absolute, or reality, the source; it is also used to symbolize the teacher. 'Father and son' can mean absolute and relative, or teacher and disciple.

Foguo An honorific name of Zen Master Yuanwu Keqin (1063-1135), a renowned Zen teacher in Sung dynasty China, author of the classic *Blue Cliff Record* and the Measuring Tap, works which are repeatedly quoted by the commentator of the *Book of Serenity*.

food This can mean sense data, experience, the sustenance of life, the experience of life.

four mountains Derived from the idea of the four gross elements (earth, air, water, and fire), this refers to the body, physical existence.

formless realm Or formless world; this is the realm of experience of formless concentration or aborption in the infinity of space, infinity of consciousness, in total nothingness, and in the state where there is neither perception nor nonperception. Arhats, or saints, are often mentally in the formless realm; the bodhisattvas or great saints experience the formless realm but avoid intoxication by it.

frozen river This symbolizes the stilled mind or totally concentrated mind. 'The frozen river bursts into flames' refgers to great awakening bursting forth from great doubt, the great function of the whole potential appearing after the cessation of habit and conditioning.

Furong Furong Daokai (1042-1118), Zen successor of Touzi Yiqing, whose verses on Zen stories are quoted in the *Book of Serenity*. "Furong revived the

Cao-Dong school"—his teacher Tozi was at the time the only living bearer of the Cao-Dong transmission; Furong was an outstanding Zen master, and was the teacher of the teacher of the great master Tiantong Hongzhi, the poet of the *Book of Serenity*.

G

gates of the face   This is usually understood to mean the senses.

gathering and release   Or gathering and letting go: gathering refers to cessation, to transcendent wisdom, to nirvana, to emptiness, to detachment, to essence, to denial; release refers to action, to compassion, to life and death, to form, to integration, to function, to affirmation.

general   This refers to the active edge, to function.

good steed   Well-cultivated potential.

great being   This can mean a guardian of enlightenment, an enlightening being on the threshold of complete enlightenment; it also can refer to the potential of enlightenment which is inherent in everyone.

great function   Great life after annihilation of egoism and restrictive habit-patterns; clearing the mind and merging with thusness. Also, it can refer to the universe itself, thusness itself, as it manifests in all workings. Also, the fully awakened human potential. "The great function does not remain within fixed patterns."

great vehicle   Conveyance through life and death for the universal liberation and ultimate welfare of all beings; this is contrasted to the lesser vehicle of individual liberation (which nevertheless is included as an aspect of the great vehicle).

Guifeng   Zongmi (780-840), a master of Huayan and Chan (Zen) Buddhism, a distinguished scholar and author.

H

hair clothes   The animal self or physical being (said of humans).

halcyon days   Great peace, enlightenment; "In the halcyon days we don't sing the song of peace" means "when the other shore is reached, the raft is left behind," and also that enlightenment has no self-consciousness of enlightenment.

hall of extinction   The nirvana hall, also called the life-prolonging hall, was the infirmary of a monastery.

hammer   Often used to refer to techniques and ability of a Zen teacher to smash apart students' mental fetters, also to pound and forge students like iron or gold, to perfect the 'sword' of wisdom and refine the 'gold' of enlightenment.

Han   China, also a region of China. Sometimes the names of ancient kingdoms or regions of China, like Han and Chu, are used together without reference to history in order to convey the sense of unity within difference and difference within unity.

highest meaning   This means the emptiness of ultimate reality, emptiness in the highest sense; that is, not emptiness by annihilation, but lack of inherent individual reality in relative existences.

holy truths   The four holy truths of elementary Buddhism are: the truth of suffering (as exemplified by birth, aging, sickness, dying, parting of loved ones); the truth of the cause of suffering (selfish grasping, clinging); the truth of extinction of suffering (nirvana); the truth of the way to extinguish suffering (the eightfold noble path of right seeing, right thinking, right speaking, right action, right living, right effort, right mindfulness, right meditation—'right' in the sense of being true to reality and conducive to liberation from bondage).

home   The original nature; nirvana; the mine or womb of realization of thusness; oneself (not in the sense of ego, but in the sense of being as is, not seeking outside).

host and guest   Teacher and student; absolute and relative; mind and environment; permanent and transient.

house   A school; people.

hundred plants   Or, 'hundred grasses,' this refers to the world, all creation, myriad things, myriad beings, differentiation.

I

ignoramus   This can refer to someone who is actually ignorant, blind to reality, or it can refer to someone in intense concentration who is not distracted by anything, or it can refer to an enlightened person who appears ordinary and makes no show of knowledge.

Indra In Hindu mythology, Indra is the emperor of the 'thirty-three heavens.' In Buddhism, Indra is sometimes used symbolically to represent the absolute within the relative, the fact that emptiness is in the relative.

iron ox A colossal monument of antiquity, used as a metaphor for the state of the enlightened person, connoting imperturbability.

iron tree blooms with flowers Returning to life after the 'great death'—see 'frozen river bursts into flames.'

J

jewel This can refer to mind, and to enlightenment; also, 'the whole universe is a jewel.'

jewel mirror samadhi The clear, equanimous mind, mirror-like awareness; also, a classic Zen poem by Dongshan Liangjie dealing with the simultaneous realization of the absolute and the relative in one whole.

jowls seen from behind the head This means an appartition or a monster; it can be applied to a formidable adept, or to a suspicious character.

K

king This often refers to mind, mirrorlike awareness.

L

leaking This refers to attachment, indulgence, defilement, the playing of the mind on objects; it also can refer to unrestrained compassion, meaning divulging.

let the first move go A term from a game, this means not making the obvious move, not pressing the advantage, or letting the other make a move to see what he will do.

Linji succession The Zen lineage descended from Linji Yixuan, a great ninth century teacher; one of the five houses of classical Zen in China.

lion A buddha, an enlightened one; the lion's roar means non-acquisitiveness, ultimate emptiness. "The roar of a lion bursts the brain of a jackal" means that the teaching of true ultimate emptiness cuts through all attachments.

lord and minister   Absolute and relative; emptiness and matter; also, enlightenment and its active expression, mind and body.

lotus of reality   Enlightenment, the middle way, thusness; also a well-known Buddhist scripture.

M

market place   The world, society.

manifestation buddhas   Incarnate buddhas, human buddhas; the active manifestation or human actualization of buddhahood, enlightenment.

medicine   Teachings and practices prescribed to cure mental-spiritual ills.

melting illumination   Inner experience of emptiness or nothingness which 'melts' illusions, dissolves fixed ideas of solid reality of objects. See case 32: the statement "no one can surpass this (melting illumination)," meaning, as it is said, "Even if there were something beyond nirvana, it too is a dream, an illusion," can also be read "If anyone goes through it, it will not be right (anymore)," meaning that one should not be attached to the formless realm or to individual liberation or nirvana, that one must go beyond the inner experience that melts illusions; the sense of 'no one can surpass this' also means that all illusions are dissolved or debunked, nothing can be held back, everything is included in the overwhelming insight into emptiness. A Zen founder said, "Bodhisattvas first realize emptiness, then realize nonemptiness; after that, they do not see emptiness or nonemptiness—they have no views at all."

mirror   Fundamental awareness; also, reality itself. Enlightened awareness is likened to a mirror reflecting whatever comes before it without partiality.

moon   Symbol of truth, reality, enlightenment; "The Buddhas' true body of reality is like space; it manifests forms in accord with beings, like the moon reflected in the waters."

mote of dust arises and the whole earth is contained therein   As soon as a thought stirs in the mind, the world exists to it. Also, the existence of the earth (universe) and each particle of it are mutually dependent—"All in one, one in all." This is particularly emphasized in Huayan Buddhism.

Mount Sumeru   The polar mountain of a world in Buddhist cosmology, highest mountain in the world, center of the world.

mouth hung on a wall   This means there is nothing to say, nothing that can be said; refers to facing the inconceivable and unspeakable true reality beyond conception. 'Hung on a wall' means unused.

moxa   An herb burned on certain spots of the body for curing and pain relief; hence means 'medicine,' a specific, a remedy.

N

nation   The world, the relative, existence: "The nation (or state) is established and the peasants frown" can refer to being bound by the view of existence without insight into the emptiness of conditional things, or, similarly, attachment to forms, organizations, rules, formulae, formalities.

noumenon   Emptiness of inherent reality in relative things; also called principle or inner truth or inner reality.

O

ocean   Used to symbolize reality, thusness, enlightenment, the unbound mind, and the Buddhist teaching. "All streams return to the ocean"—all the Buddhist teachings are aimed at enlightenment, liberation; all things are within one reality. Also the Buddhist teachings are said to be like the ocean in that they become deeper the further one enters, and also like the ocean they have a uniform flavor, which in the case of Buddhism is the uniform flavor of liberation. The 'oceanic reflection' or 'ocean seal' refers to the calm mind clearly reflecting all things.

old awl   This refers to an old, mellowed adept.

on the road   This refers to being in the world; going along with conditions. "There is someone who never leaves home yet is always on the road, and someone who is always away from home but not on the road."

one color   Uniformity, equality, equanimity; it is often referred specifically to such a meditation state, but also can refer to the metaphysical reality of the equal inherent emptiness of all things.

one eye   This is usually referred to seeing only the emptiness of form, but also refer to nondiscrimination or nonduality without the negative connotations of only seeing one side.

one or half This can mean a very few, a minimum, or it can refer to the great and lesser vehicles of Buddhism. The great vehicle is called the 'full word teaching' and the 'one voice teaching,' while the lesser vehicle is called the 'half-word teaching.' A 'half' may be someone with 'only one eye,' someone who only transcends the world but cannot integrate with it.

ox The human being; also used to represent the real self or the buddha-nature.

P

pain and itch Distinguishing these, or feeling these, refers to being awake, being aware of what's what.

phoenix Symbolic of an enlightened one, rising from the ashes of the death of ego, just as the phoenix immolates itself to be reborn.

phoenix feathers A literary expression meaning a worthy successor.

poison The 'three poisons' which afflict people are greed, hostility, and ignorance. Also, the teaching of the 'universally equal' aspect of the great vehicle Buddhism is said to be like poison to those who cannot digest it, because when they hear the teaching that life-and-death and nirvana are not two and affliction and enlightenment are identical, they mistakenly cling to their former greed, aversion, and ignorance, and call that enlightenment, unaware that the nonduality lies in the inherent emptiness of the relative. True nonduality is being in the world while at the same time transcending the illusions of the world. Also, 'poison' is a term for the methods of a teaching master to 'kill' delusive ideas and tendencies in seekers; in this sense, terms such as 'poison hand' are often used.

pole As an acrobat's pole, the term represents the body or human being, and having the pole at one's side at all times refers to self-mastery and being in control of one's faculties. 'Atop the hundred foot pole' refers to being at the peak of meditation or detachment, or having reached individual liberation; see 'fall at the pinnacle.'

prehistoric buddhas The term 'before the prehistoric buddhas' means before definitions are fabricated, before self-consciousness of awareness, the original state before the distinction of 'buddhas' and 'ordinary beings,' and also refers to what is known as 'teacherless knowledge,' or spontaneous knowledge.

probing pole Speech or action used to test the 'depth' of a student, to see the mentality or state of the seeker. In understanding Zen sayings, it is necessary to see when they are being used to test or reveal someone's state, as in general it is necessary to see the use to understand the meaning; that is, something might be said not to propound a doctrine, but merely as a test.

pull nails out of eyes   To remove views, which impede true insight.

public case   The 'presently forming public case' is reality right before our eyes, which is always becoming. 'Public' means without partiality. Public cases also means Zen stories, which are based on 'present becoming,' essential and immediate reality, which is always 'coming from the absolute into the relative.' The sense of public case as a Zen story, a 'precedent' on the basis of which decisions are made, refers to the use of stories to test students or for students to test themselves.

Puha turned a flip   When Banshan was going to die, he asked his disciples if anyone could depict his true likeness; Puha just turned a flip and left. Puhua was the chosen successor of Banshan.

R

red-bearded barbarian   Alluding to Bodhidharma, the Indian founder of Zen in China, this term came to mean an enlightened person.

reed flowers   These flowers are white, and symbolize the world, where things are apparently separate, yet are equal in being relative and conditional. Reed flowers in the moonlight symbolizes the identity within difference and difference within identity of emptiness and form. Being 'white,' the moonlight is the same color as the reed flowers, representing how all conditional things are empty and inherently equal; yet there is a slight difference between focus on the aspect of emptiness and the aspect of relative existence, even though they are 'two faces of one die.' Also, it means that though things are in essence equal, their characteristics differ, and in the pure light of the enlightened mind (also symbolized by the moonlight), what is known as 'spontaneous' or 'inherent' discrimination (that is, not produced by thought and imagination, not bound to names and concepts) remains: as it is said, "Arrayed, they're not the same; mingled, you know where they are." Similar terms used to symbolize the integration of the absolute and relative and the merging of sameness and difference are the 'heron in the moonlight,' 'snow on the reed flowers,' 'heron in the snow,' and 'snow in a silver bowl.'

robe and bowl   Emblematic of the Zen succession, these are passed on from teacher to disciple.

roc A gigantic mythical bird, used to symbolize the function or actualization of great enlightenment, soaring beyond the power of mind to conceive.

rope mistaken for a snake A metaphor for delusion which is pure thought-construction; in the dark someone mistakes a rope for a snake, just as people project imagination or conception on what they perceive in the darkness of ignorance. The 'snake' stands for the level of pure fiction; the 'rope' stands for relative reality; yet just as the rope has no inherent nature of its own but is actually a bundle of strands, similarly what is perceived as the objective world is actually only a combination of senses, data, and consciousness, upon which conceptualizations are projected.

S

scale armor Intellectual clinging, intellectual defenses, views and opinions.

scriptures Documents of Buddha's teaching; sutras.

second moon 'Another reality;' a reflection; illusion; also, the conditional world.

shadowing grass Sometimes interpreted as camouflage, or like a hunting blind; also interpreted as bundled grasses used to cast a shadow on water in order to see through the surface. See 'probing pole'.

sharpness of the awl, squareness of the chisel The former refers to transcendent wisdom or insight, 'penetrating through,' while the latter refers to knowledge of the world, skill in means, 'carving.'

Shenguang's three bows At the end of his mission, the Zen founder Bodhidharma asked his disciples to express their understanding; Shenguang (Huike), the last to express his insight, just bowed and stood there; Bodhidharma said to him, "You have my marrow."

six compounds This refers to the six sense faculties, the associated consciousnesses, and sense data, which compound to form the experienced world.

sky This symbolizes the open mind, clear mind, mind.

snake A phony 'dragon.' A 'dead snake' refers to the subdued self, or to dwelling in nothingness. The 'deadly snake' refers to the passionate self. The 'turtle-nosed snake' is you.

snow This may symbolize purity, or equality, uniformity; it is also associated with winter, cold (qv). "Standing in the snow" is an allusion to Shenguang and represents enduring hardship, non-attachment to the body. "When the snow melts the horse's feet are light" means that when clinging thoughts cease, the mind functions freely.

solitary peak This refers to nirvana, to individual liberation, to detachment, to being beyond the world.

spiritual seat "Getting rid of the spiritual seat" refers to 'descending' from one's own enlightenment to deal with others, not being attached to the experience of transcendence or enlightenment, also means 'no-mind'.

spring Symbolizes life, especially spiritual rebirth after the death of egoism

sweating horses This refers to the effort of putting the teachings into practice; in speaking of sudden enlightenment, it is said, "Everyone wants to talk more about the achievement that crowns the age; no one talks about the sweating horses of the past."

T

Taishan Mt. Wutai, a sacred mountain in northern China, a popular place of pilgrimage.

teaching(s) This refers to the Buddhist teachings, and is frequently used in Zen texts in contrast to the Zen way outside of doctrine; or it can be used for any or all Buddhist teaching, including Zen.

ten shadowed This refers to the ten bodies of buddhahood—the body of sentient beings, the body of lands, the body of rewards of actions, the body of saints, the body of individual enlightened ones, the body of enlightening beings, the body of those who realize thusness, the body of wisdom, the body of reality, the body of space. "Ten shadowed horse" refers to Zen Master Mazu as a living buddha.

third patriarch Sengcan (d.609), successor of Shenguang (qv) and author of the first Zen classic, a famous long poem.

this is it This refers to thusness.

this side, that side This refers to integration and transcendence, to form and void, to the relative and the absolute, to life-and-death and nirvana.

Tiantai A sacred mountain in China, after which one of the major schools of Chinese Buddhism is named; the Master of Tiantai was Zhiyi (Zhikai, Zhizhe), a great sixth century teacher and author of many texts.

tiger's cave The inmost mind.

titles crumble, ice melts This refers to the resolution or 'melting away' of doubt, the liberation of the mind, the dissolving of a sticking point, hindrance, or encumbrance.

tortoise hair Pure fiction, mere imagination; something that can be logically expressed in words but doesn't exist in reality.

treatises Crystallizations of the Buddha's teachings made by later teachers.

turn around This is often used of 'turning' from personal liberation to dealing with the world; not clinging to one's state; also, transforming or changing direction at an impasse.

turtle heads for fire Something unthinkable; a paradox.

twelve causes of conditional existence Ignorance, activity, consciousness, name and form, sense media, contact, reception, craving, grasping, becoming, birth, old age and death.

U

unicorn Symbol of an enlightened being.

universally good one Samantabhadra Bodhisattva, personifying the principle and practice of bodhisattvahood.

W

whisk Emblematic of the rank of teacher; also used to indicate the objective world.

white As contrast to black, white symbolizes the relative world, differentiation; it also can be used to symbolize purity and uniformity.

wisdom scripture   One or all of a large body of scriptures known as the perfection of wisdom (prajnaparamita).

X

Xuedou   A great Chinese Zen master (980–1052), the poet of the *Blue Cliff Record* and commentator of the Cascade Collection, quoted in the *Book of Serenity*.

Y

year of the ass   'A blue moon'—never. The year of the ass does not appear on the Chinese calendar.

Z

Zihu's dog   Master Zihu set up a sign outside his gate, saying, "Zihu has a dog: above he takes people's legs; in the middle, he takes people's loins; below, he takes people's legs. If you hesitate, you'll lose your life." When monks would come to his place, Zihu would say "Watch out for the dog!" If a monk turned his head, Zihu would immediately go back to his room.